my life and the

PARADISE GARAGE

KEEP ON DANCIN'

24 Hours For Life Inc.
New York, New York

My Life and the Paradise Garage / Keep on Dancin'
by Mel Cheren
as told to Gabriel Rotello
with assistance from Brent Nicholson Earle

24 Hours For Life Inc.
318 West 22nd Street
New York, New York 10011

Design and production by Scott Ashwell
Edited by Brad Rumph

Printed in the United States of America

ISBN 0-9678994-0-0
Library of Congress Card Number 00-102926

acknowledgements

I'd like to thank the people who agreed to be interviewed for this book: Vince Aletti, Bill Ash, Arthur Baker, Tom Baratta, Larry Basile, Carolyn Bird, Daryl Branch, Jane Brinton, Nathan Busch, Kenny Carpenter, Joey Carvello, Peter Castagne, Barry Cherin, Linda Clifford, Steve D'Aquisto, David DePino, Michael Ellis, Kenny Eubanks, Manuel Fernandez, Michael Fesco, David Forrest, Dino Georgiou, Daniel Glass, Florence Greenberg*, Thelma Houston, Maye James, Grace Jones, François Kevorkian, Frankie Knuckles, Ed Kushins, Barry Lederer, Robbie Leslie, Ellwood Letterlough, Minnie Levan, Monica Lynch, Louis Malkin, Alan Mamber*, David Mancuso, Willy Marquez*, Larry McDevitt*, Howard Merritt, Carol Mitro, Pat Monaco, Tom Moulton, Kenton Nix, Shep Pettibone, Timmy Regisford, Mark Riley, Cory Robbins, Ruben Rodriguez, Victor Rosado, Judy Russell, Michael Sampson, Brenda Sanchez, Michelle Saunders, Bill Scott*, Tee Scott*, Tony Serafino, Bobby Shaw, Nicky Siano, Tom Silverman, Russell Simmons, Mickey Smolar, Will Socolov, Gigi Soto, David Spada*, Henry Stone, Diane Strafaci, Junior Vasquez, Richard Vasquez, Bobby Viteretti, Allison Webster, Judy Weinstein, Dennis Wheeler, Denise Wiggins, and Ricky Willock.

My appreciation to Andrew Holleran for passages quoted from his book, *Dancer From the Dance,* and to Vince Aletti, for citing his interviews of Kathy Sledge, Judy Weinstein, Gloria Gaynor, and August Darnell in his article, "Lost in Music," published in

*deceased

Rock & Roll Quarterly, Summer 1993. Additional material came from "Roll Over Rock," an April 2, 1979 *Newsweek* cover story, and from "Feeling Mighty Real," by Walter Hughes, in *Rock & Roll Quarterly*, Summer 1993.

Since this book has been a seven-year labor of love, there are many people I would like to thank. Gabriel Rotello and Brent Nicholson Earle for the manuscript, Brad Rumph for the revised book, and Scott Ashwell for finally bringing the book to print. Additional thanks to Tom Faucett and Danny Lemos.

I am thankful that Kenny Nix and Taana Gardner have come back into my life, and back to West End Records. Thanks to Andy Reynolds, general manager of West End, and the entire staff of the Colonial House Inn for their continued support while compiling this book.

Two very special new friends to whom I'd like to give thanks: Lorenzo Ramos, for being a true friend in deeds and not just words (Calvin Klein, Look Out!), and Roberto Novo for being an exceptional mensch and extraordinary stylist.

mel cheren
new york, february 2000

love is the message

contents

dedicated in loving memory

the disc-o-la fortune 500 discothèque songs of the '70s
Compiled by Ed Rothschild, with assistance from Johnny Tripp and Chipper McKearnin

discography   SCEPTER RECORDS (out-of-print)
                   LARRY LEVAN PRODUCTIONS/REMIXES
                   WEST END RECORDS CATALOG (out-of-print)
                   WEST END RECORDS CATALOG (currently available)

music to read by   Larry Levan Live at the Paradise Garage (double CD)
                      Larry Levan's Classic West End Records Remixes
                      (Made Famous at the Legendary Paradise Garage)

information on this book, mel's charitable endeavors, west end records, and much more
can be found at http://www.westendrecords.com

prologue

This is a story of my gay generation, the world we built and the world we lost.

There are actually two lost worlds for gay men of my generation: one is the generation of James Dean and Elvis, kids who were teenagers in the 1940s and '50s, and the other is young adults in the '60s, successful by the '70s, when all heaven broke loose in the gay world... and then all hell. We have two Befores.

My generation of gay men remembers a time before you could dance with another man in a dance club, or walk down a gay street in a gay neighborhood, or read a gay newspaper in a gay restaurant, or list your lover on your mailbox, or in your obituary. A time when everything was a scary, sexy, secret code that only "friends of Dorothy" or "members of the committee" could decipher. Gay men today have no need for that code. If they think about the time before Stonewall, which unfortunately most rarely do, it is usually regarded as some dreary closet that burned down in the late '60s. In some ways I suppose it was and it did, but it was a brighter and wider and gayer closet than they can imagine.

This book is not about that Before, however, even though I'll start with that, because that's where I started. It is about the other

Before: the golden moment of openness and music and drugs and beauty beyond measure, and sex beyond limit, the moment when dance floors were palace courts and DJs were kings – drug dealers and models ruled the world. It seems like a dream today, on the far side of what I call the decade of hell. A dream whose background music was the soundtrack of freedom. From where we stand now the dream was a brief one, before the shadow of death would descend and silence my world, and blot out my generation.

I am a survivor of both Befores, but I want to tell you about the second one. In particular I want to tell you about its pulse, the music that pounded in our blood, the music I lived and breathed and helped to develop and surfed like a sonic wave through those years. And I want to tell you about a place called Paradise, and the people who built it – my people, a lost generation. Sometimes now, in these gray After days, echoes come wafting through my window from a passing car, streaming into the night from a boom box playing "I Will Survive" or "We Are Family" or "YMCA," and I'm transported back to the sweat and the ecstasy, and I realize yet again how powerfully this music will always define, at least for me, the Great Gay Before. So before you snicker, let me tell you this about disco.

There was a time when we had the whole world dancing. It didn't last long. Innocence never does. It didn't last anywhere near as long as the backlash against it, which persists to this day, a backlash that began with a campaign called "Disco Sucks!," a radio campaign suffused with homophobia and racism, the rage of the straight white guys against the gays and blacks who were taking over the dance floors and the music business, a backlash that grew so strong that eventually if you mentioned disco at a party people would be sure to sneer, even though if you played a disco record at that same party, those same people would jump up and dance.

I have been called the "Godfather of Disco" by the dance music press. I guess in a way I am. This book is about my life in that music's golden age, which was and will probably always be the golden age of gay men. It is also about the end of that age, when we flew too close to the sun and crashed into silence. If gay kids today know very little about the time before Stonewall, they know even less about the time between Stonewall and AIDS, an era that embodies the essence of two great mysteries entwined: sex and death. The age of disco was, after all, the age that gave rise first to hope, then to hopelessness. My generation, my crowd, is not only portrayed in Andrew Holleran's book, *Dancer from the Dance*, and lampooned bitterly in Larry Kramer's book, *Faggots*. It is also the generation swept away in Randy Shilts' novel, *And the Band Played On*.

Young gay men walking past my house in Chelsea these days, living in the shadow of AIDS, have a strange conflicted relationship with my generation, and well you should. Envious because we lived the life of your fantasies. Angry because, having lived that life, we precipitated a deluge that still laps at your shores. Some of you consider us like older brothers who spent the family inheritance, leaving you little but ashes and bitterness. Some of you say that when we had our chance to build a utopia on solid ground, we danced that chance away in a cloud of disco dust. This book is for you. Decide for yourselves.

chapter one
NEW YORK, NEW YORK

I was bursting with pride that day in 1959 when I reported for work at 1501 Broadway, ABC/Paramount Records. Their offices were right above the Paramount Theater, where some of the greatest stars in show business performed. The name Frank Sinatra, for example, was practically synonymous with the Paramount. ABC/Paramount was a hot record company with major stars and an impressive string of hits. Sam Clark was its president, a former Boston taxi driver, who had worked his way up from the bottom. I considered this an excellent omen since I too was beginning at the bottom, and was also from Boston.

The famous Paramount Building sat smack dab in the middle of Times Square, already fabulously seedy and destined for a long, slow, delicious slide for the next several decades. I had just come to New York from Boston, where I had a boring, miserable, deadend job counting paint brushes at the Colonial Paint Brush Company. My college degree in marketing and advertising and my life experience in the army, I had discovered, were no insurance policy against underemployment. ABC/Paramount put me in inventory control, which meant that I was counting again. But this time it was records instead of paint brushes, and that made all the difference.

New York came about through a guy I met one evening cruising the Public Gardens in Boston. He took me to his apartment on

Beacon Street. As usual in those early days, I didn't tell him my real name. I was not out in gay life, and this was my way of keeping my two lives separate. We liked each other though, and a few weeks later I dropped by his place on a Sunday morning, hoping for a quickie. As it happened, he had guests for the weekend, and I instantly connected with Rick, a handsome guy who, it so happened, was up visiting from New York. Rick was Assistant to the President at ABC/Paramount Records. I was terribly impressed. Rick was bright, open, incredibly organized, a real "take charge" guy. He quickly took a liking to me and we began an affair – this time using my real name. I guess Rick saw something in me, a hunger for success or for some kind of meaning maybe, and I was desperate to escape my claustrophobic life in Boston with mama.

Rick decided to take charge of my life. I should come to New York City, he said, where I would stay with him while he found me a job in the music business and a suitable apartment. He was so confident that he could work this magic, so assertive, that I was totally hooked. Rick wasn't necessarily my romantic ideal, but I went down to visit him in New York and we continued our hot and heavy affair. The glamour of New York, Rick's aura of success in the record business, the whole thing was so far removed from my drab black and white existence at home. New York was like a Technicolor Oz, and the idea that I could be a part of it thrilled me. I was not so thrilled, however, at the thought of having to tell my mother, to whom the very idea of moving was high treason.

to be part of it

Considering how she was, my mother would never let me move to another city for any reason she didn't consider promising, a job with a future, good enough for her Melvin. Amazingly, that was exactly what Rick came up with. He found me a job at ABC/Paramount that paid a respectable $65 a week, and he also found me a room in a decent apartment with a friend of his in Jackson Heights, Queens (a perfectly respectable neighborhood, as mom well knew). I prayed that these boons would prove sufficient to persuade mom that this was my golden opportunity. I could not turn down the prospect of a good-paying job in New York in the glamorous record business and a decent apartment with a decent fellow in Queens. Thanks to Rick, Mom was trapped. She didn't want me to move, but what excuse did she have? So almost before I knew it, I was on my way to the big city.

Before I go on, I would like to emphasize the fact that my whole life changed through this casual trick I met in the park. The importance of this is to always remember: *Nothing happens by accident.* This is my motto.

rocking at abc/paramount

I arrived at ABC/Paramount at a pivotal moment in music. The saccharine, string-laden sounds of the early '50s — the Mitch Miller Chorus, the McGuire Sisters — had been swept away by the explosive arrival of Bill Haley in 1955 and Elvis Presley in 1956. By 1959 the record industry was dominated no longer by careful arrangements and four-part harmonizing, but by the raucous rhythm of early rock'n'roll. My first years at ABC/Paramount were, in a sense, the golden age of rock. The years 1959, 1960, 1961 were the period that kids today generally think of as the '50s — bobby sox, blue jeans, and greasers, as seen in the movie *Grease* and the TV show *Happy Days*. Aside from Elvis, cleancut rebels like Bobby Darin, Frankie Avalon, Paul Anka, and Fabian were the biggest stars — white teenagers whose music was derived from black people. ABC/Paramount stood astride the music industry as one of the biggest labels, with an impressive roster of stars and a steady stream of top hits. Danny & the Juniors, Paul Anka, and Lloyd Price were all on the label, and all selling millions. Fabian and Frankie Avalon were on Chancellor Records, which was distributed by ABC/Paramount.

The signing of Paul Anka to the label created an instant, showbiz legend. He had won a Campbell's Soup contest in Ottawa by collecting soup can wrappers, and the prize was a ten-day trip to New York City. He spent those ten days trudging from record company to record company, shopping "Diana," a song he had written about his babysitter. Although nothing happened with it, New York seduced him and in a few months he had borrowed a hundred dollars from his father and returned. This time the first person he went to see with "Diana" was Don Costa, the head of Artists and Repertory at ABC/Paramount. Don Costa was extremely outgoing, a wily negotiator with an infallible ear and a sterling reputation as a hit maker. Fresh-faced Paul Anka walked in from Canada flat broke, and Diane, Costa's secretary, was the first person he saw. Paul was so broke he didn't even own a belt, Diane quickly discovered, so she took him out on her lunch break and bought him one.

Diane and Paul immediately hit it off, partly because his song was called "Diana," a fact that also impressed a superstitious man like Don Costa. But Don was also impressed by the whole package. He could smell a star a mile away. Since Paul was only 17, Don sent for Paul's parents, and the minute they arrived he signed Paul to an exclusive contract. In the magic, serendipitous way of the record business, "Diana" became a No. 1 smash in 1957, and Paul would release 17 more hit songs before he left ABC for RCA four years later, a major star at the age of 21. In the equally fickle way of the record business, he would not have another No. 1 hit until 1974, when he was 34. Throughout all of the ups and downs of his career, however, Paul never forgot the kindness and respect Diane showed him when he was a nobody. I learned a great lesson in life from the way he always remembered her.

When I came to work at ABC/Paramount, Paul had another No. 1 smash, "Lonely Boy." At No. 3 was "Personality" by Lloyd Price, who previously had a No. 1 hit with "Stagger Lee." Frankie Avalon had a huge No. 1 smash with "Venus." We (in my mind I was immediately a part of all of this now) virtually dominated the top hits in the U.S. And the hit streak continued with Paul Anka's "Put Your Head On My Shoulder" and "Puppy Love." ABC/Paramount was hot, and I was proud to think that my humble job was essential to the success of the company. True, I was starting at the bottom, but the lowliest job is just as important, and everything that went out of or came back in to the label passed through my hands in the inventory department. Mistakes in inventory were easy to make if you didn't pay attention and think creatively, and they could cost huge amounts of money. I actually grew to enjoy my job and I was good at it, and I eagerly started throwing in my two cents' worth, whether it was requested or not.

They liked me from the start. I was a spunky young guy with lots of energy. I enjoyed being there, I liked them, and I guess it showed. My immediate boss was the vice president of ABC/Paramount, the legendary Harry Levine. Harry was a bachelor in his 60s, a real character who used to carry his false teeth around in his back pocket. He took a liking to me, nicknamed me *"Melvilla,"* and soon he was letting me hang out with him in his office at night after everyone else had gone home. I remember how he would take little shots of J&B scotch while sitting behind his enormous polished desk in his beautiful wood paneled office on the 12th floor, and he would ask my opinion about music and then listen while I took his inch and ran my mile. I was on cloud nine just being a part of it all.

One thing amazed me at Paramount. In spite of the fact that everyone seemed to know that Rick was gay, he seemed very well respected. He was not exactly "out" in today's sense, but everyone clearly knew about him in an unspoken sort of way and they still liked him and left him alone. This was not, by the way, because the record industry at that time was in any way liberal or progressive. Far from it. ABC/Paramount was extremely straight laced and conventional. But Rick was excellent at his job, and people respected him for it.

I, on the other hand, remained as tightly locked up in the closet as ever. Even though Rick and I were involved in an affair, I made a conscious decision to keep my distance from him at the office to avoid gossip by association. When I think about this now, I shudder. This was the guy who had found me my first decent job, put a roof over my head, the guy I was sleeping with, and I'm acting like I hardly know him at work. It was sad, but it was typical of the kinds of things a lot of gay men went through in those days, twisted by a homophobia that was so commonplace that it wasn't even questioned.

can't fake the feelin' without feelin'

After working at ABC for awhile, I began to realize that Diane had a crush on me. I could easily have seemed to be a hot prospect: single, young, outgoing, energetic, and most important, Jewish. Nobody suspected that I might be anything but straight as an arrow, least of all Diane, and her hinting around soon grew difficult to ignore. Since she and I worked for the same company, I was able to duck behind a lame ethical excuse — I explained that it wouldn't be right of me to go out with someone in my own department. This hedge worked for precisely a split second. Before I could congratulate myself on my brilliant escape, Diane recovered from her disappointment and turned from a potential match to a persistent matchmaker. She was not about to let an eligible bachelor like me go to waste, and of course she had her girlfriend Gladys, an eligible bachelorette who worked in another department. (As gay men learned to their chagrin in those days, there was always a Gladys.) I might have been able to go along with this charade for awhile if poor Gladys had been remotely attractive, but alas Gladys was, as my Yiddish mama would say, a real *"miskyte."* Nevertheless, it seemed that Diane recruited the entire music industry to push us together as a couple.

This was a typical predicament for closeted gay men in those days. People think you can stay in the closet by just remaining discreet, but it's not that easy. Society presumes you're heterosexual unless you say otherwise. The more that people feel close to you or like you, the more likely they are to act on that presumption and interfere. What are you supposed to say when your family, friends and coworkers apply daily pressure on you to go on a date with someone of the opposite sex, to have a romance, to get married and settle down? The answer is, either you have to lie or tell the truth. For me at that time, ten years before anybody coined the phrases *"gay is good"* or *"out of the closets and into the streets,"* telling the truth was out of the question.

And the truth was that I was increasingly thinking of myself as gay, and slowly coming to terms with it. Rick and I continued our affair during my first several months in New York, and he helped introduce me to gay life in the city. We socialized with other gay men, went to gay parties, had brunches, did what gay guys of that era did. Discreetly, of course, but a far cry from my life in Boston. We would dance together, since you always danced with a partner in those days, and I remember that guys dancing together seemed strange to me. I was used to dancing with a woman, and with a woman the man always had to lead.

It began to dawn on me that it was possible to live life as a gay person, to have friends, family, some sense of community. Life suddenly seemed less furtive, not so alienating. These guys were fairly open, at least within the confines of their social circles, and the sky did not fall. Soon, however, Rick and I stopped dating, and my introduction to that world at the hands of an older, more experienced guide was interrupted. I suppose we had too little in common, a fact that became more apparent with each passing scowl. Rick ultimately went off looking for other projects, other lives to arrange, and I went off to face the question of how to be a single gay man in New York, a decade before Stonewall.

This much I knew. The sailors, the bushes, the horny teenagers kneeling in alleys — Boston was over for me. But at the same time, it was still hard for me to fully accept myself as gay. I had heard about a place called East 47, a genuine gay bar in Manhattan on the East Side near a famous cruising strip, and I was dying to go. But the first time I found myself walking down the long block toward it, screwing up my courage to enter, I just walked on by. I walked around that block for hours, it seemed, trying to build up the nerve to go inside. I was afraid I'd be seen and afraid of what lay inside. This might seem strange coming from somebody who had been cruising sailors since he was 16, had a lover in the army and another in New York. What, exactly, was I afraid of?

I suppose I was afraid of what going into a gay bar would mean. Homosexuality in those days was considered an undisputed mental illness. Coming out of the closet was a process that you were urged to resist rather than embrace. It wasn't like today, where coming out is seen as a healthy phase of development. In those days it was seen as giving in to illness, surrendering to a life of vice. So even though I had experienced plenty of gay sex, I had not fully accepted that I was, well, one of them. I could cruise the parks using my alias Bill Hallowell, or have a crush on an army buddy, and still think of myself as separate from the gay world. But going to a gay bar was, even more than sex itself, the quintessential gay social act, the thing that defined you as queer. Entering East 47 would mean entering a life for which there was no exit. Needless to say, I eventually screwed up the courage.

It wasn't long before I became a regular bar habitué. One of my favorite early haunts was Julius in Greenwich Village, particularly well suited to my ambivalent state of mind. Julius' was a straight bar in the front. It had big picture windows facing out onto W. 10th and Waverly. It was widely known to be gay in the back, where there were no windows and you could mingle and meet in the hazy darkness. Because of this, you didn't have to think of Julius' as a gay bar, really. You could walk in from the street, have a drink or two and loosen up, and then wander into the back out of curiosity. I got over my squeamishness soon enough and began frequenting several much more frankly gay bars, as well as the 47th St. YMCA, where it was easy to meet men. Soon I had an active gay life in New York, which happened to be the world center of active gay life.

I've never thought of myself as a hunk, exactly, but I certainly wasn't bad looking. I was young and slender and in good shape, with regular features, and people found me attractive. I remember being seduced into my first three-way by Wyatt Cooper, who became Gloria Vanderbilt's husband and the father of her two kids. I was in bed with Wyatt and his roommate came in and joined us. Once I figured out the score, I found I could be pretty outgoing and even aggressive myself, when I saw what I liked.

I also discovered some of the sadder aspects of gay life. At the apartment Rick found me in Jackson Heights I lived with a man who, like so many gay men of that era, was a very heavy drinker and smoker. Mick, with his raspy voice, scared the shit out of me.

He'd bring home all sorts of strangers, go on terrible binges, and regularly pass out piss drunk with a lit cigarette in his hand. I lived in terror that some night I'd wake up with the house in flames. That never happened, but there were incidents with Mick that made me realize that some gay souls, caught in that era's twisted morality, led pretty twisted lives.

One time, someone broke into the house when we were both out, trashed the place deliberately, and robbed us. I remember coming home in the dark to this incredible scene of sofas ripped open, everything strewn everywhere. I picked my way through the ruins from room to room until I arrived at the bathroom door, which was closed. Swallowing my fear that the robber might be lying in wait, I slowly pushed it open. And there was Mick's poor cat hanging by its neck from the shower. It turned out that the perpetrator was a jealous queen who was having some kind of abusive friendship with Mick. He broke in during a drunken rage, and kittycide was his idea of revenge. As a result of that episode I lost all my photos from Europe, meaning, among other things, all my photos with Jim, my army romance, and me. It was as though fate were telling me that the good side of gay love could easily be erased by this other darker side that came with too many drugs and drinks, and too little hope. I would learn this lesson over again in the coming years, and echoes of the violent, vengeful lover pounding on the door in the middle of the night would follow me around forever.

hitting the road

In my first foray into life as a semi-open gay man, then, I found good mixed with bad, freedom mixed with fear. In fact my biggest problem, one that was beginning to crush me, was the avalanche of pressure at the office to get married. But I lucked out. In 1960

ABC/Paramount decided to place sales reps throughout the country to act as middlemen between the company and its independent record distributors. The job entailed traveling from city to city to visit our distributors and promote our product, and the big honchos thought I would be perfect.

Unfortunately, the job required a car, which they were not supplying, so I went to my Uncle Abe for a loan. I couldn't very well ask my parents, who were the poorest of the poor in our family. But Abe, my father's brother, owned a sheet metal shop in Chelsea, Massachusetts with his wife Annie, and everyone in the family knew they were loaded. Abe was a hunchback with shocking red hair, one of the most unattractive men I've ever seen, and his idea of family seemed to match his looks. He turned me down flat. He explained that another cousin had once borrowed money from him and never paid it back, so to him every request for financial assistance was a potential rip-off. And he added that he hated losing money foolishly, and considered my plan the peak of foolishness. Up until then I had naively assumed that family would never refuse family. I learned that this was not always the case. I was deeply hurt by Abe's rejection, especially since it was obvious that the paltry sum I needed wouldn't have set him back a bit.

In a way, though, his rejection helped me, because it drove me to prove to him and everyone else that I could do this on my own. I also learned an important lesson in gay life — perhaps all life — that you can often depend on the family you have chosen, your circle of friends, than on blood relatives. I somehow managed to scrape together enough money for the move and the brand new black 1960 Valiant, and I was in heaven until I went to pick up my license plates. QJ 435. To me, anybody reading those plates could have only one reaction to QJ: Queer Jew 435. This might seem ridiculous today, but that's how I felt in 1960. I got over it though, and soon I was off, a rookie music mogul with a real job and a real car, zipping down the highway of life, ready for the '60s.

adjusting to middle america

Cleveland was the base for my territory that included Ohio, Michigan, Indianapolis, Buffalo and Pittsburgh. I arrived on a Saturday night during the middle of a snowstorm, checked into a hotel and found to my chagrin that nothing, not even a coffee shop, was open. After the 24-hour whirlwind of New York, I wondered what was I getting myself into. Cleveland's idea of nightlife appeared to be silent, dark, deserted streets. But despite my bad first impressions, I knew that Cleveland was important in the music business as a place where hit records were broken. It was, among other things, the home base of Alan Freed, the ground breaking radio DJ who coined the term rock'n'roll. His "Moondog Rock'n'Roll Party" on WJW was credited as the first to introduce the "corrupting" influence of black rhythm and blues on "pure" white teenagers. For some reason this modest Ohio city was, and still is, a town with a crazy ear for rock'n'roll.

The practice at ABC/Paramount originally was to have company representatives fly only to the biggest cities — Chicago, Cleveland, Pittsburgh and so on. No personal attention was paid to all the little mom-and-pop record stores out in the hinterlands that were only able to obtain their products through mail and phone service from bored, indifferent sales reps. But as part of the growing sophistication of the business in the early '60s, ABC/Paramount sent the sales reps out to service these small establishments in person.

Most of the sales reps faked it, however, despite the new company mandate. They'd report that they had been to places they'd never been, figuring *"who's gonna check?"* But I quickly grasped how individual, personal attention in the stores from the label actually did sell product. In a small location something as simple as a countertop promotional display could make the difference between selling ten records or none at all. So I always went to every one of the places on my list and volunteered to do window displays in smaller stores. It usually wasn't until I was finished that the owners would notice that I had made the display exclusively from ABC/Paramount product, or that I had written *"Have Yourself A Beautiful Christmas!"* on their storefront windows.

I loved dreaming up novel ways of promoting our records. One time I promoted an album, *Sing Along In Italian,* by mailing a bottle of Chianti and a loaf of Italian bread to all of the distributors and major buyers for the record stores in my region, with a little handwritten note on a cloth napkin promoting the record. It was a simple idea but all the bigwigs at the company loved it, and all of the sales reps were ordered to follow suit. This, needless to say, did not endear me to my fellow reps since management insisted that each sales rep write out each message personally to each store, and there were a lot of stores. And we did have one small snafu. A bottle of wine broke in the post office and ABC/Paramount got in trouble because sending wine through the mail was illegal.

If my eager beaver approach tended to alienate my fellow reps, the distributors didn't exactly jump for joy when they saw me coming either. Some of the biggest labels distribute their own product directly to the stores, and therefore don't have to go through outside distributors. But most labels can't afford the expense of maintaining an entire distribution network, which includes warehouses and personnel and inventory controls, and so they contract with independent distributors to service the stores and do promotion as well. The built-in problem with this arrangement is that a distributor does business with as many as 20 different record companies and does not always give your records the attention they deserve. This leads to a certain love/hate relationship.

I was bound and determined to stand out in the minds of every distributor in my region and to give them hell when they needed it, which most of the time they did. We had 20-odd album releases every quarter and even more single releases, and we also carried other lines like Impulse, the jazz label, and later, Enoch Light's Command Records. Command was the biggest selling label at the time and introduced *stereophonic,* a whole new wave of sound reproduction. I had to struggle with our distributors to get all of our records the best exposure, but I really loved my work and was passionate about it. Much later, I happened to be dating a guy who was the son of a local sales rep who had worked with me in Pittsburgh, and he told me that his father used to take tranquilizers when he had to canvass the stores with me. The son was part of a popular '60s group, who, according to my lawyer, I can't name.

gay in the provinces

Cleveland wasn't all work though. By chance I had met Mike Mancini and Carl Santa, two gay Clevelanders, the night of my going away party in New York. I looked them up as soon as I got to Cleveland, and they found me a room in a house owned by Carl's lover, Nick Basil. Through them I found my way into gay Cleveland, and it found me.

We never called it the gay community back then. This term was a couple of decades away. But Cleveland actually had something back then that, today, we would call a gay community. There was a big gay bar there at that time, Jacques, a family affair run by an Italian man and his wife, and it was the center of a whole crowd. We practically lived there when I was in town. Nick worked for the Cleveland Playhouse, which meant he was deeply involved with all the touring shows that came through town. This meant that I was too, a fact that didn't hurt my love life any. There was a big gay contingent among actors and dancers in the touring shows, and most of them were amenable to a quick romance while passing through. It soon became a standing joke that I had earned my Actor's Equity union card thanks to my close backstage associations. Another part of the emerging gay scene were the porn bookstores. Originally these were just cruising places, but over time they turned into places to have sex, if you liked that kind of sex. We had one friend who was heavily into it. We used to joke that the porn shops lowered their flags to half staff whenever he left Cleveland.

Since I spent a lot of time on the road, a friend introduced me to the world of roadside truck stops, where men stopped for quickies. There was a regular system for approaching such places, a sort of horny highway etiquette in which you'd blink your lights twice at a truck, and if the driver was interested he'd pull over at the next rest stop. This didn't appeal to me very much, since it reminded me of sailors and parks and the kind of closeted world I was trying to leave behind. But it was a big part of the traveling scene in rural America back then, as I suppose it still is to some degree.

I grew to really love Cleveland. It was so different from New York or Boston. Friendly, with a close knit group of gay men who valued camaraderie more than attitude. Sometimes I would be on the road for a week or two and return to Cleveland for only a few nights, savoring the town, hating to leave it again. I found a small apartment of my own and began seeing a married man, a fairly common thing in those days when so many gay men were married. This one was a decorator, and he spent endless months decorating my new place, since this was the perfect excuse for us to be together. His wife kept nagging, *"How long does it take to decorate a studio apartment?"* I suppose the poor thing didn't suspect that more than the carpet was getting laid.

I was still under some pressure to sleep with women, but not as much as in New York. Jerry Herman, who ran the distributorship in Indianapolis, was the most persistent. I suppose he figured that if I was on my back, I would get off his. I politely declined until it became clear that I couldn't refuse forever, and finally one night in Indianapolis I let him procure me a hooker. She announced the minute she sashayed in the door that she was having her period, and offered to give me a blow-job instead of her *"usual."* I was young and impressionable, but I remember thinking this was really not her forte. *Teeth.* Throughout the experience I couldn't help thinking of all the guys who could have done the job much better, since only a man knows how it feels and so how to do it really well — not to mention for free.

teen idols and me

One of my major responsibilities for ABC/Paramount was to escort our recording artists around to various promotional events in my region. Since most of our top artists at the time were in the teen idol category, I often found myself driving around with these teen idols, acting as tour guide, chaperone, and sometimes confidante.

People have asked me how it felt, as a young gay man, to spend my days and nights and share hotel rooms with the hottest male sex symbols and heartthrobs of their time. There was a certain heavenly quality to this aspect of the job. These were after all the boys who, with their slicked back hair and tight pants and peaches-and-cream complexions, literally defined sexy for a whole generation of Americans, including a whole generation of gay men. And here I was, paid to be their pal. Some of these young guys were at the pinnacle of a kind of success that hardly existed before, or since. Their fans, mostly girls, would go into spells of hysteria at the mention of their names, like with Sinatra years before and where it would reach its giddiest heights a couple of years later with Beatlemania. But things didn't always stop with just screams and fainting spells. There were sometimes riotous attacks, as hysterical young fans tried to touch their idols, rip out locks of their hair, tear off their clothes as souvenirs.

I remember one particularly scary incident in Pittsburgh in 1961. I was escorting Fabian to one of his concert appearances, and as our limo pulled up to the theater a huge crowd of fans surrounded us and we suddenly found ourselves in the middle of a screeching, flailing mob scene. They began to rock the limo back and forth; arms groped us. One girl stuck a pair of scissors through the window for a lock of Fabian's hair, waving the scissors wildly in our faces, practically poking my eye out. Fabian came close to getting pulled apart in the hysteria, and only when a phalanx of cops intervened were we saved. Recovering in his dressing room before he went on, we could hear the screams rolling like thunder out of the auditorium every time the emcee mentioned his name. For this naive golden boy, just 17-years-old, who had already scored seven hit singles and two hit albums after only one year in the music business, it was immensely difficult to comprehend what was happening. He seemed dazed by it all. I remember him confiding to me that, just a year or two earlier, he never would have believed that he could be where he was that night. But of course, he probably had an equally hard time grappling with what lay ahead. Fabian's recording career was completely finished one year later, before he reached his 18th birthday.

That's the way it was at the dawn of the '60s. In the capable but cynical hands of rock'n'roll Svengalis, beautiful boys who could barely sing were transformed into instant pop stars and marketed as mass sex symbols. I was amazed by the ruthless starmaking machinery that could drive a career to the top and then dash it against the rocks in the mad rush for the next big thing. I've always felt that being able to create a brilliant career for someone I liked, someone whose talent I respected, must bring an immense sense of fulfillment. But I've also been acutely aware of the toll such instant fame can take on impressionable young people, particularly if that fame is followed by instant obscurity. (I was reminded of how Fabian was manufactured into a star the first time I saw New Kids On the Block on MTV. Styles change, but the circle of pop remains unbroken.)

One of my strongest suits at ABC/Paramount was that I was constantly bombarding my superiors with ideas. Two of my best really added to the feathers in my young man's cap. I had heard "Heartbreaker" by Jon Thomas, a hot regional record in my area. Other companies were bidding for it, but I moved quickly and was able to secure "Heartbreaker" for ABC/Paramount, where it went on to become a huge hit. I also lobbied the company to sign B.B. King, which they eventually did. I remember how thrilled I was when I went to Cincinnati to pick up B.B. King's master tapes from the label he was with before. Not bad for somebody who had begun in inventory just a year before. I was definitely moving up.

Or so I thought. In actuality, the record business was going through a periodic slump at this time, and it wasn't long after my B.B. King coup, while I was thinking I was as safe and secure in my job as if I had tenure from Harvard, that ABC/Paramount decided to cut costs. One of the first things they cut were the very things they had most recently added: us field reps. I still remember the numb sense of shock when, one fine day early in 1961, the call came like a bolt in the blue. Jobless in Cleveland.

But not for long. Milt Saltstone, who owned M.S. Distributors in Chicago, heard that I was one of the best field reps in the Cleveland area, and when I approached him he hired me immediately to work for their new branch in Cleveland. And so I remained in Cleveland for almost a year, working M.S. product and building a gay life for myself in the city I had come to love.

One day towards the end of 1961, Al Parker, my old boss at ABC, called to tell me that a job was opening up at ABC/Paramount in New York. I would have to think about this over the weekend and get back to him. It wouldn't be easy to leave Cleveland. Many people were making names for themselves in the music business because of the work that they were doing in and around Cleveland at that time, and some of them would become major moguls. (As an example, Dave Glew, who was a sales rep for a local record distributor, is currently chairman of Epic Records.) I was torn because I really loved Cleveland. I liked my job, my employers were happy with me, and I had established close friendships with a lot of wonderful people. But Cleveland was definitely not New York, and the prospect of living at the eye of the storm was very exciting for a 29-year-old gay man.

M.S. wanted me to stay with them, but once I had made up my mind I could not be dissuaded. I trained a young man named Tommy Lipuma to take my place, and Tommy eventually became another example of someone who started in Cleveland and made it big. He went on to produce such artists as George Benson and Natalie Cole, and he rose to President of GRP Records in New York. Once Tommy was trained, my work in Cleveland, my life in Cleveland, was over. I had arrived there on a cold snowy night two short years before, an unknown kid in the music business, unable to find a cup of coffee on dark streets, wondering if I had made a terrible mistake. I left in January 1962 a grown up, a success, a gay man from the provinces ready to try again to make it in the big city. This time I would never leave.

chapter two
SEXUAL FEELING

My gay life had begun two decades before when I was 16. There wasn't much of a gay world then, in 1949, at least not in proper old Boston. No real bars to speak of, except the worst kind of Mafia dives. Nothing you'd call a community. How could there be? Almost nobody was open back then, certainly nobody I knew. Nobody sane. Life was not kind to those who dared exist as *"admitted homosexuals."* But that didn't mean there was no gay sex. There was plenty of that.

My problem, as I turned 16, was that I didn't know how to get it. The absence of a visible gay community meant, among other things, that there were no mentors or role models, nobody to show you the ropes, nor any books or movies that would give you a clue. Just your own raging hormones, and your own imagination, and your own guts, if you had any. I guess I did, because as I grew into adolescence and my thoughts got clearer and more pressing, nobody had to tell me what I wanted. By 16, I just knew.

On weekends I worked for my father, a flower peddler in Boston, riding with him into the great city from our little suburban town of Revere. Dad had a stand on Winter Street near a sort of alley where there was a famous restaurant with a room for men only, Locke Ober's. The Kennedys would go there all the time, handsome young Jack and Bobby emerging from their little black Buick and striding right past me into history.

Boston was alluring to a gay 16-year-old in 1949. On Saturday nights in the sumer, the streets would empty out around six when the stores closed, and after that the only thing walking on the streets were sailors, tanned skinned, wearing their skintight, 13-button blue uniforms, very different from the illfitting garbage that sailors wear today. If a sailor had a good build, his uniform could be incredibly revealing and sexy. Visions of sailors swaggered through my dreams, their buttoned bell bottoms bulging, their muscled legs shifting beneath clean blue cotton. I didn't really know what these dreams meant, or what they meant I was. But I knew what I wanted, and finally one hot summer night, mentor or no mentor, I decided to get it.

I walked down to the station where the sailors got their trains back to the naval base, and zeroed in on this handsome one by himself — young but several years older than I — and struck up a casual conversation: *"Where you from? Where you going?"* Beyond that I had no idea what to say or ask. But after we talked for awhile, about sports or women or whatever, and he seemed friendly and open and safe, I just asked him, point blank, like a lamb to the slaughter, would he like to get sucked off. It was instinctive and innocent. I didn't know anything about gay life, or cruising, or tricking, or how you were supposed to ask, or even what men did with each other sexually. I just knew what I wanted to do, and that he was the one I wanted to do it to, or with. And so I just asked him. And as it happened, that one person, that very first person, said yes. He must have been horny, having been out to sea for months. He must have heard a million sailor stories about queers giving blow jobs to guys like him, and how good it can feel. He probably knew much more than I did. Whatever, he said yes.

We went into the train station. In those days you could rent a changing room with a shower by dropping a few coins in a slot. I don't remember much about that first time. I know it didn't last long. But it was exciting. Thrilling. I've often thought that if he had acted differently, if he had called me a queer, or slugged me, or called a cop, I might have been so frightened I would never have tried this again. Or at least it might have been years before I did. But as it was, the magic drug of sex, my first and best intoxicant, snared me from the first hit, and I was instantly hooked.

With this success under my belt, I began cruising at night near South Station, striking up conversations with every handsome sailor I could. I quickly developed a technique that worked so well that it only took me a minute to tell whether a guy was interested or not. I'd start chatting and ask him what was up and he would usually say something like *"not much, looking for action,"* that kind of thing. And I'd say, *"Christ, you're not gonna believe what just happened to me. I just got one of the best blow jobs I've ever had."* This would almost always get his attention. And then I'd say, *"And the incredible thing is, it was a guy who gave it to me."* Some guys would act offended or even disgusted, and when they did, fine, I would just change the subject and eventually wander off. But every so often, in fact pretty often, a sailor would act interested. He'd start asking questions, and we'd start discussing this novel experience, me explaining how good it felt, how there really wasn't anything wrong with it, how delicious it was to be with someone who really knew what he was doing. Eventually I'd ask him whether it had ever happened to him. Or if not, whether he thought it ever would. And if he said yes to either question, I would pop the question. By that point in the conversation, bingo.

Within six months of that first experience my technique grew confident. Bristling with excitement and shame, I developed all sorts of clever refinements. I found out, for example, that whenever navy ships arrived in Boston the newspapers would publish phone numbers so that relatives could call. So I would go to phone booths — they actually had booths in those days — and call these numbers right out of the paper and ask for some unknown person, and then begin talking to whoever answered. Soon I'd be deep into my routine, and if the sailor was receptive, I would arrange to meet him somewhere in Boston. I guess I was pioneering phone sex, 40 years before it was invented. I was also pioneering my own brand of promiscuity. By the time I went off to college two years later, I figured I had racked up about 250 conquests.

It may seem odd to gay kids today, but thinking back on my paramours of those years, the fact is that most of them were probably straight. Straight guys had a very different attitude in the '40s. As long as they were the ones being approached, and as long as they didn't really have to do much of anything but sit back and enjoy, they didn't seem to have much of a problem with it. Today, by contrast, any kid hanging around a navy base asking strangers if they wanted blow jobs would probably get bashed a lot more easily than he would get lucky. I don't know why things were so different back then, but I know this: *gayness was utterly invisible.* There was nothing political about it, no discussion, no movement, no controversy, no openly expressed anger on either side. No issue. Just silence. A silence so big it wrapped us in a strange safety, and made what we were doing not so much controversial as simply covert.

But it was also very dangerous. For one thing, sex was almost always outside, in an alley, in the bushes, in a car. The risk of getting caught was obviously immense. Luckily for me, that never happened. In fact, the only time I came close to getting caught was once when I got greedy and tried to pick up two sailors at the same time. To my horror, they wanted to take me to *"get help."* To the police, of all people. It was only through some fancy fast talk — I promised I'd meet them the next day and go with them — that I managed to get away.

I know it may seem strange, but I did not know I was homosexual when I was a teenager, or at least I didn't think about it in those terms. I didn't read books about it. Nobody talked about it. I actually thought I was probably the only Jewish guy doing what I was doing, and I worried that I might embarrass my religion if I got caught. I would see other gay men out cruising, but I never tried to meet them. We were competitors in this particular pursuit, rather than allies or prospective partners. We were both hunters after the same prey — straight guys, sailors. I didn't think of this lifestyle as my lifestyle or these people as my people. Not at all. I had my world of family and friends and, later, college and career. This was just what I did for sex.

Still, even though I didn't exactly analyze what I was doing in political or psychological terms, I considered it wrong, and bad, and was ashamed of it and afraid of it, and afraid of myself for doing it. Which is why I kept it so tightly wrapped in a veil of secrecy, why I emptied my pockets of all identification whenever I went out, why I invented a new, non-Jewish name — Bill Hallowell — for my cruising alias. I lived in fear of getting caught, and worried about what the future could have in store for someone so different, so driven, so lonely and alone. On dark nights, out searching for sailors so far from the psychic home I was raised in, I wondered if this was going to be it. If these dark nights in rainy side streets, these furtive looks from strangers, were glimpses of my future, of myself as an old man in a raincoat under a streetlight. The idea that a community would someday arise from this forbidden sexual world, a warm family with its own psychic home, its own lights, a community that would draw me into its bosom, was inconceivable to me. There was no one to whisper *"Gay is Good,"* much less yell it out loud; no one to tell me that in 20 years a thing called Stonewall would happen. Or a pounding Paradise Garage. No one to tell me, and no one to ask. And so I kept everything utterly to myself, and learned to separate sex from life, to seek out love as a stranger even to myself, and to fear a lonely old age. Now I realize, I am a creation of God and if it's good enough for God, it's good enough for me.

At Northeastern University in Boston, I continued leading two lives. One, the popular fraternity guy, the other, the active secret homosexual. Aleen and Bert, my closest friends during college, never suspected I was gay. Or if they did, they never said a word about it. They used to joke about a mutual friend they suspected of being into *"that world,"* as we described being gay back in those days, and they made it amply clear that such men and their sicko urges were a race apart. As my generation graduated into active sex lives, as friends around me began doing more than holding hands and necking, as the pressure grew to begin serious dating, I buried my secret life even deeper and began, on the surface, to lead the life of an active heterosexual. In the way of over-compensators everywhere, I went out of my way to appear straighter than straight, even becoming the one to arrange dates for my frat brothers. We often double dated in my car, and in a sense I kind of liked it. I certainly never felt that I was pretending during my hot necking and petting sessions with local girls, because I genuinely enjoyed being with them. Sometimes I would take a girl out on a date and we would neck in my car, getting as worked up as we could without actually *"doing it,"* and then I would drop her back at home, proud of my virtue. I always thought of myself as someone who could be trusted by a girl's father, someone who would have absolute respect for his daughter. After I dropped the girl off, I would go looking for sailors. Respect was not an issue with them.

soldier boy

I finished college, was drafted into the army and was stationed in Colorado. Over Washington's birthday, three army buddies and I drove to Las Vegas. I came up with the idea of calling several of the artists who were performing on the strip — Patti Page, Victor Borge, and Marlene Dietrich — who invited us to be their guests at the performance. Marlene also invited us back stage after the show. She thanked us for coming and said that she could feel the presence of young people in the audience. She ran up the steps, two at a time, to get an article to show us. (She was being criticized at the time for appearing in a skin-colored gown. The women in the audience wouldn't let their husbands react to her.) I had my arm was around her shoulder like an old friend. I'll never forget it. She was in her late fifties, had on a pair of shorts and a sweater, and was extremely beautiful and charming.

I was sent to Stuttgart, Germany, and was assigned to a tiny army base in what looked like a miniature college campus, just three buildings that had once been a queen's castle during World War I and later Rommel's headquarters during World War II. Our barracks were cozy, the town was beautiful, and even though I was celibate — it was far too dangerous for a soldier to go out cruising soldiers — I was reasonably happy.

One morning I was in the bathroom shaving when a guy walked in and I was instantly smitten, a classic case of love at first sight —Jim, from Wichita Falls, Texas. Blond, blue eyes, crewcut, cleft chin, broad shoulders, thin waist, a perfect WASP ideal of a soldier. He had come from the Counter Intelligence Corps in Maryland, and although he worked in another department, he lived just down the hall from me in the barracks. Jim and I quickly became friends, though from my side it was a lot more than friendship right from the start. Just being near him, his easy smile and his hard body and butch blonde face, filled me with agonizing desire. I was sure, however, that there was no way that anything more than friendship could happen between us. The policy of *"don't ask, don't tell"* was decades into the future, but the reality of not asking and not telling was a basic part of army life. So although Jim clearly liked hanging around with me and accepted me as his buddy, and although I made passionate love with him in my dreams, that would have to be it. Friendship and dreams. And perhaps the occasional peek in the shower.

On Christmas Eve, 1957, a lot of the guys were going to hear Christmas carols in a nearby church and they asked Jim and I to come along. Jim shot me a look that seemed to say, *"Let's not,"* and so we declined, and the two of us ended up in the town square instead. A light snow was falling, transforming Stuttgart into a Holbein etching, a Christmas card. We walked along in the snow, talking about our jobs back home and our dreams. In the train terminal a group was singing Christmas carols and we stood together for a moment listening to the familiar songs, lost in a kind of reverie. All of a sudden, I felt Jim's little finger grab mine and pull on it. The sensation was like a bolt of electricity that knocked my breath away. I turned to look at him but he said nothing. After a few endless moments we went to the station restaurant, ordered stout German beer, and the pinkie holding graduated to knee rubbing under the table. We didn't talk about what was happening. Our bodies just seemed to find each other.

When we arrived back at the barracks no one was there and we just fell into each other's arms — and into a big broom closet, the closest thing to privacy you're likely to get on an army base like that. It was delicious and passionate and tender and all the things I never thought sex with a man could possibly be, especially in a broom closet. I could hardly believe it was happening. Then suddenly we heard the other guys come back and enter the room and stand right in front of the broom closet door talking. Our hearts stopped. What would we say if someone opened the door? What would happen if they stayed in that room for hours? I don't know exactly what I felt during those ten minutes or so, so much surprise and sudden anticipation and passion followed by so much fear of discovery and shame. Luckily, the guys eventually wandered from that room and Jim and I emerged undetected, moles in the barracks of love. But from the beginning ours was a broomcloset love, meant for shadows, not to be spoken of, not to be shared with anybody but each other.

From then on, Jim and I were inseparable. Falling for Jim, and feeling it was reciprocated, marked the first time I realized that I could actually love another man. Which meant, I suppose, the first time I could imagine loving myself as I was. Up until that time, my idea of sex with men was strictly anonymous and furtive, severed from everyday life. Love, romantic love, was what decent people did. Normal people. What dad did with mom. Sex between men was what queer shadows did in alleys of shame with sailors who had their own decent lives somewhere else. I used to think that unless a guy was a male idol in a Navy uniform, I couldn't possibly be interested. I never thought that the tender connections of love — emotional, romantic, heartbreaking love — could exist between two men, or that I would ever be part of a male couple. There were absolutely no models like that, or none that I knew of. No one had ever even suggested to me that such a relationship could exist. If a trick tried to kiss me — and on occasion a few did — I was repulsed. Jim changed all that.

But having a secret romance in an army barracks was not exactly an exercise in gay self-esteem. We had to keep our affection totally hidden because we knew it was totally forbidden. The opening we made to ourselves had to stop there, a little atom of pride surrounded by an ocean of shame. Even the most basic physical aspects of our love — not only sex but even kissing and touching, even holding hands — were crimes punishable by court martial, imprisonment, dishonorable discharge. We had to think logistically, to plan our kisses like military exercises, our sex like D-days. In this sense we were still not that far from shame. On one occasion Jim and I rented a room in another town, since two army men renting a room together didn't draw any notice, and we spent a delirious weekend together. But that was expensive, and obviously a special treat. The vast majority of the time we were in the barracks, living together but unable to touch each other except in stolen moments. Fortunately, my roommates and I co-owned a 1949 Mercedes Benz, a huge Gestapo looking showboat we named Betty, and she became our ark, our refuge. Jim and I would drive to the movies in Betty and then go and park somewhere afterward like high school sweethearts, fogging up the windows. I don't know if my roommates were suspicious, but they always seemed curiously interested in what time I came home. *"The movie was over hours ago,"* they'd interrogate me, *"What time did you say you got in?"*

There was one other little break in our closet wall, however. Jim had developed something of a social life with a few other gay men, a little circle that included a couple of sergeants and even a fairly obvious gay guy, a screamer. We would socialize with them from time to time, discreetly of course, and that gave me an inkling that there might be a more open world somewhere, at least among men who didn't care as much as I did about convention and safety and fitting in. Like the screamer. He couldn't fit in, and so he just went with it. Flaunted, as they say. I suppose the obviously effeminate, the naturally flamboyant and fey never had the luxury of hiding the way the rest of us did. But what struck me was that his relative openness seemed to have made him happier, freer. He had seen the other side of rejection and scorn, and it wasn't so bad.

I, however, conventional to my Boston Jewish core, was nowhere near ready to contemplate such a life for myself in the mid 1950's. I cared deeply about safety and my reputation, my family, my religion, my self-respect. I was so tightly locked up in the closet that it even made me nervous being seen around somebody so obvious. In our little group we sometimes talked about being gay, but only when we were in a very safe environment, and only in a way I'd describe as bitchy conspiratorial. We'd talk about our suspicions about who else might be gay, or we'd talk about who was hot, or dangerous, or available. We'd dish the dirt. It may have been superficial and a bit self-hating, but it was our little discrete society, and with Jim at my side I began to loosen up and glimpse the possibilities in my own heart. And then Jim did what lovers often do. He broke my heart. He confided to me one day that he had met someone else before coming to Germany, and that he was madly in love with this someone else, although it was apparent to him that his feelings were not reciprocated. What's more, this had been going on for quite some time. Our relationship, he implied, was more a diversion, something to keep him busy while he pined for his one true love. I suppose he thought that I would think nothing of this, but it absolutely crushed me. And it probably showed, more than I realized. We continued to be friends, and I carried a torch for him for years afterward. In fact, I think I still do, 40 years later. But the romance was over. Not long afterward I was discharged from the army and went back to Revere, back to my parent's house, back home.

home from the army

I soon discovered that my college degree in marketing and advertising and my life experience in the army were no insurance policy against unemployment. After a few months searching for a job in my field, I ended up at that miserable job doing inventory at the Colonial Paint Brush Company. For a measly dollar an hour, we counted paint brushes and stocked them, about 20 of us in a room, watched over by a horrible hawkeyed "Nurse Ratchit" bitch. If we so much as took a breath to relax, she'd fix us with the stare of doom. I dreaded going to work each day, but this drudgery taught me an important lesson — that one of life's greatest blessings is to work at something you love. Colonial Paint was something I most emphatically did not love. I considered it worse than prison, because at least in prison I could have done what I spent all my time daydreaming about doing. Having sex with men.

The only time I could do that now was on the weekends. When Friday night arrived, I was primed for the hunt. Somehow the experience of the army and Jim and the romance — the experience of loving another man and of feeling loved in return — did not seem to translate to Revere or Boston. That kind of life belonged to another world, a European world of villages and falling snow and a great Mercedes parked on romantic country lanes. Back in gritty Revere, in my parent's house, in my old room, it was as though I had never left. As though I were 16 again, guilty and horny. And so the Public Garden in Boston became my weekend escape from the crushing weight of being a grownup homosexual living in a child's room under a mother's watchful, jealous eye. And it was there, at the Public Garden, that it first became apparent that a great change was taking place in gay life, even though that change seems much more vivid in retrospect than it did at the time. Today gay historians write about it and analyze it, but when you live these things you both notice them and do not notice them at the same time.

What was happening was this. The very beginnings of modern gay life were stirring in darker corners of the park, and the first ramparts of a gay ghetto were beginning to go up on Beacon St. and Commonwealth Ave., a little community of homosexual men loving each other. Nothing as big as today, of course. But the seeds of today. Those seeds were planted in the rich, expectant soil of young men like me, back from the service, back from experiences, back from affairs, not completely ready to return to kneeling before straight guys who loathed us except for the momentary pleasure of our mouths. We had been kissed on the lips by handsome gay men in village inns. We had been cuddled in trenches, or Mercedes Benzes. We had met like-minded men, from screamers to sergeants, who talked of injustice and dabbled in drag and knew the lyrics to Broadway show tunes and weren't ashamed to sing them out loud, and we weren't completely ready to go back to being shadows. And so gay men, guys like me, started to spend less time cruising sailors and soldiers, and more time cruising each other.

Now this happened very slowly, so that in my forays in the Public Garden I was still having sex with sailors, still kneeling in alleys, still trying out my best lines on farm boys from Peoria. The difference now was that I was also meeting men who did not wear uniforms, men who had tasteful apartments and drank very dry martinis, men in whom I saw myself reflected. Men who tried to kiss you, and expected you to kiss back.

return to the womb

It's funny the way people's lives can be so easily influenced, and so deeply hurt, by myths. Especially myths masquerading as science. Thank God, the truth has finally been told — a gene is what determines our sexuality. We don't just wake up one day and decide to switch. All the years I was growing up, the word was (the myth was) that guys became gay because they had a domineering mother and a weak father. Today the mainstream scientific establishment scoffs at that idea. But in those days, before people got the bright idea of actually testing Freudian theories against the real world, that was what people believed. It was long ago proven that there is no correlation at all, that huge numbers of gay kids have just the opposite — strong fathers and unassertive mothers — and that huge numbers of straight kids have the supposedly gay combination. Look at inner cities, where in some neighborhoods two-thirds of the kids have strong single moms and no dads at all. No big surge in homosexuality there, so far as I can see. But in my case the dominating mother theory caused me a lot of pain. Because in my case it happened to be true. My mother Sophie walked all over my father. He would work like a dog, out at 5 a.m., back home late in the evening, beat. Then on his one day off, she would have him do all the cleaning and the household work while she'd sit there complaining of how "*exhausted*" she was. Right. Exhausted from giving orders. Of course, this was their problem, not mine. It was the way they were, and they were probably perfectly happy. To hear my father tell it, their marriage was a genuine love affair from the very beginning, and it remained so throughout their 58 years together. But it became a problem for me because, as I realized I was gay, I blamed them, and carried a grudge mixed with love, the most dangerous kind.

My mother was a bona fide Jewish American Princess. She never cooked or cleaned. Her routine was to get dressed and spend the whole day at her girlfriend's house, watching *her* cook and clean. If someone dared ask if she liked to bake, her favorite line was, "*Are you kidding? With a bakery right down the street?*" She did work one day in her life, or at least she went to work one day. After half an hour on the job she called her brother to come pick her up, disabled by a migraine. After that, she patiently explained to whoever asked that she couldn't work because she got headaches, even though it was obvious to everyone else that she got headaches because she didn't want to work. Since mom wouldn't lift a finger, she never invited guests to her home. In our closeknit, family-based world, it was a rudeness my father's relatives could never fathom. But he always stood by her. He was standing by her on January 21, 1933 when she went into a difficult labor that ended with my birth by cesarean section. I did not come easily. My painful birth was like an omen of the stormy relationship that my mother and I would weather our whole lives. We always seemed to be struggling with each other somewhere between love and murder.

I'm sorry I didn't realize how serious migraines are. I wasn't particularly happy growing up. I hate to admit it, but I was kind of a mama's boy. My mother would not let me ride a bike because she thought I might hurt myself, and she never let me go swimming, so I never learned to swim. Extremely embarrassing in a beach town. My mother used to mortify me about it in front of my friends, screaming after me, *"Remember, Melvin, Don't go in the water. YOU KNOW YOU CAN'T SWIM!"* Thanks, mom. But though she was overbearing and smothering toward me, she was very popular with my friends. She may have hated work, but she loved life, and around my pals she acted more like a friend than a parent. Unfortunately, for the most part, that attitude didn't extend to me. I was definitely overprotected and spoiled, and I began to show I was precocious at a very early age, including sexually. When I was six I needed several teeth removed and was deathly afraid of going to the hospital, so I insisted that the dentist come to our house instead. Both Dr. Goldfarb and the family dentist came to the house and put me on the kitchen table for the extraction. As the ether took effect, I began to swoon and dream that I tried to kiss Dr. Goldfarb on the mouth. It was the first time drugs would liberate my libido. Not, as you will see, the last…

chapter three
MICHAEL

Immediately upon arriving back in New York I rented a 5th-floor walk-up on E. 83rd St. in Manhattan for $115 a month (such things were possible then), and reported back to work. I was brought in to run all production, and within months I literally became a one-man production department, handling both singles and LPs.

I couldn't believe how much work there was. ABC/Paramount issued more than 20 releases every quarter, and I had to coordinate the placement of orders to the pressing plant, an extremely detailed job that had to be maintained at a hectic pace under immense pressure and, of course, without the aid of computers. In addition, all of the records required artwork, covers had to be printed, liner notes coordinated, the records had to be packaged, and everything had to be pre-ordered in advance of sales. I have to admit that I didn't really know what I was doing at first, but this wasn't the first time I'd had to fake my way through — or the last. It took years for me to realize that nobody else knows much about what they are doing either — from the president of the U.S. on down. But whatever you do, you must be passionate to be truly successful.

Musically, a lot had happened while I was in Cleveland. The era of the girl groups had dawned with songs like "Will You Love Me Tomorrow" by the Shirelles and "Please Mr. Postman" by the Marvelettes. (I didn't realize it at the time, but that first hit by the Shirelles was also the first hit for a new company called Scepter Records. In several years time I would join the Scepter team, and there, in the early '70s, would help inaugurate a whole new form of pop music unknown in 1962.) Chubby Checker had introduced "The Twist" in 1960, and he and others had been turning out twist variations ever since, until we found ourselves swept away by dance craze after dance craze. The year 1962 alone saw the introduction of the Locomotion, the Mashed Potato, the Limbo Rock, the Watusi — even a dance parody, the Monster Mash.

I arrived back at ABC/Paramount during a period when one peculiar genius, Ray Charles, dominated both the business and the output of our company. Ray was already a headliner and a No. 1 charter before I got back to the city. "Georgia On My Mind" held the No. 1 slot for ten weeks in 1960, and "Hit the Road Jack" held the same position for 11 weeks in 1961. Now Ray was about to produce one of the most historic albums in popular music history, his ground-breaking *Modern Sounds in Country and Western Music*, and I was in charge of production. It was a far cry from schlepping product around to mom-and-pop stores in Ohio. I knew right away that I had made the right decision. *Modern Sounds in Country and Western Music* was a major departure for Ray Charles, and the whole project was suffused with brilliance, talent and extraordinary teamwork. That's what I love most about the record business — creating something great from the efforts of many. *Modern Sounds* gave us "I Can't Stop Loving You," one of Ray's greatest hits, as well as "You Don't Know Me" and "You Are My Sunshine," also Top Ten smashes. It seemed that 1962 was the year of Ray Charles — anything he recorded turned gold, and I was smack in the middle of it. But *Modern Sounds*, produced by Sid Feller, was more than a huge financial success. It was also an enduring cultural and musical landmark. For the first time, a black r&b artist had crossed over into country and western, with strings added to the arrangements. The fact that this sounds so banal today is a testament to how successful an innovation it turned out to be. But back then, it was revolutionary.

Just as Ray's new album was entering production, a salesman from a company making equipment that pressed records began pressing me about a new machine he wanted us to use in production. Up until then records were packaged in thick cardboard covers with no other protection of any kind. Unfortunately the cardboard covers often warped, thus warping the vinyl inside, and we sometimes were obliged to take back hundreds of spoiled returns from distributors. This salesman was now urging me to adopt a brand new shrink-wrap device that encased each album in its own airtight plastic cocoon. I became convinced that even though the initial investment in this new technology was very expensive, it would ultimately save us money. So I prevailed on ABC/Paramount to make the investment. Because ABC owned the pressing plant, they had jurisdiction over packaging. They resisted at first, but I had all my fiscal pegs in a row, and could prove how much could be saved by investing in a technology that was sure to end the endemic problem of warpage and returns. *Modern Sounds in Country And Western Music* thus became the first album ever shrink-wrapped in plastic (something I cringe to think about every time I struggle to open a compact disc today). Needless to say, "I Can't Stop Loving You" more than paid for the shrink-wrap machine. Ray Charles remained in the Top Forty with six more releases through Christmas of 1963. He dominated the charts for years without a break — 19 Top Forty charters, ten Top Ten hits, and three No. 1 smashes. For awhile, nobody could touch Ray Charles.

Others were not so lucky. It was sad to watch Frankie Avalon's slow slide from pop icon to music industry has been. His success had been closely tied to his producer Pete DeAngelis, and after that relationship was terminated Frankie put out one flop song and then another, his last release. "You Are Mine" was a midcharter, stopping at No. 26, and the second stiff in a row that DeAngelis did not arrange and conduct. These last two disappointments seemed ample proof that DeAngelis had been largely responsible for Frankie's earlier hits. The mediocre "You Are Mine" was rushed into release for no other reason than to cash in on Frankie Avalon's box office success. I always thought that this was a pretty shabby way to end a great recording career.

But these ups and down were typical of those heady years that many people think of as the golden age of American pop, before the British invasion. Motown was big. The girl groups were big. Harmony and melody and lightness, the trademarks of the songwriting music factory known as the Brill Building, were big. Great pop songwriters like Carole King, Gerry Goffin, Neil Sedaka and Ellie Greenwich dominated the charts. Out in California the Beach Boys had begun the whole surfer craze. The one thing that marred that era was the assassination of Kennedy, the president who symbolized the self-confidence and vigor of the early '60s. His assassination seemed to undermine everyone's sense of security and confidence.

Then, just a few months later in early 1964, the music business suddenly changed forever. The Beatles touched down at the newly renamed Kennedy Airport, were mobbed by thousands of frenzied teenagers — both boys and girls — and proceeded to spark a mass hysteria that made what had happened to boys like Fabian and Paul Anka seem small potatoes. The Beatles and the subsequent British invasion not only set the music industry ablaze, but also shattered the self-confidence of many of America's brightest songwriters and producers. People who had produced hit after hit suddenly went dry; a whole musical generation felt their moorings slip away. Within a short time the industry seemed in the throes of a real English invasion and the charts were suddenly dominated not just by the Beatles, but also by the Rolling Stones, Peter and Gordon, Herman's Hermits, the Dave Clark Five, and many others.

The one musical style that did not collectively lose its bearings beneath the British onslaught was black American — particularly the Motown sound. After all, r&b was in some ways being imitated by the British boys, and it remained the font of cool. In 1964, the Beatles dominated the charts with "I Want to Hold Your Hand," "Can't Buy Me Love," "She Loves You" and several other smashes. But right up there at the top, holding their own, were the Supremes with "Baby Love," "Come See About Me," and "Where Did Our Love Go," Mary Wells with "My Guy," Martha and the Vandellas with "Dancing in the Streets." While the rest of the world screamed for the moptops from England, I and a lot of my friends were happier boogying down to the cooler, smoother, more danceable sounds of Motown and r&b. In a way, the later distinction between disco and mainstream rock had roots right back here. British boys were masturbating their guitars; black Americans were working out rhythm and dance routines, and exploring novel ways to make you boogie.

Exciting for me were the positive changes blowing in the wind. A month after the Beatles swept through America, Sidney Poitier became the first black person to win an Oscar for Best Actor. I took this as a sign that black people might finally begin to garner some clout in the entertainment industry, an industry to which they had made gigantic contributions but from which they rarely received their due, either financially or any other way. The entertainment industry might help society sweep away the vast self-fulfilling prophecy of racism, I thought. It felt like my dream was coming true the night in 1964 when I turned on the television to hear President Johnson address the nation about the Civil Rights Act. After the tragedy in Dallas the year before, it seemed as if the world was regaining its positive spin. The Summer's Olympics in Tokyo that year showed humanity united, different races and cultures playing together in peace. It was a sweet moment. Vietnam was still a minor story, the horrors of the late

'60s — war, demonstrations, crushing disappointments, riots — lay in the future. Idealism ruled, and set itself up for a grand fall. From my vantage point in Manhattan, looking at the world through the often racist prism of a music industry that thought in terms of black music and white music, I dreamed of a music and a nightlife that would do for us what the Olympics did for the world — bring everyone together.

There was no place in New York City in 1964 where whites, blacks, Hispanics and other minorities could party and play together. Segregation, the cultural kind if not the legal kind, remained the rule. And there was certainly no place for gay men to party with each other in peace. As the decade progressed, the general loosening up of society was not reflected in its treatment of homosexuals. In fact, things seemed to be getting worse. The silence that had blanketed my cruising life in Boston with a certain safety in the late '40s was now shattered by police sirens. Bars were raided more frequently. Men cruising in parks and streets were busted more often. A series of noxious Freudian experts produced book after book about the supposed pathology of homosexuals. Whatever loosening was occurring elsewhere seemed to lead to a tightening of the screws on gays. But we had at least one solution. If we could not be free in the straight world, we could create little worlds of our own. And perhaps the most idyllic world we created was on a long, narrow spit of sand, 60 miles from New York.

fire island

They say that Venice arose in its lagoon when the barbarians swept over the Roman empire and a few enterprising Romans began to build a city far out in the water, inaccessible to the barbarians who simply left it alone. That's kind of what happened with Fire Island. You can only get there by a ferry from Sayville, Long Island, and on the island itself there are no roads or cars, just winding boardwalks and sweeping sand dunes and dense woods. You have to really want to go there to get there. And so, as the barbarians swept Greenwich Village with their paddy wagons and their billy clubs, we fled out onto our lagoon, and built a little paradise where they mostly left us alone.

In terms of pure natural beauty, Fire Island is a paradise. Fairy tale houses and boardwalks nestled in among primeval holly and pine forests. Pristine beaches. The complete lack of cars. The tiny, everybody-knows-everybody communities, the warmth and camaraderie. For a young, still-closeted gay man trying to juggle a professional career with a clandestine social life, it was a dream come true. I would have loved to go out there all year, but unfortunately Fire Island was just a summer place. The season started on Memorial Day and generally lasted through Labor Day weekend or a week or two after. For those who could not afford to rent an entire cottage for the summer, myself included, the solution was a summer share in which several people leased a house for the season on a rotating schedule. A full share usually meant sharing a room every weekend; a half share, every other weekend. For big holiday weekends, everyone was usually allowed to come out, which meant doubling up in rooms or sleeping in shifts. No one minded. During those big party weekends, sleep was beside the point.

As the ferry drew you closer to the island you could feel the restrictions of city life fall away, feel yourself wrapped in safety, security and acceptance. Well, almost. Even in paradise the barbarians and their stupid rules had a toehold. Boys were not allowed to dance openly with other boys, for example. There always had to be a girl in the group somewhere. This farce was taken so seriously that the owner of the Boatel would literally force guys to leave the dance floor if they did not have a girl in their midst. It seems so ludicrous now — four guys dancing in a circle with a girl in the middle. Still, when the police burst in to check, which even out there they sometimes did, we could point out the few women with us and commiserate with the straight cops about Fire Island's poor ratio of women to men. Right.

in walks love

On the 4th of July, 1965, at the peak of the season, I went out to the island to party the weekend away in a room Wayne Stellmacher and I had rented in a crowded little house in the Pines. That weekend I brought along my friend Dick Fisher, a good-humored, lanky, sexy, blue-eyed Ichabod Crane whom I had met through mutual friends from Cleveland. Over the years Dick became like a brother to me, a confidant, a therapist and a constant advisor — though I didn't always heed his advice about so many things.

The night that changed my life began like any other on the Island. I went dancing at the Boatel until closing at 4 a.m., and instead of going directly home I took a walk. The rain had recently stopped, and the ocean air was like pure oxygen after a smoky night in the disco. For some reason I was oblivious to the charms of the scores of hunky boys cruising the boardwalks, and I wandered aimlessly in the cool night, savoring the hours before sunrise, when the dull world is asleep and only the spirits of pleasure are out. Suddenly a young brown-haired guy walked by, stopped and gazed back at me. I mumbled a quiet hello and immediately, without the slightest hesitation or self-consciousness, he introduced himself. Michael Brody, he said. Nineteen-years-old, just one year out of Lafayette High School in Brooklyn, currently working on Wall St. as a messenger. In the intermittent moon the blue of his eyes sparkled like gems, and his flashing smile reminded me of the foam on the waves washing the beach below — sudden bursts of white in the darkness. But although he was strikingly beautiful, there was something else about him, something so warm and open and easy that our age difference — I was 12 years his senior — seemed utterly unimportant. As he casually chatted away I sensed some strange subtext, as though his words encoded a mysterious, lovely message I couldn't understand, a language meant only for me. He had come out to the island with a date, he said. There was a quarrel, after which the date had asked him to leave. These things happened on Fire Island all the time; he knew that. No big deal. Now he was hanging out on the boardwalk, waiting for the dawn. My honest-to-God thought was, I can't let this nice Jewish boy walk around without a place to stay. It could easily start raining again. And so, of course, I did what any gay gentleman would do under the circumstances. I invited him back to my house, even though I had only the couch to offer as a place to sleep. He accepted. It didn't surprise either of us that he did not sleep on the couch that night.

Who knows what perfect alchemy of elements blends into love? Why one soul is incompatible or indifferent, while another becomes the passion of a lifetime? The professional shrinks of that era were telling us with icy scientific detachment that gay men could not love, that ours were stunted hearts. Many of my friends believed it, and were destroyed by that belief. I think I believed it too, at least on the surface. But beneath that surface my heart was not stunted, it was just lonely, and Michael began to ease that loneliness from that first morning, as dawn filtered through the curtains and bathed us in gold.

Did I love right at that moment? Many people have asked me that. After all, it was a moment that, in its small way, changed so much. Developments that would alter gay music and change the ways gay men socialized in the '70s, that would give rise to new kinds of communal celebration, integrated and without regard to race, developments that would lead to a legendary place called the Paradise Garage and the worldwide ascendancy of its famous sound, the rise of disco and house music — so much would flow from that chance meeting on a rain-soaked boardwalk between a lonely 30-something man and a smiling messenger boy. Circles of people would arise and flourish — and perish — all within echoes of that golden morning. Michael himself would perish. But no, I cannot say I fell in love that morning. I only know that's the moment when the possibility of love began.

The next day, Michael proudly offered to drive me back into the city in his hot little yellow Corvair convertible. Poor Michael. Broke as he was, a messenger boy on Wall St. without a pot to piss in, that Corvair was his only material possession, and passion. Before ferrying out to the Island that weekend, he had lovingly draped it with a blanket to keep the sun from destroying the seats, but the rain had completely soaked the blanket, which had fallen into the car and filled it with water. I had to help him bail out the Corvair before we could drive back to Manhattan, scooping up and wringing out and laughing together, funny but not funny. I could hardly have guessed what a metaphor for our lives this would become: me bailing him out, over and over again.

From the start, being with Michael was like living in a new, uncomplicated world. We had fun together, plain as that. We got along. For my part, I was immensely flattered that this beautiful youth 12 years my junior, who could have anyone he wanted, wanted me. He confided in me his dreams of success; he hung on my every bit of advice about his sometimes stormy relations with his family and his problems in school. And he was interested in everything I did, including my newfound passion for painting. It was perhaps because of the unlikelihood of our relationship that

I hesitated at first to plunge into a full-time commitment, and it soon became obvious that Michael wanted far more than I seemed prepared to give.

As the months progressed, my friends were appalled at my ambivalence. What the hell are you waiting for? They'd ask. He's an unbelievable catch. My reply was that I didn't really want a heavy romantic involvement with someone so young. In today's pop psychology lingo, you might say I had low self-esteem, not really believing that something this good could last, and not wanting to get too close so that I wouldn't get too hurt when it didn't. Maybe. It's just as likely that going slow was simply sensible. But there was danger in hesitation. To keep his options open, Michael started dating John Rodriguez, a handsome blonde and blue-eyed Cuban. And to keep mine open, I dated someone else as well. In the end, though, it was a useless charade. Neither one of us could deny that we were falling in love, and it wasn't long before we decided to become full-time lovers.

I remember asking Michael, *"Why did you choose me? Why not John?"* His response was not as romantic as I had hoped, but honest. *"One star in the family is enough,"* he said. I interpreted this to mean that he didn't want to have to deal with the kind of competition that would have existed in a relationship with a stunning hunk like John. But I also liked the casual way he said *"family,"* as if he already thought of me as someone permanent in his life, someone who would be there until the end. And so, as it turned out, I was.

This is not to say that Michael wasn't romantic. He could be positively giddy, sending me postcards from the floor of the New York Stock Exchange, brief but wonderfully sentimental: *"Hi, Baby! Volume at noon: 3,120,000. Love at noon: Always."* On one he drew a facsimile of the famous little red wagons so popular on

Fire Island. On the side of the wagon he wrote *"Weekend,"* and on the boards he drew sticking out of the wagon, he wrote *"Week,"* with the message, *"Thoughts of the weekend will carry my week...Forever, M."* I still have them all, fading artifacts from another age, shards from before a deluge.

For the first couple of years of our relationship we spent weekends together and Michael lived at home with his parents during the week, while he attended college. We started spending a lot of our weekends together out on Fire Island, and once I even took time off from work in the middle of the week, a first for workaholic me. He loved it out there, but I began to realize Fire Island was not necessarily a great place to take a handsome young lover. I shared a house with two men, Gil Johnson and John Robinson, who had been together for over 20 years, and like so many other gay men of that era, their relationship had evolved to include other sex partners. Lots of them. It was an *"anything goes"* kind of house, free-wheeling and wild and a ton of fun, and it soon became clear that everyone was lusting after Michael. So the next year we decided — well, I decided — that we would rent one of the little co-ops on the ocean instead, just the two of us.

It was thrilling to be this handsome boy's lover, but I often found myself overwhelmed by caustic little jealousies. When we would go dancing at the Boatel I'd catch guys slipping him their phone numbers, and my stomach would tie up in knots. But I had to go with the flow. The sexual revolution sweeping the rest of the country was positively inundating gay New York and Fire Island. Everywhere around us people were expressing their sexuality with abandon, and it soon became clear that despite his genuine love for me and our growing intimacy, Michael was a true child of his age.

I began to realize that a lot of the time he wasn't with me, he was, as we used to say, tricking. To him, these were just innocent dalliances, and he took great pains to make sure that I didn't find out about them so that we could maintain the pretense of monogamy. For example, he'd call every night and coo that he wanted to say goodnight and *"take the phone off the hook to study."* This seemed both romantic and sensible — the boy was in college, he had homework to do. But I began to discover that after taking the phone off the hook, he often went out cruising. After awhile it became clear that this was the way it was going to be. He apparently loved his little adventures, and our mutual friends assured me that it was perfectly natural and that it would be foolish of me to think otherwise. After all, I was 31, he was 19, and the world was young. Especially gay New York.

It also became clear that these dalliances could not really threaten our relationship as long as I didn't let them. So I decided that what was good for the goose was good for the gander, and one day I tried to prove it, with rather disastrous results. An attractive guy named Bill Rifkin had moved in across the street. One day, after one of Michael's more outrageous lies about where he had been the night before — some elaborate story about three flat tires — Bill and I happened to meet up outside my building, one thing led to another, and we ended up in my bed. Suddenly, there was this timid knock at the door. It was Passover, and Michael had brought over some treats baked by his mother. I put the chain across the door, opened it a crack and said, *"Sorry, I can't let you in. I'm busy. Understand?"* And to my utter amazement, he began to cry and ran for the elevator.

I was completely flabbergasted. How could Michael, who had tricked with someone only the night before and concocted some outrageous lie about it, be so upset with me for this? I got dressed and ran after him, leaving poor Bill naked in my apartment, and found Michael sobbing despondently on the front steps of the building next door. I tried to console him, but he seemed beyond consoling. Obviously he loved me more than I had realized, despite certain rather blatant inconsistencies. Finally he began to calm down, and I was thankful that Bill, who had dressed and let himself out of my apartment, had the grace not to acknowledge me when he left the building. Without so much as a glance towards Michael and me, he crossed the street and disappeared into his own building — a true professional. Those were the kinds of games we played, especially in the early stages of our relationship.

But eventually it became clear that if Michael was going to have his dalliances, so was I, and we developed a rationale to accommodate our behavior. It was simple: we were not hurting anyone, including ourselves. Far from it: a struggle for monogamy that neither of us really wanted would probably hurt our relationship far more. We had seen how fights between possessive lovers never really brought them any closer together and usually pushed them further apart, and we didn't want to fall into that trap. So over these first few years one of the ways we evolved to deal with our wandering eyes was to bring our outside adventures into the relationship. Once in awhile I'd go out to get cigarettes or ice cream and come back with some hunky guy for dessert. I'd look for someone who would turn Michael on, and for the most part it was fun adding a third party to the mix. I considered this far preferable to being tortured by jealousy. At least I knew where Michael was.

true love

Despite our age difference, we had very similar backgrounds, both having grown up in Jewish families without a lot of money. Money was so tight in the Brody household that Michael was forever being pressured by his family to leave school and find a decent-paying job. I encouraged him to stay in school and get his degree, but with the continuing pressure from his family, exam time became hell, he would become a wreck, his anxiety attacks would get worse, which would only increase his feelings of inferiority within his family. The fact that they downplayed his need for an education and constantly urged him to get a full-time job hardly bolstered his self-esteem.

Michael was also nagged by feelings of inferiority toward his popular, straight brother Jerry. Jerry was a hunky jock, every parent's all-American dream son, and gay Michael felt his parents loved Jerry more, and he could never measure up. It didn't help that his father Ben preached a rigid masculinity, insisting that men always *act like men*" and keep their emotions in check, which Michael felt was directed against him. Years later Michael vividly recalled one incident when he tried to greet his father with a kiss. Ben pushed him away brusquely and made a big scene in front of everybody — a son doesn't kiss his father — insisting they shake hands instead. Michael was very slow to forgive, and he carried the memory of that for the rest of his life. But it's funny how different people have different perspectives. Years later, when I finally got to know Ben Brody, I found him to be as fiercely proud of Michael as any father I've ever met. Sadly, I was never able to convince Michael of that.

We used to have long discussions about money. I knew that Michael could not afford things like vacations, so I was happy to provide them. Any extra money that Michael had was poured into the other love of his life — his convertible. It was a car crazy age — the Beach Boys' songs about cars gave the Beatles a run for their money — and Michael's Corvair was extremely important to him, his most tangible status symbol. Unfortunately it was falling apart, and I began to realize that his credit payments would probably out-live the car. Which is exactly what happened: the poor thing finally gave up the ghost one morning during exam week.

For months Michael had been ogling a 1957 Mercedes Benz 190 SL that was parked on the street by my apartment with a For Sale sign in the window, drooling over it every time we passed. Now, since he needed a new car and didn't have the money to buy one, I secretly called the owner of the Mercedes. I had a mechanic check it out, and decided to buy it for him. I parked it in Michael's garage, and on the day of his last exam I phoned him from work and told him that Dick had left his keys in the garage. *"Could you possibly go down there and see if you can find them?"* He told me afterwards that he just stood there and cried when he found his dream car instead. The fact that this little surprise made me, if anything, even happier than Michael, made me realize how much I had fallen in love.

But I wasn't kidding myself. No matter how much you give to someone you love, you cannot give them a sense of pride or self-accomplishment. Michael's self-esteem had to come from within, from being able to support himself and manage his own life. So despite the fact that my job paid vastly more than his, I did not keep him. That would never have worked. He always took care of himself financially and even took pains to spend money on me. On the 4th of July, 1966, our first anniversary, he gave me a stunning gold and diamond ring with the inscription *"Our love forever."*

We were in love, simple as that. There were nights when he would come bursting into my apartment, eager to share exciting news about school. There were nights when we would just laugh and laugh like children, chasing each other, falling into each other's arms. Sometimes, when he reached the end of his rope emotionally, he would drop his defenses and let himself cry in front of me. I can remember holding him in my arms and feeling his warm tears on my neck. I don't think I can recall any stronger memories of loving him than those.

But I could also see that Michael was struggling with too much, vainly trying to keep up with his studies while struggling to earn money, and I finally convinced him to start looking for a full-time, well-paying job. He was worried that his lack of college degree would hobble him, but I assured him that if he fibbed a little on job applications and told prospective employers that he had already finished college, they would probably never question it. I knew he'd do well once he found the right job: he was a go-getter, eager to please, desperate for something to immerse himself in. Michael had a very winning way with people, exuding honesty and reliability, and just as I predicted, no employer ever checked his mythical college degree.

So I was able to find him an office job at a printer that I had with ABC/Paramount. Michael was thrilled to be off Wall St. and making better money. We even started discussing the possibility of living together. Up until now he lived at home and spent weekends with me, which was fairly easy to explain to his parents: convenient for seeing friends in Manhattan. It was not going to be so easy explaining living with me on a full-time basis. And so it was high time I met Ben and Jean Brody.

Michael and I decided to add a couple of friends to this initial meeting with my unsuspecting in-laws, just to keep things casual, read — *closeted.* We invited Vince LaMonica and his beautiful girlfriend Dawn. Vince was a fiery Italian with weird notions about his sexual identity. One day he was gay, the next he was straight, the next that he liked to *"keep people guessing."* Dawn occasionally acted as a beard for Michael when he had to attend straight functions, and the four of us often hung out together, so Vince and Dawn were perfect for meeting Michael's parents. The evening went smoothly and everyone seemed to get along well. The next day I asked Michael what his mother had said. Apparently she couldn't say enough about Vinnie and Dawn.

They were just fabulous. Terrific friends to have. That Vinnie, what a hoot. And that Dawn, such a gorgeous girl. Such a figure. And, I asked... and? *"Oh, and Mel is nice, too."* At least she remembered my name.

my life as an artist

During our weekends together, Michael would often drive me to the art fairs to sell my paintings. My life as an artist had begun during a brief fling with an artist named Joe Abraham back in 1962. One day at the Museum of Modern Art, we stood looking at a painting by Mark Rothko, whom I had always idolized as a unique and brilliant colorist. Swept away by Rothko's genius, I confided to Joe that I had this sudden sense that I could create something as full of emotion and expression as these abstracts. Although I didn't realize it at the time, that moment changed my life forever.

Joe suggested I try my hand at painting. *"Whatever you paint is bound to be better than those prints you've got hanging on your walls,"* he joked. So I bought some tubes of paint and a little canvas board, and then the feeling passed and I didn't go near them for a long time. Then one night coming home from the bars I saw the stuff staring at me from the corner of my apartment. It was 3 a.m., and I was restless and depressed. I didn't have any brushes, so I just plunged in with my fingers. I had never taken an art lesson, but while I was painting, the colors seemed to pour out of me and onto the canvas. In the stark light of day the next morning, I was dubious about the result. *"What is that?"* I asked myself, worried I had created a monstrosity. But before throwing it away I decided to show it to Joe, the only artist I knew. My jaw dropped when his jaw dropped and he praised it effusively, strongly encouraging me to keep painting. I kept that first attempt, and many people have told me they think it is one of my best paintings.

Not too long after that I tried to copy a Modigliani print. My copy turned out to be so close to the original that when I called the framer to find out if it was ready, he told me, *"Your Modigliani is ready."* That was certainly encouraging. Soon I was secluding myself in my apartment and painting like crazy. A turning point came the day President Kennedy was killed. In a state of shock, almost in a waking dream, I began a kind of simple line drawing. Without even thinking I watched as it became a distinguishable profile of a woman. When I came out of my trance a glowing silhouette of Jacqueline Kennedy shone from the canvas.

Someone suggested that I exhibit my paintings at the Washington Square Art Show. The first day I sold two to a couple from Great Neck and was a bonafide, if part-time, artist. Pretty soon I was a regular in the art shows, where to my amazement my paintings sold well. I began making money painting, and winning awards as well, from prestigious places like the Salmagundi Club. Painting seemed to provide the perfect release, and the only thing that could have made things better would have been to combine work with painting. And then even that miracle occurred.

One night Michael and I were spending a quiet evening at home listening to music. I pulled out Ray Charles's *Genius Plus Soul Equals Jazz*, produced by Creed Taylor, a protégé of my old boss Harry Levine. Creed was a very successful producer who used to spend a lot of money on the albums he produced. Harry Levine, his mentor, always covered for him and allowed him enormous budgets. Together they created one of the first ultra-exclusive packages, Impulse Records. Thinking about this I suddenly remembered that Creed, after starting his own label, CTI, had used an abstract impressionist painting by Olga Albizu as an album cover. I started pulling out more of my jazz records and found that plenty of other labels were using abstracts for their covers as well. Michael jumped on the idea that this would be a perfect venue for my paintings, and I, not being the shy type, immediately showed some of my paintings to Bob Thiele, the well-known jazz producer. He loved them so much he used my very first painting for the cover of Archie Shepp's *Fire Music.*

Soon my paintings were gracing the covers of albums on several major labels, including Impulse, Bluesway, ABC and Riverside. Bob Thiele told me that the inspiration for the title of an album by Archie Shepp, *Fire Music,* came from a painting of mine that he'd chosen for the cover. I was particularly proud of my covers for *Latin Shadows* by Shirley Scott, and *East Broadway Run Down* by Sonny Rollins, both on the Impulse label, and for a John Lee Hooker album that came out on Bluesway Records. Five of my covers were nominated for Grammys, yet I was paid only $50 or $100 a cover. Who cared? I would have paid them. And anyway, it was so simple. I lent them a painting, a photographer would photograph it, I'd get paid and get the painting back. Of course, artwork for albums isn't that easily negotiated nowadays. What they paid me back then wouldn't even cover the cost of a lawyer to make a single phone call today.

michael moves in

Not too long after that dinner with the Brodys, Michael moved into my apartment on W. 20th St., and the best time in our lives together began. I wanted to crow about this happiness to those I loved at home and at work, but I couldn't. Instead, the opposite. My closet door remained iron shut. My mother nagged constantly about who I was dating, and one day, when I evaded her questions too breezily, she announced her opinion: I had decided to wait until she died before I got married, so she wouldn't have the pleasure of seeing any grandchildren. Oy. I would have loved to say, *"Don't worry, Ma, I already am married. To a nice Jewish boy."* I would have loved for her to love that. But that seemed impossible in 1966.

It was another family member, cousin Barry Cherin, who offered Michael his break into show biz. Barry worked as a publicist for Paramount Pictures, and one day he called to suggest that Michael apply for a temporary position in publicity under advertising director Everett Olsen. Michael got the job and it was perfect: exciting work, challenging, good money, and in the movie business. He loved it, and within a short time he became Paramount's fair-haired boy. This became quite obvious when the employee he had temporarily replaced returned to the company — and was shunted off to another position. There was no way that Everett was going to let Michael Brody, this golden catch, get away.

It turned out there was another reason Olsen was so keen on keeping Michael. Olsen was often out of the office on business, and Michael knew that the main reason for his absences had to do with a serious bout with the bottle. Michael ended up covering for him extensively, not only doing his own job but Olsen's as well. Michael found himself returning memos and phone calls, chairing meetings, and eventually handling million-dollar budgets. His self-confidence soared, and I prayed that the praise lavished on him at Paramount would compensate for the lack of approval that he felt from his family and father.

the mamas and the papas, and macarthur park

Over the next several years, as Michael and I consolidated our relationship and learned to live together, the music industry was on one of the great historic rolls of all time. This was the second golden age of rock'n'roll. The period from 1965 to 1969 is now remembered for giving birth to many of the sounds that still dominate music today, 30 years later. The mod era evolved into the psychedelic, heavy metal was born (although it wasn't called that at first), Motown redefined glamour, the Beatles continued their unstoppable streak of success with *Sgt. Pepper's*, and some of the greatest sounds ever produced by pop music vied for control of the airwaves. The biggest artists from those days still have enduring popularity today, including the Stones, the Doors, the Who, Janis Joplin, Simon and Garfunkel, Aretha Franklin, Diana Ross and the Supremes, Joe Cocker, Marvin Gaye, Jefferson Airplane, the Grateful Dead, Creedence Clearwater Revival, Jimi Hendrix, Steppenwolf, the Band, and a group that would have its bigger heyday years later — the Bee Gees. It was the era of Monterey and Woodstock, flower children and antiwar protests. Rock was the music of rebellion and freedom, and for awhile it seemed that music itself was driving the immense cultural changes that still reverberate today.

Things were certainly interesting at work. At the very beginning of this amazing era, ABC acquired the Dunhill label, and I sat in on the meetings that launched this important move. Dunhill's original owners were Lou Adler and Jay Lasker, and it was decided that Lasker would be the president of the new ABC/Dunhill label. (Years later, he became head of Motown Records.) Lasker and I had a good relationship, and he would often call and ask my advice about new product. Steppenwolf and Three Dog Night were assigned to Dunhill, groups right out of the Love Generation, and also part of the Dunhill stable was a group of troubadours formed in the Virgin Islands and recently relocated to California. The New Journeymen consisted of John Phillips, Cass Elliot, Denny Doherty and Michelle Gilliam. Lou Adler brought them to California to record backup vocals for

Barry McGuire, whose darkly pessimistic single "Eve Of Destruction" hit No. 1 in September of 1965. For McGuire's next album Lou produced "California Dreamin'," which was written by New Journeyman John Phillips, and Lou used the Journeymen for the backing track. Then he signed the New Journeymen to their own deal.

They toyed around with the name the Magic Circle, but finally settled on the Mamas and the Papas. Lou produced "Go Where You Wanna Go," which he was planning to release as the group's debut single but changed his mind and went with "California Dreamin'" instead, using exactly the same backing track that he'd used on the Barry McGuire version, except that this time with the Mamas and the Papas handling the lead vocals. We released the song to huge acclaim and the Mamas and the Papas, along with ABC/Dunhill Records, were off to a great start. Which meant that I was going out of my mind with work. Over the next four years we churned out hit after hit, and were sometimes responsible for major innovations in the industry.

One of those innovations occurred in June of 1968 when ABC/Dunhill released an album with Richard Harris singing Jimmy Webb songs, including "MacArthur Park." "MacArthur Park" should be the single – we decided – but it was over eight-minutes long, and radio programmers at that time refused to play songs longer than three-and-a-half minutes. We held a big pow-wow to decide the fate of this potentially ground-breaking single, and some executives suggested that it fade out after three-and-a-half minutes, while others thought that we should split the song and put it on two sides of a 45 rpm single. I couldn't believe it. *"You can't take a masterpiece and fade it out or cut it up,"* I objected. I argued that we had to release the song as is, that radios were bound to play it anyway. Fortunately, other executives rallied to my support, and after a lot of arguing, we won.

"MacArthur Park" was released on a single side, all eight minutes of it, and it climbed the charts like a rocket, blocked from the No. 1 spot only by Herb Alpert's "This Guy's In Love With You." Since I had loved "MacArthur Park" from the first and was certain it would become a smash, I was thrilled that hundreds of thousands agreed with me. A serious song like "MacArthur Park" really stood out from the rest of the Top Forty songs of the time, and it paved the way for many other innovative songs that might not have otherwise become hits. Within just a few months Simon and Garfunkel released "Mrs. Robinson" and the Beatles came out with "Hey Jude," both of which far exceeded the radio programmers' previous three-and-a-half-minute time limit. I like to think that these great songs benefited from the ground-breaking "MacArthur Park." It was thrilling to be in the middle of all this, to help make these little revolutions happen. From 1965 through 1969 we rode the wave.

stonewall

By 1969 a great wave of freedom had swept the nation, raising women's skirts to the pelvis, dropping men's hair to the shoulder, turning the college campus and the ghetto into battle grounds and a farm in upstate New York into a hippie nation. Everyone clamored for freedom, and practically everybody was getting it. But not us.

In Greenwich Village and other gay neighborhoods, more and more gay men and lesbians were coming to terms with their homosexuality and trying to build an affirming community. But that just irked the establishment, and by 1969 a vicious backlash was in full swing. Vicious but silent. Reactions to the black movement and women's movement and hippie movement may have been front-page news, but the anti-gay backlash proceeded silently, out of sight. Every week teams of police harassed gay people just for the sake of intimidation, and police paddy wagons were a familiar sight outside gay establishments. It seemed like we were always having to duck out of bars that were being raided, and the possibility of police interference became a determining factor in our decisions about where, or even whether, to go out. But nobody fought back. We just accepted it, the way we accepted the closet, the way we accepted our second-class status. Until one night in June.

That weekend, Judy Garland's body was laid out at Campbell's Funeral Home on Lexington Ave. The fanatical worship of Garland was a big part of gay life back then (writer Vito Russo would call it Judyism). The fact that I was not much of a Judy Garland fan was almost enough to get my membership in certain gay circles revoked. But I did come into contact with her when she was performing with her son and daughter, Joey and Lorna Luft, at the Palace theatre on Broadway. I was invited along by Bob Thiele, the ABC A&R man who was producing the album *Judy Live at the Palace*. A drug store delivered a prescription for Judy, and she shouted to someone, *"Tell that fuckin' trumpet player to tone it down. He's drowning Joey out."* She came off the stage and declared, *"Oh, I split my pants." "Let them see it Judy. They'll love it,"* I told her. *"No,"* she winked, *"It'll be our secret."*

Garland's sudden death was a galvanizing event in gay New York, and emotions ran high on that unusually hot weekend. The Stonewall bar, a slightly seedy dance place in the Village's main square, was packed with customers when the paddy wagons pulled up outside. As the cops started pulling people out, a couple of drag queens jeered back, *"reading"* the policemen and drawing a small crowd. It never takes much of a commotion for people to gather in New York City, and those drag queens were playing to their audience. Then something just collectively clicked. The crowd began to join in. Someone started throwing coins. Then, as a lesbian was being dragged from the bar, she turned, saw the mob gathering, sensed the rage building, and recognized her moment. The next push from the cop was one push too many, she resisted, and the world changed forever. Rocks flew, bottles blew up against cop cars, an airborne trashcan shattered a cop car window. The cheers became a chant. Within minutes, the police sent in their big guns, the Tactical Police Force, with their helmets and riot shields. The crowd divided, forming a wall of *them* versus *us*. Fires were lit, one of which almost burned down the Stonewall with cops still inside. One detective actually waved his gun, shouting, *"Let's kill some faggots!"* People began to stream out of nearby bars, shops and restaurants to see what was going on. Traffic on Seventh Ave., normally busy, came to a complete halt and backed up for blocks.

Michael and I were out for a walk, and as we came down W. 4th St. we were drawn to the commotion by what seemed like thousands of flashing police lights. Suddenly I found myself — at 36, with a rising career in the music business, and firmly locked in the closet — smack in the middle of a homosexual riot. Becoming an activist was the furthest thing from my mind, but the mood of the crowd was contagious and it drew you in. You could sense our power as a group, and I found myself unafraid to shout back and scream at the cops. There were thousands of us, with more gathering as the night wore on, and Sheridan Square became a glorious, hysterical, hilarious mob scene, perhaps the most tasteful riot in history. Michael and I could have ducked behind someone and got away if we'd wanted, but it was too exciting. We had all suffered humiliation at the hands of the police; we all knew that no one else was going to fight this battle for us. My memory of a man in high heels and a dress kicking back at a cop — *"You bitch, this dress cost a fortune"* — symbolizes the entire episode. On that steamy summer night we discovered that as individuals we may have been no match for the police and their billy clubs, but as a community we had tremendous power. It was a lesson I have never forgotten.

Throughout the weekend the oppressive heat held fast and people couldn't wait for nightfall to get over to Sheridan Square and see what was happening. Every time the cops tried to disperse the newly forming crowds, things began all over again. On Saturday afternoon, a new group called the Gay Liberation Front circulated flyers asking people to meet July 1st to organize an official response from the gay community, an act that stands as the official beginning of modern gay liberation. But frankly, in the heat of the moment most of us probably were not that interested in official responses. We were fired up. The fracas continued until the wee hours of Monday morning, and by the end of that weekend a new era had begun. It would be my era, my golden age. My great Before.

chapter four
AGAIN,
NOTHING HAPPENS
BY ACCIDENT

In 1970 the music business was once more in the throes of change. The Beatles, who had epitomized and personified the happy spirit of the '60s, broke up in rancor. The free love ethos of Woodstock was smashed in the violence and murder of the Rolling Stones Altamont concert, and the optimism of the hippie era began to give way to a pervasive cynicism. Simon and Garfunkel's ambitious, heavily arranged "Bridge Over Troubled Water" hit the top of the charts, a new Motown group with an 11-year-old lead singer — the Jackson 5 — had a smash hit, "I'll Be There," and Diana Ross, now shorn of her Supremes, had a solo smash, "Ain't No Mountain High Enough."

The industry itself began to change, growing more professional and less freewheeling. In line with that change, ABC/Paramount renamed itself ABC Records and began moving its operations to the west coast. Los Angeles was fast becoming the magnet of the industry, and most music honchos in grimy New York jumped at the chance to relocate to the sunny, laid-back canyons of southern California. There was just one hitch: I loved the grimy canyons of Manhattan. My close circle of friends were here, and so was the most important thing in my life, my five-year relationship with Michael. I was also falling in love with New York's energized nightlife, then just on the cusp of the disco explosion that would form the center of my world and entice a whole generation of gay men to dance our way through the coming decade. Gay life was blossoming in the wake of Stonewall, and like many other New Yorkers I felt I was in the center of the world. 1970 was no time to leave — things were just getting good. So while my co-workers started shopping for suntan lotions to lubricate their bronzed new lifestyles on the coast, I started looking for a new job.

I landed first at a place called Commonwealth United Records. My mentor at ABC, Sam Clark, didn't think Commonwealth had much chance of surviving and advised me not to take the job, offering instead to let me remain at ABC and handle production from the New York office. I was tremendously flattered that Sam liked me enough to try to create a special position for me with the company, but I also knew production well enough to know that you could never run that department from New York if the rest of the company was out in California. So as my giddy colleagues winged off to the coast, I started my new job with Commonwealth.

Unfortunately, Sam was right. Commonwealth had only two artists in 1969, Lenny Welch, who had a hit with "Since I Don't Have You," and Cissy Houston, a transcendent singer in her own right long before she became known as Whitney's mother. But Commonwealth lasted only four months before it folded, owing me $16,000 on my contract. My lawyer advised me that to recover the money I had to show good intentions by quickly finding another job, so I hit the streets again. And that's how I fell into the charmed and sometimes cursed orbit of Florence Greenberg.

florence

Florence owned Scepter Records, a small but flourishing outfit churning out hits with such artists as the Shirelles, Dionne Warwick, and B.J. Thomas. Florence was one of the great characters of the '60s and '70s music world, the toughest of tough cookies, a loud, brassy Jewish "Ma Kettle" on speed. Scripts about her life have been knocking around Hollywood for years, with Bette Midler often mentioned to play the role of Florence. That would be truly casting to type. My earliest memory of her is the day we met. Slightly trembling, I asked for $400 a week. *"Do I look like a fuckin' money tree?"* she snarled. Then she turned all Jewish mother: *"Look, dear, I can offer you $350 a week. That's decent money for a single guy like you. Surely."* And then she turned Mrs. Hyde again, barking, *"And if you don't dick around with me, I'll think about giving you a raise."* This, I could immediately see, was not going to be a walk in the park.

But while everybody agreed that Florence could be hell to employees she didn't like, she was reputedly a great boss to employees she did like, and she knew how to throw around generous perks as well as gutter profanities. I crossed my fingers and took the job. Then I discovered a slight problem. She didn't like me.

This woman who was to have such an impact on my life rose to power in the music industry almost by accident. For years she had owned a tiny local record label, Tiara Records, in New Jersey, where she otherwise lived as a suburban wife and mother. One day in 1958, her daughter Mary Jane brought over a girl friend, Shirley Owens, the lead singer of an obscure girl group called the Poquellos. They played Florence a song called "I Met Him On A Sunday" and Florence saw her chance to grab the brass ring. She renamed Shirley's group the Shirelles, recorded the song, and worked it into an immense smash. It is often considered the song that inaugurated the era of the girl groups (although the Chantels, with their 1958 song "Maybe," probably deserve that distinction just as much, since they actually preceded the Shirelles) and the Shirelles were followed by a slew of Ronettes and Marvelettes and Dixie Cups and Chiffons and Shangri-Las and, supremely, the Supremes. After negotiating a lucrative deal with Decca Records, Florence went into business with Marvin Schlacter to form her own company, Scepter Records, and throughout the '60s she produced hit after hit, becoming by far the most successful woman in the music industry. The name Scepter was in royal company with her earlier label Tiara and a later subsidiary, Wand. As far as Florence was concerned, it was all about being a queen.

As far as I was concerned, at least for the first few months in 1970, it was all about being the queen of mean. My start at Scepter was a season in hell. Florence swaggered around the office finding unique combinations of Yiddish and four-letter words to describe my work. I was *"a fuckface schlmiel, a putz."* She'd grab orders out of my hand, sandwiches out of my mouth. I had knots in my stomach all day, but I still somehow managed to throw myself into the job with my usual cheerfulness and energy, and suddenly one day, completely out of the blue, the dragon lady turned into snow white. Or at least snow white with a marine's foul mouth. Florence suddenly loved my work, loved my ideas, fuckin' loved fuckin' me. She even began inviting me to her Florida condo.

Years later, when I asked her about the abrupt change, she told me that she had started out distrusting me because I originally worked for her competitors, Sam Clark and Larry Newton. In her savvy but slightly paranoid way, she thought I came to Scepter to pull some of their *"bullshit schtick"* on her. When she finally realized I was not some secret agent, she said, *"I fell in love with you."* The feeling was mutual. Florence was to become a treasured friend throughout our association, long after I stopped working for her, right up to the day she died.

As it turned out, the Shirelles were no one-hit wonder (unlike the Chantels), and that was no accident. The girls recorded "Dedicated to the One I Love" in 1959, watching it top out at an embarrassing No. 83. But Florence believed in that song, and nothing like a little commercial flop was going to dissuade her. She reworked it, and with her faith, tenacity and timing, it shot up the charts to No. 3 in 1961. After working closely with her, I discovered that what it really boiled down to was how much Florence believed in herself and the close circle of trusted friends she gathered to assist her. Her boyfriend Luther Dixon (she had separated from her husband) became the Shirelles producer and arranger, and Luther and Florence wrote "Soldier Boy" in five minutes of spare studio time left over from another song. The Shirelles recorded "Soldier Boy" in a single take, and it became the biggest of a string of hits that included "Will You Still Love Me Tomorrow," "Mama Said," "Foolish Little Girl," and "Baby It's You."

When I arrived at Scepter in 1970, the company's most famous songwriter was Burt Bacharach. He came to Scepter with Dionne Warwick, whom he had employed as a demo singer for the songs he and Hal David were sending around to record companies. Florence saw the genius of the combination, put Burt and Hal to work writing songs for Dionne on the Scepter label, and by the time I joined the company, they had written 17 hit singles for Dionne Warwick and several for other singers. Florence's complex relationship with Burt is an example of how, even though she was capable of brilliant moves, she was also capable of disastrous ones. At some point along the way Burt meekly suggested to Florence that he wanted to start his own publishing company. Some of the biggest money in the music business comes from publishing royalties, and with Florence's power she could easily have told Burt that she wanted to control the publishing rights herself. But for some inexplicable reason she had what she called a *"friggin' attack of Jewish mother crapola"* and gave Burt permission to start his own company. She ultimately lost millions in publishing fees because of that lapse.

There were other lapses as well. Florence started Mace Records, a budget classical line run by her son Stanley, who was legally blind, and Florence's heart-of-gold quality showed in her relationship to Mace and Stanley. Because the label was run by her son, she would get more excited about orders for two Mace records than an order for 10,000 copies of any other release. But as I discovered when I started working in production, her motherly devotion blinded her to even the simplest business decisions. The problem was that Columbia pressed Mace records, and whenever a Mace product was selling slower than slow, which was always, Columbia just put it in dead storage. The little classical Mace label simply didn't sell the kind of quantity Columbia required to keep the records available in current stock. So when an order would come in for two measly Mace records, Florence would call up Columbia, discover no records were in current stock — she didn't realize that they were simply in dead storage and nobody at Columbia ever mentioned it — and she would excitedly demand the minimum production order of 300 new records pressed, all to sell two pieces of Mace product. When I discovered this problem and its easy solution, Florence's respect for me grew even more.

Despite these business lapses, Florence was flourishing. Not only was she the first female owner of a record company, she had several subsidiary labels aside from Mace. Groups like the Kingsmen, Wilson Pickett, and Chuck Jackson were signed to her predominantly r&b label, Wand Records. She had a gospel label, Hob, with artists such as the Mighty Clouds of Joy, Albertina Walker, the Five Blind Boys, James Cleveland and Shirley Caesar. Hob was run by tall, distinguished Mancel Warwick, Dionne's father, a great co-worker and a true gentleman, an unusual combination in the elbow-in-the-gut music world.

Dionne herself was starting to have problems with Burt when I arrived at Scepter, primarily over her dissatisfaction with the material they were churning out. I remember the day she recorded the mediocre "Paper Mache" and I overheard her saying, *"I'll bet Burt wrote that one on the way to the race track."* It never made *Billboard's* Top Forty, sputtering out at No. 43. Her confidence in the Bacharach/David team was revived the next year when she won a Grammy for Best Female Contemporary Vocal Performance with "I'll Never Fall In Love Again." But then it was a free fall. Her next two songs were disappointments, and her last record on the label, "Amanda," stalled at No. 83 and then completely dropped off the charts. Dionne packed her bags at Scepter and went looking for greener pastures at Warner Brothers. She didn't have another hit for years.

I only glancingly knew Dionne in our days together at Scepter. I was coming and she was going, and so we never had a chance to become friends. But I sometimes wonder what we would have thought back then if somebody had told us that someday decades later, we would both end up as leaders of charitable organizations fighting a modern plague. It seems so strange to think of us then — still kids as the swinging '60s roared into the go-go '70s, the great youth explosion reaching its feverish peak — and then to think of us now — older, having lived through hell itself, raising money in a desperate attempt to save lives. I can't speak for Dionne, but as for me, if you had told me in 1970 what was going to happen to my world, I would have said you were nuts.

ed and maye

Two other people at Scepter were destined to play big roles in my life and in the disco explosion of the coming years. Ed Kushins was Scepter's hard-working and meticulous Sales Manager. He used to keep a 3 x 5 card to list every penny that he personally spent. Despite our vastly different styles we immediately hit it off, listened to music together, exchanged ideas and generally clicked.

We didn't realize it then, but we were laying the groundwork for the cooperative spirit that would animate us when, a few years later, Ed and I would form our own record company.

Maye Hampton James was the production department secretary. Maye was a smart, sassy black woman who had been Mary Wells's best friend and road manager in the early '60s. When Mary's career waned after her hit streak with Motown, Maye packed up and moved to New York, a divorced single mom looking for work. Even though a couple of advertising firms offered her well-paying jobs, she came to work at Scepter as our humble receptionist *"because,"* she later said, *"I could hear the music coming from the studio all day."* Maye quickly went from company receptionist to secretary of the promotion department, which pushes the company's product in stores and onto the airwaves. Though she was only paid to be a secretary, Maye immediately started calling the contacts she had made on the road with Mary Wells, using them to promote Scepter product. She also began calling all the disc jockeys she had befriended during those record hop tours, cooing into the phone in that way she had, using her considerable charms and personal friendships to get them to play our records.

Whenever Maye got a record added to the playlist of an important radio station, which was often, the staff was blown away. Chris Jonz, Scepter's head of promotion, was astounded by Maye's initiative and success. As far as Florence was concerned, however, Maye was just a secretary. We were a small company in which it was normally easy to get ahead. Whenever someone left, Florence, suspicious of outsiders, usually promoted from within. But when Chris Jonz left to work for Stevie Wonder at Motown, we were shocked to learn that Maye was passed up for the promotion job, which she richly deserved. Ed believed that Florence was simply biased against women. That might seem odd for a woman who had made it in a man's business. But it also seemed true. Florence may have been a feminist icon, but she was hardly a feminist herself, and she rarely gave women a fair shake. Maye, however, was soon to emerge as a power in her own right. Florence couldn't hold back a tidal wave.

building a life

As the '60s flowed into the '70s things were going well for Michael and me. I loved my painting and my job, Michael was blossoming in his, and our five-year relationship had matured into a mutually supportive, trusting partnership. It may seem odd to say that we also slept with other people, that we sometimes had threesomes, that our relationship did not involve or even require the pretense of sexual monogamy. But that was the way things were back then, and we thought we had things figured out pretty well. We had a circle of close friends we loved and with whom we shared summer houses on Fire Island. And gay life itself, that vast conglomeration of spirit, sex, politics, partying and camaraderie, was booming like never before.

The aftermath of Stonewall almost took your breath away. Gay New York seemed to explode, bars popping up like mushrooms, splashy bathhouses opening across the city, discos and demos and books and magazines and a radical new spirit proclaiming *"Gay is good!,"* that we're not sick or evil, that gay people don't have to be ashamed, that it's society that's got the problem, not us. Underneath the sex explosion, underneath everything else, this newfound pride was the real change. Gay men had lost what Allen Ginsberg called *"that wounded look"* that everybody had in the '50s and '60s. A lot of guys replaced it, at least in part, with a lumberjack masculinity of boots and muscles and mustaches: the Marlboro Man cruising Christopher St. with a key ring in his belt loop and a colored hankie in his back pocket that advertised his sexual tastes.

Michael and I didn't really go in for that, any more than we had gone in for the hippie thing a few years earlier. My hair was a bit long, but Michael kept his curly brown locks cut short, and we were both fairly clean cut, our casual jeans and t-shirts reflecting our casual approach to life. Of course, whatever you wore, decades of shame are not erased overnight by a slogan or a manifesto or a pumped-up set of pecs. I and many others had been conditioned to be ashamed, and I was going to have to be conditioned out of it. And so as life opened up around me, and as I opened up to that life, I remained tightly closeted at work and to my family. In a way, though, it seemed to matter less. There was such a marvelous new world to be open in, that popping back into the closet during business hours and in long-distance chats with my family seemed less onerous. I had a life. We both did.

As we began to feel more financially secure, Michael and I decided to try to become property owners and establish ourselves financially for the long haul together. We couldn't yet afford a building in pricey Manhattan with the modest sum I'd saved from doing art shows, but from doing those shows on the Brooklyn Heights Esplanade I had become familiar with affordable Brooklyn, the borough of the Fonz, and so we looked around there. We soon found a house at 240 Warren St. in Cobble Hill, and by juggling loans and cash and credit cards, we were able to scrape together the down payment.

Warren St. was far from a dream house. In fact it was an ugly duckling, a five-story oddity sticking out like a sore thumb in a row of classic brownstones. We chose one apartment for ourselves, tore down walls and carted away enough wire mesh and plaster to fill a two-ton truck. I remember those as days of hope, stripping old paint, coughing plaster dust out of our lungs, laughing and hammering and dreaming of how it would be when we were secure, when all our struggles were behind us, when we could relax and enjoy a happy middle age and beyond because of our hard work, because we had done it together. It probably sounds corny, but that building became our child, the visible symbol of our love and commitment to each other. And when it was finally done a year later, it worked. We had a fabulous place to live, equity, money from rents. We'd done it.

It was very important to both of us that Michael have an equal partnership in the new building. His enthusiasm and labor were more than comparable to my larger monetary investment, and he took care of all of the financial records, collected rents from the tenants and made sure that the mortgage was paid. Managing the business side of the building came naturally to him. I saw in Michael what his superiors saw at Paramount — an intelligent, hard-working young man who only needed opportunities to realize his potential. The savvy that he would later show as one of the great entrepreneurs of disco was evident in the way he oversaw every little detail of renovating an apartment or haggling with contractors. He was born to do business.

But Michael was also showing glimpses of a somewhat darker side. Shortly after we moved into Warren St., he started palling around with Dennis Tomasetti, one of his co-workers at Paramount. Dennis was an Eddie Haskell type, good-looking but calculating and a bit shady, the kind who takes three-hour lunches and thinks he's getting away with something. He started luring Michael away from the office during working hours, taking him on lunch-hour tours of the seamy side of the gay world, the bookstores and X-rated theaters and porn palaces of Times Square. Michael was fascinated with this underworld of zipless sex, and Dennis did everything he could to make it seem alluring. With Michael's innocent youthful good looks he was probably an instant star in this jaded, mostly middle-aged realm of trench coats and flickering images in the dark. I sometimes think these forays were more motivated by some need to establish independence from me and gain affirmation than by his sexual curiosity. But it was a sexual world he was stumbling into, a world of excess, one that would sweep up almost all our friends, one way or another, over the coming years.

This was also the period when Michael and I started smoking grass. In retrospect it's odd that it took us so long to experiment with drugs. I was now in my late 30s, Michael in his mid 20s, and somehow we had arrived at our respective ages virtual virgins in the ways of substance abuse. Whenever we went to parties and someone passed a joint, which was often, Michael and I politely declined, saying we didn't smoke pot. In my case, I hardly even drank. But as time went by the opportunities increased. Drugs — poppers, lsd, cocaine, angel dust, speed — flooded into gay life, it seemed like everyone was doing everything, and one night a friend pressed us with a joint and we smoked it and liked it, and that was that. We began smoking, first occasionally, then regularly. That friend, by the way, bears a lot of Catholic guilt, particularly about his sexuality. He prays a lot. And to give you a hint of what's to come, I can only say that years later he told me that every single day he prayed for forgiveness that he ever got me started on grass.

a house is not a home

As the '70s progressed our financial position improved even more, and in February 1973, I put up $23,500 and Michael put up $7,500, and we bought a very large rooming house on W. 22nd St. in Manhattan. If Warren St. was our little experiment in gentrification, 22nd St. was to be our endless ordeal by fire. It was a total, utter mess. The shabby facade was covered with peeling white paint; the only exceptional features were two antique etched-glass front doors that were soon smashed by a drunken tenant. Every room was filled with sad, sometimes alcoholic, sometimes mentally ill single people, and the whole block, which had been elegant when it was built in the late 1800s, was sagging.

It's hard to remember sometimes that despite the blossoming of gay New York during the early '70s, the rest of New York was on a one-way ticket to Palookaville. The city fell into bankruptcy; President Ford declared in a famous *Daily News* headline that New York could "Drop Dead;" and entire blocks in (what are today beautifully restored and expensive) Manhattan neighborhoods were at that time consumed by growing ghettos or were burning down altogether. The middle-class Chelsea neighborhood where our building stood was teetering on the brink, which is probably one reason we could afford such a large building. It was impossible to predict which way the neighborhood would go on the day we closed the deal, and realtor Paul Gay asked us if we wanted a bicycle or a tree as a gift. We chose the tree, and he planted it in front of the building. Today it towers over Colonial House, the elegant gay inn that our building became, which I own and operate and where I have a beautiful duplex garden apartment. But Colonial House wasn't even a glimmer in our eyes back then. We had almost no funds to renovate the building, and although it was really just a shabby rooming house, it was rent controlled. So that even fixed up, it didn't pay. For the time being we decided to leave things as they were and just collect the rents and make the mortgage payments. Michael took over the management, and as usual excelled.

But there were rumblings in our relationship. Part of Michael's allure was his moody streak, but now he began having more pronounced up-and-down mood swings, growing darkly angry and depressed one day, buoyant and optimistic the next. We were both having extracurricular adventures, him scouring the porn districts, me trotting off to the newly opulent bath houses for liaisons that may have been sudsier but were just as clandestine. We continued to have threesomes. And more ominously, we were both starting to do a lot of drugs as well. At some point in 1973 someone brought over some funny tasting joints that absolutely blew us into outer space, then made us violently sick. We found out later they were laced with angel dust, which was fast becoming a popular hallucinogenic party drug made from phencyclidine, a potent psychoactive drug. Angel dust was to become my nemesis for years.

Michael gave me a card for Christmas in 1973 that exemplified how good things still were, despite troubling omens. The printed message read, *"Wishing you a year filled with everything beautiful."* Beneath this he wrote —

> What more can I add to this? It's everything I want for you. I offer you my love and my friendship. I don't know if you comprehend the depth of either of these, but I hope in time you'll realize that what I give to you is the deepest and purest of any emotion or total feeling that one person can give to another. I'll always love you!

With things starting to get a bit bumpy between us, I think he was trying to reassure me that regardless of whatever might eventually happen, his feelings for me would never change. I suppose, in a way, they never really did.

chapter five
THE DAWN OF DISCO

From time immemorial, the making of music and dance was seen as inseparable, two sides of the same rhythmic coin. It was only in this century that the invention of recorded music introduced the possibility that this could change. As early as the '20s, flappers began to flap at home to the music of the gramophone and the radio, and the widespread dissemination of records had a huge influence on the development of popular music, bringing the new sounds of jazz and swing directly into the living room. But at least until the '50s, the experience of going out to dance had not changed very much. You might dance to records or the radio at home and boogie to canned music at private parties or sock hops or while watching TV programs like *American Bandstand*. But when you paid money to go out and dance, you still usually danced to a live band.

Throughout the '50s, record and sound technology advanced and eventually reached a point where the proper investment in equipment could produce a professional sound system that rivaled the experience of live bands. As that occurred, nightclubs based solely on dancing to recorded music became feasible. And clubs that could dispense with musicians were potentially highly profitable.

Disco has its own hotly debated genealogy — which club came first, what trend led to what. But there's fairly broad agreement that the direct precursor of New York's modern nightlife was a place called Le Club, which opened, spectacularly and tellingly, on New Year's Eve of 1960, the dawn of pop's pivotal decade.

Owner Oliver Coquelin had converted an old garage into a fantasy hunting lodge — heavy tapestries and rugs — and only allowed the beautiful people past the intimidating doorman. Le Club immediately became the watering hole of the international jet set. At the center of the club was a postage-stamp-sized dance floor and a little booth in front of a marble fireplace. The club's first DJ was Slim Hyatt, a tall, graceful black man who worked as the butler for society bandleader Peter Duchin. Hyatt had no previous experience spinning records — but then, nobody did. In fact, he was so terrible that at first Coquelin tried two or three other disc jockeys. No one was any better, so he rehired Hyatt, who eventually grew into a major draw — the first DJ as star, and as such, the father of a whole profession.

After Le Club, many other discothèques opened up throughout the early and mid '60s, not just in New York but all over the world. By the mid '60s America was in the grip of its first *disco* craze. It was not that far removed from the twist craze and the hula hoop craze and all the other crazy crazes of that crazy era. The button-down '50s were melting away in a youth quake, and after the Beatles invaded in late 1963, everybody was suddenly swinging. In the popular imagination, the discothèque was imported from France, and a proper French discothèque was not complete without go-go girls — young, mod, mini-skirted ingenues paid to dance *au go go*, whatever that meant, often dangling in a cage.

The next Manhattan night spot that really grabbed the public's imagination and exploited the British invasion to the max was Arthur, which opened in May of 1965 in a space that had been the old club El Morocco. It was the brainchild of actor Richard Burton's ex-wife Sybil, who based it on a popular English loft club, Ad Lib, which dominated swinging London nightlife in the mid '60s. Arthur's democratic door policy was the opposite of snooty Le Club. All the hip young swingers of the day were welcome, and in they flocked, making Arthur the center of mod New York's most happening scene.

the idea of disco

It was in these clubs, in the first half of the '60s, that the idea of disco began, although it bore little resemblance to what would later bear that name. At first, a discothèque was simply a commercial dance club based on records rather than live bands. No one realized its revolutionary potential for many years. There were no dance records, per se, designed specifically to make people boogie, and no one dreamed of an art of spinning those records in ways that would maximize the experience of dancing to pre-recorded music. It would take almost a decade before people grasped the implications of these possibilities, before the producer's art and the DJ's art began to emerge.

Indeed, during the first disco craze of the '60s, we were years away from the creation of a dance music category in the industry. There were no producers who specialized in creating music especially to dance to, no groups whose main claim to fame was their ability to get people on their feet. Instead, virtually every popular group and singer turned out a variety of product: some ballads, some medium-tempo numbers, some blues and r&b-flavored songs, some classic pop songs, and some up-tempo tunes suitable for dancing. Certain musical styles were obviously more intrinsically danceable than others: you were a lot more likely to tap your toes to a song from Motown than one from Peter, Paul and Mary. But dance records could come from anywhere, and they did. One of the most important jobs of the early DJs was to wade through the ocean of material being released each month, seeking out the most danceable songs. It could be anything from the Beatles to the Temptations, from Otis Redding to Herman's Hermits, from Petula Clark to the Supremes. And the best DJs, like Terry Noel at Arthur, often dropped in eclectic tunes by totally unexpected artists like Frank Sinatra and Bob Dylan.

Aside from searching out the most danceable songs, the pioneer DJs began experimenting with new ways of playing records. Prior to the mid-'60s, the proposition that spinning records could itself be an art form would have seemed ridiculous. Sure, some DJs were better than others, and the best were able to judge their audience's mood and try to modulate an evening's energy based on the songs they played and the order they played them. But beyond that, creativity was limited. With only one turntable in the DJ booth, what else could a DJ do?

In general, a song would end, there would be a moment's pause while people left the dance floor or changed partners or just stood chatting, and the next song would begin. All this seemed perfectly natural, since that was the way live bands played. So a turning point was marked when, around 1965, Terry Noel set up *two* turntables at Arthur and began to play records back to back. As the final notes of one song faded, he would begin the next, depriving the dance floor a chance to stop and catch its breath. This seems obvious today, to the point of primitive. Contemporary DJs not only play songs nonstop, but mix them and blend them into intense sets that evolve over hours, taking dancers on an elaborate voyage. But simply spinning records non-stop, back to back, was radically new back then, and it drove people wild.

Terry Noel also pioneered a somewhat darker aspect of his art: the DJ Diva Hissy Fit. Noel was so integral to Arthur's success that he was able to make the most outrageous demands and get away with them. One night he got into a heated argument with John Wayne over a record Wayne insisted he play, and he

smashed the record on the floor: the Diva facing down the
Duke. He also sometimes let his eccentric moods dictate his
performance. On one famous occasion the management decided
he had had enough to drink, so he simply shoved the needle off
the record and refused to play another note. A mini-riot
ensued, with the crowd screaming *"Give him a drink! Give him
a drink!"* He got the drink.

Dancing remained popular in mainstream pop culture throughout
the Carnaby St. era of the mid '60s. Later, as LSD burst on the
scene and the mod era mutated into the spacey psychedelic late
'60s, dancing remained just as popular. There was something
about the whole psychedelic style — the body painting, the black
lights and day-glo, the free love ethic — that made people want to
go out and express themselves even more outrageously.
Everybody it seemed was tuning in and turning on during the
1967 "Summer of Love," and a brash young talent agent with the
William Morris Agency saw his chance. Jerry Brandt decked out
an old Polish working-man's club on St. Mark's Pl. in the East
Village with a huge tent upon which he projected massive, trippy
images, colors and lighting effects. His Electric Circus was an
instant, mind-blowing success, like the musical *Hair* come to life.
On opening night, more than 3,000 people jammed a space that
had a legal capacity of 740, and at $15 a head the place became an
instant cash cow. It started a whole new craze for psychedelic
dance palaces that lasted through the rest of the decade.

By the time I arrived at Scepter in 1970, however, the
psychedelic era was winding down, and so was the dance
explosion. Some observers have argued that once downers and
depressants replaced psychedelics as the drug of choice,
dancing became passé. Hippies who had been tripping their
brains out a few years before were now staggering around
zonked on Quaaludes, and while they still wanted to go out,

they did not necessarily want to dance. And so, as the '60s flowed into the '70s, the big dance palaces faded from the mainstream, giving way to trend-setting clubs like Max's Kansas City, where you could sit down and, if necessary, pass out.

Though gay men and blacks kept dance alive, nightlife remained sadly segregated in general; there was little mixing going on despite all the peace and love rhetoric. Black people had succeeded in battering down legal segregation only a few years before, but cultural segregation persisted, fueled if anything by new tensions in society. This was the era of Black Power. Martin Luther King had been assassinated, the Black Panthers were on trial, seething riots were fresh in people's minds. But one group of people embodied both the party spirit of newly visible gay men and the long, brilliant musical tradition of African-Americans. Namely, black gay men. They served as a bridge between these two largely segregated communities and would have a huge impact on the emerging disco scene.

where the party people go

Despite segregation in society, gays were hardly about to be segregated out of nightlife. We were going to reinvent it. And we were hardly about to give up dancing; we were going to dance for what was, in effect, the very first time. Gay men had not even been allowed to dance together in a club up until 1969 when the Stonewall uprising ended all that almost overnight. The first and most persistent demands of gay activists were to get the cops out of our spaces — out of our bars and baths and cruising areas, and off of our dance floors. And the activists won. Now, in the fertile, idealistic climate of 1970, filled with experiments in communal living and group love and alternative lifestyles, gay people were ready to boogie like they could never have boogied before.

As part of the spirit, gay men lobbied for a new kind of communal gay dance space, a place to organize and raise consciousness, and party at the same time. In response, the fledgling GAA (Gay Activist Alliance) opened a building known as the Firehouse, a sort of gay community center carved out of an old firehouse in SoHo, then an area of decrepit, half-abandoned warehouses. The GAA held dances at the Firehouse every Saturday night, great jubilant shindigs that crystallized the magic of the pleasure revolution, a world being born in free love and drugs and a call to pride. Michael and I loved dancing at the Firehouse, bopping off the walls as DJ Barry Lederer spun his magic on the turntables.

It was at the Firehouse, with its mix of hippies and macho men, outrageous glitter queens and intense politicos, that I first began to understand the relationship between the DJ, his music, and the dancers on the floor. It struck me that certain elements in music could practically force people to jump up and dance. If a DJ was good, he would pick records that were not the known top radio hits of the moment, but would focus instead on more obscure records that had a certain infectious something, a beat or a hook that would drive even wallflowers off the wall. I noticed this, too, at other small gay clubs that were opening across the city: Moscow, Stage 45, Andre's, the Round Table, Jay's, Mr. D.'s, Tamberlane, Charades. DJs at all these clubs to varying degrees were playing records for their ability to make people dance, not because they were already popular radio hits. And so, as early as 1970, a second track began to emerge in music, almost in secret. The first track consisted of whatever was popular on the radio and on the charts — mainstream popular music. The second track consisted of what was popular in the underground clubs, where many of the hottest tunes never made it onto the radio or sold in record stores. Some people however, especially gay men, were to become connoisseurs of these obscure records, and many a passionate dinner conversation revolved around songs, artists and DJs that were virtually unknown to the wider world.

It might seem ridiculous or obvious today, but it struck me like a bolt one night at the Firehouse as I was watching the migrations of the dance floor. I suddenly realized that a savvy record executive could predict which among these obscure records had the potential to become mainstream hits simply by haunting the clubs and watching what people responded to. A dance floor was like a ready-made focus group, with an unforgiving and sometimes fanatical audience that was quick to vote with its feet. And so I decided to become that savvy record executive, to spend my nights in the clubs and seek out obscure songs, emerging trends, whatever I could discern from the experts — those who lived to dance. From the moment I made that decision, partying and dancing ceased to be forms of recreation for me. They became a part of my job.

As the early '70s progressed and mainstream nightlife grew smaller and more intimate, gay nightlife grew bigger, spaces grew more elaborate, and everything became more irreverent and outrageous. In 1971 an old German Baptist church in Hell's Kitchen was converted into the Sanctuary, the first really enormous gay dance space. Located on W. 43rd St. between 9th and 10th Avenues, the Sanctuary was what today we would call *"in your face."* The DJ booth was constructed where the altar once had stood, which was appropriate given the diva status of its star DJs, and the church was draped with porn and pagan images guaranteed to shock the god-fearing and delight the irreverent. When the Sanctuary was used for several scenes in Klute, a film in which Jane Fonda plays a high-class hooker, its notoriety and popularity increased even more. Roman Catholic authorities were appalled, and lobbied desperately but unavailingly against the sacrilege.

The Mafia long had a stranglehold on gay nightlife, and were not amused when gay men began to open dance clubs after Stonewall. The Sanctuary's main DJ, Francis Grasso, was the first (and hopefully the only) DJ to be kidnapped from his booth at gunpoint. When Francis finally staggered back to the club, his handsome face had been beaten to an unrecognizable pulp. The rumor that the incident had Mafia overtones seemed supported by the fact that he never filed a police complaint. The Sanctuary was more than just a fledgling bulwark against the Mob though. It was a hotbed of musical experimentation. Another Sanctuary DJ, Michael Capella, distinguished himself as a cutting-edge figure. His way of mixing records had a tremendous influence upon a young teenager from Brooklyn named Nicky Siano. Soon Nicky began playing at the Round Table and was to make a major mark on the coming disco explosion.

drag

Drag balls, with their Las Vegas showgirl extravagance, their massive headpieces perched atop even bigger egos, their unique language of *"shade,"* have provided an outlet for the roiling creativity of black gay New Yorkers all the way back to the turn of the century. It was at one of these balls around 1969 that two young black teenagers from Brooklyn, big burly Frankie Knuckles and tall, skinny Larry Levan, were to meet while helping bead a gown for a lavish queen named the Duchess.

The Duchess held sway over a drag house, a sort of gay gang of (mostly black) junior drag queens and their friends and admirers who were *"ruled"* by an older member. The houses competed — and still do today — at deadly serious drag contests held in ballrooms around the city, contests that mean as much to their participants as Miss America means to Oklahoma cheerleaders. At that first meeting, sewing beads to some faux fabulous gown, the 15-year-old Larry Levan and the 14-year-old Frankie Knuckles found an instant sense of communion in their shared love of music and fashion and realness, their keen sense of mischief, and their larger self-awareness as outsiders in a straight white world in which black gay men were — and are — twice excluded. But there were differences between the two friends as well. Larry was undisciplined and impulsive, glued to the groove of the moment, and paid for his intense creativity with a scattered sense of self. Frankie was the grounded one, just as brilliant as Larry, but down-to-earth and determined to survive. They fit each other perfectly, their fierce friendship based as much on their differences as their similarities.

They were little hell raisers from the start. *"We used to run around at Stage 45 back then,"* says Frankie, about a popular midtown gay nightspot.

> We had no business being up at Stage 45. We were 15, 16, much too young. But there we were, two nappy-headed banjee boys racing around at five o'clock in the morning, raiding pie trucks, grabbing boxes of pies and racing down the street.

Their devilish partnership, begun by beading gowns and stealing pies, would soon blossom into lives at the center of music. The day they met they could hardly have guessed that one day they themselves would rule, not as drag queens but as the reigning high priests of New York and Chicago nightlife, Larry Levan as the undisputed founder of the New York Garage sound, Frankie Knuckles as father of Chicago House music. Today, Frankie Knuckles remains one of the industry's most respected and admired producers, writers, and remixers, a hugely successful Grammy-winning DJ constantly in demand around the world. Larry Levan is dead, victim of a life in which he applied his genius as much to self-destruction as to creation. His ashes rest in an urn on my mantelpiece, where I can see them as I write, but the world of Garage music he set in motion spins on. A wall of sound stretching from here to Japan attests to the time he spent on earth.

the loft and the lofts

The future careers of Frankie Knuckles and Larry Levan would be hastened by developments far downtown in Manhattan, miles from where they first met as teenagers uptown in Harlem. In 1971 David Mancuso, a young white gay entrepreneur, opened a now-legendary private gay club downtown at 647 Broadway in the area of light industry that was beginning to gentrify into Soho, the city's new artist district. David may have looked like a leftover hippie from the previous era, but his long hair and spaced-out attire belied his keen business sense, and the Loft he created was a wholly new phenomenon in gay nightlife, the true precursor of what was to come.

The Loft was, for one thing, private. You had to be a member to get in, or be brought in by one. As such the Loft inevitably became the favored domain of disco snobs, more desirable precisely because it was more exclusive. But it was also racially and culturally integrated, a democracy of dance with an almost equal mix of rich and poor, white, black and Latino. David Mancuso had a strong sexual attraction to black men, and some say he wanted to create an integrated space where he and his friends could mingle. But this preference had other benefits as well, and other results. Dance music, and particularly disco, grew largely from black roots, and black gay men were among its first and most fanatic adherents. The racial integration that characterized early underground gay dance clubs like the Loft provided a crucial link between a moneyed, mostly white group of gay men eager to party with tribal abandon, and a mostly black gay world suffused with music and style. These worlds cross-pollinated in that uniquely American way that has produced so many musical innovations of this century, from jazz and swing to rock and r&b. In this case, it produced disco.

The Loft did not serve liquor. This meant at least two things. First, it was exempt from the draconian rules imposed by New York's obnoxious Liquor Commission, and so could stay open all night and well into the next day. Parties grew later and later, and by the end of the first season the peak hour for dancing had migrated to around six in the morning. Disco denizens became the ultimate night people, and those who partied several nights a week found themselves living in a time zone of their own, the graveyard shift of dance.

Second, no liquor meant a lot of drugs. Throughout the '60s drugs had grown more and more pervasive in nightlife, but many people still chose old-fashioned booze instead, and the two essential forms of dance lubrication rubbed shoulders and bumped behinds in clubs everywhere. But the Loft's lack of liquor meant that drugs were virtually mandatory, and what to take, when to take and how to get it became a passion. Amyl nitrate poppers —which provide a momentary whoosh of ecstasy — became all the rage, and the floor of the Loft was littered with the tiny broken snap canisters that poppers came in. Angel dust, coke, MDA, LSD, speed and a host of other drugs turned the Loft into a dreamscape, or if you were too high or had mixed the wrong drugs or the acid was bad, a bit of a hell.

In all these respects the Loft represented something wholly new. But the club's main claim to fame, its mystical centerpiece, was its sound system. Richard Long, a sound designer who had created, among other things, the special speakers for the film

Earthquake, worked to create a system of crystal completeness, from a bass so low it vibrated your heart strings to highs so translucent that violins and voices shot through you like arrows. No expense had been spared, and Long produced a bass-driven sound no one had ever heard before. Because the room was so small — hundreds of beautiful drugged men and a scattering of women crammed into a space that could barely fit 200 — the effect was totally overpowering. This was no Firehouse, with its quaint mix of politics and partying. This was serious business. The men in the Loft at six in the morning had banished the oppressive reality outside and created their own fantasy world within, a fantasy of compelling, almost hypnotic allure. It was fabulous that first season, and yet it was only an inkling of what was to come.

our dream

At some point early that first season, Jerry Rosenbalm, a handsome A-list friend who was a Loft member, offered to bring Michael and me along. I was thrilled by the idea of a racially integrated dance space, and while we stood on the stairs waiting for Jerry to get us in, watching the colorful parade of beautiful black, white, Latino, Asian men swirl by us, I got carried away with excitement and told Michael about a dream I had. I want to do what the Loft is doing, I said, only bigger and better. I want to build a place where everyone can party together, where it won't be just a black crowd or a white crowd or a Latino crowd, but where all men and women, gay and straight, can come together to party and feel safe and free to be themselves. Michael looked at me skeptically. *"You mean open a disco?"* he said. *"We don't know anything about that."* A big disco, I dreamed. The most fabulous club ever. Michael frowned for a second, then smiled, and a small light went on. We made a silent fantasy pact, laughing that someday we would open the biggest, most fabulous dance club ever, a disco democracy. After all, we were young, the world was new, gay was good, we could do anything. Years later Michael and I would remember that as the moment the Paradise Garage began. A momentary remark on a stairway, an idle thought shared in a crush of bodies and the throbbing of a distant bassline from a magical room beyond.

Of course, back then our dream was still only a dream. But others took their own dreams literally, and following Mancuso's lead a number of loft clubs sprang up, so that for a year or two it seemed as if everybody was opening a gay dance club in a loft, virtually all of them private. The 10TH Floor, another new club, became very popular among the Fire Island crowd. James Jessup and his lover David Brewy teamed up with David Sokoloff — three designers who were already known for their theme parties in Fire Island Pines, one of which featured an erupting volcano on a barge floating in the bay — and they put their visual expertise to practice and designed a magical environment for the 10TH Floor. Arriving at midnight on a Saturday, guests would ride what was fondly called the "Enchanted Elevator" to a party space that had white walls with sparkles embedded. The look was tropical, swaying palm trees surrounded by lounge seating and large bowls brimming over with fruit on the bar. Ray Yates, who had made a name for himself creating the music for Halston's fashion shows, was the primary DJ at the 10TH Floor. Bill Ash, Retail Advertising Director for *Mademoiselle* magazine at the time and a regular at the 10TH Floor, remembers the club fondly. *"It had a very light, very up feeling,"* Bill says.

> It reminded me of the 400, New York society in the 19th century. This was like the 300. The 10TH Floor was a stepping-stone, absolutely the right thing at the right time to catapult us to the next level and the level after that, a bridge to future places like Flamingo and 12 West.

Andrew Holleran, in his famous gay novel, *Dancer from the Dance*, wrote this about the denizens of the 10TH Floor:

> They lived only to bathe in the music, and each other's desire, in a strange democracy whose only ticket of admission was physical beauty — and not even that sometimes. All else was strictly classless: the boy passed out on the sofa from an overdose of Tuinals was a Puerto Rican who washed dishes in the employees' cafeteria at CBS, but the doctor bending over him had treated presidents. It was a democracy such as the world — with its rewards and penalties, its competition, its snobbery — never permits, but which flourished in this little room — because its central principle was the most anarchic of all: erotic love. If their days were spent in banks and office buildings, no matter: their true lives began when they walked through this door — and were baptized into a deeper faith, as if brought to life by miraculous immersion. They lived only for the night.

the education of frankie knuckles and larry levan

During the first years of the '70s Frankie Knuckles and Larry Levan began hanging out at the Planetarium in the East Village. It was less A-list exclusive than clubs like the Loft — no membership passes here — and the still underage Larry, who was 17, and Frankie, who was 16, had no problem getting in. One night Larry was spotted by the roving eye of Loft owner David Mancuso, and they soon began dating. Their relationship was short-lived, but pivotal for Larry and Frankie both. David brought Larry to the Loft, and Larry began dragging Frankie along, exposing these two uptown boys to a whole new downtown world, a world in which the city's most beautiful gay men merged with its most hedonistic scenes and most exceptional sounds. They fit right in, and for the rest of 1970 and early 1971 they were regulars. Pretty soon they knew everybody, and everybody knew them.

David closed the Loft for the summer of 1972, and the main beneficiary was the gay Italian teen from Brooklyn, Nicky Siano. Although Nicky was about the same age as Larry and Frankie, not even old enough to legally enter a nightclub, Nicky and his brother were getting ready to open their own gay club, the Gallery, in Chelsea. From so many long nights dancing at the Limelight and listening intently to pioneer DJ Michael Capella, Nicky had developed a powerful sense of what a DJ was capable of, although he had yet to put that into practice. And from his nights at David Mancuso's Loft, he had also developed a set of strong opinions about what went into the perfect club — the room, the dance floor, the sound, the lighting. Nicky was a perfectionist, and he worked like a demon to realize his dream. *"I wanted to be like David Mancuso,"* Nicky later said. *"And I wanted it so bad I made it for myself."* Once the Loft closed and its crowd needed a new place to go, the Gallery was the obvious choice, and became a hit almost overnight. Nicky Siano was hailed as a rising star. He had both created a club and emerged as its star DJ, a double whammy for a 17-year-old. As his business boomed, he invited Frankie Knuckles to come work for him at the Gallery. This time it was Frankie who dragged Larry Levan along. *"One day,"* Nicky recalls,

> Frankie Knuckles said, "Listen, I have this friend who's a little fucked up, always late and into this and that, but he's a great kid. I'd really like for you to give him a job." So I said, 'Sure, Frankie, for you, anything." The next week he brought in Larry Levan, we became good friends, and Larry became the club decorator.

Some people have said that Larry's innate talent, above and beyond his talent as a spinner of music, was as a creator of a total mood. Once he became a DJ, of course, he primarily accomplished this through music, but I've always thought it was interesting that he began his career not as a DJ but as a decorator and promoter — someone who worked to create an atmosphere and then worked to draw people in. His weekly concepts grew more insane and elaborate, and Nicky, the perfectionist, loved it. *"He was always late and always fucked up,"* Nicky recalls, *"but incredibly creative."* Larry began to experiment with the light board, and soon became expert. His wild side emerged, and he began doing things like spiking the punch with acid. As the summer progressed, Larry and Nicky became close personal friends and eventually moved in together. Their relationship included occasional sex, but Nicky recalls that Larry was essentially asexual, and they weren't exactly lovers. In any event, it soon became obvious that Nicky Siano was having an enormous influence upon Larry Levan, including a musical influence. *"Larry and I would be at the Gallery working,"* Frankie Knuckles remembers,

> pulling down decorations, putting up new ones — and in between Nicky would show us how to play. He used to tell us that he could show us how to operate the sound equipment but he couldn't really teach us to be DJs. We had to have that inner ability to really do it. But he let us watch him very closely.

No teacher ever had more attentive students, and Larry soon began to spin occasionally at the Gallery. Frankie, meanwhile, began getting a chance to spin at Better Days, a black club that boasted another pioneering DJ, Tee Scott. Both Nicky Siano and Tee Scott had a big influence on their protégés. *"Nicky and Tee were the first two people that Larry and I had ever heard who actually made a conscious effort to make two records fit,"* Frankie says.

> They made a conscious effort of doing that, and Larry and I worked on that all the time, until we pretty much perfected it on our own. Before that it was just putting one record on after another.

Soon Nicky's Gallery was becoming an industry watering hole that regularly boasted soon-to-be-famous people like Steve Rubell and Ray Caviano. When real estate problems forced Nicky to move the Gallery in 1973 from W. 22nd St. to Mercer and Houston around the corner from the Loft, he took Frankie and Larry with him. The highly motivated Nicky Siano was emerging as one of a handful of DJs whose influence extended beyond the dance floor and into the music business itself. Michael Capella, Tee Scott, David Rodriguez, David Mancuso, and Nicky Siano all numbered many promoters and industry bigwigs among their friends. With a small but fanatic loft scene now flourishing underground, savvy executives were starting to frequent these places, as I had, and some of them were also beginning to recognize the influence that star disc jockeys could wield. But until Nicky Siano came along, the record companies supplied very few of the DJs with new releases, seeing them more as avid customers than what they really were: advance promoters, stalking horses of the next big hit.

Nicky was perhaps the first to realize that if he went directly to his friends at the major labels, they would almost be forced to supply him with free records to try out at his club. And so they did, beginning a trend that would eventually shift the relationship between record companies and disc jockeys. Nicky took Larry along with him on these forays from company to company, and began to allow Larry to spin records at the Gallery. And he began to notice something odd. Larry was copying his style, precisely and brilliantly. Nicky was surprised and flattered by how fast Larry had picked it up. In addition to his obvious talent as a decorator and promoter, the kid was a natural born DJ.

By this time, two turntables were now standard equipment for most club DJs, but one night while sleeping, Nicky had a dream about playing on a third turntable. The next day he disconnected his home unit and hauled it into the Gallery, becoming the first DJ to mix with three turntables. Larry jumped on the idea. As the months went by and he and Frankie began to develop the signature techniques that would later make them famous, beginning a lifelong obsession with newer sounds, better sound systems, the best ways to mix. And since Larry was obviously limited to playing second fiddle to Nicky Siano as long as he remained at the Gallery, he began thinking bigger thoughts, dreaming of a dance floor of his own.

the continental baths

The dawn of disco was also the golden age of the baths. These great multistoried institutions included pools, steam rooms, showers and saunas in which men could frolic and have sex, as well as small bedrooms for more private encounters. Gay bathhouses were both sexual and social institutions, places to relax and places to hunt. None was more famous in the early days than the Continental Baths, in part because this huge establishment in the ornate Ansonia Hotel also had a space for dancing and entertainment, where straight patrons in street clothes mingled with gay men wrapped in towels. Bette Midler is not the only famous entertainer who rose to fame thanks to the unique venue of the Continental Baths. Two others were Larry Levan and Frankie Knuckles.

Larry began hanging out at the Continental while still learning the DJ's art at the Gallery. Since he had learned how to run a light board, he was hired by the Continental's DJ Joey Bonfiglio to work the lights. One day Joey got very upset about something and stalked out of the booth, forcing Larry to take over the turntables. The next day the owners fired Joey and announced that whoever got their records together first would be the new disc jockey at the Continental. Since Larry had numerous contacts at the records companies thanks to his forays with Nicky Siano, he raced from company to company amassing a major collection almost overnight. And he got the job. Suddenly this skinny, spacey kid who had been on the far periphery of mainstream gay nightlife just a year before, was now at the center, spinning at the Continental.

Frankie Knuckles, meanwhile, had been spinning on Mondays and Tuesdays at Better Days. When the managers decided business was too slow on those nights and dropped him, Larry came to the rescue, inviting Frankie to play Monday and Tuesday nights at the Continental. And so this pivotal disco partnership matured in the steamy, sexy environs of the city's most famous bathhouse. Gradually they built up a loyal following at the Continental, and soon their names were included in any list of the city's up and coming DJs. They were still teenagers.

"We were living at the Continental by this time, in apartments in the back, and I was still in school," Frankie recalls. *"It used to piss me off, since Larry wasn't and he could sleep all day."* Like kids everywhere, they talked about their futures and shared their dreams. But the whole underground DJ thing was so new, so untested, that they didn't really consider that line of work a lifelong option. It was an extension of adolescence, a game to play when you're young, a way to pay for your future, perhaps, but not a future in itself. *"I remember telling Larry, 'You really ought to think about doing something else,'"* Frankie says.

> The life expectancy of a club DJ was three years back then. Larry asked me, "What are you going to do when your three years are up?" And I told him, "Baby, I'm going to have a career. I'm not going to wake up one day when I'm 35 and still be spinning records!"

goin' dancin'

While Frankie and Larry were perfecting their techniques at the Continental, the mainstream music industry was changing yet again. The huge megagroups and stars that had dominated the airwaves were giving way to, or at least making room for, new trends. Teen idols became big again, and teeny-bopper artists like the Osmonds and David Cassidy scored huge hits. In the mainstream world of rock, the hippie era had now mutated into the glitter era, and the public went wild for the critically acclaimed David Bowie, whose 1972 release *Ziggy Stardust* started a virtual cult of androgyny. Synthesizers began to come into their own on albums by Stevie Wonder and Roxy Music, a development that would have major implications for dance music in years to come.

In these last pre-disco years, the industry did not yet recognize what was about to sweep over it. But disco's seeds were already firmly planted. Although there were no actual disco artists yet, and nobody called any particular style of music disco, plenty of great dance songs became smash hits, like "Crocodile Rock" by the platform-shoed Elton John, "Midnight Train to Georgia" by Gladys Knight and the Pips, and "Superstition" by Stevie Wonder. But in 1973 not a single song emerged in the Top Ten that would be considered disco by today's standards. It would be the last year in which that could be said.

Still, in 1972, and even more in 1973, the growing gay underground dance scene began to coalesce around a particular kind of dance music, and a distinctive style emerged that would later be called disco. It's important to recognize that although disco is often considered largely a gay invention, the earliest musicians and producers were not themselves gay, at least at first. The music we were dancing to was produced mostly by a variety of artists and producers (with a few notable exceptions) who were probably unaware at first that they were being adopted wholesale by a tiny gay elite in underground clubs. Several strains of music coalesced into this proto-disco. Motown was a major precursor, as was the stripped down funk of artists like James Brown and a more lush and almost pornographic type of r&b popularized by Isaac Hayes, especially his influential soundtrack for the film *Shaft*. Released in 1972, the *Shaft* soundtrack, with strings and horns and a sophisticated electric guitar riff, was funky and dangerous and smoothly infectious at the same time, an archetype of the evolving sound.

Another important influence in proto-disco, perhaps the single most important influence, was the "Philadelphia Sound," an r&b style pioneered by Philadelphia producers Kenny Gamble and Leon Huff. The Gamble and Huff team assembled a racially mixed group of session musicians and produced a rich, sexy, soulful music, upbeat while stripped down. Their impressive string of hits such as "Me and Mrs. Jones" by Billy Paul and "Love Train" by the O'Jays became immensely popular in the clubs and influential with other producers.

Crossover is the name of the game in music. A musical style may have a devoted and even fanatical audience, but until the general public picks up on that style — until it crosses over — it is likely to remain just a footnote to the music of its time. And when it comes to cross-over, radio is the ticket, since most music consumers first hear the newest sounds on the radio. In that respect, a little-noticed event occurred in 1973 that now looms as a turning point. Frankie Crocker (the top radio DJ at New York's top black station, WBLS, and a close friend of Larry Levan and Frankie Knuckles) had been haunting the clubs, listening intently to the sounds that Larry and Frankie and other pioneer club DJs were discovering. He fell in love with a completely obscure

French import, Manu Dibango's African-based funk "Soul Makossa," then popular in the clubs. He began to play it on the radio, and within weeks it rose on the charts to become a modest hit. Virtually no one recognized what this meant at the time — funky but obscure foreign song with no promotional budget, no star, no tour, suddenly becoming a hit because one intuitive radio DJ saw crowds go wild for it in tiny, underground clubs and began to play it on his station — but from that moment on, nothing would ever be the same.

the disco pest

During this period I was gaining a reputation at Scepter Records as the annoying guy who checked out the underground clubs and kept coming in to the office with enthusiastic reports about this new trend or that new group, pestering people who didn't really know or care what I was talking about. It wasn't easy at first. The concept of a *club* or *dance* record was not yet in the vocabulary of the record labels, including my own. Most head honchos, including Florence Greenberg, still believed in making hits the old-fashioned way, through traditional promotion, strategic concert tours, radio airplay. From my frequent nights out I was convinced that the dance floors, particularly the black and gay dance floors where the most fanatic fans gathered, had the potential to generate major retail hits if only the record companies had the ears to hear. But they rarely listened, even when events practically forced them to.

One of those events occurred in 1973 when Scepter signed a new Philadelphia group, the Independents, who came out with a modest hit called "Leaving Me." The b-side contained "I Love You, Yes I Do," a song that was considered simply a throwaway, fodder for the flip side. Months after "Leaving Me" faded from the charts, several DJs including Larry Levan and Frankie Knuckles discovered "I Love You, Yes I Do" and put it into the equivalent of heavy rotation on dance floors across the city. Audiences loved it, and suddenly, from nowhere, the record began selling again. Everyone at Scepter was flabbergasted, since records don't just spring back to life after they fade. I enthusiastically explained that this was because the b-side was a *disco* hit in these new underground gay lofts. No one knew what I was talking about.

I was thrilled that Scepter had signed the Philadelphia girl group, First Choice, even though their first song, "This is the House Where Love Died," didn't make the Top Ten. When producer Norman Harris delivered a follow-up, "Armed and Extremely Dangerous," I recognized its potential as another dance floor hit and could barely believe it when the creative folks at Scepter announced they were not crazy about the song and were making a deal with Bell Records to transfer it to them. Too much like the old Supremes, they said. I yelled and screamed, but I lost. Bell put out the record, and Scepter was deeply embarrassed when it began to sell. This mistake at least seemed to make Florence and the others a bit more receptive to my insistence about the new underground disco movement. But not much.

the birth of the b-side

A lot of innovations go into creating a landmark style in music — a new way of writing songs, new ways to sing, new forms of instrumentation and arrangement and rhythm, new marketing ideas, new social trends, new technologies. I'll say it again – *nothing happens by accident* – and what was happening now was anything but accidental. From all corners, a flood of innovation came together in 1973 that would, collectively, set the stage.

As the disco style coalesced, DJs began to seek out new ways to spin records. They wanted to go beyond merely fitting one record seamlessly into the next — already old hat for pioneer masters Nicky Siano and David Mancuso, Larry Levan and Frankie Knuckles. Now they wanted to figure out new ways to alter songs themselves, to jump into the middle, extend a song, create a personal signature of their own to a song. Of course, to do this was almost impossible. Most DJs had two turntables, and they often bought two copies of the same record and tried to mix the two copies together. This created room for a bit of creativity, but since both copies were exactly the same, there was not that much they could do. Several of my DJ friends thought they had a solution. If they could get a copy of the song that contained just its instrumental mix — the background music without the vocals — then they could really do something. In the middle of a vocal they could suddenly switch to the instrumental, extend the song, isolate various riffs and hooks, build up the energy. Then, when the audience was wild for release, the DJ could jump back to the vocals, and the room would explode.

These were the dark ages before the 12-inch, when every single was released as a seven-inch 45 rpm, and the record companies traditionally recorded a second song for the b-side that rarely got noticed and generally ended up a throwaway. So an idea popped into my head. What if record companies placed an instrumental mix of the a-side on the b-side? DJs could then buy a record, listen to both the vocal and the instrumental, and decide what the song's possibilities were. Then, if they wanted to, they could buy a second copy of the record and mix the two together. Of course, the idea would only work for dance records. You wouldn't want to release a ballad with an instrumental b-side. But for dance tunes, it made eminent sense. It would encourage DJs to play the song in clubs, which would translate into increased sales. And as an added bonus for the record company, it would even be less expensive, since the label wouldn't have to record a second, throwaway song. And even with a ballad a different mix would be less costly than recording a throwaway b-side.

In 1973, I saw my chance. Scepter had traded First Choice's "Armed and Extremely Dangerous" with Bell Records for "We're On the Right Track" by Ultra High Frequency, which I knew was a potentially hot dance record. The problem was, we now had only this one song by Ultra High Frequency, with nothing to put on the b-side. I cornered Sam Goff, vice president of Scepter, and explained the DJ's problem, and suggested we put an instrumental mix of "We're On The Right Track" on the b-side. Sam was shocked. *"We can't do that, Mel,"* he shot back. *"People will think we're trying to cheat them."* The institution of the b-side was so long established, so inviolate, that Sam assumed that record buyers would suspect a fast one if we didn't offer two songs on one record. But this time I persisted. I was the only person at the label who knew and avidly followed what was happening in the clubs. Sam and Florence certainly didn't. I reminded them that I was the one who predicted the unexpected comeback of "I Love You, Yes I Do." This time I wasn't going to give up, and they finally and reluctantly agreed, probably just to get me off their backs. (By the way, "Armed and Extremely Dangerous," which Scepter had traded with Bell, saying it sounded too much like the Supremes, became a big hit for Bell and, with its screaming police sirens and campy all-points bulletin — *"Be on the lookout for a dangerous man!"* — was a fierce hit on the dance floors.)

And so it happened that "We're On the Right Track" became the first single ever released with its instrumental track on the b-side. The DJs went wild, and played the grooves out of the record. It became an immediate dance floor hit, and other savvy record executives and producers took note. Within months the practice spread, and by the end of 1973 the instrumental b-side began to play an enormous role in the development of the DJ's art. It became an industry standard, and persists to this day. Eventually, even records that were not dance, per se, put extended instrumental mixes, or another mix, on the b-side.

bustin' the charts

Then, in 1974, everything seemed to come together. Producers were producing songs with a coherent style, and there was now an infrastructure of disco — a network of clubs, a roster of star DJs, a growing number of radio jocks, and executives like me who understood what was happening and haunted the clubs. Everything was in place, and the dam burst.

In one of his trips to the record companies, Nicky Siano plucked a record out of a pile of what Twentieth Century Records considered dead records, began playing it at the Gallery, and soon "Love's Theme," by Barry White's Love Unlimited Orchestra, was causing a major sensation in the clubs that winter. "Love's Theme" is a lush, 40-piece string arrangement that lasts 17 minutes, and certain DJs probably appreciated it mostly because its extraordinary length gave them a breather and saved them from having to urinate in a bottle. But its length hardly argued for its crossover appeal, so practically everyone was surprised when "Love's Theme" drifted from the clubs to the airwaves and then literally exploded onto the charts. On February 9, 1974, it hit No. 1. A month later "Boogie Down" by Eddie Kendricks, another big club favorite, hit No. 2. In April the Gamble and Huff production "TSOP (The Sound of Philadelphia)" rose to spend two weeks at No. 1. The flip side, "Love is the Message," would go on to become the great disco anthem. And then things really got hot. On July 6th the Hues Corporation's "Rock the Boat" rocketed to the top spot, and was bumped from No. 1 a week later by George McCrae's "Rock Your Baby." Suddenly, as if from nowhere, something new was climbing the charts.

This new sound was different from anything else. The rest of mainstream popular music continued on its rock-driven course. This was the year Elton John signed his huge, eight-million-dollar deal with MCA, the year Steve Miller's "The Joker" hit the top album spot, the year Kiss debuted. Billy Joel scored his first hit with "Piano Man," crowds rioted at David Cassidy's concert in London, and rock critic Jon Landau attended a Boston concert by a new artist and wrote afterwards that he had seen *"the rock'n'roll future — and its name is Bruce Springsteen."* Rock rolled on, but something new was rolling in. Its appearance seemed somehow official when *Billboard,* and then everyone else in the business, began referring to this musical revolution as "disco."

The new songs like "Rock Your Baby" and "Rock the Boat" had a definable sound, a genuine signature: funky rhythms, snappy, upbeat and sexy, with a genuine lightness of feeling. Their lyrics repeated a simple theme — *"I'd like to know where you got the notion"*..."shake, shake shake/shake your booty" — a theme that seems mindless until you're on the dance floor, probably high on something and falling in love with someone, at which point it resonates like an eternal truth. Beyond an infectious rhythm and an uncomplicated approach to lyrics, the new music represented something radically different from the rest of pop. For years, virtually all the big acts had been what some rock critics call *"head driven."* That is, their most profound messages were found in their lyrics, and the audience's attention was focused on what the bands meant, what they were trying to say. The acts were the stars, we were their followers, and our job was to worship them and deduce their meaning. But this new music wasn't meant to be pondered. It was meant to be surrendered to on a dance floor. It was not intellectual; it was ecstatic. And its stars were not the singers or the producers or the writers. Its stars were us. The dancers. Years later in a Vince Aletti article, Kathy Sledge would say that, when her Sister Sledge song "He's the Greatest Dancer" came out,

> Everybody thought that *they* were the greatest dancer. We literally had people come backstage and say, "I am the person you're singing about."

Given the fact that disco eventually came to dominate the record industry and sell billions of dollars worth of records, it produced relatively few bona fide stars. Almost none. And that was no accident. Some have argued that the primary reason was that disco was more a producer's medium than an artist's medium, and that is certainly true. But it's just as true that, unlike rock, disco did not need stars; they were beside the point. The point was joy and ecstasy and self-expression. The point, for many gay men and many African-Americans and working-class urban kids, particularly Italians, was building a community out of dance.

Nobody realized this at first, of course. Those of us in the clubs had been dancing nonstop for several years already, and the fact that our music was suddenly being adopted by a mass audience hardly affected us — although it affected me as a record executive. Nor did we intellectualize what was happening. But without realizing it, we had precipitated a seismic shift in music. From now on, rock, and all it stood for, was going to get a run for its money.

billboard catches on

The trick that Nicky Siano had taught Larry Levan early on — go to the labels and get free copies of their danceable records to play in the clubs — had now caught on in a big way. Record label offices were now besieged with DJs, to the point where Florence was driven to distraction. But I was always receptive. I relished these visits that gave me a chance to dish with those who were, to me, the most important forces driving the new music. Then one day a young DJ and aficionado of popular music came by the Scepter office to ask Maye if he could get free records for tapes that he was making for the Sandpiper disco on Fire Island.

Tom Moulton was a model, so blindingly handsome that Maye says she *"just couldn't look at him too long, he was so good-looking. He made me nervous just talking to him."* Tom Moulton actually was the Marlboro Lights man, or at least one of them, dark mustache, chiseled features, a god. But he was a god who lived and breathed disco. Although he was not much of a night owl and never did drugs, he was an encyclopedia of all aspects of dance music, and has a thousand theories about how to move people on the dance floor. Unlike almost any other DJ, Tom mixed records onto tapes at home, using his own equipment. Then, instead of standing in the DJ booth and basking in the admiration of the crowds, he would haunt the Sandpiper's dance floor as his tapes were played, fascinated by the effects his music had on people.

Tom was excited about the great reception that our hit "I Love You, Yes I Do" by the Independents was getting on dance floors, and asked Maye whether we had any more records like that. Knowing that disco was my department, Maye brought him into my office. It was an instant connection, two kindred spirits hungry for someone who was as excited as he was about this music. Tom was eager to make contacts with anybody in the industry who thought the way he did, and we grew close very quickly. I sort of took him under my wing, and decided to try to help promote him in the business. It didn't take long. Tom almost immediately emerged as disco's most pivotal early figure.

One day, not long after Tom and I met, Florence got a call from her then-boyfriend, Bill Wardlow, who ran *Billboard's* record charts out of Los Angeles. Bill Wardlow worked in one of music journalism's most influential jobs, one that required him to be up on every latest trend, and he had heard the buzz about the influence that the new underground New York clubs were having. He asked Florence whether she knew anyone who could take him around to the fabled Manhattan discos, and since I was the obvious choice, she asked me. But I was already committed to attend a cousin's wedding that weekend, so I hooked Bill up with the one other person who knew as much as I did: Tom Moulton.

Tom asked Bill whether he wanted to go to the straight discothèques or the underground gay clubs where the real action was, and Bill replied that he had not flown three-thousand miles to miss the real action. So Tom shepherded him through a maze of clubs, dazzling him with his vast knowledge of the scene. At one point they stopped by the Limelight, where David Rodriguez was playing. Rodriguez had always been a classic DJ diva, famous for playing what he wanted to play whether the crowd wanted it or not, and this night he was into a Gladys Knight song, "Make Yours a Happy Home," to which the crowd was not responding with sufficient enthusiasm. They kept calling for an Eddie Kendricks favorite, "Date with the Rain," but Rodriguez announced that unless they put more feel into Gladys Knight, they were not going to get Eddie Kendricks. When the demands for "Date with the Rain" became unrelenting, Rodriguez said fine, you want "Rain," I'll give you rain. And for the next thirty minutes all he played were thunder sound effects, nothing else. The club's owner was pounding on the booth, screaming *"Open this door!,"* and Rodriguez screamed *"Fuck You!"* right back. Then he played Gladys Knight again, at which point the audience, exhausted by the battle, reluctantly got up and danced. And "Date with the Rain," in the end, was their reward.

This was the kind of intense, almost intimate relationship that existed between the best DJs and the dancers, but Bill Wardlow had never seen anything like this before. He was amazed by the fanaticism, the vitality, the intensity of the people's likes and dislikes. He was also amazed by his guide, and the next day he hired Tom to write the first disco column for *Billboard*. The creation of a disco column in the bible of the music business meant that the industry now had a focus, a forum in which to analyze and exploit this new underground force. The fact that Tom Moulton was the columnist meant that the industry was going to get an earful from perhaps the most knowledgeable man in the business.

persistence overcomes resistance

The industry may have been poised, but Scepter Records wasn't. Back at the office I was continually harping that disco was the wave of the future and that it should also become the future of Scepter, but no one paid attention. It is true that Florence hadn't exactly been playing at the top of her game. She had been in ill health and had moved out to California, so she was less and less in contact with what was going on back in the office in New York. Despite being on what was the wrong coast from the disco perspective, she got to hear more than enough about disco from me, and she just wasn't buying it. One time Florence brought some records back from Europe and I told her they were great club records, that we should put these out for the disco market. She and Ed Kushins both said, *"What disco market?"* This, when disco was already climbing the charts. Another time she returned from California for a meeting and stormed into Ed's office. *"The next time that schmuck mentions the fucking word disco,"* she barked, *"Fire him."* She had always been used to a huge volume of sales and Scepter's sales had been dropping. I suppose the last thing that she wanted to hear about was the potential of a new genre of music, one that she didn't understand, one that could leave her in the dust.

But she had to hear about it, because like it or not it was the future of the industry. And of course she didn't fire me. Instead I forced her to listen, and slowly her impatience grew into receptivity. As I persisted I began making more headway with others at the company, particularly Ed and Maye. Both were in positions to sign and promote dance music, but Maye was about to rise to a top creative role in the company. Our head of promotion left us for a lucrative position at Motown, and after trying to replace him with outsiders who were simply unacceptable, Florence finally broke down and went in to see Maye. *"Would you mind ... would you be interested in trying to do it?"* Maye recalls Florence asking. And so Florence finally gave Maye the national promotion job, and the Scepter team was now complete. It was more like a family than a group of co-workers. From outside the company Tom Moulton was pushing me to get Scepter to put these hot new records out. From inside I continued to push Ed Kushins and Florence to do just that. Maye began to take my side, Ed and Florence caved, and collectively we pushed and pulled each other into the hey-day of disco.

chapter six
DON'T
LEAVE ME
THIS WAY

This was an exciting time at work, but it was a confusing and tumultuous time for Michael and me. On the surface of things we should have been perfectly happy. We had, in addition to each other, a close circle of friends, a vibrant social life in the city, beach houses in the summer. We both had jobs that were not just well paying but exciting and rewarding. We had a growing sense of financial security thanks to our real estate investments. And because we allowed ourselves sexual liaisons outside the relationship and even menages within it, we seemed able to balance the potential restlessness of a nine-year relationship with the freedom and sexual experimentation that was so much a part of gay life at that time. What more could we want?

I wanted nothing more. I was happy as a clam. But Michael was not. People often say that if you get into a relationship too early in life you may end up feeling that you missed something, and that if your partner is older, or dominates the relationship, you end up aching to declare independence. Such was the case with Michael. Beginning in his late adolescence and then for his entire adult life, he had always been known as half of Mel-and-Mike. And not just half, but the lesser half, or so he felt. I was the older one, the established one, the one with money and contacts and experience. I moved with fluidity in all sorts of situations, knew everybody, was the one whose opinion people sought about everything from business affairs to music to politics. Michael remained the permanent junior partner, the kid.

At first, of course, this difference between us was not only natural, it was an essential part of the magnetism that pulled us together. I loved him and he loved me, but also because he was young and beautiful and needed someone's help in order to blossom in life, and I could be that person and offer that help. And he loved me because I loved him, but also because I believed in him and encouraged him and pushed him, and because I was in a position to back up that encouragement with connections and financial security. We were like a pair of ancient Greeks, the older helping establish the younger.

Those Greek relationships were never built to last, however, at least not past the younger man's coming of age, and I can see why. As Michael grew into himself he grew to resent his permanent junior status. He was making it on his own, had a successful job, plenty of reasons for self-assurance. But in his larger life he was still the minor half of Mel-and-Mike, living, as he increasingly complained, in my shadow. At first this didn't bother him, or just caused a dull ache, but over the years through a thousand little grievances it grew more acute, and at some point along the way he became unhappy.

Unfortunately, I was not very sympathetic to all this, partly because in an odd way I felt as subordinate to him as he felt to me. He was so handsome and sexy, so effortlessly able to light up any room he walked into, especially a room filled with gay men, that it was him I thought of as the star of the family, not me. Guys were forever whispering in his ear, forever slipping him phone numbers, forever kissing him hello or goodbye a bit too long. When we were out in public it was hard to suppress a bit of jealousy, harder still because I was jealous both for him and of him. For him, because any one of these hunks might steal him away, and I had to face that fact everywhere we went. Of him, because he was the one getting showered with attention and I wasn't, or at least nowhere near as much. It seemed to me that despite my experience and connections, he had what people really value the most, or at least what gay men valued most in that time and place: youth and beauty. I was the shadow, the way I saw it, and he was the light.

But my complaint was relatively minor, the painful but common pang any older lover naturally feels. His was more serious, the complaint of a grownup child desperate to fly, tied to an image of inexperience and subordination that no longer fits. My insecurity about Michael was a slight problem for our relationship. His insecurity about me was a major problem for his life.

And so he chafed, and as he chafed he got edgy and moody and things grew tense. He began making little declarations of independence, gestures designed to wound and bind at the same time. Out at the discos he would flirt as we danced, shooting little knifelike smiles and winks right past me. His forays into the porn palaces and sex clubs of Manhattan with his Paramount co-worker Dennis Tomasetti grew more frequent, and from what I heard on the rumor mill, more jaded. It seemed that the more forbidden something was, the more Michael desired it. It didn't seem to matter how much space I gave him, he needed more. He had to *"experiment,"* as he would say. This made little sense, since he was actually having as much casual sex as the fastest gay man in the fastest gay lane, but consistency is hardly an emotional strong suit to anyone who is unhappy. Michael also increasingly let it be known that he was developing a strong attraction to black men. This by itself hardly bothered me, since I also had liked black and Latino men and even introduced Michael to his first black partner during a three-way I arranged. But when he began to hint that the attraction was perhaps becoming exclusive, I shuddered. After all, an exclusive attraction to black men could hardly mean that he was still attracted to me.

fantasy becomes reality

As things spiraled downward we began partying a bit heartier, perhaps trying to dance the tension away. Since I was always proselytizing about the dance clubs to my coworkers at Scepter, I did the same at home. Michael heard my spiel more often than anyone, and he was as receptive as Tom Moulton. We went out to research the trends together, and he and I developed our musical taste in tandem. Soon his opinions were as pointed as mine, even more so. I encouraged this, since it gave us something to do together, a project. And we continued talking about our dream of opening our own disco, and how we would do it right, how we would combine the perfect elements of dance and beauty and sound and avoid the mistakes and flaws we saw in other people's clubs. But it also gave Michael more opportunities to circulate in the fast lane, and it gave both of us more opportunities to take drugs. Including a new drug that would change a lot of lives beginning around then, including mine.

Angel dust and I did not begin our long relationship very auspiciously. I've mentioned that the first time Michael and I unintentionally tried it, when someone slipped it into a joint without telling us, made us violently ill. That memorable experience alone ought to have been enough to keep me away from the stuff, and it probably would have except for a person who was to become the center of my existence for years, both my lover and my nemesis.

Julio Velez began as my fantasy. Ever since the '60s I had noticed and lusted after a remarkably hot man I would occasionally see working out at the 47th St. Y, but whom I had never met. His chiseled Latin looks and perfectly sculpted body would have been enough to explain why so many found him attractive, but he also had this inner quality that oozed sex appeal, the kind of quality that makes even a not particularly good-looking person sexy. Julio was the strong and silent type, macho but also warm, sensitive and sensuous, both a real man and a palpably gay man, which meant he was both a fantasy and a possibility. Since Michael was often out on sexual forays with Dennis, I often indulged myself at the baths, and every so often I would see Julio there, if anything even more alluring in his revealing white towel, prowling the halls, relaxing in the steam room. After one such foray I confided to Michael how much I was attracted to Julio, and he readily concurred. Julio became one of our shared fantasies, and whenever we saw him out and about, we would drool.

During the Christmas of 1973 Michael came home with a story about having been followed around Bloomingdale's by *"I would never guess who... Julio!"* he said triumphantly. *"He was chasing me all over the store, and when he caught up with me he tried to pick me up."* Tried? I asked. Why didn't you go home with him? *"I didn't have time,"* was Michael's vague reply. *"I told him I'd give him a call, and maybe the three of us could get together. But now I'm not sure."* What do you mean? Go ahead and call him, I said. But Michael hesitated. *"Perhaps he won't like you. Or be uncomfortable."* I was puzzled, considering that we had both been dreaming of Julio for ages, but I let it pass.

A short time later I saw Julio again at the baths. This time, when he ducked into a room I screwed up my courage. Having watched Julio in operation, I knew that he could be cruelly dismissive to those he was rejecting, but I figured that if this was to be my fate I might as well find out now. His door was ajar, as doors at the baths often were, and I slipped in. Julio was sitting there with Robert Christian, an actor from the *Boys in the Band*, but I only had eyes for Julio. And, to my very pleasant surprise, he only had eyes for me. When he saw me enter he kicked the door closed and we grabbed each other like drowning men. That settled that. I don't even remember Robert leaving, I was so caught up in my fantasy made flesh.

Julio, Michael and I got together for a three-way pretty quickly after that, and Julio brought along some angel dust and shared it with us. It was our first time smoking dust intentionally. Angel dust is a powerful anesthetic that loosens inhibitions more than perhaps any other drug. People who use it either soar to stellar heights or plunge into hellish depths, feeling close to life's essence or close to death itself, which I suppose is why it's called angel dust. It changes you. Even at this early stage Julio was already heavily into it, and always smoked it whenever we played together. At first, of course, I did dust as a treat, just one of the many drugs that were part of the seemingly innocent play that made up our social lives. But even at this early stage my growing fondness for angel dust indicated the direction I was going, and soon I began doing it more and more. If I was not yet barreling down some pretty dangerous tracks exactly, I was certainly picking up steam.

death in the family

The tension between Michael and me continued to grow. Things were certainly not helped by our threeways, by our increasing forays into the night — which were meant to give us freedom within the relationship but which inevitably became sources of friction — and by our increasing drug use. Things really got bad when Michael announced that his sexual tastes were now almost exclusively oriented toward black men. I could see our future slowly being squeezed off.

And then Michael's father died. Michael was very bitter about the fact that just when his father was finally able to start enjoying life, he was cut down by lung cancer. Ben Brody had been a cutter in the garment industry, and the asbestos in the fiber of some of the materials probably caused his disease. When his condition became inoperable and the pain grew unbearable, Ben wanted no one near him except Michael and me. A couple of weeks before he died, he grabbed my arm, looked me in the eyes and said, *"I'm glad you're Michael's friend."* He had never spoken before of our relationship, and if he'd had problems with our being gay and being lovers, he kept it to himself. But now, in his extreme pain facing death, he was telling me that he was glad I was Michael's lover, and glad that I would be there to take care of him.

Michael, however, didn't want anyone taking care of him. He wanted to take care of himself, and in the trauma of his father's death something clicked. After Ben died Michael grew very restless. He talked of wanting just to enjoy life, to make money quickly and then retire, maybe to some Pacific island. I began to realize that this claim was a code that masked his real meaning, which was that he wasn't enjoying life right now, his life with me.

As the clouds gathered I took a trip to Puerto Rico by myself, moping around the island, remembering times when Michael and I had visited there together, two lovers in love on a tropical beach, planning a life together. Now the beach looked desolate and I felt the deepest loneliness I had ever felt before. As I wandered around wondering how to fix things, wondering if they could be fixed, I had the bad luck to run into Jaime de la Cruz, a blond, blue eyed local. Michael and I had met Jaime on a trip to the island one or two years before and bedded him one delirious night in a three-way. But this time it was Jaime, myself, and Frankie Garaton, an airline steward. Jamie seemed even more sexy, a golden memory of a happier time. And so we made love again and we became reacquainted. A time would come when I would curse that very day. (Years later, I learned from Frankie that Jaime had told him that he'd had a crush on me.)

the love I lost

As the summer of 1973 progressed, Michael began to get serious about achieving independence. We went out to Fire Island, the place where we had met so many years before, and had what we called a truth session. One of the unspoken rules of our open relationship was that we were free to do what we wished with other partners, but that we should not tell each other too much about our private dalliances. Now, in desperation, it seemed that perhaps the only thing that could help would be getting everything out in the open. And so we admitted everything. All of our tricking around, Michael's lunch hours on 42nd St., the works. In retrospect, the truth session was a disaster. We discovered things about each other, and had to face things about our relationship that until then we could conveniently ignore.

Between the shock of all this and Michael's continued demands for more freedom, I was at the end of my rope. How could I possibly give him any more freedom and still maintain some semblance of a committed relationship? And so I made one of the biggest mistakes of my life. I forced the issue. I asked Michael point blank if he wanted to end it. I had thought I was being rhetorical, but he jumped into the subject eagerly and the discussion didn't go much further before he matter-of-factly asked me, *"Do I move out, or do you?"* It seemed as though he had been waiting for this opportunity, and I, the fool, gave it to him. But I was drained and fed up. *"You move,"* I told him. *"I don't have the energy for it."* He didn't have to be told twice. Before I could reconsider, he had found an apartment in Manhattan.

Even though I thought I had braced myself for this, I was completely undone. The man I had based my whole life around was leaving. To make matters worse, I realized that he could not really leave. We owned property together, ran a business together, were tied together in a deliberate web of entanglements that I had thought, had planned, would bind us forever. Now they seemed like chains that might just drag us down. Amid my hurt and confusion, Michael kept sending me mixed messages that only confused me more. A card summed up his feelings:

> Who needs the world, when I have you! Please don't be jealous... I'll always love you just as I know you will me! This isn't the end, it's just the beginning. To Mel from Mike. To my only love!

I had never been this confused before, and had never been hurt this badly. And so I made an even worse mistake. After he moved out he still wanted to maintain the ties between us, to remain close friends, do the books for our buildings and conduct business as usual. In retrospect, I have often thought that perhaps he saw his moving out not as a final break but as a temporary respite. Perhaps he wanted to continue the relationship, but just on a different plane, or even just on a different plane temporarily. To establish himself, get some space, but otherwise just keep on keeping on. I, however, would have none of that. As far as I was concerned, if Michael wanted to be out on his own, then he could damn well be out on his own. I withdrew the love and support he'd taken for granted over the years, and I felt completely justified in doing so because I was so devastated. It was so ironic. He had always been the one who wanted a relationship, and now that I had finally fallen deeply in love, he wanted out. From my wounded perspective, he was the bad guy, the traitor. I had met a wonderful, innocent 19-year-old kid on a Fire Island boardwalk, an adorable messenger-boy who became my lover, and we had lived and loved and grown together. And now, ten years later, that sweet boy finally had what he wanted — money, a good professional position — and he wanted out.

It was betrayal, it deserved punishment, and I punished him with gusto, lashing out whenever I could, cutting him down, pushing him away. And in the process, I punished myself. Of all the mistakes that I have made in my life, this I regret the most. Michael really did want to remain close to me, but what might have been a momentary break in our lives, a bad patch, I turned into a wall of ice. The fact that we were tied together in business, that we had to keep seeing each other on financial matters only gave me more opportunities to hurt him. I buried myself in work by day and partying by night, assuaging my damaged self-esteem with drugs and with the hapless idea that he was losing something just as good as I was. But I was wrong.

doin' the best that I can

After we broke up, Michael had a fling with some close mutual friends. I suppose he wanted to make his independence tangible to everybody, and an effective way to do that was to sleep around within our circle. This only hurt me more and gave me another reason to want to push him away. But it also gave me permission, of sorts, to start dating with a vengeance. And in this I was lucky.

One of the greatest gifts Michael gave me during our years together was his encouragement to stay in top physical shape. He may have had some ulterior motives (including the fact that we'd attract hotter guys for our three-ways) but ultimately the body I achieved helped me after we broke up. Since this was also the summer when disco was exploding onto the airwaves, the summer of "Rock the Boat," and since I was in the middle of that, I suppose I was even more of a catch. In any event I was easily able to land dates with the most desirable guys on the A-list. In a way I was on it myself.

And so I had a series of affairs with a series of hot guys. I smiled at Bill Scott from across Christopher St. on a Sunday afternoon in 1974, and the rest of that summer our romance helped take my mind off of Michael. When I met Bill he was just coming out and needed a gay role model, so I became his mentor, taking him to discos and concerts, getting Julio to cut his hair. He used to call me his gay father. To complete his coming out, Bill took a job as a waiter on Fire Island and we would often meet out there and dance the night away in the Ice Palace. But even in the flush of a new romance, ours wasn't an exclusive affair. Like practically everybody else, we were both dating other guys.

That was the way it was in those days. Most romances like ours petered out after the first attraction and excitement wore off, but afterwards, if you were lucky, you had a new friend. Sometimes a good friend. It seems like many of the longest lasting friendships in our circle began as short-lived affairs, and eventually my friendship with Bill Scott evolved into a very close friendship as well. The romance ebbed but the love and support grew for years.

A few months after Bill and I stopped dating I met young and strikingly handsome Dennis Lasker at Ty's bar on Christopher St. Suddenly this dreamy, blue-eyed, golden boy came right up and asked if he could buy me a drink. I thought I was dreaming. Apollo, with his luscious lips and burning eyes, buying little old me a drink. We retired to his place for the night, and another romance began, a hot one. Whenever he came over he barely got past my front door before we were all over each other, our clothes leaving a trail all the way to the bedroom. I still have a memento of that wonderful time on one of my paintings. The painting hung over my bed in Brooklyn, and at the culmination of a particularly intense session, Dennis's climax hit the painting and dried on the canvas, where it can still be seen. The painting is appropriately titled "The Summer of '75." Dennis wasn't just hot for me, he really liked me, and things could have easily developed into something lasting. But we remained more playmates than lovers. He was a free spirit, and in any case I didn't have the stomach for all of the jealousy and other baggage that inevitably seemed to move in with a lover. I also thought it would be unfair to try to tie him down and hold him back, since he was determined to go to Hollywood and make it in the movie business. In the meantime he did some modeling work. In one spread in *GQ*, Dennis is seen hanging suspended from a tree by a parachute, shirtless in army fatigues. With his flexed arms and stunning face and those lips, it remains a classic. Dennis and I ended up becoming great friends, and true to his plans, he moved out to California a year later.

my real family

Over the years on Fire Island, my housemates had become a surrogate family, more real to me in many ways than my own family. Dick Fisher originally found the house on Ozone Walk in 1972 and filled it up with his friends, including Michael and me. It was a wonderful house and a wonderful group, funny and irreverent but also deeply supportive like many extended friendships among gay men.

Dick Fisher and Ray Ford were my therapists. They would listen to me go on about my problems for hours, and were not shy about sharing their opinions. Sometimes, during the stormy end of my relationship with Michael, they told me that I was being too controlling, too bossy, and after we broke up, that I was foolishly pushing him away. I listened. I only wish I had heard.

One of my favorite stories about Dick illustrates his slow, methodical, deadpan character, the way he was always two beats behind in everything. One night he made dinner for the whole house and just as we were finished, he asked in all seriousness, *"Would anyone like salt and pepper?"* We were in hysterics.

Ray was brilliant, with a vocabulary so capacious (a word he'd probably use), that the first time he visited our house on Ozone Walk, we turned to each other after he left and said, *"What did he say?"* But he was also caring and gorgeous — tall, blonde, handsome, seemingly emotionless, always proper, the WASP prototype.

One afternoon in 1973, Dick brought over a handsome young man with piercing blue eyes, and it wasn't long before Larry McDevitt was a member of the family. It was truly a magical environment, an easygoing place where you did your own thing, yet always managed to share meals together. We all shared the cooking chores — I loved cooking for a big crew — and when Terry Fu (who ran the Hong Kong Tourist Bureau) cooked, it was an all-day exotic Oriental production. He would start at nine in the morning and wouldn't serve until eight in the evening.

These were carefree, innocent times. The house was forever filled with laughter and good-natured teasing, and the love and camaraderie was accepting and unconditional. We may have started out only as housemates, but we became lifelong friends.

Since Michael chose to remain in the house on Ozone Walk for the summer of '75 after our break up, I decided to look for another house. I ended up taking a share with another bunch of guys that included Julio. We christened that house "Camp Tommy," after the Who's rock opera and Ken Russel's film *Tommy*. It wasn't far from the house on Ozone, and I continued to maintain close ties with my friends there. My family from the Island was an essential support system for me during that difficult period in my life, when I was working to regain my equilibrium after Michael.

reade street

It wasn't too long after Michael and I split up and he moved out that I discovered, unbeknownst to me, that he had withdrawn $5,000 from our joint banking account. He intended to use the money to open his own nightclub with two new friends. Since he was now primarily interested in meeting black men, what better place to meet them, he thought, than in his own racially mixed dance club? (It was common knowledge that this had also been David Mancuso's and Richard Long's motivation for opening The Loft.) I could feel the last ties to Michael beginning to unravel when I received this mailing from the trio of new entrepreneurs:

On Saturday, at midnight, we are opening a discotheque club for our friends at 143 Reade Street. The woofers and tweeters will be blasting every Friday and Saturday from midnight till six. Enclosed is your personal invitation for you and a guest. In order to make it a smooth, hassle free evening each time you come, we ask you to respect the following guidelines:

1- If you invite guests, please bring them with you. There is no practical way to meet guests there or to leave names in advance.

2- It is absolutely imperative that there be no congregating in front of the building. This causes hassles with the city and interruptions in our music. So please no congregating outside.

3- No alcoholic beverages. There will be plenty of fruit punch in our kitchen.

Enough of the rules. Come share the same good vibes and the same party people we had upstairs at W. 20th St.

— Dean, Marc & Mike

The Reade Street club sat in an old building between Hudson and Greenwich Sts. in lower Manhattan, now known as Tribeca. About a month after opening, Michael ditched his partners and asked me to invest with him. Despite all my pushing away, he was still trying to pull me closer, still wanting me as a partner in his life, one way or the other. But I was not about to get into another business venture with Michael. I figured that the buildings on Warren St. and W. 22nd St. were already tying us together far too much. I was also stung that Michael had planned Reade Street without even telling me, secretly withdrawing money from our joint account. So I said no. And I consider this the second biggest mistake of my life: letting stupid wounded pride stand in the way of what might have drawn us back together and what might also have been a wonderful business partnership. I'm sure things would have had a far more positive outcome, for Michael, for me and for thousands of others in the clubs he founded, if I had done things differently. But as it turned out, Reade Street would be the forerunner of a legend in the evolution of disco: the Paradise Garage.

Like many new places, Reade Street did not do very well at first. Michael struggled with one difficulty after another, especially with the landlord. Whenever he had problems, he would ask my advice, or even ask me to go help him sort things out with the landlord. And I always went, always helped out. We were like that. Former lovers with a lot of baggage, but too close really to separate. As time went by, though, Michael grew certain of one thing: the club needed something major to boost its popularity. One day he called me and said, *"Mel, I've found the guy that's going to make it happen for me."* He had been to a club called SoHo Place and heard a great new disc jockey. Michael was sure this DJ was going to provide Reade Street with the boost it needed. His name was Larry Levan.

chapter seven
LARRY LEVAN'S
LEAP TO
STARDOM

In the late spring of 1974, audio designer Richard Long asked Larry to leave the Continental Baths and come play at Richard's new club, SoHo Place. *"It was a loft at 452 Broadway with too much sound equipment,"* Larry later recalled, *"and it was Richard's workshop as well, basically a very energetic black club."* After many months at the Continental, Larry was growing bored, and he grabbed the opportunity to experiment in the playground of the leading audio designer of the day, the bass-heavy master who had created the Loft's revolutionary system. Once Larry arrived at SoHo Place the club became so popular that it was soon closed down for overcrowding — I suppose a testament both to Larry Levan's drawing power and Richard Long's sound system. Then, as the club was being shut down, Larry got a call from Michael Brody.

Larry had no idea who Michael Brody was, but he returned the call, and Michael introduced himself. *"I own a new club downtown,"* Michael said, *and I think you might be interested in becoming its DJ."* Michael later recalled that he had already decided to offer Larry the DJ job at Reade Street, while Larry remembered that he was the one who decided to go to work there. Either way, a deal was made, and Larry Levan began working for Michael Brody, although it sometimes seemed the other way around. Their timing was perfect. It was the summer of 1974, the breakthrough moment of disco.

Oddly, that breakthrough didn't matter much to the dancers in the gay clubs. True, the clubs got more crowded. But internally, the club scene continued to form a tight community that was almost impervious to mass acceptance or rejection. Most gay men in the dance scene did not seem particularly to care how they were viewed by straight America, so disco's sudden popularity simply did not much affect them. But it certainly made a difference in the way straight America viewed gay men. Suddenly, emanating from what was still considered a shadowy, mysterious gay world, was this music. This happy, joyous revelry. For a lot of people, the vision of gays as lonely, sad people isolated from society — my own vision from back in my Boston youth — began to be replaced by a vision of rotating disco balls and glitter and bodies undulating under flashing lights. Some even began to credit the burgeoning dance scene with the rise of open homosexuality, almost as if the music itself was propelling gay people into visibility. Which, in a way, it was. Bill Scott, who was my first lover after Michael (and who eventually became a leader in Houston's gay community), summarized the impact that we were having on music, and it was having on us:

> I don't think that those of us on Fire Island and in the clubs in the city could have danced the way we did without our new found sense of freedom. We were a bunch of recently liberated people, and when we came together to celebrate in a free environment, it was explosive. Even my straight brothers came to watch us dance, and they couldn't believe that people could be that happy and full of love and express it to each other. These people didn't want to hurt themselves or anyone else. They were good people, and discos were places where they could express themselves and be happy about their goodness.

This confluence of music and gay life was integral to what Larry Levan now began to do at Reade Street. Although the club remained troubled by various real estate problems, the atmosphere was almost fanatically supportive, and Larry felt free to experiment. It was at Reade Street that he first began playing records through a crossover device that allowed him to pull certain frequencies out of the music, distorting and altering the timbre of a song. Crossover lent an eerie element to the music. With the flick of a switch, Larry could bathe the vocals in a tinny reverberation or make them sound like an echoing jet soaring overhead or a subway train rumbling below. Since he loved deep bass sounds, he often used the crossover device to create a virtual earthquake. In his quest to create a total experience, Larry also took advantage of something unique to Reade Street. The club had been built inside a huge old meat locker, and from controls inside the DJ booth Larry could raise the heat to ovenlike temperatures or cool the club down to subfreezing in minutes. Tweaking the atmosphere was an extension of his mania for control, but it also made for an intense experience: the sensurround of night clubbing. *"Everybody would pack into that meat locker and Larry would let it get intensely hot in there,"* Frankie Knuckles recalls,

> pitch black and an inferno. Then, all of a sudden, he would drop the temperature down to subzero. I would go up into the booth and yell at him, 'Somebody's gonna catch pneumonia, you can't do that." And he'd just say "Miss Thing, you're getting on my nerves!" and throw me out of the booth.

This kind of experimentation was hardly confined to Larry Levan. Throughout the rest of 1974 and into 1975 the recording and club industry produced a series of innovations that helped disco mushroom into what it became: the single most popular form of popular music. And by far the most influential figure behind most of those innovations was Tom Moulton.

moulton the inventor

Since the dawn of recording, records have been produced by people called, appropriately, producers. Their job is similar to that of a film director: they oversee the whole production from arrangements to final release, and put all the pieces together. In the '60s this job became much more creative and complex with the widespread introduction of overdubbing. Using this technique, each instrumentalist and singer can be recorded on a separate track, so musicians do not even have to be in the studio at the same time, and they often aren't. A producer will usually lay down a rhythm track using just bass, drums, and perhaps guitar playing together. Then the producer progressively adds more guitars, keyboards, horns, strings, synthesizers or what have you, each on separate tracks. Later, the singers come in, to a usually empty studio, and sing along to the tracks. Finally, the producer mixes the whole thing, in a process similar to film editing. Since each instrument and voice is on a separate track, the producer is able to boost one track, tone down another, add more bass, add effects to the voices, pass instruments through filters and equalizers and other devices, and generally play around until things sound the way the producer wants. And bingo, a record.

Producers are sometimes musicians themselves, sometimes recording engineers, sometimes both. But back in those days, one thing they usually were not was a dancer. Because of that, they often did not have a clue as to how a song is heard and experienced by people dancing to it. Dancers might want a particularly infectious guitar hook to repeat over and over, while they dance themselves into a frenzy. Or they might want the bass way up. Or concentrate on the pure rhythm. The dynamics of dancing are very different from the dynamics of simply listening, and back then most producers didn't have a clue.

But DJs did. They spent their time figuring out what makes people dance. And with the increasing sophistication of their equipment, and the introduction of the instrumental b-side, they were now able to experiment with a form of live mixing right there on the dance floor. Extend this. Boost that. Cut back and forth to the vocal. This wasn't traditional, studio mixing, of course. It involved tweaking and blending a premixed record, and indeed some argue that we should call it *"blending"* to distinguish it from the type of mixing that goes on in the studio. Whatever it was called, DJs were now doing it like crazy. In the process, they got the feel for complex equipment, and they could see before their eyes the instant reaction that their experiments produced with the fans on the dance floor. Far more than traditional producers, the top DJs quickly became masters of a kind of instant, on the spot, *remixing* designed specifically for dancing. The problem was, their raw material continued to be the original mixes, released by the original producers. So a few DJs, particularly Tom Moulton, began to wonder. What if you could go into the studio and get your hands on the original, multitrack tapes, and remix them according to your own tastes? Actually boost the bass, or put the vocals through a different effect, right there on the original tape? Imagine the kinds of dance records you could produce then!

This idea might seem heretical, almost like asking a different director to go in and reedit a Hollywood movie after it had been finished by the first director, just so that it might appeal to a different audience. Still, as record companies began to realize the importance of the dance floor in breaking new records, the idea of turning to the dance experts seemed less than outlandish.

By mid-'74 Tom Moulton was already a star. He was writing the new disco column for *Billboard*, which everybody read and respected. And even though he did not actually spin in clubs, and so was not, strictly speaking, a DJ, he produced for the Sandpiper disco on Fire Island what may be the most influential disco tapes ever made. Turning his home into a veritable studio to make the tapes, he gained considerable mixing and studio experience. His Sandpiper tapes, important in the development of disco, introduced a whole new way of mixing records. I've already mentioned how back at Arthur in the mid-'60s, DJ Terry Noel pioneered using two turntables to keep the music going non-stop from one song to the next. This had now become standard — people would kill a DJ who stopped between songs — but Tom Moulton was about to take back-to-back a giant step further. *"I wanted to perfect a system to keep people dancing through the end of one song and into the beginning of the next,"* Tom recalls,

> By carefully watching how people danced, I noticed that they would always finish the step. In other words, they would go *one-two-three-four* and then they would walk off the floor on the one beat. The trick was to get them to begin dancing to the next song before they realized it actually was another song.

Tom began to mix his tapes so that they played over each other and blended into each other, making it impossible to distinguish where one ended and the next began. This came to be known as slip-cueing. *"It was a way of trapping them,"* Tom says, *"and it worked."* It still does, to the extent that slip-cueing is now standard in clubs throughout the world. Of course, to do this properly the tempo of both songs, the beats per minute (or bpm) had to be very close. You couldn't slip cue something fairly slow into something much faster (and God help you if you mixed something fast into something slow). So as Tom's innovation spread, the bpm of each song became more important. DJs began to make a conscious effort to build sets from relatively slow to furiously fast by gradually increasing the bpm. Eventually this became so standard that today some complain that there's almost a tyranny of bpm — that DJs are hostage to matching the beats of songs, and that this limits their creativity and spontaneity. Be that as it may, slip-cueing was a major influence, but was just one of Tom's many innovations.

In the early days, it was still something of a challenge for DJs to introduce new songs into their sets. Many people would get off the dance floor if they heard too many unfamiliar songs, and Tom was so committed to the newest music that the Sandpiper crowd would sometimes stomp off the floor in disgust. After a rough week in the city and a long slog out to the island, the disco queens wanted to hear their favorites. But Tom was determined to challenge his fans constantly, and he hit on a solution. He started putting most of his new music on the tapes for Saturday night, when people were more relaxed and probably drugged, and were more open to new material. Then the Friday the following weekend, he would use the tapes from last Saturday. By now the new music would be a bit more familiar, and people responded to it. Then, on Saturdays, when the crowd was again more open to new material, he would challenge them with the breaking songs. He was thus able to introduce new stuff continuously. Besides slip-cueing, Tom's Sandpiper tapes were constantly the first with the latest sounds.

One day I introduced Tom to Freddy Frank, an independent producer working at Scepter. Freddy had produced for us "Dreamworld" by Don Downing, and he had an extra copy of the master. I encouraged Tom to take it home and experiment with it on his own. He jumped at the chance, remixed it and brought it in a few days later. We were amazed: a so-so record was suddenly snappy, upbeat and ten times better. But there was something more. Right there, on his first try at remixing, he did something so radical I could hardly believe my ears. "Dreamworld" was only about three minutes long, so Tom decided that he wanted to extend it. But there was a hitch. The song modulated into a higher key near the end, making it impossible to get back to the beginning without modulating back down. Generally speaking, in music, you can modulate up all you want, since that makes a song seem brighter. But you can't modulate down. Tom stripped the song to the bare percussion tracks, eliminated all singing and musical instruments until what he had left was a sort of tribal pounding that went on and on, perfect for dancing yourself into a trance. Then he built the song back up by layering the instruments back into the rhythm. Eliminating the modulation allowed him to extend the song and finally get back to the lyrics.

I was so impressed that I made a suggestion: *"Tom, when you break it down, keep it going for a while so the crowd can really get into it."* And he did. Right there, on his very first time in the studio, not only he had remixed a song into a classic, he had also invented a standard that would sweep the record industry almost overnight, the *disco break*, in which the music stops but the beat goes on. Although his purpose was to get rid of the modulation, he had accidentally achieved something far more important. Stripping the tracks down to just the basic rhythm, and letting that play for awhile, was perfect for dancing and was also perfect for DJs. They could now jump back and forth between their two turntables, play the bare rhythm track on one turntable and blend in elements of the vocals or instruments on the other, or even play little snippets of the next song over the rhythm of the first. As Tom is the first to say, his discovery was an accident, the obvious solution to a technical/musical problem. But his solution was a DJ's solution, the kind of thing that would never have occurred to anybody who doesn't have the soul of a dancer. When "Dreamworld" was released, dance floors went wild. Soon disco breaks were being added to countless songs, and they still are. Nothing happens by accident.

Tom was suddenly in demand as a remixer. Producers and record labels began calling him in to add breaks, change drums, add strings, add backgrounds, add whole new rhythm sections, speed up the tempo or slow it down. Almost everything he touched turned gold, and because of his growing string of hits, jealous producers could hardly afford to say no to his offers to remix. They often didn't have the chance. The record company would simply assign him to fix a record. *"After I had a number of hits no one would ever question me,"* he told me years later. *"I had carte blanche to do whatever I wanted."* He tried not to ruffle feathers, taking care to talk with the song's producers, and making sure he never erased anybody's original tracks, preferring to work off a copy. But this did not always go over so well with original producers who sometimes saw their creations altered beyond recognition. Tom remembers one time being confronted by an angry producer who accused him of *"ruining"* that producer's record. *"Yeah,"* Tom replied. *"I ruined it all the way to the top."* The producer had to smile ruefully and agree.

As 1974 drew to a close, I introduced Tom to Jay Ellis, Meco Menado and Tony Bongiovi (Jon Bon Jovi's uncle), who were producing Gloria Gaynor's debut album. It included her hits "Never Can Say Goodbye," "Honeybee" and "Reach Out, I'll Be There," and the three producers asked Tom to mix the album. He decided to blend these three songs together without a break, just like on a disco tape, but right there on the album. This was something unheard of in album production, and the record's producers thought it was idiotic. *"How are we going to separate the songs?"* they asked. *"Why separate them?"* Tom replied. *"DJs will love it because they can take a break, and fans will love it because they get eighteen minutes of nonstop dance music."* He was right. The new medley format caused a sensation. People found that they could put the record on at home and suddenly have the impression that they were at a top-notch disco.

Gloria Gaynor's debut album became a classic, and helped fuel her meteoric rise to the top as the first bona-fide disco star. Her ascent was so swift that a few months later, in March of 1975, she was crowned Queen of the Discos by the National Association of Discotheque Disc Jockeys in a coronation ceremony in New York, a title she held for two years. But Gloria's album also fueled Tom's reputation. He was soon known in the industry as "The Doctor," the man who took sick records and brought them back to life. The words *A Tom Moulton Mix*" on a record practically guaranteed success. The list of songs that Tom either remixed or produced over the years began to read like a disco hall of fame: "Do It Till You're Satisfied," "That's Where the Happy People Go," "Disco Inferno," "Where Do We Go From Here," "Free Man," "Feel the Need," "La Vie en Rose," "More, More, More." He became a role model for a whole group of top DJs who saw what he was doing and wanted to emulate it. The concept of DJ as remixer became firmly established, and over the next few years many prominent DJs trooped into the studio to make remixes: Larry Levan, Frankie Knuckles, Jim Burgess, Walter Gibbons, Jimmy Simpson, Rick Gianatos and many others. Sometimes they did what Tom did: go back to the original tracks and modify them. Other times they created a new production by mixing record to record, just like they did in the clubs. Today, a whole generation of DJs has entered the ranks of top record producers. All of them are, in a sense, following in Tom Moulton's footsteps.

At the beginning, however, a technical problem sharply limited creativity. Disco records were produced on 7–inch vinyl singles, a format originally designed for short, three-minute songs. As remixers began to produce longer, extended mix versions of songs, they had to cram a lot more grooves onto a side, which reduced fidelity. Even then, they were limited to about six-and-a-half minutes on the 7–inch discs. Again, Tom would stumble on the solution. Producers usually auditioned their works-in-progress for the record company by pressing them on 10-inch discs made of acetate, an inexpensive compound so soft that the discs would lose their fidelity after a few plays. Tom began taking these unfinished productions — ref discs — around to a few of the key DJs, to let them audition works in progress right there in the club. Even though acetate discs were not durable, they became the first promotional records made especially for club DJs.

One day Tom was working at Media Sound, finishing a mix of Al Downing's "I'll Be Holding On" for Chess Records. It was Friday afternoon and Tom wanted to get a ref disc out that weekend to several DJs. But his engineer Jose Rodriguez told him that the studio had just run out of 10-inch acetates. The only thing left in stock were the regular 12-inch, hard vinyl discs used for commercial LPs. These were considered too large for a single song, even for an extended mix, and too expensive for a mere ref disc. But here was an emergency, so Tom asked if there was any way to spread the grooves so the song would fill up a 12-inch. Jose said sure, and to their grand surprise, the process of spreading the grooves over the surface produced a sound that was much sharper, cleaner and hotter than anything they had ever heard.

Tom told me about this accidental discovery, and it didn't take long to realize its implications. He had stumbled on a superior format for disco, one that would not only give DJs a higher quality product, but would also allow remixers to extend their creations for far longer than possible on a 7-inch disc. He thought we should immediately start providing DJs with 12-inch ref discs made of vinyl on a regular basis. My idea was not to sell, but give them to the clubs free as promotional tools. I broached the idea to Ed Kushins, who had no objections, and we immediately began to distribute our mixes on 12-inch. It spread like wild fire. Salsoul Records got the bright idea of releasing special limited edition 12-inch mixes for sale to the fans, and they proved wildly successful. Before long the 12–inch became the workhorse of disco. It still is.

So it was that Tom Moulton came up with a slew of innovations — slip cueing, DJs as remixers, the disco break, the medley format, the 12–inch — all within a year of disco's cross-over in 1974. These techniques and technologies provided the basis for much of the coming disco explosion as well as Tom Moulton's reputation as the most important innovator in the new style. I'm immensely proud of the opportunities I gave him to make many of these things happen. There was just one more innovation to come.

the birth of the record pool

The Loft owner and DJ David Mancuso had long realized how important it was that DJs be able to get their records for free, directly from the labels. It was good for the DJs, who got instant access to the latest songs, and good for the labels, who got instant reaction to their product from the very market most important to their success. Like Nicky Siano and Larry Levan, David Mancuso impressed this fact on his protégés, who used it to good effect. For awhile it was a cozy, almost private relationship between a handful of mostly gay DJs and the labels, and everything seemed fine. But by the end of 1974 discos were opening everywhere and DJs were proliferating along with them. Not only were there an increasing number of gay and black clubs, but a whole new disco scene began to emerge in outer boroughs like Brooklyn, where young working class kids, particularly Italians, were picking up on the trend. The record companies were swamped with DJs and DJ-wannabes demanding free product and began to look on them as low-life spongers. Florence hated them, complaining that they ruined the workday with their constant interruptions. Some labels simply refused to cooperate. Between DJs there were charges of favoritism that some labels only cooperated with a select elite of DJs, freezing others out. It was a mess. The last straw came when the CTI label issued a hot new song by Idris Mohammed, and a CTI promotion man, Tony Serafino, refused a copy to popular DJ Steve D'Aquisto because the company claimed that they had only pressed two copies which were already promised to two other DJs. Steve D'Aquisto was furious and called Tom Moulton. *"The only way for disco to survive,"* he argued, *"is for the DJs to band together. We should have an understanding that if every DJ doesn't receive a certain record, then no one is allowed to play it."* Steve was, in effect, advocating a disco strike to force the industry to distribute their dance records to DJs freely and fairly. Tom agreed with Steve and realized that the best way to create such a system was not to strike, but to organize a record pool of disc jockeys and institutionalize the distribution of free product. He championed the idea in his disco column in *Billboard,* and DJs took notice.

As a result, Steve D'Aquisto, David Mancuso and Eddie Rivera got together and launched the first record pool. Based in David Mancuso's Loft, the idea was simple. DJs would pay a monthly fee to join the pool; the organizers would make sure they were bonafide DJs and not wannabes trying to sponge free product. The participating record labels would then send their new dance releases each week to the Loft, where members of the pool would drop by and pick up the records. This was good for David Mancuso, whose Loft became a center of attention and power among all the subscribing DJs. And it seemed good for the DJs and good for the labels as well whose normal business day would not be interrupted by their visits.

DJs were charged a $5 a month token fee, and each was given a bin to hold the records that came in to the Loft from the labels. I represented Scepter at the record pool's first meeting, and in the excitement I volunteered Scepter to donate money to help build the bins. Juggy Gales, who represented RCA, was violently opposed to my suggestion because he couldn't make a decision about RCA's contribution without first checking with his superiors. We got into a terrible argument. I think Juggy was pissed because I had the authority to speak for Scepter but he could not for RCA.

The birth of the first record pool wasn't without labor pains. David Mancuso almost immediately ran afoul of a SoHo neighborhood association, which was already leery of this wild-haired, erratic entrepreneur who looked like a cross between Jesus Christ and Charlie Manson. They had never liked the ethnic mix of people trooping over to Prince St., and now that such people were coming around all day, they liked it even less. Before long they brought the matter to the city, and David was in trouble.

One day I got a call from DJs Steve D'Aquisto and David Rodriguez. They told me that David Mancuso was in danger of losing his license for the Loft unless respectable industry executives like me went down and testified at a hearing of the Community Review Board. I panicked. At Scepter I was still firmly in the closet, and now I was being asked to testify publicly about the goings-on at one of the preeminent gay dance clubs. They might ask me anything, not only about gay topics but also about drugs. The Loft was now, for example, giving out tabs of acid at the coat checkroom, a fact that I (thankfully) did not know about at the time. But I did know that the city's attack was aimed at the very core of the new gay nightlife emerging in New York, and particularly the aspect of that nightlife I loved the best. The Loft was not only a patently gay club, a type of establishment that had not even been allowed to exist just a few years before, but also a racially integrated club, something that was rare in nightlife, gay or straight, in the mid-'70s (and still is today). So my desire to defend David Mancuso prevailed over my fears. I went into Ed Kushins and told him what Steve and David wanted, and Ed advised me to go down there and tell the truth.

I took direct aim at what I believed the city was trying to pull, testifying that *"the only thing David Mancuso is guilty of is helping people come together with music — black people, white people, gay and straight."* I also pointed out that the eccentric and somewhat disheveled Mancuso hardly fit the image of the rapacious, greedy club owner. *"If David is as materialistic as you claim,"* I asked, *"why would he be wearing a green velvet suit in the middle of July with one white sock and one black sock?"* When I finished, David's lawyer Mel Katz was ecstatic and told me, *"You said exactly what I wanted them to know about David."* David won the case, and afterward Katz told me that my testimony had been instrumental. A few weeks later I ran across David in the street. He lifted up one pants leg and said, *"Look!"* revealing two different colored socks. Apparently he had affected this little eccentric fashion statement all of his life.

The Loft survived, and so did the record pool. Unfortunately, we failed to recognize any potential for trouble. There were immediate disagreements within the pool about various policies, and there was a lot of friction between gay DJs and those from the new and growing straight scene. Many straight DJs complained that the gays were essentially running the show, which of course they were. Eventually there was a break and a straight DJ, Eddie Rivera, started his own pool. There was also friction between blacks and whites that eventually splintered the original pool even further.

Moreover, the pools created the opportunity for DJs to flood the market with free product. Promotional records started showing up in the stores, and eventually swelled to huge proportions. The concept of the record pools had become a monster, to the point where hardly any record company could now afford to participate. After all, there are not many businesses that can afford to give out five thousand pieces of product to sell only fifteen thousand. Although the worst problems and excesses were mostly in the future, at their inception, the record pools were unquestionably instrumental in building the excitement around disco. They raised the prestige of club DJs, and they would allow ideas and trends to cross-fertilize between record labels and their most fervent audiences.

honors without honor

As the new year dawned, my idea of putting instrumental mixes on the b-side had become so widespread that Scepter was honored with *Billboard's* 1974 Trendsetter of the Year Award. As head of the company, Florence was officially invited to accept the award, which was nice irony since it was she who had fought tooth and nail against the new trend in the first place. Florence was now living mostly in Los Angeles and suffering from poor health but, never one to turn down glory, she flew into New York for the ceremony at the Friar's Club. She and I and several others sat at the Scepter table with her boyfriend Bill Wardlow from *Billboard*, and when she got up to receive the award, I was kvelling. It was such sweet vindication.

I prepared to stand up for my acknowledgment, that I was sure to come. But Florence accepted the award as though the b-side instrumentals had been her idea. I couldn't believe it. She was taking credit for something she had opposed. When she got off the dais, it took me a second to realize that she had not even mentioned me. I looked at Maye with what must have been a very sarcastic smirk, and Bill Wardlow noticed. He never forgave me, thinking I was showing disrespect to Florence. But Florence was showing disrespect to everyone at the table who had made that award possible, especially me. *"Poor Mel,"* Maye said afterward. *"We got very quiet at the table. I just felt so sad for him."*

Years later I would be acknowledged many times as the "Godfather of Disco" for my role in the development of dance music. But this was still in the future. For now I was furious. This might have been the moment when I realized that if I was ever going to get full credit for my ideas, I was going to have to run my own company. I didn't know it then, but my own label was right around the corner.

chapter eight
THE GOLDEN AGE

By 1975, disco hit its stride across the nation. It emerged as a multi-million, then billion-dollar business, and began its climb up the charts. "Fly, Robin, Fly" by the Silver Convention was 1975's second most popular single, and several others made it to coveted No. 1 slot: "That's the Way I Like It" and "Get Down Tonight" by K.C. & the Sunshine Band, "Lady Marmalade" by LaBelle, and of course "The Hustle" by Van McCoy. A slew of others made Top Ten, tons made Top Forty. Disco had really arrived.

The increasing number of disco records released by the major labels was mirrored by the growth and quality of the clubs, especially in New York. No longer an exclusively underground phenomenon, disco also ceased to be exclusively gay. In fact, the first disco to receive major media attention was Infinity, and — not surprisingly in an era where homosexuality was still largely banished from the media — Infinity was primarily a straight club. Almost as soon as it opened, on Broadway just north of Houston St., Infinity became the haunt of celebrities and the nexus of a major scene constantly written up in the papers. New York has always had celebrity hangouts where paparazzi stalk the stars and publicize their goings-on in the gossip columns, but Infinity was the first to cater to the new music: the first disco as star haunt. There would be plenty to come.

Infinity got most of the mainstream attention, and more clubs opened up in black and working-class neighborhoods, but gay clubs remained disco's driving force, and many new ones sprang up around Manhattan to cater to the burgeoning gay crowd. In the fall of 1974, arson gutted the Firehouse, ending its eclectic mix of politics and dancing, but by now there were so many other places for gay men to dance that although the Firehouse was mourned, it was hardly missed. Gay men followed their favorite DJs around: Walter Gibbons to Galaxy 21, Bobby "DJ" Guttadaro to Le Jardin, Tony Gioe, Joey Palmenteri and Richie Kaczor to Hollywood, Jonathan Fearing and light man Peter Kinnard to the Cock Ring. Its name notwithstanding, the Cock Ring showed that gay men were not necessarily size queens when it came to discothèques. The dance floor was minuscule, but the crowds jam-packed Saturday nights and its famous Sunday tea dances. Many DJs who later grew successful learned their way around a booth in that hot little club at the end of Christopher St.

12 west and flamingo

Amid this profusion of discos, two in particular, 12 West and Flamingo, stood out as paragons of the new gay spirit. 12 West, located on the West Side Highway, was created for the young, acid-taking gay men who wanted to experience hallucinations as they danced the night away. Alan Harris and Carey Finkelstein constructed the club inside a one-story garage whose roof formed a huge arc, and they surrounded the dance floor with bleacher-type platforms that created a sort of amphitheater. This not only lent a trippy, theatrical effect to the room, but also did amazing things to the acoustics. The music would literally resonate back and forth between the arced ceiling and the wooden dance floor, sucking the crowd into this fulcrum of sound. The general consensus among serious dancers was that sound designers Barry Lederer and Peter Spar had given 12 West the best sound system in town. And unlike other clubs, it was a real dance democracy: no membership, no velvet rope. Everyone was welcomed, and people flocked in like mad: boys with big hair, hip fashion queens, fan dancers, body builders, punk rockers, everybody.

But even 12 West paled before the vision of disco as paradise that Michael Fesco created at Flamingo — the direct predecessor of the ultimate gay nightclub, the Saint. Flamingo opened in December of 1974 at the corner of Broadway and Houston in a second-floor loft that ran the entire length of the block to Mercer St. By the end of the first month Flamingo was so popular that Fesco had to close the membership rolls to new people — there was simply no more room. This only raised the hysteria to get in — to the extent that the door was mobbed by desperate queens pretending to be members' guests, using members' names, phony names, any excuse at all to gain admittance. Fesco was quickly forced to restrict the guest policy, and within weeks memberships were selling on the black market for as much as $500. It was rumored that Calvin Klein himself, king of the A-list, had to lobby for a membership.

The most striking thing about Flamingo was the sheer physical beauty of the men. No one had ever seen anything quite like this before. The A-list, the thin fashion set, the bodybuilders — all of them beat a path to Flamingo, and different cliques of miraculously handsome men could be found in the same corners week after week. Entering Flamingo was like stepping into the sexiest, most alluring fashion spread on earth, *GQ* and *Playgirl* and *Colt* come to life in mindboggling 3D. When first timers entered you could see their eyes widen at the profusion of cheekbones, jawbones, shirtless torsos glistening with perfection. Men who would have been the center of attention at any other gay bar or club were, here, a dime a dozen. In an era before the gym became a center of gay life, when staying skinny was still the easiest way to stay sexy, the Flamingo presented the prototype of the future: chiseled abs, bulging pecs, oiled, moisturized skin, amazing hair. The overall effect, the pounding music, the lights, the shirtless bodies, was overpowering. This was clearly the ultimate realization of the fantasy that gay men had been reaching for since Stonewall: Heaven on Earth, Olympus with a beat.

If the gods on Olympus had their manna, the men at Flamingo and 12 West had drugs. Both clubs adopted the policy of serving no liquor, only free punch and juice, and drugs flowed like water. By now I had surrendered enthusiastically to the drug craze. I was smoking angel dust fairly often, as were a lot of people. But we also snorted coke, took uppers and downers, mda, lsd, mescaline, you name it. Poppers were everywhere, and some men were developing such intense popper addictions that the little vials seemed almost surgically implanted to their noses. Reality was altered for almost everyone: surreality ruled.

In such a drug-saturated crowd the best DJs had a system for staying ahead of the game. *"I would call drug dealers up and ask, 'What's been your big seller this week?'"* says Flamingo's DJ, Howard Merritt.

> Then I would know what kind of music to play that weekend. If they'd sold a lot of mda, the music had to be more high energy. Cocaine and speed, that's the kind of music I played. But if they'd sold a lot of dust, then people weren't coming to hear me — they wanted to hear Richie Rivera, because he played a lot of heavy music.

Flamingo's long, rectangular room was quite simple. The moveable banquettes could be placed around the room or stored on other floors of the building. There was a constant flow of cross-ventilation from open windows that let cooler air blow through and out the back, so that as you moved through the space it went from cooler to hotter to very hot. This influenced where various cliques hung out, depending on whether they wanted to be cool and comfortable (fashion types) or hot and sweaty (muscle boys). Except for the special theme parties, the decor was minimal, the lighting wasn't elaborate, the sound system excellent but not innovative. But the disc jockeys were the best in the business, and at Flamingo the same passions, the same violent adoration or disdain, that had led earlier gay generations of opera queens to worship Maria Callas or despise Joan Sutherland, was now pumped into disco. We all became connoisseurs, the Flamingo our Met.

The focal point of Flamingo was the DJ booth, located along the right wall directly in the center of the long space. It was coveted as the best booth in town by New York's hottest DJs. *"Visually, it was the best disc jockey booth I ever worked in,"* Howard says. *"At eight feet off the ground, just above the dancers' heads, you could see everything and pick out anyone you wanted."* Howard Merritt was typical in that he never planned his program, just sensed the direction the crowd was going and how to grab them. *"Then once you had the crowd, you could do anything you wanted. They trusted you. Sometimes in the middle of the music they'd all stop dancing and just applaud."* Or, if the DJ was out of synch that night, hiss and boo.

The first DJs at Flamingo were Armando Galvez, Luis Ramero and Vincent Carleo. Vincent was temperamental and could toss turntables if he became angry. The next year Howard Merritt, who had been roommates with Vincent in San Francisco, shared the turntables with Roy Thode. Although owner Michael Fesco maintained a stable of regular DJs, the mainstays at Flamingo became Howard Merritt and Richie Rivera. *"I'd play the gay white boy music,"* says Merritt,

> and Richie played very intense dark music. Between the two of us it worked out quite well. I always played the White Party, and he always played the Black.

Despite the intimidating beauty of the men, there was none of the standoffish snobbery you might expect. This was a sexual brotherhood, an elite family at the cutting edge of a musical and cultural and sexual revolution. The men at Flamingo didn't have to pose: they were secure at the apex, they could just relax and let go. Men made love with each other in endless chains of him and him and him (although not right there in the club — that would come later at the Saint), and I fondly remember one night when I looked around the floor and counted 32 ex-bed partners who had since become friends. Love permeated the air along with the sweat and poppers, and no matter how high I got, I felt utterly safe, taken care of. Every weekend, with Saturday night shining on our Sunday morning faces, the dance floor throbbed with the shirtless, the sweaty, the yearning, the yearned after, all of them floating in a miraculous dream. This was our gay utopia, the ultimate Before.

the bruise

My star was certainly rising at Scepter since the obscure dance movement I had been championing for years was now, finally, breaking into the mainstream and generating huge sales. Instead of an annoying kvetch, I was now the prophet who had seen it coming. In June '75 *Billboard* held the first disco convention at the Roosevelt Hotel, which Boston producer Arthur Baker recalls as a landmark in disco's evolution. *"Everyone,"* says Arthur, *"was thinking that since Billboard was doing a convention, disco was now real, something you could keep doing. Something you could make a living at."* And so despite my lingering sorrow over my breakup with Michael, I soared through 1975. I even became known during the summer for a dance that reflected the exuberance I was feeling.

The disco craze had spawned a craze for new dances, just like the early '60s when the Twist and the Locomotion were the rage. The

Hustle was now the biggest, but there were also the Freak, the Bus Stop, and many others. I had developed a particularly muscular sort of dancing that featured about as much bumping and grinding as you could get outside the bedroom, or for that matter, the boxing ring. It was essentially "dirty dancing" — long before Patrick Swayze and the movie — and after one particularly hot round on the Island, Ray Ford said to me, *"Whoa, Big Mama, I can't do this anymore for awhile — you've bruised me!"* The title stuck (as did his outrageous nickname for me: Big Mama). Soon, it seemed, everybody was doing the Bruise.

A particularly fond memory of these golden days is my birthday in January of 1976. Since it was also the birthday of several friends, I decided to throw a dance party at my Brooklyn place on the Saturday night following my birthday. This was going to be the first party I had thrown without Michael, and DJ Vincent Carleo agreed to make a special tape of music to bruise by. In early January all of my A-list cronies from Flamingo and the Island received this invitation:

> Do you Bruise??? If you don't, here's your opportunity to learn the Bruise, the new dance sensation sweeping such places as Fire Island Pines, Flamingo and 12 West.

> Mel Cheren is holding the first Bruise Dance Party on Saturday, January 24th, at his Brooklyn building (240 Warren St.). Bruise all night to special bruise music prepared for this gala occasion by one of New York's most popular Disco DJs. You will bruise with people you never imagined bruised before! Bruise and cruise!!

In the midst of planning the party, Michael secretly decided to throw me a surprise party at Reade Street on the actual night of my birthday, even though he knew I was throwing the Bruise Party a few days later. He quietly got Tommy, my assistant at

Scepter, to pass him the guest list to my party and then sent everyone invitations to come to Reade Street for this surprise. It might seem that Michael was doing this as a great kindness, or at least a way of staying close, and perhaps it was. But he obviously had another motivation. Reade Street was cooking since Larry Levan had taken over the turntables, but it could always do better. Having over a hundred A-list friends from the Island and Flamingo dancing in his club couldn't hurt. On the night of the surprise, Dick Fisher held a small dinner for my closest friends, including Michael, Julio, Ray Ford, Terry Fu and a few others. On arriving I didn't smell anything cooking, and when someone suggested that I give Dick a hand in the kitchen I thought I was going to have to start from scratch. But as I walked into the kitchen, I was grabbed and handcuffed, a pillowcase was pulled over my head, and I was led out of Dick's building and into a waiting car. (Later, I learned that my kidnappers were terrified when, as they were stuffing me into the car blindfolded and handcuffed, they noticed a cop across the street.) They drove me around to confuse me, and when we finally arrived at Reade Street they put me on a chair to make it seem that they were carrying me up a flight of stairs. Once inside the club they set me down, and before pulling the pillowcase off my head they stuck poppers under my nose. The rush was incredible when I realized that I was at Reade Street surrounded by all of my friends.

Tommy, dressed in white tie and tails, acted as Master of Ceremonies, and Nathan, who prepared the Loft's food, whipped up a banquet. My cousin Barry found a photo of me dressed up as a nun on Halloween (the first and last time I ever did drag), and had it made into coasters and a huge poster. (The lady in the photo shop remarked, *"Oh my! I've heard about those lesbian nuns."*) The beautiful Dennis Lasker gave me a gorgeous black-and-white pen-and-ink drawing he had done of clouds and feathers that had a wonderful sense of whimsy, and on the back he inscribed the words *"Pleasure — delight — chance."* Dennis fulfilled that promise later by spending the rest of a delirious night with me. The next day I kept getting calls from friends who said they had a great time but just couldn't seem to get to sleep afterwards and ended up ironing all night, or even, in one case, washing the windows. I just thought it was just the excitement until I found out that Michael had spiked the punch with acid. It was, needless to say, a fantastic party; a memory.

I was concerned that my party a few nights later was going to pale in comparison, especially since the same people had been invited to both. How could I top Reade Street with a house party in Brooklyn? Then I got an idea, called up my business friend Jerry Sanders at Queens Litho and asked him to print t-shirts for me. Since he only had one day to produce them, the lettering had to be simple. And so on Saturday night 124 men got t-shirts that said, simply, *"I BRUISE."* The party turned out great, and there was a buzz for weeks afterward about the bruising that went on out in Brooklyn.

reade street closes

Throughout 1975 Michael struggled on with Reade Street. It was not the biggest of clubs, not the sexiest, not the trendiest. But it had Larry Levan, whose reputation continued to grow.

Larry was developing a style that was almost the opposite of what most DJs were doing. The new trend was to pay extremely careful attention to the technique of spinning and slip-cueing, seamlessly blending one song into the next. But Larry was a free and anarchic spirit, and as such he grew to care less and less about technical perfection. He would stop a song in the middle. Play two songs back-to-back with totally different beats. Play the same song over and over. *"Technically, he was an awful disc jockey,"* says Flamingo DJ Howard Merritt. *"He couldn't mix two records together, but somehow they still sounded great."*

This first part wasn't exactly true. Larry was a master of the mix when he wanted to be. It's just that as the years passed, he yearned for more than technical perfection. He wanted inspiration. Ecstasy. He wanted to spin the way he lived — in inspired anarchy. In an interview years later, he was asked about his eccentric style, particularly his habit of suddenly stopping the music in midstream. *"It's boring when it's the same thing all the time,"* he replied. He argued that a lot of disco was growing monotonous, that dance music should look to rock, which had more contrasts and natural variety. This, of course, is what a lot of disco's critics were saying. So it bears noting that the man who would become disco's most legendary DJ shared many complaints about the new music with its harshest critics. Perhaps this is what made him so great. He wanted the best from disco — its energy and abandon — but he saw that in over-emphasizing a relentless beat, disco was in danger of smothering creativity, which, in the end, is precisely what happened. Larry Levan moved to the beat of his own drummer, and it is partly because of this that his reputation has grown as it has.

And partly because of his obsession with sound. From sound designer Richard Long, Larry had learned the lesson that many club operators have never learned: the crucial quality of sound. Larry was fascinated with electronics, speakers, effects. He was always listening, wrapped up in wires, always tinkering. He took dancers on his long, strange trips on the most intense, bass-heavy sound anybody had ever heard. The combination was unique, and throughout 1975 more and more people frequented this off-beat club with the great sound system and the eccentric DJ who might do anything, and often did.

Michael was convinced that Larry was his ticket, but he also became convinced that Reade Street was never going to be the venue for that ride. Despite growing success, the club was still struggling, especially against its uncooperative landlord. Michael's real estate problems were overwhelming his energy, and he realized that to create the type of club he envisioned he would need both a better and more secure space. He was also going to need a lot more money if he were to satisfy Larry's requests for the latest and most innovative sound equipment. Michael recognized Larry's genius very early on, but he also recognized that Larry was like a mad scientist, unconcerned with small details like money. Larry's acoustic obsessions would eventually prove more than worthy of the cost, but by 1976 Michael was painfully aware that he was going to need much more cash to make his dream club a reality. And so in early 1976, after some epic dispute with the landlord, he announced he was closing Reade Street. It was time for a new start.

The closing was not without trauma, even for me. Reade Street had a huge, unpaid bill with Con Edison, and Con Ed duly added that amount onto the tab for the building that Michael and I owned together in Brooklyn. I was furious, and I called them to try and buy Michael more time. Since he had already closed Reade Street and did not actually have to be around, I told them that he had died in a car crash. I'm not proud of this, but it was all I could come up with at the time. Even so, it took me quite awhile to extricate myself from Michael's debts. We were no longer lovers, but I was still bailing him out.

finding paradise

Michael immediately began searching for a better site, and one day he found an old garage located at 84 King St. in SoHo. It had previously housed a defunct disco, the Chameleon, which was only open for a brief period, and it wasn't hard to see why. It had such a cavernous dance floor — a massive, 10,000-square-foot second-floor above a huge parking garage — far too big for anyone to feel comfortable in. The space was being used for truck maintenance when Michael first saw it, and hardly looked like disco material, but Michael had a simple solution. The space could work if he just split it up. But transforming the vast garage into a disco paradise was going to take money, and when Michael needed money, he always started with me.

This was the age of the Hustle, and "Do the Hustle" was more than just a song lyric or a dance step to Michael. It was how he worked. He informed me that he wanted us to sell our joint properties and split the profits so that he could pursue his dream. I had grown to like the security of owning property, however, and I was not about to give that up for anyone, Michael included. Since the real estate market was lousy, I decided instead that I would buy him out. This would have the added advantage of severing our business relationship for good and was one of the smartest moves I've ever made. I signed the documents on tax day — April 15, 1976 — and I now had my own buildings, my independence, and Michael had his money, and he left his job at Paramount to devote his full attention to transforming the King St. garage into his dream disco.

surprise

Julio and I were becoming closer and closer. I was in love with him, although I suppose I didn't really consciously recognize it at the time. To me, he was a paragon, the ultimate gay man: macho, sensitive, stunning, an inexhaustible party animal, the hottest guy on almost any dance floor he graced. I dreamed of being his lover, but he was so sought after that he seemed beyond my reach. We had sex occasionally, but then, everybody had sex occasionally with everybody else in those days. It hardly meant that we were on the road to a relationship. So I adopted the solution many gay men have adopted with their unrequited flames: if I couldn't be his lover, I would become his best friend. It wasn't that difficult. He was caught at the time in a horrible, abusive relationship — at one point his hunky boyfriend bit his finger so badly he wound up at the hospital — and I tried to show him that there were people who loved him for himself by being one of those people myself.

That April, in part to console Julio over his unhappy relationship, I decided to throw him a lavish surprise birthday party. Since Reade Street was now closed, I picked the Loft, and David Mancuso agreed to play. Everybody clamored for an invitation, even people Julio didn't know. Since the world was in love with him, it seemed as though people who called to RSVP mentioned that they would be bringing 10 or 15 guests. In the end, the surprise was spoiled by the buzz. The night before his birthday the Flamingo held its annual Tropicana party and a stream of gorgeous guys kept coming up to Julio wishing him a happy birthday. It didn't take him long to figure out why everyone at Flamingo knew.

On the night of the party David Mancuso was late, so Judy Weinstein took over as emergency DJ. Judy had been a faithful disciple of both incarnations of the Loft, and a few months earlier had taken a job working as David's secretary. She was so wrapped up in the scene she even slept in the disco for a while. Judy would soon emerge as a power in her own right, and on this night she proved how indispensable she could be, covering for David on the turntables or dishing up ice cream, doing whatever needed to be done. Julio was a big Maria Callas fan, so Paul White, a graphic designer and one of our "Camp Tommy" housemates, created a huge blow-up card of the Maria Callas/Blackglama ad, "What Becomes A Legend Most,"inserting Julio's face in place of Callas's. Everyone signed the card and Julio pretended to love it, but I think he was horrified at the heresy. He tossed it in the garbage the second the party was over. More than four hundred people showed up, the party was a smash, and Julio and I grew closer than ever — for better or worse.

the hits just keep on coming

Danceable r&b and even pop continued to dominate *Billboard's* charts throughout 1976. A slew of disco songs hit the No. 1 slot, including Johnny Taylor's "Disco Lady,"Wild Cherry's "Play That Funky Music," Diana Ross's "Love Hangover," K.C. and the Sunshine Band's "Shake Your Booty." Walter Murphy's "A Fifth of Beethoven" launched the often questionable trend of adapting classical music to disco. The Bee Gees had their first No. 1 hit in years with "You Should Be Dancing." The Sylvers hit No. 1 with "Boogie Fever." And a parody — "Disco Duck" by Rick Dees and his Cast of Idiots — also hit No. 1. This was the year of "More, More, More" by Andrea True Connection, "You'll Never Find Another Love Like Mine" by Lou Rawls, and a ton of other great songs. I got some studio experience of my own, mixing "Nice and Slow" by Jesse Greene and "I Get Lifted" by Sweet Music on my lunch hour. I had 200 copies pressed back-to-back with my own money. "Nice and Slow"was picked Best Disco Record at the 1976 Billboard Convention.

A new musical element entered the disco mix that year. Up until now, disco was an American phenomenon, its roots firmly embedded in Motown, funk, and the Philadelphia sound pioneered by Gamble and Huff. But in 1975 Neil Bogart, a record executive largely responsible for the bubblegum sound of the '60s, launched his new Casablanca label and was approached by Giorgio Moroder, a Swiss-Italian producer. Moroder had produced "Love to Love You, Baby," a three-minute single by an unknown singer named Donna Summer. "Love to Love You" had a radically new sound: mechanistic, synthesized, robotic. Neil Bogart thought the combination of this new, European sound a brilliant match with Donna Summer's rich, soulful vocals, and convinced Moroder to extend the song to 16 minutes, taking up a full side of an album. It rose to the No. 2 spot and launched Donna Summer's career. She would soon become one of the most popular recording artists in history, arguably disco's greatest star. "Love to Love You, Baby" also launched a whole new sound that would soon sweep the genre — Euro-disco. Americans, it seemed, could not get enough of any kind of disco in 1976.

One song released that year always transports me back to the time. "Cherchez La Femme," by Dr. Buzzard's Original Savannah Band, was about the lives and loves of record producer Tommy Mottola. I have vivid memories dancing to this classic and of Cory Daye's rich vocal contrasting with the song's rather misanthropic lyrics:

> All I can say / Of one thing I am certain/
> They're all the same / The sluts and the saints
> For misery / Cherchez la femme

the end of scepter

For several years now Florence Greenberg had been in ill health, and as a result Scepter was beginning to languish. Florence was spending so much time in California that she gradually lost touch with the business and with what was happening musically. Her heart really wasn't into the record business anymore. Her era of girl groups and clever, pretty pop, had passed. She had her pile of money, she was tired, she didn't need the constant struggle to stay ahead of the game anymore. A year earlier Ed Kushins had taken me into his confidence and told me that Scepter might close, and I had kept that in the back of my mind.

Now, in July of 1976, just as the new music was becoming a billion-dollar industry with limitless opportunities, Florence made the momentous announcement: she was closing down Scepter Records. It probably wasn't difficult for her to shut the company from 3,000 miles away — she wasn't as emotionally attached to the day-to-day battle of the record business as we were. But her decision was devastating for many of us. The dream of lifetime employment, of climbing the corporate ladder, of security, vanished in a day. Shortly after Florence's announcement, Ed came to me with a plan. He had always wanted to start his own record company, he said, but his contract with Scepter had made that impossible. Now that Florence was determined to close the business, he was free to do what he wanted. And what he wanted, he said, was me as his partner.

Ed's idea was simple. He had the business savvy, was the famous penny pincher, the one who could bring things in on time and under budget, but he had little connection with music itself. I, on the other hand, had the music savvy, was the famous talent seeker, the one at the center of disco, who knew everybody and every trend, but I was no businessman. It seemed a perfect match. So as we began the complex business of closing down Scepter, Ed and I began serious discussions about starting up our own label. I was laid up with hepatitis, and my Fire Island housemates were trying to convince me to spend the whole summer on the Island, something that I had always wanted to do. But Ed insisted that if we were going to start a label, we needed to get busy right away, and he promised that once the label was launched, I could take all the time off I wanted. So the day Scepter closed its doors, Ed and I made our decision.

It was the Bicentennial. The city was throwing a spectacular party celebrating the nation's independence, and hundreds of elegant tall ships and thousands of hunky sailors crowded New York harbor. If I hadn't been so focused on starting up our new company, I might have been tempted to revert to some of my old habits. But I was in the process of declaring independence myself. My own record company would mean the end of having to beg and argue for a hearing, the end of watching somebody else get the credit for my ideas, the end of falling on deaf ears. Disco, my music, was everywhere, wafting out of every bar, booming from every boom box, cresting over the airwaves and out of record stores like a tidal wave, no longer just a phenomenon of the clubs, but big business. Now I could ride that wave on my own, captain of my disco ship. Things were just getting good.

chapter nine
WEST END
RISES

Ed and I named our new company West End Music Industries, Inc., after Ed's favorite resort in the Bahamas. I came up with our slogan, *"Where the sun sets and the stars rise,"* and we printed it over a cityscape on the sleeves of our records. Our new office, in the same W. 54th St. building Scepter had just vacated, was just one floor below, on the 6th floor, a small reception area and one little room with two desks facing each other — a record company in a shoebox. But even though the office seemed cramped, it worked. When producers came in to audition new songs, we would listen together, me playing the good guy and Ed frowning and playing the heavy. We would read each other's faces for reaction, fill in each other's blanks, feed off each other. Once we became successful and moved into spacious separate offices, we lost something vital that we never got back. Sometimes, I guess, it pays to be poor.

In keeping with our respective talents, Ed ran the finances and I was responsible for finding producers and artists and going out to the clubs to promote our records. Ed loved the arrangement, loved that he got to sit there and wheel and deal during the day while I roamed the clubs at night. For my part, I trusted Ed so much that I never bothered to look at the books.

We didn't have a single record in the pipeline when we started, but specialty records had been very successful for Scepter, so Ed and I signed Eddie Kochak, the "Belly Dance King," for our first venture. We created a subsidiary label for specialty product, Amaraba Records, and Kochak ended up recording three albums for us. But we had hardly gone into business to promote belly dancing. Disco dancing was what we were about, and product came our way almost immediately.

Our first call was from Joe Auslander, head of E.B. Marks Music Corporation, an old-line music publisher. Joe told us about an album he had from Italy that he thought we could turn into a disco hit. It was from the film *How Funny Can Sex Be?* released in Italy under the title of "Sessamato." Since we didn't have a name for the group, we called the song "Sessamato" by Sessa Matto. And we were off and running. We needed a hot DJ to mix the song, and I immediately thought of Jimmy Stuard, a friend from Boston who was making a name for himself in New York as DJ at 12 West. Jimmy had the makings of a star DJ, and I wanted to give him his first shot at mixing a hit song. He grabbed the chance. While he was mixing the song, he mentioned that he had a piece of tape left over and asked if he could experiment with it. I said sure. He jerked the tape backwards over the heads of the tape machine and produced a scratchy noise, the kind of noise you get when you jerk a needle over a record. Jimmy loved the sound, and insisted that we add it to the song. To my surprise, that particular sound became immensely popular. Some pioneers of rap music argue that it was the very first scratch mix ever put on record. Grandmaster Flash told me years later that "Sessamatto" was the first record ever used for rapping, and the portion of it that the Uptown Rappers used was the very portion that contained Jimmy's scratch sound. DJs began scratching on their turntables, and the whole scratch thing became huge. It's funny to think that poor Jimmy helped initiate that trend, maybe even invented it altogether, on his first and last session in the studio.

Right from the start our philosophy at West End was to nurture DJs like Jimmy. One of the thrills of having my own company was that I could finally put my ideas about the relation between

DJs and labels into play. So we announced that Thursday would be DJ Day at West End, and at least 50 spinners from Manhattan and New Jersey regularly showed up, eager for new product and intent on sharing their experiences and their philosophies with the people actually producing the music. These guys knew everything. They could build a sound system from scratch – take it apart, rebuild it – they were the auto mechanics of disco. And none was more talented than Jimmy. But my dreams of nurturing Jimmy's success ended one horrible night when someone left a cigarette smoldering on a mattress in one of the cubicles at the dingy Everard Baths. There was no sprinkler system in the building, the place was a darkened maze, and in the smoke and confusion men suffocated and burned, some so grotesquely that they were never identified and became the focus of legends: Who were they? Why did no one claim them? Some of them were hanging from a small ledge outside the second story, clad only in towels, screaming, falling to the sidewalk below. And Jimmy, who I truly believed was destined for stardom, was caught in there. The loss, the suddenness, the unexpectedness floored me. Young men in our circle were not supposed to die.

I was in grief over Jimmy as West End began to soar. Tom Moulton mixed "Mary Hartman, Mary Hartman" for us, which clawed its way onto the disco charts. It probably would have done even better if we had called the group by its real name, Vince Montana and the Salsoul Orchestra. Tom also mixed our next release, "You Are The Star," by Jakki, and we released "Na Na Hey Hey, Kiss Him Goodbye" by Garrett Scott, a remake of the hit by Steam several years before. Then came "Spirit of Sunshine" by Chuck Davis, and later that summer Tom Moulton remixed *Magic Love*, a French album by Michelle with okay tracks that Tom churned into a smoking dance medley — "Can't You Feel It, Disco Dance," "Magic Love," "Hold Me, Squeeze Me"— it became quite successful. Although we were still waiting for our first unqualified smash hit, we were up and running, pumping out product, racking up sales, a real record company.

My love life was flourishing as well. One Saturday night at the Eagle's Nest I noticed a very attractive blond across the bar staring at me with this rakish grin while rubbing himself suggestively up and down on somebody else's leg. Wade Benjamin was a classic hot number, sexy and sleazy and lewd and lascivious, into tit clamps and orgies and what have you. He was perfect for that time in my life and we soon tumbled into a glorious, almost exclusively physical relationship. We didn't have much in common, but who cared? I took him to Europe, and I remember him carrying a dildo in his luggage. Every time we went through customs I told him, *"Baby, if the agents pull out that horse dick, I don't know you."* I thought it was hilarious that this raunchy sex machine was in the process of becoming an Episcopal priest. I attended his ordination, as did his ex-lover and a woman who was also in love with him.

construction parties

While Ed and I were starting West End, Michael was hard at work on his new space, which he decided to call the Paradise Garage. Even though he had sold me his share of our properties, he still needed a lot more money. He began to borrow from everybody: me, Larry Kramer, Lou Malkin and Dino Georgiou, his mother lent him $20,000. In September, as the Bee Gees "You Should Be Dancin'" hit No. 1 on the charts, the old tenants moved out of 84 King St. facility and Michael moved in. It was a vast, lumbering wreck of a building.

At first Michael thought he had borrowed enough to renovate the space and get the club started, but paying the landlord five months' advance rent and buying a modest-sized sound system ate up most of his $110,000. He had little money left for the actual renovation. The extra money he had coming in from operating the parking garage on the ground floor was barely enough to pay the monthly rent. *"After parking cars myself,"* Michael said later, *"working 6:00 A.M. to 6:30 P.M. five days a week, it was plain to see that I was getting no place. A decision had to be made. Either open the place as is, or give up my lease."*

And so Michael decided to open the club in stages. He began throwing what he called construction parties, a classic real estate technique, enabling the club to pay for itself. First he built the Grey Room, an intimate enclosed area about 900 square feet, carved out of the larger void and renovated. In the spring of 1977, word spread that the much talked-about Paradise Garage would open in bits and pieces, a disco-in-progress. The construction parties in the Grey Room caught on fast, even though the new space was slapdash at first, even primitive. Sawdust covered the floor, freshly spackled walls were left raw, the speakers were stacked up on one side of the small room, Larry Levan mixed from the other side on makeshift tables. The main dance floor was left dark and sheets of plastic obscured it from the Grey Room, but you could see it anyway. And what you saw was this looming cavern, the biggest dance floor in the city outside the famously gigantic Roseland Ballroom. It was clear that the intimate Grey Room was just a small corner of Michael's plans. There was an electric sense among those in the early crowd that they were in on the ground floor of something huge.

From the start, the Paradise Garage had two acknowledged stars — the space itself (including its sound system), and Larry Levan. Michael recognized that in this age of star DJs, Larry was his ace in the hole, so he decided to build the club around Larry, indulging him with the best, the latest, the most cutting edge (and expensive) equipment. It is probably every DJ's dream to have a club built to their specifications, but few ever get the chance, and Larry was not going to let his chance go to waste. He knew exactly what he wanted, and he obsessed over every detail: the perfect sound, the perfect floor, the perfect lights…

Particularly the perfect sound. *"The greatest thing about Larry,"* says Frankie Knuckles, *"was that he set a precedent for DJs to not only be educated about music, but also about sound."* Although Larry lacked a formal education in electronic engineering, he constantly sought out opportunities to further his electronic education. By now he had pretty much mastered the field, to the point where he began actually designing "Levans" — his own line of speakers. As the Garage's sound system evolved, Larry came up with the idea of a five-way crossover, a completely revolutionary component of sound design that he created with Richard Long. Larry could manipulate the five-way crossover to pluck out certain lyrics, and by omitting or emphasizing different voices make records actually talk to each other (and to the crowd). *"When he manipulated the new crossover,"* says Joey Llanos, *"he would drop everything out until you'd hear a specific part of the vocal that was really meaningful."* Then he might pull a line out of a different song, commenting on or adding to the first. You'd suddenly realize that a message was coming down from on high. And if the drugs were right, or the mood was right, you would get the message and it would blow you away. Larry would send specific messages to friends in the crowd. I'd be dancing and suddenly I'd hear this voice in the music telling me in a very specific way to fuck off, or sending me its love, or commenting on some recent conversation or fight I'd had with Larry. And I'd look up to the booth and there he would be, glaring at me, or throwing me kisses, or just flashing that impish grin. Larry used the crossover to communicate with his crowd, his flock. It came to be known as "disco evangelism:" preaching through the mix.

Larry was extremely protective of the sound system at Paradise Garage and fought over practically every piece of equipment with Michael. As far as Larry was concerned, music was the sole purpose of the Garage and the sound had to be perfect, which, in his mind, it rarely was. If Michael refused him some toy, he might pout and show up late, and Michael would have fits worrying that he wouldn't show at all. This was even more outrageous since Larry actually lived at the Garage. He would disappear for hours at a time, like the Phantom of the Disco out there somewhere in that vast cavern, and would return only when he was good and ready.

Larry's vision of disco perfection stood poles apart from that of Flamingo, the reigning gay disco at the time. Since the Flamingo crowd was mostly white, DJs there focused on the happy, energetic disco that appealed to this crowd. Larry focused on heavier black music, the r&b-disco style that was also a favorite at the mostly straight black clubs uptown. He would not play the high-energy, white records that were huge hits in 1977 — "Dancing Queen" by Abba, "Romeo and Juliet" by Alec Constantinos. Instead Larry was playing "Don't Leave Me This Way" by Thelma Houston and "Let's Get it Together" by Pam Todd. He was pulling together the threads of a musical style that would be named after the Garage itself and ultimately would flow into house music. Larry's style shunned the happy mainstream and embraced something dark, sexy, and sometimes dangerous. He not only entertained, with titles such as "Ain't No Stoppin' Us Now" and "Now That We Found Love, What Are We Gonna Do?," he educated his audience with his music.

Although Michael took pains not to peg the club racially, the Paradise Garage quickly established a reputation as the premier underground black gay club, the flip side to the white Flamingo. Not that either was exactly segregated: people of all races were welcome at both clubs, provided they had style and were fabulous in their own way. But each club established its separate culture, one mostly white, the other mostly black. Each would ultimately lead to two disparate schools of dance music, so that years later the genealogists of disco would carefully chart the family tree of a dozen styles and a thousand clubs on several continents back to these twin roots, black and white, Garage and Flamingo.

There was one unfortunate incident during the early days of the Garage that really damaged my always rocky relationship with Michael. I lent him over $30,000 to buy sound equipment, and my lawyer advised me to have *"Property of Mel Cheren"* stamped on the back so that if the club failed, Michael's creditors would not be able to repossess the equipment. I was finally smart enough to listen to my lawyer, and I thought his suggestion made perfect sense. But Michael went into a rage. Such legalisms were insulting to him, unnecessary, unfaithful. *"You're my friend,"* he shouted, *"and friends don't need lawyers."* I suppose he resented the fact that he still needed me, and this visible reminder pushed him over the top. I wasn't particularly angry; I had just wised up. But to Michael it seemed like betrayal, and Michael kept score. He never really forgave me.

dario, can you get me into studio?

On April 26, 1977, just as the Garage's construction parties were getting underway downtown, the ultimate disco opened uptown in the whoomp! of a thousand flashbulbs and a barrage of publicity no disco had ever seen before — or since. Studio 54's final pieces of furniture were not delivered until three hours before opening, and the fake waterfall still leaked until the last minute, but so what? Owners Steve Rubell and Ian

Schrager had built the crown jewel of discos, and their million-dollar investment paid off almost overnight. They converted an old television studio that happened to sit right next door to West End's new offices, so Ed and I got a bird's eye view of what amounted to the opposite way of creating a disco from Michael's — namely, with tons of money. Everything about Studio 54 was state-of-the-art. The sound system was an uncompromising masterpiece designed by Richard Long. The lighting system included more than 400 separate programs. The decor was fabulous, the help gorgeous, the DJs inspired, plus there was the door policy.

To help foster the sense that this was the ultimate nightclub, Rubell and Schrager made people wait for hours outside before they were admitted. That is, if they were admitted at all. A desperate mob often numbering in the thousands spilled out into the street almost every night, even though there were often only a few hundred people actually partying inside. This was a formula based on snob appeal, and it worked brilliantly in fashion-victim New York. Every time some movie star or powerful executive stalked away in disgust after being made to wait, another ten thousand secretaries and Wall Street traders gritted their teeth and swore that no matter what it took, they had to get in. Standing on a pedestal outside the door, picking and choosing, Mark the doorman resembled some elitist Nazi youth. Capricious and certainly cruel, the door policy was designed to create a stellar mix inside. And even though this was the nation's hottest "straight" discothèque, much of that mix was gay. Steve Rubell, who was gay himself, was quoted as saying that he liked to admit gay men (*"guys with guys"*) because they made the dance floor *"hot."* It was almost a reverse of society's then-pervasive antigay discrimination, since Steve Rubell's policy openly scorned single straight men for gays. *"I wouldn't let my best friend in,"* he boasted, *"if he looked like an*

East side singles guy." He was after the perfect mix: androgynous, stylish, exclusive, trendy, and fashionably gay; anything but macho and singles bar. From Halston and Calvin and Capote at the top, right on through John Q. Fashion Victim clamoring at the ropes outside to get in, the Studio mystique drew heavily from the gay explosion downtown. On opening night Rubell casually remarked, *"I think we have a winner."* He barely knew.

Following close upon the heels of Studio 54 came three other mammoth midtown clubs — Xenon, Bond's and New York, New York. All aspired to Studio-dom, and although none really came close, Xenon mustered a certain panache. Initially owner Howard Stein commissioned a monster sound system from Paramount Pictures, which designed systems for large movie theaters. But what seemed like a brilliant PR move turned into mush when the much-vaunted system proved to be nothing more than a huge, one-sided movie theater set-up. You didn't have to be a disco audiophile to hate the bloated, blurry sound. Eventually the system was completely redesigned by Jonathan Fearing and Peter Kinnard, and Xenon had a healthy run of several years, although all of them were in the shadow of Studio.

an inevitable tragedy

That summer of '77 Michael was far too busy renovating the Paradise Garage to take a share on Fire Island, so I felt comfortable rejoining my old family in the wonderful house on Ozone. I brought wild and wicked Wade into the house, and we shared a room with Edmund White, who was already establishing himself as our world's most accomplished writer. To complete the circle, Julio moved over from Camp Tommy with his beautiful young lover Kenny Sheibley. The house seemed perfect, complete.

Kenny was an immensely beautiful young man who had traveled a million psychic miles from Des Moines. In New York he had the great misfortune to fall madly in love with Julio. When they first got together, many thought that Kenny was the more handsome of the pair, and in one sense he was. Blond, blue-eyed, sleek, feral – his beauty was almost the opposite of Julio's – dark and Latin –and they made a stunning pair. But this was hardly how Kenny felt. Despite the effect he had on others, he was fragile inside, a bruised survivor of school-yard taunts and bullies urinating on him, and his father's brutal rejection of his homosexuality.

Into Kenny's unstable life blundered Julio, who by now was smoking dust regularly. He began sharing dust with Kenny, which must have made things much worse. Under the influence of dust, Julio could have epic, operatic mood swings. He was all love, valor, and compassion one minute, all depression, rage, and cruelty the next. But Julio at least was able to fly to extremes and still land somewhere in the middle. Kenny, with less of a center to begin with, was turned inside out by dust and by Julio's craziness, and was swept into deep depressions where he sometimes languished for weeks.

Even though I knew about the drugs, and was doing them myself, I had no idea that things were so bad. Not that I was exactly looking for signs. You almost might say that we believed in the power of drugs in those days. A lot of us drew a connection between the fact that moralists rejected gay people and rejected drugs. If they were so wrong about homosexuality, we thought, what else were they wrong about? Wasn't it all just some conspiracy against pleasure? And if we, for our part, rejected their views on gay people, shouldn't we also reject their views when applied to drugs and, for that matter, to everything else connected with pleasure? I don't know if we ever put it exactly this way, but it is how a lot of us felt. We were storming the gates of ancient hypocrisies, and drugs were among our weapons. In retrospect there were warning signs, but at the time they seemed more like innocent occupational hazards than hints of looming disaster.

At any rate, there were plenty of warning signs with Kenny. While working as a TWA flight attendant, he was so wired from angel dust one day that he threw a piece of luggage at a female passenger. He wasn't fired, but TWA put him on restriction, and he had to wait by the phone to be called back to work. He was far more devastated by this than any of us would have expected. I spent one afternoon consoling him on the beach at Fire Island, trying to make him see that he was lucky he hadn't been fired, that he should take advantage of his second chance. But the fact that he had been dusted at work, that he had flipped out and lost control in the only place left where he had some control, seemed to pull the bottom away. He kept insisting he was worthless.

He hardly seemed worthless to me. Far from it. I was entranced by him. One night I stopped by Julio's right after one of their big fights and Julio sent me into the bedroom. Kenny was there, stepping out of the shower, glistening naked, and within moments the three of us were making passionate love. Another night that summer Wade and I had a spontaneous four-way with Julio and Kenny. (This was a period when making love with friends was taken for granted, and Julio and Kenny were good friends to have.) And then one day the curtain fell. I'll never forget the moment. Peter DeAngelis, who had produced Frankie Avalon and Fabian back at my days at ABC/Paramount, brought us "Speak Well" by the group Philly USA. It had a rap segment that went, *"It's not the size of your pencil, but how well you write with it that counts."* I was in the office that evening listening to the final mix when the phone rang. Kenny had been out on the Island with Julio. They had had an argument. Kenny fled back to

Manhattan while Julio remained on the Island. And back in the city, alone, Kenny killed himself in a horrible, bloody, self mutilating suicide.

Andrew Holleran fictionalized this in *Dancer from the Dance*:

> That 23-year-old beauty who had his whole life before him; that boy from Idaho — who had slashed his wrists, and then his throat, and then hurled himself nine floors from the top of his apartment building to the steaming pavement below on this hottest of all afternoons...and now the boy, with his fine bones, his gazelle-like grace, his long thighs, and high buttocks, had slashed his veins...hating his youth, his beauty, his lover.

Andrew Holleran's description altered minor details (Kenny jumped from the Y on 23rd St., not his apartment building; he was from Iowa, not Idaho) but was true in its larger sense: Kenny had indeed hated his youth and beauty and, for whatever reason, Julio. And he had slashed at his own perfection and thrown himself from a great height as if to make sure that Julio would never be able to forget him, to make sure his ghost would haunt Julio forever. Which it did.

We were all torn up. Julio blamed himself, and no amount of assurance that he was not at fault could take away the sense that he was. As the initial shock wore off, I found that I was very angry at Kenny. It seemed so selfish, so inconsiderate to his mother and Julio and everyone, even me, even himself. I had come to know his mother earlier that summer when she visited the Island — we were about the same age and liked each other — and after Kenny died she told me she had spoken to him that fatal morning, thought that he sounded strange, considered calling me to check on him, but decided not to follow her intuition. Now she had to live with her regrets. For some reason, as my anger toward

Kenny grew, I never really factored in the drugs, the angel dust, our uncentered disco lives, the effect of Julio's wild emotional outbursts on a fragile mixed-up youth. His death seemed tragic, but not especially prophetic.

media — more categories, more confusion

The losses of Jimmy Stuard and Kenny Sheibley were like dark undercurrents in what was otherwise the ultimate boogie summer, 1977, the year disco became the most popular form of popular music. The second biggest song of the year was the Emotions "Best Of My Love," which sat at No. 1 for five weeks that summer. The third and fourth biggest were "I Just Want To Be Your Everything" by Andy Gibb and "How Deep Is Your Love" by his brothers, the Bee Gees. A slew of other disco favorites made their way to the coveted No. 1 spot, including "Don't Leave Me This Way" by Thelma Houston, "You Make Me Feel Like Dancing" by Leo Sayer, "Dancing Queen" by Abba, and "I'm Your Boogie Man" by K.C. and the Sunshine Band. And these were just the No. 1 hits. Disco was all over the Top Ten and Top Forty.

The media began to analyze this shift in popular taste, and some critics divided the disco genre into three styles, which made basic sense: pop-disco, r&b-disco and Euro-disco. Pop-disco was the song-oriented, hit-oriented style that was eating up the charts. In this genre, producers simply took the time-honored practice of generating hits with strong, melodic songs and infectious hooks, and added a disco beat. The main emphasis was on commercial success, and soon many of pop music's biggest stars were issuing pop-disco songs, cashing in on the style.

R&B-disco was the original article: African-American music with roots in funk, Philadelphia, and Motown soul. Artists like

Gloria Gaynor, LaBelle, Loleatta Holloway, Sister Sledge and Rick James kept the r&b flame alive, and DJs like Larry Levan emphasized this style, particularly popular in black clubs.

Euro-disco was the sound introduced by Giorgio Moroder. Euro-disco was mechanical and spacey, favoring synthesized sound effects and minimal, synthesized rhythms. The idea that dance producers could use synthesizers and drum machines instead of live musicians was revolutionary back in the late '70s, and reached its next milestone when Moroder produced *From Here to Eternity*, the first all-synthesized disco album. This gave ideas to a lot of young kids with musical aspirations but without a lot of money. If you could produce a hit album by yourself on a few synthesizers and drum machines, without expensive musicians, practically anybody could become a producer. And within a decade, practically anybody would. The house sound of the '80s was synthesizer-driven, often produced in peoples ' homes, so in a sense, Moroder's style would be the most enduring, the direct precursor to today's electronic dance music. My definition of house music, by the way, is Garage on a budget. Garage was Barry White, Salsoul, the Philly Sound, live musicians and big budgets. House was talented guys in Chicago trying their hand at producing the Garage sound electronically and, in the process, making it funkier.

While some critics analyzed the new music as an innovative and interesting addition to the panoply of pop, others began preaching against it. Rock critics in particular hated the new sound, saw it as a threat, and made fun of it as mindless garbage. There was a strong streak of anti-gay sentiment in all this, since disco was so closely associated with gay life. But that was about to change. Out in Hollywood, producers were finishing a new film about a straight, working-class Italian guy in Brooklyn obsessed with disco. It would be out at the end of the year.

west end's first anniversary bash

That summer *Billboard* held its second annual Disco Convention at the Sheraton Hotel in an atmosphere of intense excitement. Ed and I realized that the convention offered us our best chance of establishing West End's presence in the industry. But we also knew that legitimacy doesn't come cheap in a business where people spend themselves into Chapter 11 on a regular basis. We had to appear successful, and to do that we had to appear to be rolling in dough, so we paid an exorbitant fee for a huge reception suite in the Sheraton, and another small fortune for a Presidential suite as well, money that (rumor had it) found its way into the pocket of a certain former *Billboard* executive. But even this wasn't enough. Parties were the staple of any music convention, and the best way to demonstrate your deep pockets was through sheer party power. This, of course, was right up my alley.

The major record labels traditionally threw their parties in hotel suites. But now, as disco became the focus of the industry, hotel suites were being replaced by discos and hot nightspots. Alan Mamber, who was doing our promotion at West End, booked our party into the spanking new gay club Les Mouches. With low ceilings and obstructive pillars, Les Mouches wasn't the greatest dance space, and it never really attracted the hardcore dance crowd, but it had something new in discos: a full restaurant, very stylish and high tech, with carafes that brewed coffee right at the table. Perfect for a party.

Carey Finklestein, Les Mouches owner and a personal friend, wanted to show off to people in the industry his new concept in clubbing, and our party was his ticket. We hired horse-drawn carriages and stretch limousines to shuttle guests from the Sheraton down to the club, and once there we served a huge buffet breakfast to the music of Boston DJ Danae Jacovides. We converted the West End logo into a neon sign, and as guests entered they saw us, the West End welcoming committee, next to our name in lights. We outdid everybody. Conventioneers who had only nibbled cheese and sipped red wine at the Casablanca party that previous night at 12 West were in awe of our several course breakfast for fifteen-hundred people. It was so lavish that people kept coming up asking if we had signed Diana Ross.

It seemed like everybody posed in front of the neon logo. My lover Wade and my closest friends — Julio, Dick Fisher, Ray Ford, Norman Marine and Mark Rosenfeld — all wearing West End t-shirts and acting as hosts, mingled with their disco idols, and we took tons of pictures of the crème de la disco crème: Andrea True, Marilyn McCoo, Billy Davis, everybody. At one point I told Grace Jones I was a bit surprised to see her there and she threw her arms around me and cocked her head back in arch amazement, *"I always come to your parties, Mel,"* she intoned, dragonlike, *"because you always throw the best parties."* High praise indeed, considering the source. Someone snapped a picture of Grace and me with Tom Moulton, Maye James from Scepter, Wanda Ramos, program director at WKTU, and singer Tamiko Jones, who had a hit with "Can't Live Without Your Love." It still sits on the piano in Grace's New York apartment.

If our party established West End as a major player, this was the *Billboard* convention that cemented Studio 54's reputation as the industry's premier disco. In one famous incident, record producer Arthur Baker went to a party that *Billboard* was throwing at Studio 54, and Steve Rubell wouldn't let him in. Arthur stormed off and got *Billboard* head honcho Bill Wardlow, who stormed back and got into a huge fight at the door. To no avail. Even the kings of disco were not fabulous enough to enter the castle of their own domain, at least if Steve Rubell gave them the thumbs down. The tabloids loved it. "Dance King Barred By Studio 54!" screamed the front-page headlines.

me and julio

As summer drew to a close, so did my affair with Wade Benjamin. Our attraction was mostly physical, and by now the fires had ebbed. Without the heat there was little point in staying in the kitchen, so I initiated our breakup. On the day he moved out, Wade startled me by announcing that in his opinion he and I were breaking up *"because of Julio."* This was news to me. Julio and I had become closer since Kenny's suicide, and of course we occasionally had sex as well. Who didn't? But that was it. Or so I thought. Wade was apparently paying closer attention to Julio's expanding role in my life than I was. And a few months later, at one of the Garage's construction parties, Wade was proved right.

Julio and I were in the middle of the dance floor, high on angel dust, when suddenly he looked at me and declared that we were *"a lot more than just friends."* There was real passion in his voice. Perhaps I should have just smiled and pretended not to have heard him. If I had, many things would have turned out differently. I remember the song that Larry Levan was playing at that moment, by a young singer named Jeffrey Osborne:

> Every time I turn around / Where I look, I've been
> Every time I turn around / I'm back in love again.

It took me exactly one split second to decide to go for it. Julio had always been my great fantasy, and there was simply no way that I was going to pass up the chance to have him all to myself. Within a few days it was clear to everybody in our circle that Julio and I were now an item. I'm sure that after Julio and I became lovers, more than one queen stuck pins in voodoo dolls hoping I'd drop dead. But nobody needed to. My relationship with Julio would eventually become its own punishment.

Michael was absolutely furious. He was still mad with me about my name on the sound equipment, and the fact that I was now with Julio seemed to send him over the top. He warned me repeatedly that Julio was only after me for my money, and he couldn't stop ranting against our relationship. I'm sure that if I had ended up with anyone other than Julio, Michael would not have been so upset. But I certainly wasn't going to let Michael's resentments bring me down, even though I knew that in a sense, he was right. It was pretty obvious that Julio wasn't in love with me, at least at first. Years later, during a late-night drug confession, he so much as admitted that money was a big reason he had kindled our romance. It seems that when I took Wade on a fabulous trip to London and Paris, Julio took notice. He saw how well I treated my boyfriends, and asked himself why should he be left out. *"And so I let you chase me,"* he said, *"until I had you caught."*

Nothing happens by accident; we receive the lessons we are meant to learn, even the bad ones. There would certainly be many lessons with Julio over the years, both good and bad, but back then I wasn't analyzing the situation. How could I listen to Michael's voice of warning? The man of my dreams was in my bed at night. The world was going crazy for the music that I had been crowing about for years. How could I listen?

The next month *Saturday Night Fever* opened in movie houses across the country, and the disco momentum reached its crest. John Travolta received an Academy Award nomination for his portrayal of Tony Manero, Brooklyn hardware clerk by day, king of disco dancers by night. In the film's most famous scene, the climax of a dance contest at a Brooklyn disco, Director John Badham pays hommage to Larry Levan. In a slow-motion dream sequence, Tony meets his girlfriend's face as the music is cross-phased, punching out the lyrics, *"more than a woman to me."* Crossphasing was Larry's invention, his signature.

Many people think *Saturday Night Fever* is an ode to disco, but it was really anything but. Its premise — that disco was a highway to nowhere — was a marked and ironic snub at the fans who were forging disco's multi-billion dollar market and who made up the majority of the film's core audience. Disco fans snatched up tickets and soundtrack albums by the millions anyway, oblivious to *Saturday Night Fever's* implicit criticism. The Bee Gees' "Night Fever," "You Should Be Dancin'," "More Than A Woman" and "Stayin' Alive" had permeated the airwaves before the film's actual release, and Yvonne Elliman's "If I Can't Have You" became the unrequited love song of the year. As 1977 dissolved into 1978, the *Fever* soundtrack sold like crazy. It still holds the record for biggest-selling soundtrack album of all time. For the next year-and-a-half until disco's sudden demise, the dance culture represented by *Saturday Night Fever* would be the biggest and most lucrative force in the music industry since the birth of rock'n'roll.

chapter ten
THE GARAGE

The grand opening of a New York City disco is like a Broadway debut — both a declaration of arrival and a moment of truth. A great opening can make you. A bad one can guarantee empty nights and bankruptcy. Michael planned the grand opening of the Paradise Garage in January of 1978 to be the moment he would finally take his place as the king of downtown. But in reality the grand opening was worse than bad; it was a disco disaster so total that it took him at least two years to recover.

It didn't have to be that way because the Garage didn't really need a grand opening. The humble construction parties that Michael had launched early in 1977 to raise money to renovate the space had blossomed into successful events. Even though the club began as an empty shell, membership grew in a slow, steady way throughout the year. With money dribbling and drabbling in from these events Michael plunged ahead, systematically renovating each section of the club, and finally building the dance floor of his dreams in the huge central space. Now, as the new year began, the Paradise Garage had come together to the point where it actually looked like a major disco, not some makeshift parking garage with a few crazies boogying in the corner. The fact that Michael had done it, that he had pulled it off through incredibly hard work, that he had built his disco paradise mostly by himself, without me looming over him and pulling his strings, made him want to show it off. The Paradise Garage was virtually finished, and everybody agreed that it deserved a major debut.

You entered through the ever-grungy first-floor parking garage, walked past a security check to a membership desk and were handed a slip of paper showing how much you would pay upstairs. You were then led to the bottom of an immense ramp leading to the second floor. The ramp ran the entire length of the building, hundreds of feet in all, and was painted pitch black and lined with chaser lights like an airplane runway. As you trudged up this black tilted tunnel to paradise, a lightness overcame you, a momentum — you began to take off. The pounding grew louder, the roar of the dance floor grew closer, reality receded further behind, and by the time you got to the top of the ramp, paid the fee and were admitted into the Grey Room, you were in another world.

This Grey Room had constituted the entire club back in the beginning. Now it was an anteroom, its sawdust-covered floors and banquettes providing a refuge from the disco inferno beyond. (In later years Michael redesigned and renamed it the Crystal Room, and Woody Allen used it for a scene in his film, *Radio Days*.) Looming beyond, filling the remaining space, was almost an entire city block of flailing darkness, arms akimbo, passion, thousands of square feet of what Frankie Knuckles remembers as *"the best floor in the world."*

It was a different kind of dance floor, in part because of its size, in part because the people on it were so different from those at every other major disco at that time. For one thing, they were without question the city's most serious dancers. There was no attitude here, no cliques defined by their muscles, no fashion victims, no A-list. These people were dancers. Or perhaps you might say, dancing was their posing. Artists vogueing into new realms of realness, macho men competing furiously with "Miss Things" for attention — the intensity of the disco pyrotechnics was unlike anything anywhere. Venturing onto the dance floor was like swimming into an undertow — you were sucked into the vortex, and you surrendered, for hours at a time.

Michael's concept (the concept I had dreamed about and preached about, and that he was now trying to realize) was that the Paradise Garage would be the first big-time, mainstream gay disco to enthusiastically court black and Latino gay men, not just whites. True, the Loft had tried to do the same thing, but the Loft was small and underground, and it was an exception. True, there was also tokenism in the big mainstream places — you saw black and Latino faces almost everywhere. But mainstream gay nightlife remained largely segregated by race, and most of the spaces that welcomed minority gay men were basement dungeons, cheap walkups, firetraps. Michael made it clear that the Paradise Garage was going to change all that. Given the tenor of the times, the reaction of much of the disco world was predictable. The Paradise Garage was quickly stereotyped as a black club, even though it was simply a very integrated and balanced one. Probably about as balanced as the city, and the gay community, that surrounded it.

Still, the fact that the Garage included a much higher proportion of African American and Hispanic gay men gave it its second major distinction. The potent intersection of rhythm, race and realness that had produced disco in the first place — black as it was gay, gay as it was black — all came together here. What Louie Armstrong was to Benny Goodman, what Chuck Berry was to Elvis, the Paradise Garage was to Flamingo and Studio 54 and almost every other major disco: the absolute, rock bottom, real thing. These girls were serious, they knew what they were doing, and it was manifest. The fierce rules of the Apollo Theater — the wild cheers, the cheerfully heartless boos and hisses — ruled with this crowd. If they liked the DJ, he knew it. If not, he was dead meat. And this applied to performers as well. This fact remained glaringly apparent years later when a rising star named Madonna bombed big time in front of this crowd. Long before it officially opened, the Paradise Garage had earned the reputation not only as the hard core place to dance, but also as the one place that truly reflected the rainbow that had produced disco's pot of gold in the first place.

But there was an unforeseen irony built right into our original idea of a safe space for all gay men. The irony was that to accomplish this, you had to exclude the straight and (all too often) female, those whose place in the rainbow clashed with the vision. And so Michael found himself applying the time-honored rules of the exclusive private club to this supposedly democratic place. Prospective members had to apply in person during specified hours that were never advertised or posted. You had to hear about it from a member, know someone who knew someone. Fashionable straight people who thought it was chic to go slumming with the gay boys, à la the Bette Midler crowd at the old Continental Baths, were rigorously rooted out. As a paradox, this became increasingly difficult as word spread about Larry Levan's awesome music and the equally awesome atmosphere. More and more straight people clamored for memberships, and eventually straight male disco ducks took to masquerading as gay in the interview process, hoping to outsmart Michael and his perceptive staff. Few did. Most of these gay impersonators were outed — or perhaps inned — through a series of coded questions. Had they ever been to a leather bar on the West Side called the Spindle? (Its real name was the Spike.) Did they know what it meant to wear a yellow hankie in the left back pocket? The wrong answer meant exile from paradise.

Eventually the demands of straights to be admitted grew so insistent that Michael, who operated the club only on Saturday nights, introduced a second night on Fridays, designed to mix both straight and gay. A core member (read: gay) could attend on either night, but straight men were confined to Fridays only. This largely solved the straight problem, but it didn't do much for the female problem. It's sad and strange that women were even considered a problem, but despite the feminist rhetoric of gay liberation, this was an era of iron-curtain separation of the sexes in gay nightlife. Women, including lesbians, were routinely dissed in big city gay bars, and for that matter gay men were not exactly welcome at lesbian haunts. So when women clamored to get in to the Paradise Garage on Saturdays with their gay friends, Michael felt he had to do something, even though he himself loved having women at his club. His solution was a rule that core members could bring as many as four guests on Saturday nights, but only one could be female. This assured that the ratio between the sexes would overwhelmingly favor males, but even then Michael sometimes got letters from misogynist members complaining that there had been too many women in the club on a specific night. Then he might stand at the door himself, admitting only the most stylish and fabulous gals at his discretion.

The doors opened at midnight and closed at 6:30 the next morning, after which no one but the occasional VIP was admitted. Then, depending on Larry's musical mood, the crowd's stamina, and the quality of the drugs — again, there was no booze served, and most people were high on something, or many things — the party carried on well into the late morning hours. Those who stayed to the very end of Larry's epic sets often found themselves straggling home in the sunshine of an early afternoon.

The earliest employees were all friends of Larry's, part of his extended self-made family. Tommy Baratta, my assistant at West End, took tickets. Nathan Busch, today a famous make-up artist, prepared the food. Shamako, a flamboyant young black gay man, did the club's decor. But the Garage was more than just a place for Larry to construct a symbolic home. It actually was his home. He built a bedroom right behind the DJ booth and lived there, the ultimate DJ workaholic. It didn't take long before this arrangement began to make Michael nervous. He didn't particularly mind

Larry living in the club, but realized that it was dangerous for Larry's friends to occupy all the major positions. Larry was already powerful enough. Michael needed his own allies.

So in his clever way, Michael casually began replacing Larry's friends with his own friends and allies, until eventually everyone but Shamako was gone. And to his credit, Michael did this in such a way that nobody seemed to notice, preserving a strong feeling of camaraderie among the staff. This family atmosphere trickled down from staff to members and guests and created a spirit that made the Garage the antithesis of most of the other great posing palaces of disco. Not surprisingly, that family atmosphere attracted some of the city's most fashionable mavens, some almost despite themselves. *"My friends kept urging me to come to this new place called the Garage,"* recalls Diane Strafaci, a popular East Sider.

> But I was a victim of Studio, and I wasn't about to miss my Studio for anything. Then one night after we left Studio some friends finally dragged me down to the Garage. I remember walking up that ramp, paranoid that my heels were clicking too loudly, seeing these incredibly interesting people racing to get inside. When we walked in and I heard this music blasting I was so petrified I thought I was tripping. But once I relaxed and got into dancing, that was it. I became a "victim" of Paradise Garage.

the wrath of mother nature

By the end of 1977, things were going well for Michael and his dream. From the sawdust and makeshift tables to the final renovation of the main space, and thanks to the construction parties and a lot of hard work, Michael had done it. Men were trickling over from Infinity, from Flamingo, from Studio, from all the other happening spots, to this more expansive disco democracy. The place was being discovered. And then came the grand opening, and all the bustle that was pushing the club toward success almost unraveled in a single night.

Michael dreamed about a cosmic opening where all the fabulous fashion, music, sex and beauty boys would flock to his creation and mingle with the home boys, the banjee boys and the fanatic Larry Levan disciples, and we would finally achieve disco apotheosis, paradise in a garage. But several funny things happened on the way to Paradise. Starting with the weather.

New Yorkers still remember the blizzard of January 1978 as one of the city's greatest all-time storms. The city was entirely shut down for a couple of days, after which a frozen wave of icy air fixed the mounds of snow and ice into immovable mountains, Himalayas at every corner. When Saturday arrived the city was still a frozen mess, which was a serious cause for concern. I dropped by the club that afternoon to bring Michael an opening night gift — two thousand little pillboxes to distribute to his members, perfect for holding their pills. I planned to attach a cover to each box, and took the whole project down there to complete. Not smart. There was no heat in the club, and during this coldest of cold waves the club was like a deep freezer. Wearing gloves, I struggled to affix the little covers, and the job took forever.

But I wasn't the only one struggling. Michael had ordered a spanking new sound system to be flown in; unfortunately, the snowstorm that had buried New York had also closed the Louisville, Kentucky airport for several days. The airport had finally reopened, the equipment had finally arrived, but it was days late. A mad, panicked scramble to hook it up only made things worse, and things fell hopelessly behind. Grand opening was now only hours away, and the way things were going, Michael needed another whole day to fine-tune the sound system. Larry Levan, the perfectionist, wasn't helping matters. Miss Thing made it plain that there was no way he would spin unless the system was flawless, and that hardly seemed possible under the circumstances. The atmosphere was so tense you could cut it like an iceberg. I turned to Michael and asked, *"Are you going to be able to open tonight?"* I'll never forget the look in his eyes: panic drowning in tears.

I couldn't wait to escape. I finally finished attaching the covers to my 2,000 pill boxes and raced back home to change and meet up with Julio and the other couple who were our guests for the night: the poet and folk singer Rod McKuen and his boyfriend Ed. Julio and I had recently met them on a cruise, where the still-closeted Rod introduced Ed to everyone as his brother. But it was pretty clear that lover was more like it, and sure enough that was confirmed when Rod put the moves on Julio (as everyone eventually did). I would have thought no more about it except that along the way Rod discovered two things: that I owned a record company, and that the opening of Paradise Garage coincided with my birthday. So after the cruise Rod recorded a song he titled "Mel's Song (Mon Ami, Mon Amour)." He then called my partner Ed Kushins from London, told Ed that he had recorded a song in my honor, and coyly suggested that they *"surprise Mel with it at the opening night of the Garage."* Rod then sent the master tapes to New York, requesting that Ed dash out to Kennedy Airport in the snow to collect them and have five hundred copies pressed in time to be given out at the Paradise Garage opening. I knew none of this as we headed downtown in a cab. I was just horribly anxious for Michael, praying that things were ready, knowing how important tonight was. This was the first visit by most of the A-list, and if it was favorable they stood a good chance of making the Paradise Garage a regular hangout, and making Michael rich in the process. But if their impression was unfavorable, it would probably be the end. These queens never gave a disco a second break.

As our cab approached King St. we saw hordes of people walking down 7th Ave., their breath crystallizing in the bitter cold. It seemed eerie and electric, a mass migration, but when we turned the corner it really hit us: Thousands of people were swarming in the middle of the block in front of the Garage, its facade illuminated in bright yellowish glare. My first thought was that this swarm of people was like a scene from *Day of the Locust*. My second thought was elation and success. Look at the turn-out! I yelled to Julio. This is bigger than Studio 54!

My third thought, however, was disaster. The Paradise Garage was not some trendy club that manufactured cachet by snottily making its guests freeze on the sidewalk. Quite the opposite. So why were all these people milling around in subfreezing 17-degree wind? Why weren't they inside dancing? And I knew there could be only one reason. They were out here because it wasn't ready in there. We hurried past friends and acquaintances and were quickly admitted into the empty club. As we did, I tried to avoid meeting anyone's eye, but I could plainly see that people were freezing and furious. I was embarrassed to squeeze past them, but once we entered it only got worse. The place was still an ice box, there were a million problems and glitches, Michael was frantically trying to fix the bugs in the sound system, and Larry, needless to say, was playing the grand diva, insisting things were not ready, insisting he would not spin unless they were. He had no idea of the conditions outside — he probably hadn't been outside himself for days — and he could have cared less. He was an artist, the sound system was his medium, it had to be perfection or nothing. This insistence of his would make him famous. But on that night, it almost ruined everything.

In retrospect, Michael made a major mistake. If he had just allowed the crowd to gather in the parking garage below, where it was much warmer, and perhaps explained the problem and begged the crowd for patience, he might have been forgiven. But Michael was overwhelmed, and he had not thought to delegate anyone to deal effectively with the door — a fatal oversight. And so people cooled their heels — literally — in sub-freezing temperatures for hours until Larry finally gave his grudging consent, and the throng of frozen people — or at least those who had not already stormed off into the night — were allowed in. By now goodwill had evaporated, and everyone's anger was compounded by even more glitches. My friend Larry McDevitt worked the coat check that night with Noel Garcia; it was the first time they had ever done it. They had over three thousand coats to deal with, and as they were trying to take a count by tag, they ran out and started using the tags over again. They were overwhelmed, and the whole thing was a devastating mess.

In the meantime I was involved in my own little drama. I had finally been informed of my birthday surprise — that Rod McKuen had convinced my partner Ed to press 500 copies of my supposed birthday song and have them distributed to the first 500 lucky guests. This was one of the most blatantly self-promotional stunts I ever saw, and I was furious. For one thing, the song was a soapy choral number that had about as much to do with disco as... well... a song by Rod McKuen. For another, the song had absolutely nothing to do with me. It's real title was "Mon Ami, Mon Amour," and Rod simply tacked "Mel's Song" on to get it played at this event. Nonetheless, he had now convinced himself, probably due to some merely polite remark of Michael's, that Michael had promised that "Mel's Song" would be played five times over the course of the evening as my birthday present. Larry, of course, would have sooner dynamited the Garage than play anything by Rod McKuen, and the last thing on Michael's mind was to make Larry play that or any other song. (One difference between Michael and Saint owner Bruce Mailman, by the way, was that Michael never told his DJs what to play.) So now Rod turned to me. I had to intervene, he said, to get Larry to play the song. Trying to please everybody, I made what I thought was a reasonable excuse. *"This is a disco,"* I told Rod, *"and it's not even a disco record."* He was furious, flipped me the bird, turned on his heel, and it was "Bon Voyage, Mon Amour."

That incident pretty much summed up the night. Years later Michael tried to minimize the extent of the disaster, even hinting that the opening had been fabulous and the Paradise Garage an overnight success. The sad fact is that if the opening had been a success, in all likelihood the Garage would have been an instant hit. But after this fiasco, none of the A-list guys ever wanted to darken the club's door again. I ended up apologizing to friends for months afterwards, explaining the problems, promising that they had been corrected, begging them to give the place a second chance. I went after key individuals like Mark Rosenfeld, the leader of a very popular crowd of Flamingo boys, who had dragged a huge number of friends to the opening. But there was nothing I could say to make things right. After that ill-fated night, most of them stuck to Flamingo and didn't return to the Paradise Garage for years, if ever. For Michael, the event that should have launched him into orbit instead ground him back down, and his struggle for success had really just begun.

ain't no stoppin' us now

The terrible disappointment could have been the end of the Paradise Garage. For any other club it probably would have been. But Michael was not about to let one disastrous night derail him. He still had his club, he had a growing clientele, and he still had

Larry Levan. From those seeds he would continue to nurture the Garage. More slowly, to be sure, but also more steadily. After the bad word of mouth about the grand opening, membership sales slowed down, and Michael decided that the construction parties had to continue. He, Larry and the rest of the staff worked furiously to improve the Garage, continuing to renovate its nooks and crannies, adding to the sound system and light system, improving the decor. It was like a replay of our efforts years before at Warren St. in Brooklyn, a daily grind but a true labor of love... a baby. And the staff was as game as anybody. Each week when the club was closed, they would redecorate entirely, so that members and guests were amazed every weekend to find the place transformed into a whole new environment, with a whole new theme, sometimes elaborate, sometimes plain. I loved helping out. Late one night, for example, I drove down to Canal St. in lower Manhattan, swiped a bunch of blue police sawhorse barricades and fluorescent traffic cones, and turned the Garage into a construction site. It could hardly have looked more authentic, or illegal. It was often said that the construction barricades probably saved more lives at the Garage than they would have left on the highway.

Michael realized that successful theme parties could eventually offset bad word of mouth about the opening, which, after all, was a kind of theme party itself. His first big special theme party was in mid-April, the "Night of the Bats." Members were told to dress in black, which meant leather for most, and it seemed delightfully twisted since it happened to be Easter weekend when the world was awash in white. One of the highlights of the night was, of course, Larry's music. As usual he would select a theme for the night, and it was never hard to guess how he felt on any given night. If he was in love with somebody new, he might select "Love Is the Message" by MFSB (which became one of his signature songs), or "Lost In Your Love" by John Paul Young, a bouncy, lovesick cha-cha. If he was dumped by some beau, or was mad at somebody, he might play what we called a Fuck-You song. During the "Night of the Bats," Larry introduced Evelyn "Champagne" King's debut song to his repertoire of Fuck-You songs. It was remixed by Larry's fellow DJ and bunkmate David Todd. And it tore the house down.

> Shame! Only love can relieve the pain.
> If we don't, our love is a shame!
> I wouldn't want to live with the pain!

Larry kept the conga drums beating, utilizing the crossover to phase out the rest of the instruments and punch up the lone crying sax, mixing in more congas, bringing them back in with the sax, then adding the now familiar rhythm guitar licks. The song came to a peak as it arrived at the vocal, and the crowd responded by trying to stamp the dance floor to dust. "Shame" immediately spread to discos in Boston, Philadelphia, Miami, Ft. Lauderdale, Chicago, Los Angeles, San Francisco, Washington — most of them underground gay dance clubs, previously ignored because their record selling power was underestimated — and became an instant hit for the 16-year-old Evelyn "Champagne" King.

It was hardly the only hit that Larry Levan helped discover and promote. Despite the Paradise Garage's diminished reputation among the white gay crowd, the people it did attract were often the first to respond to new songs and new trends in music, and it was still the number one place for the most fanatic dancers. As such, music promoters increasingly recognized it as a place that broke records. One measure of the club's growing importance was the fact that Vinylmania, the famous record store nearby in the Village, began opening on Sundays to capitalize on the Garage's influence. The owner would arrive at the store on Sunday mornings and find a line of people waiting to purchase records that they'd just heard Larry playing.

In the end, the opening night failed to sink the unsinkable Garage. What it did instead was cement the club's black and Latino reputation. Michael's dream was an integrated dance floor, and he naturally wanted his place to be popular among his own group of Fire Island friends. But eventually he realized that the opening night disaster might have sealed off that crowd forever. And so he went with the flow, capitalizing on his assets: his room, his genius DJ, and the intensely loyal following that the whole mix had evolved into. Michael continued to fight to bring in the white crowd, and this increased tensions between him and Larry, who had grown comfortable as king of a mostly black world. And over the years, of course, the white crowd would trickle back. But this would take time and would be entirely on Michael's terms, and by the time it came to pass, long after the mainstream had passed disco by, Michael would already be a very rich man.

west end finally hits

As Michael struggled with the Garage, West End Records was steadily growing and building its reputation as a cutting-edge independent disco label. But we had yet to catch the crest of the wave of success that disco companies like Casablanca were enjoying. And when our star finally arrived, it was not in the form we might have expected.

Karen Young was a white soul singer from Philadelphia who had once dated Wilson Pickett. We met her by way of Andy Khan, who co-managed various recording projects, and Kurt Borusiewicz, a DJ from Philadelphia. At first Ed Kushins and I didn't think there was much that could be done with Karen. She was frumpy, knew nothing about makeup and clothes, loved her Quaaludes and was afraid of heights. Not exactly disco star material — at least from the outside. But she had this resilient, joyous, powerful voice, and once she got onstage (if you could get her up the stairs to a stage) she had an inner force that erupted like a volcano. We decided to take a chance and release a 12-inch mix of her song "Hot Shot;" and we set about hiring stylists, hair people, and makeup artists, hoping to transform this ugly duckling into a disco diva.

We hardly needed to bother. "Hot Shot" was an instant smash and was all over the radio that summer, making Karen an international star. With over 800,000 orders, "Hot Shot" put West End over the top. It was nominated for 12-inch Record of the Year (only losing out to Taste of Honey's "Boogie Oogie Oogie," one of the biggest hits in disco history). Karen was nominated as Best New Artist at MIDEM that year, the big international music industry conference in Cannes. I spent the week after in Paris and got a terrific high walking down the Champs Elysées, seeing *"Palace Presents Karen Young – Hot Shot"* advertised on kiosks all down the boulevard.

We did make a big mistake later, however, when we put out the album, *Karen Young, Hot Shot,* with her picture on the front. Karen was white, but people who heard her voice naturally imagined her as this smoldering, sexy black mama, and we probably should have left it that way. DJs and club owners were always unpleasantly surprised when we trotted her out to nightclubs and they saw her for the first time. So I don't know what we were thinking when we decided to put Karen's picture on the album cover. Record buyers went looking for it, found this dowdy white girl on the cover, and put the record right back in the bin. Still, although the sales of the album were disappointing, the 12-inch single was our first unqualified, mega hit.

Karen was a genuine trooper. In Boston she performed the eight-minute-and-forty-second "Hot Shot" in ten different clubs in one night — no small trick in a city where clubs close at 2 a.m. —

and she did it at the top of her energy in every one. Karen then made an appearance at a local telethon where she performed with the Village People. Due to her fear of heights, we literally had to push her step-by-step up those stairs. But once up, she brought the house down.

One time Karen was scheduled to perform at the Garage during a disco convention and Larry couldn't find a copy of the instrumental track for her song. I was mortified, since I had borrowed it from Larry for some reason and had forgotten to return it. We went on hands and knees in the booth searching for a copy through Larry's stacks, and poor Karen, alone up on the stage, finally yelled out, *"Well, if you ain't gonna play it, then I'm gonna sing it solo. C'mon, everybody!"* She started clapping and singing *"I need a hot shot!"* with no music accompaniment. She did the whole song a cappella, and the Garage crowd absolutely lost it. I guess this is another example of nothing happening by accident, since Karen's performance became a disco legend in its own right.

Our luck with "Hot Shot" continued with Bettye Lavette's "Doin' the Best that I Can." I learned a valuable lesson from this one. A young producer named Cory Robbins brought us the song, and at our first meeting I realized he had all that it took to zoom right to the top of the record industry. Cory was musically talented, possessed a great business sense, and was handsome and charismatic to boot — never a handicap in show biz. We liked him and we thought "Doin' the Best that I Can" was a good song, so we decided to release the record. I asked Walter Gibbons, Galaxy 21's star DJ, to do the remix. He went into the studio with Cory Robbins, and they came out with a mix that, much to my surprise and disappointment, went nowhere. I couldn't understand what was wrong until Alan Mamber, my promotion man at West End, called and told me the truth. It seemed that

Cory Robbins had refused to allow Walter to do anything in the studio, instructing him to sit and just keep his mouth shut, while Cory remixed his own record.

I was furious and called Cory and informed him that I was sending Walter back into the studio. *"And this time he's going in alone,"* I said. *"That's the way it is."* Cory had a big ego for a young kid, but after much arguing, he had to agree. I thought I had solved the problem until Walter brought in his own finished product. It sounded like a musical acid trip, and I had serious second thoughts. But I was surprised again. His version of "Doin' the Best that I Can" became another immediate hit, and it has grown over the years into a genuine, if quirky, disco classic. The valuable lesson I learned was this: never let the original producer go into the studio with the remixer.

high summer

By the summer of 1978 disco had become a national obsession. *Saturday Night Fever* was still drawing huge crowds, and although disco remained dominated by a gay sensibility, the film had challenged the notion that disco was exclusively gay. John Travolta had made it cool for macho, working class boys to shake their booties and primp and preen, and they took to it like crazy. Of the Top Ten No. 1 songs that year, seven were danceable r&b or pop. The most popular was the Bee Gees' "Night Fever," followed by "Shadow Dancing" by Andy Gibb, "Le Freak" by Chic, "Stayin' Alive" by the Bee Gees, "Boogie Oogie Oogie" by A Taste of Honey, "Baby Come Back" by Player, and "MacArthur Park" by Donna Summer. Never before had a new musical style so utterly conquered the charts. Rock seemed in full retreat. The year's Top Forty that were not disco were mostly ballads like "Three Times a Lady" by the Commodores, Barbra Streisand and

Neil Diamond's "You Don't Bring Me Flowers," Billy Joel's "Just the Way You Are," or quirky novelties like Randy Newman's "Short People." Rock was getting ossified and grandiose, and audiences were getting bored. A new rock style was taking shape in New York's downtown clubs, with acts like Patti Smith, the Ramones, the Talking Heads, Television and Blondie drawing big crowds and getting signed by major labels. But the punk and new wave revolution that would revitalize rock in the '80s was a couple of years ahead, and still mostly a cult phenomenon in 1978. In mainstream rock, big acts such as Foreigner affected a pose that bored almost everybody except high-testosterone teenage boys. Disco was left to rule the roost.

Unfortunately, a lot of the new disco was crap. Producers began to assume that they could make hits out of anything set to a pounding four/four rhythm track, and began flooding the market with tons of mediocre product, assembly-line clichés recycled into disco garbage. Artists everywhere were clamoring to have their own songs done disco style, and every popular trend seemed to be fodder for the disco machine. Some fading stars probably thought that disco-fying their songs would be a quick fix to their declining popularity, and for some, I suppose, it was. But mostly it was embarrassing. There were a spate of children's disco songs, and more ominously, a spate of disco spoofs. There was, "Dancin' Disney," one of the first disco clone songs, followed by "Whistle While You Work" and "Heigh Ho! Heigh Ho!" arranged disco style. There would be disco "Evita," in which the Andrew Lloyd Weber/Tim Rice musical was rearranged, and its popular theme song, "Don't Cry For Me, Argentina," became a dance floor hit. For some artists this disco conversion worked. For many others it was the kiss of death, since there's nothing more transparent and pathetic than jumping on somebody else's bandwagon, shaking your tail feathers like an idiot, and then falling off.

And then one day that summer came the final signal that we had arrived. WKTU, New York City's easy listening radio station, went "All Disco." A radio station playing our music nonstop was something I had never even dared imagine. We held our collective breath waiting for the Arbitron ratings, to see what would happen to WKTU's share of the market. It was like the second shoe dropping when Arbitron announced that WKTU had instantly vaulted to the top spot in the New York market, beating not only every other station but every other type of music — a breathtaking accomplishment for a brand-new radio format, and one that was instantly noticed by every radio programmer and owner in the country.

Because its success was so rapid, WKTU did not yet have a full-time music director for the new format, and its playlist developed in a very spotty way. The station sent questionnaires to club DJs, but their response might take as much as a month to get back, if it came back at all — a very imprecise way of charting the hottest trends. This lapse provided a niche for a young commercial scheduler at the station, Michael Ellis, who lusted after the music director position. Michael came up with a plan that would help make his name in the business. He suggested that WKTU do an ongoing, week-by-week survey of the city's hottest DJs to find out what their favorites were. *"I said, 'Let me call the DJs at home once a week, and do an actual chart,'"* Michael recalls.

> I had done sales charts at another radio station, so I knew how to make up a chart. They said that I'd never get those people on the phone, but I said, "Let me try." So they said, "Fine, try."

With the help of record pool owner Judy Weinstein, Michael compiled a list of DJs, then badgered them until they all agreed to cooperate, with one major exception. Larry Levan said he couldn't be bothered. Larry probably refused to cooperate because of his close friendship with Frankie Crocker, who was a DJ at WBLS, a major competitor of WKTU. Larry wasn't going to do anything that might hurt Frankie Crocker. So the list went ahead without Larry's help, which I think was a major missed opportunity to inject his brand of disco straight into the radio market. In any event, Michael Ellis instantly had the best music survey in the business, one that included Top Twenty lists from all the big clubs — Studio 54, Flamingo, 12 West — and all the best spinners: Jim Burgess, Roy Thode, Robbie Leslie. It became hugely influential. And as usual with show business, it also became mired in politics. WKTU executives used to wait outside Michael Ellis's door for the list to be compiled each week, and they'd grab it the second he was done and rush into their music selection meetings. But they never invited Michael to those meetings. Hours later, they would emerge with the new records to be added to the weekly rotation, most of them added because of Michael's research. Not only did he feel slighted, but also he felt frustrated because the executives often inexplicably omitted some of the most important club hits.

It turned out that WKTU was just the beginning. In Los Angeles, a corporate radio executive handed the music director of KIIS-FM a credit card and asked him to buy every disco record available at a local record outlet. By the end of the weekend, the station's promotional spots were announcing "All Disco KIIS-FM." By the fall of that year, several of the top radio stations across the country had switched their entire formats to all disco. By the next year, there were 200.

The same thing was happening across the country in the clubs. If dancing had fallen out of mainstream fashion in the early '70s, it was back with a vengeance now. By year's end there were an estimated 20,000 discos across the country, from tiny holes in the wall to big, fancy schmancy establishments in malls, to the huge urban dance palaces like Studio 54. It seemed almost unreal. The world was falling into dance step behind us (the gays and blacks who were otherwise shunned.) And we thought, naive as we were, that this meant that mainstream America was lending us its approval, that intolerance was declining. That a peace train was choo-chooing its way through the discos and out into the wider world. We would find out differently soon enough, when the backlash set in. And then, in retrospect, we would realize that this had been it, that disco had peaked in 1978, and that the craze would end even more quickly than it had begun.

paradise catching on

Michael Brody's theme parties were catching on, and the Paradise Garage grew more crowded each weekend. In June he threw "Fire Down Below," a hugely successful red party, and it seemed like the fortunes of his club and my record company had merged for one brief shining summer night.

Larry McDevitt had photographed a spectacular disaster: a fire at a Brooklyn warehouse went out of control, jumped from one side of the street to the other, and a whole block of wooden houses went up in flames. On the night of the party Larry used two projectors to cross-fade images of naked porn stars and of firemen up on ladders with hoses spraying the massive Brooklyn inferno. The slide show caused a sensation and would be much imitated, but it wasn't the only thing special that night. This was also the party when Karen Young performed "Hot Shot" a cappella, and the night we previewed the Walter Gibbons mix of "Doin' the Best That I Can." Michael was still desperate to woo the Fire Island crowd back to his club, so he hired a bus to provide round trip travel from the Fire Island ferry dock to the Garage and back. No one had ever tried that before.

The party was much talked about, although "Fire Down Below" wasn't the only reason things were hot in the club that night. Just as Michael had no heat in the winter, he had no air-conditioning in the summer, and New York's hot town, summer in the city blanket of heat and humidity was at its oppressive worst that night. *"I used to ride Michael about the air-conditioning,"* says Judy Weinstein, *"kidding him that if they can air-condition Kennedy airport, he can air-condition Paradise Garage."* But Michael knew that to stay in business he had to keep expenses way down, and with a space as huge as the Garage, there was no cheap way for him to air condition. So he chose to forego air-conditioning altogether, reasoning that heat would just become part of the overall intensity of the experience. Which I suppose it did.

That summer the famous exhibit of Tutenkhamen toured the museums and over five million people came to see it (most of them, I'm convinced, were in line ahead of me the day I went). Brian Wallach, my hit barometer out at Fire Island who was now also a successful party promoter, called me with an idea. *"What more reason do you need to have a party for gay men,"* he quipped, *"than a boy-king?"* I put him in touch with Michael, and the result was the Garage's legendary "Tut, Tut, Tut" party in September. Brian and his crew created the only Nile drag, doing the whole Garage over in drop-dead Egyptian. They smoked up the long ramp into the club and installed two huge statues of Ramses at the top end. The invitation was on parchment, as close to papyrus as you could get. That night the overall effect was spectacular, like partying inside a disco pyramid. First Choice performed on stage and their appearance was sensational. *"We saw this big gold Tut head easing toward the front of the stage,"* Shamako recalls. *"All you saw coming out of it was smoke. Then, all of a sudden, it opened up and three fierce girls in blue satin, top hats and tails emerged. I freaked."*

By chance, the party was held on the day that Sylvester's "Dance (Disco Heat)" made the Top Forty charts. Sylvester was an openly gay transvestite, and we were thrilled that the mainstream was accepting him. His success seemed like a symbol of a broader acceptance of gay people, and we thought he was forging the path for a future generation of openly gay stars. Larry adored Sylvester and his back up girls, Two Tons O' Fun — Martha Wash and Izora Rhodes — and Larry literally wore the grooves out on Sylvester's records. The admiration was mutual, since Sylvester told me on more than one occasion that the Garage was his absolute favorite place to perform. His kaleidoscopic "Dance (Disco Heat)" would become the theme of the Tut party.

show me the money

But all was not sweetness and light that famous day at Paradise Garage. Quite the contrary. The relationship between Michael and Larry was growing increasingly strained. Both were driven, and intense perfectionists; both had big egos; both were totally mutually dependent. Now, after the disaster of the opening and the failure of the club to become an instant money machine, tensions were brewing. Michael was desperate to bring back the white boys, and he was always seeking my advice about how to do it. His decision to bus them in, from Fire Island to the Garage, was a typical, desperate attempt. I suggested at one point that perhaps the best way was to make the club white one night and black another. This was a violation, of course, of my own dream of a fully integrated club. But if we could just get the white crowd back, I figured, and get them enthusiastic about Larry's music, the club would integrate and blend by itself. My idea was only a suggestion, and I would never have proposed it if I'd known where it was going to lead.

"The idea to make the club white one night and black the next really didn't work for Larry, to say the least," says Judy Weinstein. *"He thought Michael was turning on him, and he freaked."* By this point Larry had become thoroughly spoiled and he routinely broke things to get what he wanted. His tantrums grew worse, along with his drug use. Larry was never what you would call moderate at anything, least of all his drug consumption. As frantic as he could get about expressing emotion, he'd become just as energetic when it came to getting high. He loved living in a world where money was banished and emotions reigned supreme, where he was king of a feel-better place and love was indeed the message. But he could also be quite moody; he didn't really give a damn about whether or not his moods bothered you. The drugs only exaggerated his swings.

Larry's rage both at Michael and me was built over several days of increasing tension, dark looks, petty fights and silences. Finally the whole crazy atmosphere built to a head and exploded over a relatively trivial matter. Larry insisted that he needed some new piece of expensive equipment or he simply could not play. Michael refused. Larry began to abuse Michael verbally in front of the staff, which Michael hated. It was a standoff. But since Michael had ultimate power, it looked that he had won. Then suddenly, without any warning, Larry totally lost it. He dropped down on all fours and took a bite into Michael's leg, holding on like a pit bull. Michael was screaming, but Larry would not let go. Willy Gonzalez, one of the club's bouncers, a heavyweight bodybuilder, couldn't pull Larry off Michael. When finally they were separated, Michael's leg was gushing from a terrible puncture wound, and he was rushed to the emergency room.

Michael always worried that Larry might completely lose it someday, and after this freakish incident, he never again took Larry's threats idly. Violence dragged their relationship to a darker level. On the surface they seemed to forgive each other, at least to the extent that they were able to continue working together. But then, they had to, they needed each other so much. I had lived with Michael for over nine years, however, and was well aware that he never really forgot or forgave. I knew his problems with Larry were only just beginning. Larry considered himself such an integral part of the Garage that he was fairly sure Michael would never be able to find a replacement for him. But just to be absolutely sure, he took a few steps to guarantee his continued employment. *"If you looked in the back of the amp racks up in the booth,"* says Joey Llanos,

> It was a total mess. There were wires everywhere, and nothing was labeled as to what went where. Once I asked Larry: "How do you know where all this stuff goes?" I'll never forget his response. He turned around and looked at me, and he said, 'That's job security, Joe."

love and happiness

As 1978 drew to a close our disco crowd was not just riding high in the music business, we were also the center of attention in the gay world. Everybody was talking about two new novels that were essentially about us: *Faggots* by Larry Kramer and *Dancer from the Dance* by Andrew Holleran.

Faggots was a scathing send-up of what Larry Kramer saw the fast lane as — superficial, and many men in that fast lane were scandalized by the book and furious with him for writing it. Knowing Larry, I've always thought that *Faggots* was another word for sour grapes, since he was not really in this fast lane.

Dancer from the Dance was a novel about the disco scene in gay Manhattan, and it, too, frankly described widespread drug use and wanton sex. Its beautiful, romantic prose many gay readers considered a celebration of our lifestyle, an ode to the cult of disco and the worship of beauty and love. Not that its author did. He said later that he was actually depressed by New York gay life and all the things that he wasn't getting from it, and that he was shocked that people thought that he had glamorized the circuit when he wanted to criticize it. As usual with a book based on real life, everybody recognized somebody in it they knew or the friend of a friend, but no one recognized himself. I only know this: when I came to the part about Kenny Sheibley's suicide, I stopped reading. The wound was still searing and fresh. The thinly veiled description was more than I could take.

That aside, all was well with my world. By now Julio and I had been lovers for over a year, and although he had not really loved me at first, love was definitely growing. He expressed his love in the most touching ways, constantly buying me gifts and thinking of some small gesture to make me happy. He was like a dream lover; the strong and silent type who can't really say *"I Love You"* until he really means it, but tries to show it in a thousand gentle gestures. Sometimes I needed to pinch myself to make sure he was real. Things were just as great at work. West End Records was now a success, and I was extremely proud of myself for that. And the Paradise Garage was starting to take off after a year of furiously fanning the embers. At the Christmas party that closed 1978, I was on top of the world.

I don't know why the events in the wider world didn't depress me more than they did, especially the assassination of Harvey Milk in San Francisco, the first openly gay politician to rise to any real prominence. But I was high a great deal of the time, and I was perfectly content to lose myself in a disco daze. Drugs had permeated my world in a way that makes me wonder today. How did we do it? How did we keep from killing ourselves? We spent our days sleeping, shopping, working out, gossiping, smoking pot, making deals, meeting tricks, taking drugs, keeping up with the latest in everything. We spent our nights dining, drugging, running out to the clubs, popping over to the baths, sleeping with the beauty that so-and-so had last week, the gorgeous Puerto Rican trick, the flawless California number, the Marlboro Man, God; smoking angel dust, lapsing into a dream with a threesome you hardly knew, falling madly in love with one of them, waking up, starting over. Dancing itself was a way of getting high, a way to manufacture endorphins and stop processing and soar. Solitary athletes — marathon runners, skiers, gymnasts — speak of moments of absolute absorption when the endorphins start pumping. This is what dancing has always given me. Combined with cocaine and angel dust and youth, and an endless stream of dream partners and — whatever moralists may say — you have a formula for existing the way people have always dreamed of existing but were never able to: a state of pleasure, without harshness, decay and death. Like climbing onto the stage of a beautiful opera and joining the cast. From now until that black moment in 1981 when the doctors told us that lightning had struck our veins, we lived out everybody's fantasy. And for all that happened afterward, we had, at least, these memories.

Paradise Garage is central to those memories for many, many people. Today, over a decade after it closed, the Garage is referred to with the reverence of a sacred place — it was a refuge, they say, an ark, a church, a temple, a home. People claim it saved their lives, helped get them off the streets, gave them a purpose. It may seem odd to describe a disco in these terms, but we were a tribe, and we were doing what tribes have been doing for thousands of years. We were building a community through communal dance and celebration. Like our ancient ancestors, who pounded drums and painted their faces and danced in the moonlight, we were simply a new queer incarnation. All the more powerful for us, because outside the disco walls we were still outcasts. And if we had any illusion that the triumph of disco would mean better days ahead, that it would mean that we were being accepted into the world at large, we were about to learn otherwise.

mel's photo album

Mel

ABC/Paramount's executive staff, 5th-Anniversary convention, Diplomat Hotel, Hollywood, FL, 1960

Mel

ABC/Paramount's executive staff with U.S. distributors, 5th-Anniversary convention, Diplomat Hotel, Hollywood, FL, 1960

Mel (M.S. District Salesman) with Connie Francis, Cleveland, 1961

Mel's first private office at ABC Records new home, 1330 Ave. of the Americas. as Director of Production for ABC, Impulse, Bluesway, Command, Dunhill, 1967

Mel exhibiting his paintings at the Brooklyn Heights Promenade, 1966.

Mike Brody, 1966

Mike Brody, Mel, Richard Kane, Dick Fisher, Upstate New York, 1969

Dick Fisher, Ray Ford, David Lynn, Terry Fu, Don Melsop, Mike Brody, Mel, a friend
Fire Island, 1972

"nothing is more important than friendship —
not money, not fame, not death," Michael Brody, 1973

Mike Brody and Mel, Fire Island Pines, 1973

Ralph Marine, Norman Marine, Bob Siddons, Larry McDevitt, Ray Ford, Mark Rosenfeld, Fire Island, 1975

Photo by Barry McKinley

Phil Patrick, Fire Island, 1976, (later became the first office manager of GMHC in 1982)

Julio, 1976

Julio & Mel at Julio's Surprise Birthday party at the Loft on Prince Street, 1976

Paul Popham, Founder and first President of GMHC (Gay Men's Health Crisis), 1976

Frank Cioffi, Tommy Baratta, Mel, Gary Burbank, "Camp Tommy 2," Fire Island, 1976

70s

West End Record's First Anniverary Bash at Le Mouche, 1977
BACK ROW: Maye James, Grace Jones BOTTOM ROW: Mel, Tomiko Jones, Tom Moulton

Karen "Hot Shot" Young and Mel at the Billboard
Music Convention, Sheraton Hotel, NYC, 1978

Mel at the West End office, 254 W. 54th St., 1978

Mel & Gigi (age 5), 1980

Mel & Julio, Fire Island, 1981

Mel, a friend, Larry, Jose, Garage, 1981

Top of ramp, Paradise Garage, 1981

Frankie Crocker (WBLS Program Director), Larry, Garage, 1981

Michael Brody, Mick Jagger, Larry, Garage, 1984

Juan DuBois, Keith Haring, Andy Warhol, Party of Life, 1984

Diana Ross, Party of Life, 1984

Judy Russell, Manny Lehman, Party of Life, 1984

Grace Jones, Party of Life, 1984

Garage party, 1984

Michael Brody's Christmas gift to his staff, a trip to Rio, 1983

Mel painting, Fire Island Pines, 1984

Manuel Fernandez, Randy Barselo, Chaz Goward, Ignacio Zuazo, at Sophie & Jack's 54th Wedding Anniversary, 1984

Mel's mother, Sophie, and his father, Jack, celebrating their 54th Wedding Anniversary, 1984

Julio and Mel at Joe Novak's, East Hampton, 1985

Mel and Chaz at Disneyland, 1985

Mel painting "Consortium," 1985

80s

Members of the Inner Sanctum, VIP lounge, Garage, 1985

Larry, Keith, Garage, 1986

Minnie, closing night, Garage, 1987

Matty Novak, Larry, Joey Llanos, David DePino, NYC, 1987

Larry, closing night, 1987

Jack Cheren's 83rd Birthday with Carmen Marquez (Willy's mother and Jack's caregiver), and Mel, 1988

Mel with Willy Marquez at the Upstairs party, Palladium, 1987

Mel with Gladys Knight, Chairperson for 24 Hours For Life, 1989

Mayor David Dinkins with Dionne Warwick at 24 Hours For Life press conference, "That's What Friends Are For" Weekend, 1989

Florence Greenberg, Shirley Austin (orignial Shirelle), Dionne Warwick, Mel at the AIDS Benefit for St. Claire Hospital, 1989

Gladys Knight, Florence Greenberg, Dionne Warwick at "That's What Friends Are For" dinner, USS Intrepid, June 1989

Gigi Soto, Florence Greenberg, Jean Brody, Jack Cheren at "That's What Friends Are For" dinner, USS Intrepid, June 1989

Dedication of plaque at Colonial House Inn, first site of GMHC offices, June 1989. (Mel also sponsored the Thank-You party for Dionne Warwick's volunteers for the "That's What Friends Are For" AIDS charity weekend on this day)

Mel, Jean Brody, Tony Orlando, 1990

Mel & Larry, in front of the Choice, 1990

Jake Corbin, Peter, Mel going down on Robyn Byrd, Gabriel
Rotello, Ice Palace, Fire Island, 1990

Jack Cheren, Ricky Willock, Florence Greenberg, Mel, & Julio, 1990

Larry, Mel, John-John Martinez, Richard Vasquez at the Choice, 1990

Gabriel Rotello, Kendall Morrison, Mel, Michaelangelo Signorelli, night before Gay Pride March, 1991

Tom Baratta, Larry, Mel, Bernice Lynch, Jack Cheren, Minnie Levan at Salute to Gladys Knight dinner, 1990

Linda Clifford with Mel, Miracle Party, Shelter, 1991

Mel, Thelma Houston, Larry, Miracle Party, Shelter, 1991

Mel with Brent Nicholson Earle, Washington DC, 1992

Dick Fisher, Larry McDevitt, & Mel in front of the GMHC building, 1994

Jim Hyde, Mel, Lupe Flores, and Glenn Cooper, Christmas in Key West, 1993

Reunion of executive staff of GMHC at NYC headquarters, 1994

Last picture taken of Mel and Larry together, Tokyo, 1992

François Kevorkian, Larry, Tokyo, 1992

In front of Gold disco Tokyo, Sept. 1992

François, Larry, Walter Gibbons, Tokyo, 1992

Joey Llanos, Frankie Knuckles, Tee Scott, Sound Factory Bar, 1993

Tom Moulton, Danny Krivitt, François, Nicky Siano, at a party honoring Larry Levan, Sound Factory Bar, 1993

Mel, Derek Daniels, Grace Jones, Brent Nicholson Earle, Paris, 1997

Mel, Mauricio (Kiko) Mera, Junior Vasquez, Tunnel, 1997

Kevin Williams, Taana, Mel, Roberto Novo at Taana's surprise birthday party at Mel's house, 1998

Kenton Nix with Mel, 1998

Larry Basile, Buzz Hoff, Mel, Clem Pepe, Tom Faucett, Brent, Mike Mancini, Bill Scott, January in Jamaica, 1998

Mel with Jeffrey Stokes, 1999

Louis Malkin, Dino Georgiou, dear friends for 35 years

Sam Watkins, Marcos Becquer, Lorenzo Ramos, Roberto Novo, Human Rights campaign dinner, New York, 1997

Brad Rumph, someone who helped immensely to get this book finished, Paris, 1998

Mel's cousin Ilya, father Jack, Mike Mancini, Odessa, Nov. 1991

Gigi & Mel at Gigi's graduation from the University of New Hampshire, 1999

Mel's godson, Scott Herman (now a doctor's assistant) with Lisa Herman (Mel's travel consultant)

Larry Basile, Julio, Mel at Gigi's graduation from the University of New Hampshire, 1999

Andy Reynolds, Fred Held, Kenny Nix, Winter Music Conference, 1999   Minnie

Kenny Nix, Scott Ashwell, Taana Gardner, Mel at the Benefit for the East Harlem School at Exodus House, Club Vinyl, 1999

chapter eleven

THE RISE AND (SO-CALLED) FALL OF DISCO

"It's 2 a.m. in Studio 54, the Versailles of disco," began a 1979 *Rolling Stone* cover story on a party thrown by Warner Bros. Records to launch its new, supposedly multi-million dollar disco label, RFC. (A few years later, I would find out that RFC capitalization was not, in fact, six million, but sixty thousand.)

> There's such a buzz in the air that you wonder if someone has pumped amphetamine vapor through the heating system. Euphoria is rampant. Everyone knows that 1979 will go down in history as the year disco became the biggest thing in pop since Beatlemania, and possibly since the birth of rock'n'roll.

This is how 1979 began, in a blizzard of superlatives unlike anything I had seen in the music industry in 20 years. And yet it ended with the supposed death of disco. In a single year, the biggest bubble in the history of popular music would burst, and the record industry would turn viciously on the music that had fed its coffers for half a decade. By year's end, the very word disco would be so tainted that music magazine editors would change disco to *dance* to escape the dreaded association. Of course, in the gay and black worlds the beat would go on just as it had before. Disco would simply go back underground, and we would keep dancing until we met a different disaster, one we couldn't escape. But the huge public craze was about to end in a sudden collapse that amounts to one of the strangest revolutions in popular music, even stranger since the year it happened began on such a high.

"Roll Over, Rock!" exclaimed *Newsweek's* April 1979 cover story in a classic of misguided prediction — *"Disco is Here to Stay."* It was one of dozens of high-profile articles in the mainstream press that trumpeted the ascendancy of disco over other forms of pop. Record executive Rick Stevens of Polydor put it simply enough. *"We're going through,"* he said, *"the most dramatic taste shift in popular music history."*

Honchos like Stevens had good reason to gloat. Labels had tallied their balance sheets for 1978, and the verdict was in. Disco was grossing eight billion dollars a year, accounting for about 30 percent of the entire music business and almost 40 percent of the Top 100 hits. There were now 20,000 discotheques, 200 all-disco radio stations, 8,000 professional DJs, and thousands more trying to break into the business. It was astonishing. And disco-crazed optimists argued that this was just the beginning, that we were in the start of a fifteen-year cycle of non-stop dance fever.

Money was rolling in by the barrel, to the producers, the labels, the clubs, the fashion designers, the acts. And it rolled out just as fast. The response of normally stingy Atlantic Records to Chic's enormous success with *"Le Freak"* was to more than quadruple the budget for their third album, *Risqué*, from $35,000 to over $160,000. Insiders gasped, but it produced another chart-topping hit album, *Good Times*. Executives throughout the industry were literally throwing money at disco, and the money fueled a culture of extravagance and conspicuous consumption not seen since the wild era of Janis Joplin and Jim Morrison. These were truly the days of disco excess. Executives and promoters kept limousines at their disposal at all times, offices were decorated in the most lavish styles, companies like Casablanca maintained fabulous houses on Fire Island with names like "The Golden Arches" and "Eureka." After all, their promotion people needed to break records where the action was, and Fire Island was still the holy land.

And of course, there was the disco drug scene, which burst into the open when Studio 54 found itself the focus of a huge investigation. Owners Steve Rubell and Ian Shrager eventually got three-and-a-half years for tax evasion, but everybody knew that the government had really targeted them for the extravagant drug use and dealing that was going on in the club. In fact, drugs were over the top in every club, and at every label. Ray Caviano got Warner Brothers to finance his new label RFC. He was in complete control of everything, including the biggest startup budget anybody had ever seen, and a lot of it went up a lot of noses. His cocaine abuse and extravagant spending eventually left him bankrupt and in jail. But for now, anybody who could sniff out the next big hit was treated like gold.

However, not everyone was having a good time. *"With insidious speed,"* wrote the editors of *Newsweek*,

> the after-hours music first heard only by small urban groups of blacks, Hispanics, gays and insomniacs had invaded the hearts, minds and feet of all ages and classes.

Insidious is not a word you normally find in articles about pop, so it gives some idea of the misgivings. The bigger disco got, the more certain people resented it, and a backlash that had been building for several years emerged in 1979 under the general rallying cry, *"Disco Sucks!"*

Some of the resentment was well placed. A lot of disco did suck. More and more aging stars were jumping on the disco bandwagon, and more producers were applying the disco formula to horrible songs. Some of this product was great. "Miss You" by the Rolling Stones is a dance classic, and Rod Stewart's "Do Ya Think I'm Sexy?" was the third biggest song of 1979. But much of it was embarrassing, and the glut of stupid pop-disco was enough to make lots of people want to turn the beat off. It didn't help that disco's pounding rhythm did not lend itself very well to poor imitation. In the right hands the beat can become mesmerizing, a launching pad to ecstasy. In the wrong hands it's just relentless.

But these complaints were not really enough to explain the intensity of the Disco Sucks movement that would emerge and sweep the nation later that year. After all, most styles of music, including rock, produce an excessive amount of garbage. And most of the worst disco, the really rank stuff that I had to wade through at West End, rarely got released, much less played on the radio or in the clubs. People today sometimes justify the backlash as a result of things like Ethel Merman cutting a disco record, but does anybody actually remember her disco record? Most people probably never heard it.

There was certainly plenty of bad disco, but there was plenty of great stuff. 1979 was the year of "Bad Girls" and "Hot Stuff" and "Heaven Knows" by Donna Summer, "I Will Survive" by Gloria Gaynor, "Ring My Bell" by Anita Ward, "Heart of Glass" by the new group Blondie, "Y.M.C.A." by the Village People, "We Are Family" by Sister Sledge. Campy or inspiring, quirky or soulful, many of these songs remain classics that are as familiar today as they were back then. The Euro-disco, pop-disco and r&b-disco camps were churning out dance music in a wide variety of styles, and there was as much diversity in disco as in rock. Today, 20 years later, '70s disco remains among the most popular genres in the oldies business. Entire radio stations are devoted to it, and there are constant reissues and remixes of the classics. If it was so bad, why is it still so popular, especially with younger people who were not even around back then?

The sad fact is, the disco backlash was fueled by a lot more than just bad music. The clue is right there in the *Newsweek* quote that disco began as the music of *"small urban groups of blacks, Hispanics and gays."* Despite *Saturday Night Fever,* the popularity of disco continued to throw a glaring light on the lifestyles of gay men. It was one thing for us to elbow onto the charts and create a little niche for the gay and the black markets. It was something else for us to grab a third of the whole industry, and threaten to take over completely. The music market is largely a zero-sum game, so as disco rose, everything else had to fall. This infuriated those who had dominated music for years — rock critics, DJs, and producers, and lots of disenfranchised fans. Rock had defined almost two generations of white, middle-class straight baby-boomers, particularly guys. It spoke to them and for them, and now it was in danger of being relegated to a niche market itself by a new style dominated by black musicians and gay promoters, producers and tastemakers. As the disco sweep turned into a tidal wave, a near panic set in. Beneath the bitter complaints that disco was mindless, hedonistic, repetitive, pounding — exactly what critics had said about rock itself in its early years — there was this deeper complaint: disco was black and Hispanic. Disco was mindless and gay. Disco sucked.

As to the accusation that disco was controlled by gays, this much was certainly true. A very small group of people had pretty much cornered the market in terms of promotion, and most of us were gay. In 1979 *Rolling Stone* did a profile of Disco's Top Thirty and there I was in the layout, smiling from behind my desk at West End. But there, too, were many of my closest friends, from Tom Moulton on down. Things got so incestuous that at one point our West End promotion man Alan Mamber shared an apartment with two other top promotion people for different companies, Star Arning and Ken Friedman. I'm not sure what the Securities and Exchange Commission would have made of that, since the three of them collaborated as much as they competed. Alan recalls nights when they would come home from their respective labels and sit around divvying up the coming hits. *"I've got the new France Joli single,"* someone would say. *"I've got the new Instant Funk. Wait, you guys, here's the new Donna Summer."* Then they'd smoke a joint or do a few lines and get down to business.

> You're going to have to wait with your Instant Funk, because I'm putting out the Donna Summer this week, and if you release yours at the same time, she'll clog up the No. 1 slot and you won't be able to get in.

It was like musical monopoly, and gay people ran the bank.

michael and julio

I chuckled when I opened the envelope in January and pulled out the invitation. *"Last year we gave you L-L-L-LONG L-L-L-LINES AND C-C-C-COLD R-R-R-ROOMS,"* it said, in the shape of a penis. Inside, the message continued as an outline of lips: *"This year, THE GARAGE AS YOU'VE NEVER SEEN IT!"*

Although it would take another two years for the Garage to attain its legendary status, it was now a finished place, beautiful in every detail, state of the art. True, few of my A-list friends had returned, but Larry Levan's following kept the place going strong. The fact that the Garage had survived a whole year after its disastrous official opening was reason enough for me to celebrate. The song that stands out from that First Anniversary Party was Gloria Gaynor's "I Will Survive," the first major disco hit of 1979. It began its run up the charts on January 20, the day before my 46th birthday, and it seemed an appropriate song to start the second year of Paradise Garage.

Michael's feelings toward me, however, were anything but resolved. One reason was my continued loyalty to the Flamingo.

Most of my friends went there on Saturday nights, and although I loved the Garage and Larry's music, I also loved the Flamingo's special camaraderie. And since the Garage had become an industry hang-out, I never felt like I could fully let myself go there with Julio. I was, even at this late date, still closeted to most of the music industry. Michael considered my patronage of Flamingo a sign of treason. He considered me part-owner of Paradise Garage, even though I had only loaned him a large chunk of the money for his initial investment and did not share the profits. And I did feel a little guilty. But not enough that I thought I had to please Michael at the expense of my own enjoyment.

Another source of tension was the fact that my West End partner Ed Kushins disrespected Michael, and worse, wasn't shy about saying so. *"Whenever Michael wants something or needs something, he's up here with a smile on his face,"* Ed was always saying to me. He considered it his duty to steer me clear of someone who, to him, was just another in the long line of handsome faces always trying to take advantage of me. And it didn't help that in between the times Michael needed favors, he often treated me poorly.

But the biggest source of tension by far was the fact that Michael hated to see Julio as my lover. I'm sure that Michael now came to believe that our whole relationship had been a fraud because, he probably felt, I had always loved Julio. I suppose that was due to the fact that I had first pointed out Julio to Michael, after which we had both fantasized about Julio and even had threesomes with him. After Michael and I split up, he even had sex with Julio himself once or twice, as well as several love affairs of his own over the years. But all of this was blotted out. To him, my relationship with Julio was some kind of pay back. It became another rather large item on Michael's *"never forgive"* list. I'm sure that if I had become involved with anybody other than Julio,

Michael would not have resented it. As to my relationship with Julio, there were wonderful times when he was thoughtful and kind and I could count on him for things that I needed without ever having to ask. He'd find the simplest reasons to buy me gifts, and his generosity made me want to respond in kind. It became a treat for me to go out of my way to find things that would please him. But there was trouble brewing there as well.

We never lived together. With his hair-cutting business, it made sense to maintain separate apartments. It also gave both of us more opportunities to have tricks on the side. He was very tight-lipped about his trysts, and I didn't ask any questions. After my disastrous experiment with truth back at the end of my relationship with Michael, I decided that I couldn't get hurt by what I didn't know, and silence was the best way to hang on to what I had. There were very few illusions between us. We realized pretty early on that we were both independent, sexually and in many other ways, and we never seriously considered living together. Even our plans for growing older together included separate apartments in the same building. Still, if you had asked me then, I would have said we led normal lives.

Now, when I think of what I considered to be normal, I shudder. The fact is that over time we began taking larger and larger amounts of drugs, and at some point we started smoking angel dust on a regular basis. By 1979 Julio was smoking it every day. Although most of the time he had no trouble functioning, since he worked in his apartment, he simply canceled his appointments when he didn't feel up to it. Dust seemed to become his escape hatch from life, and he seemed to have a lot to escape from. Despite his thoughtfulness, he was completely bottled-up about his feelings. I guess you might say he had intimacy problems. He never wanted to talk about the things that most lovers talk about — like my work, for instance, which was pretty much my whole life at the time apart from him. He was the quintessential party boy, and as time went on it seemed like he was determined to keep the party going 24-hours a day. Since he was smoking dust constantly and joints were always being passed, I smoked it more and more myself. If I had been a late-bloomer in the drug department, I was making up for lost time.

Some of my drug experiences were really unpleasant. One time I took a hit of clear-light acid that was actually two hits stuck together. I danced off the ceiling that night with my friend David Cohen, but when we left 12 West the trip suddenly turned very bad. Hitting the quiet streets at that hour of the morning, I felt the world was coming to an end. Cars looked twisted out of proportion, and when we got to David's apartment I was hallucinating horribly, terrified to go out on the 12th-floor terrace for fear that I might try to fly off.

Angel dust did not usually have those effects, but it certainly made life with Julio more volatile. As time went on he became more erratic and we started having fights. Finally, I don't remember when, we actually broke up during one of these dust battles. We got back together pretty quickly, but soon it settled into a pattern. High on dust, our scenes would spiral out of control, and we began breaking up and getting back together so often that it became old news to our friends. Sometimes we wouldn't talk to each other for weeks, but then when it came time for a big party, all was forgiven. Even if we were still pissed at each other, we would maintain a front. *"Think of appearances,"* Julio would snarl as we entered a club. Nobody understood our up-and-down relationship. Quite frankly, neither did I.

One way I tried to knit us closer together was by occasionally presenting Julio with a third party in bed. With Julio's looks he could have brought anyone home, but it was hard for him to look for someone to be with both of us. So I would go out and search for likely candidates. Whenever I found one, I would have to warn the guy that Julio might be turned off if he felt that I was receiving most of the attention, which sometimes happened, since I was the one who was doing the selecting. But usually all it took was one look at Julio and the playing field was leveled. Occasionally the planets were aligned and things worked out great. But often Julio would be dusted and disinterested and would find some fault with our new partner, making sure there would be no return engagement.

I know it must sound like a strange relationship, and I guess it was. With the drugs, the tension, the love, the insecurity, the overwhelming pressures of work, the problems with both Julio and Michael, sometimes life felt like it was moving too fast for me. It was becoming more difficult to tell where the job ended and the party began. At the end of a long night I often found myself home alone, and I was hardly the euphoric executive when the drugs wore off. Time and again the dust would turn on me and I would wind up miserable and depressed and caught up in what I called the early morning blues. I wondered how my friends could possibly envy me, successful, at the center of my world, a handsome lover, and still so lonely. At times, the only way that I was able to deal with all the angst was through painting.

I've never used brushes. I prefer the tactile sensations of massaging the paint into the canvas with my fingers. Some mornings would find me covered in paint at the canvas, caught in a jumble of troubling thoughts: How was the dust affecting my relationship with Julio? What was becoming of my relationship with Michael? Where was that wonderful young kid I had met 17 years ago? Why had he become so afraid to show his emotions? Why did he resent my success with West End Records so much? And how long could that success last? Where was our next hit song going to come from?

The whirlwind of drugs and partying tinted my whole world view. In the third week of May, gays rioted in San Francisco when Dan White was found not guilty of murdering Harvey Milk. White was convicted of voluntary manslaughter instead, which carried only a seven-year sentence, and the verdict sparked a huge insurrection as outraged gays vandalized City Hall, overturned police cars and started fires. I watched the White Night Riots on television, but they seemed remote to me and I hardly noticed. Only later did I realize that something big had happened, when people chatted about it at the clubs. *"Wasn't it awful?"* they'd ask as they reached for their cocaine vials or sniffed another popper.

SUCCESS

But somehow, drugs never seemed to interfere with my work. In a way they may have even helped, at least for awhile. By being just as high as the most hardcore disco fans, I was hearing what they were hearing, responding the way they responded, liking what they liked. In a sense, West End was a label run by a fan. I can only remember one time in those years when I got so high it stopped me from working. I was on my way up to the DJ booth at Flamingo to bring a new record to Howard Merritt, and owner Michael Fesco stopped me and told me I couldn't go up. I was so high that I wasn't able to tell him that I was introducing a new record that night. Intimidated, I just backed off. But that's my only memory of ever being so high that I couldn't work a record. Somehow, I was always able to get the job done. Perhaps if angel dust had interfered with my work more, I would have seen the warning signs and stopped.

At West End, we weren't on the fringe of the action in 1979, we *were* the action. Our releases were among the most highly regarded records in the business. *Rolling Stone* called West End the most innovative label in disco, and I suppose it was, simply because I believed in taking chances instead of just trying for sure things. Of course, I wanted the hits to keep on coming. But I also wanted to keep pushing the envelope, and wanted to be proud of my records in the place where it really counted to me: on the dance floor. Unfortunately, the very fact that West End product was considered the most cutting-edge music in disco often meant that its critical success failed to translate into huge hits. The charts were now dominated by pop songs designed for mass appeal. We were often looking for something else.

One of the secrets of our critical success was that we were willing to listen to performers who wouldn't have a shot anywhere else. Most companies refused to audition material on anything less than 16 or 24 tracks, but Ed and I would listen to everything, even unfinished 8-tracks. Ed was usually reticent about new acts and new material, but I must say that for someone with his background, he often surprised me. He had a natural instinct for what sounded good, even though he never went to discos and when he did it was mainly during the early hours at an industry event, before things got hot.

In any event, things were going gangbusters for West End. We had another huge hit when producer Kenny Nix walked in one day with a four-track demo. He had given it to Larry Levan one night at the Garage, and even though the record had no vocals the place went wild, and Larry convinced Kenny to bring the song to us. Ed was not impressed, and I had to convince him to take it on. But he finally agreed, and Kenny went back in the studio and added Taana Gardner as the vocalist. If nothing happens by accident, "Work That Body" was a prime example. Taana met Kenny by chance at an airport, where they were both waiting for Kenny's brother. He had already finished the music to "Work

That Body" and decided that Taana would be perfect for the lead. He took her into the studio without any rehearsals, saying that the energy of a recording session is like making love — you can't rehearse lovemaking, and you only get one shot to capture the feeling. It certainly proved to be true in the session with Taana. Larry Levan mixed the record and "Work That Body" immediately shot up the charts and became one of our big hits.

I was so wrapped up in everything that I hardly noticed the Three-Mile Island nuclear disaster, which panicked New York. When it came to nuclear annihilation, the only thing that could have penetrated my disco brain was if something threatened to meltdown Flamingo or the Garage. *"Disco Sucks!"* was literally the writing on the walls all over Manhattan, furious Clash fans spray-painting it right in our faces. But I paid absolutely no attention. I was having too much fun. And according to Ed, making too much money. He told me that we were doing so well that we desperately needed additional tax deductions. So he presented me with an option: we could either pay a huge sum to the Internal Revenue Service, or spend it on entertaining our clients. Guess which one I chose. We decided to host a four-day convention for our record distributors at the Mark Hopkins Hotel in San Francisco. Since it was my parents' 50th wedding anniversary, I invited them to come out to San Francisco along with my Aunt Miriam and Uncle George, my cousins George and Muriel, and Michael Brody's mother, Jean. I also brought along Diane Strafaci, who was working with me on the Colleen Heather and Taana Gardner projects, and her husband Joe. Julio came, too, but I was so afraid my parents might find out that I was gay that I put him up in another hotel.

My parents thought that they were only going along as my guests for the convention, but I had planned a golden wedding anniversary party for them. That weekend, Ed and I had plenty of reasons to feel proud. West End was rolling in money and our partnership was a success. This convention alone was proof enough. I was surrounded by the friends and the family I dearly loved. And the surprise party for my parents was the icing on the cake. Those four days were among the happiest of my life.

touring

Since I firmly believed in utilizing live appearances to promote our records, I began to book our top performers in clubs across the country, which was almost a full-time job in itself. A lot of the best disco singers — mostly black women — were from poor backgrounds. They had street style, but they didn't really know how to present themselves in the best light. So I copied impresarios like Motown's Barry Gordy and hired professionals to come in and teach them how to walk and talk, do their makeup and develop poise, onstage and off. This could get very expensive. I remember once sending our promotion man, Alan Mamber, on a shopping trip with Taana Gardner. Alan thought my orders to dress her up included buying her a pair of incredibly expensive jeweled earrings from Bergdorfs. We fought for days over the expense, but it was justified in the long run. Taana worked those earrings.

It was a lot more difficult with Karen Young. Karen was such a mess she practically defied fixing up. She lacked the social graces that most young girls have — grooming and make-up and that kind of thing. She was also very heavy. One time she and Alan Mamber were out in Fire Island and they took a water taxi back to the Pines. The tide was low, so they had to climb up onto the dock, and poor Karen just couldn't do it. Finally, Alan and his friends had to get below her and shove her up onto the dock like an elephant. Karen was so big people actually mistook her for a drag queen or female impersonator, which could sometimes work to her advantage. When audiences saw her come onstage, they'd get ready for just another lipsync act. Then this immense voice would ring out of this immense body, and audiences went crazy. However Karen may have looked, she was real, and it came across.

Touring was not lucrative in itself, and we could never afford to hire a live band. Disco was so much a studio art form, so dependent on equipment and cross-phasing and elaborate orchestrations, that when superstars like Donna Summer did try to recreate the music live onstage, they needed a couple of dozen musicians — and still it wasn't exactly right. So instead we did what was called live-to-track singing, in which the artist sang over a tape that had the lead vocals deleted. Alan Mamber jokes that when he toured with Loleatta Holloway he used to carry the whole Salsoul Orchestra in his bag. Sometimes the tape contained backup vocals, which would come popping out of nowhere during a live appearance like disembodied ghosts. But people loved it. Most of the time they were too high to notice the difference.

For gay New Yorkers the highlight of the summer of 1979 was the party on the pier for Gay Pride weekend. It was the tenth anniversary of Stonewall, and one of the big hits of that summer was "We Are Family" by Sister Sledge. Its defiant refrain — "We are family/ I've got all my sisters with me" — was an unofficial anthem for a gay community that considered itself steeped in "sisterhood." Promoter Steve Cohn was getting his start with this party and I thought he could use my support, so I secured Taana Gardner to perform "Work That Body" and Ednah Holt, former lead singer of the Ritchie Family, whose group StarLuv was now recording for West End, to perform "People Come Dance." StarLuv's record had only been released that week and the crowd didn't recognize it, but the moment they took the stage wearing little sarongs painted with watermelons and looking very Ritchie Family, I knew that they had what it took to move an audience.

At the peak of the party two hours later, Taana Gardner came on. Taana's record was already a big hit, and when her music started, the crowd exploded. But it was only the beginning for Taana that weekend. The second she left the stage, Alan Mamber whisked her into a limo and raced to the airport. We had also booked her for the Gay Pride Parade in San Francisco, which was taking place the next morning. *"We had quite a timing problem on our hands,"* Alan recalls.

> She had to be in San Francisco on the float by noon, so she had to change costumes on the plane in the tiny First Class bathroom. Her dress was bigger than that entire bathroom, but Taana disappeared into it and came out all in white chiffon — transformed into a disco goddess. She left the other passengers gaping.

In San Francisco, Alan hustled Taana into a limousine, instructing the driver to drive like a bat out of hell. At exactly 12-noon he lifted her onto the float, and over the next two hours she sang "Work That Body" down the entire length of Market Street. As she reached the end of the parade, she barely had time to catch her breath before Alan whisked her off to the tea dances at the I-Beam and the Trocadero, before escorting the exhausted 19-year-old to her hotel.

During this period, most artists were either paid little for their promotional appearances, or not paid at all. At most, a company might pick up an artist's expenses on a per diem basis — but you could hardly expect to live in New York City on $25 a day. Still, most artists were determined to perform in public. They knew the appearances promoted their records, and there was the added advantage that they got to bask in the adulation of the crowds.

In the midst of all of this activity, we hit Boston for the Fourth Annual Disco Music Awards. For those in the Music Hall Theatre in Boston that night, it seemed like disco was at a pinnacle that would last for years. The program notes talked about disco as the music that would dominate the '80s, and devotees insisted that it was more than music, that it represented a new way of life. That rock was dead, and disco was destined to take its place. What a line up of disco hit-makers that night. Gloria Gaynor, the first ever Queen of Disco. Loleatta Holloway, with her go-for-broke vocal style. Grace Jones, fashion model/disco diva with her animalistic stage act. Candi Staton, queen of confessional songs like "Victim" and "When You Wake Up Tomorrow." Pattie Brooks, Donna Summer's former background singer with her Summer-styled Euro-disco bent. And our own Karen Young, who was nominated for Best New Female Artist for her *"scat singing style and raspy interpretations,"* as the program stated, and whose "Hot Shot" was nominated for Best Disco Single and Best 12-Inch. Also nominated for awards that night were established hitmakers like Sylvester, Peter Brown, Dan Hartman, Cerrone, Gregg Diamond, Rick James, the Bee Gees, Chic, the Village People, John Davis and the Monster Orchestra. That week "Hot Stuff" by Donna Summer debuted on *Billboard's* Top Forty chart, and would reach No. 1 just a few weeks later. Disco was anything but dead as far as we were concerned. And yet this was its swan song.

disco sucks

Then came the event that signaled an end of sorts, although we didn't recognize it at the time. Steve Dahl, a *"morning zoo"* radio DJ from Chicago, had been pushing the "Disco Sucks" thing like a fanatic, promoting t-shirts and bumper stickers and whipping up a frenzy of anti-disco backlash. Dahl announced that he would have a surprise for his anti-disco fans on July 12th in Chicago's Comiskey Park, and he did not disappoint. In between games of a White Sox/Detroit Tigers double-header, he strode out onto the field and began an anti-disco rally centered around a huge funeral pyre made up of hundreds of disco records mixed with several pounds of TNT. At the climax of the rally, with tens of thousands of fans chanting *"Disco Sucks! Disco Sucks!,"* Dahl set fire to the whole thing. There was a huge blast when the flames reached the TNT, and the bleachers were showered with flaming bits of *Saturday Night Fever.* The crowd rioted and the second game was canceled, not least because of the crater in the field. It was the explosion heard round the record industry.

The next day a rival, all-disco Chicago station played Donna Summer's *"Last Dance"* for 24-hours straight. At the end of the 24-hours, the station proclaimed *"Disco is Over"* and switched their format to Top Forty rock. The stampede was on. Overnight, the *"Disco Sucks"* campaign grew into a huge juggernaught, and everybody who ever had any misgivings about disco jumped on. Radio DJs began denouncing the music openly; disgruntled writers at music publications went on the attack; people began making fun of anything associated with disco, and it quickly had an effect. Programmers and market researchers began to encounter a visceral hatred for anything connected with the word disco, gay people included. Within months of the Comiskey Park rally, dozens of all-disco radio stations were abandoning what they now believed was a sinking ship, adopting instead a blend of rock, pop and only the most popular disco hits, a format they labeled urban-contemporary. As stations dropped disco, the fountain that had supplied the unbroken stream of disco hits dried up almost overnight, and disco's domination of the charts ended with incredible speed. The fact that a revolution was taking place could be seen in the succession of the subsequent No. 1 hits on *Billboard.* That fall the big songs were traditional rockers like "Heartache Tonight" by the Eagles, or songs that hinted at the coming new wave/MTV revolution, like "My Sharona" by the Knack and "Pop Muzik" by M.

Of course, disco did not cease to produce hits entirely. Michael Jackson's "Don't Stop 'Til You Get Enough" hit the No. 1 spot in October — for precisely one week. And the masterful Donna Summer/Barbra Streisand duet "No More Tears (Enough Is Enough)" captured the No. 1 slot for two weeks in November. This once-in-a-lifetime collaboration between two of the biggest female singers in pop history was the brainchild of Paul Jabara, who had produced the Oscar-winning "Last Dance" for Donna Summer the previous year. When it was time for the lead vocal tracks to be recorded, Summer kept Streisand waiting in the studio while she finished a previously scheduled concert appearance. *"I haven't waited two hours for anybody,"* Barbra cracked, but she knew a good thing when she saw it. Radio was not about to ignore this double-whammy. The song's aggressive screw-you lyrics about an unfaithful lover riveted disco fans, who saw it as an anthem of triumph over their anti-disco detractors. But "No More Tears" was the exception — a song so good, sung by singers so famous, that radio could not afford to ignore it. Otherwise it was all downhill. There would be a few minor disco hits over the next few months and into early 1980, but nothing like the dominance of the previous several years. With strains of the Streisand-Summer war cry echoing in the ears of fans everywhere, disco began its quick descent underground.

Never before in the history of popular music had a dominant style dropped from popularity so quickly. Rock'n'roll's famous ascendancy over swing bands and crooners took years to complete. But within six months of Comiskey Park, disco was so officially over that the word itself ceased being used by the mainstream media except as a pejorative. If you wanted to describe utter extinction, all you had to say was that something was as *"dead as disco"* and people knew what you meant. Practically everybody involved in the business has a different explanation. Gloria Gaynor later said that disco *"unfortunately evolved into a lifestyle that Middle America found distasteful."* August Darnell, of Dr. Buzzard's Savannah Band, blamed greed. *"People who don't have the heart and soul of the music,"* he said, *"but just want to cash in on it."* Judy Weinstein claimed that *"the word disco killed disco. Anything that becomes too popular is apt to be destroyed by the same people who gave it the name."* In the end, the "death of disco" could not be separated from a general backlash against the rising tide of gay visibility. This was the era of Anita Bryant's "Save Our Children" campaign, the era of the first major public reaction against the advances of gay rights, advances that were symbolized by the seeming mass acceptance of a gay music form. The "Disco Sucks" campaign was often frankly and openly homophobic — disco was faggot music. Even when such sentiments were less openly displayed, they were not far below the surface, masked in code words about frivolity and mindlessness and so on. The backlash didn't happen earlier, I suppose, because as long as disco occupied a niche, even a fairly big niche, it wasn't that much of a threat. But once it began to take over, it was. And the cultural forces that found that takeover frightening were huge and vocal and very powerful. The death of disco was engineered, and preordained.

The proof is contained in a rather interesting and often over-looked fact: The fact that disco never really died. The new style that took over was simply disco minus the overtly gay overtones. Bands like Blondie, the Human League, Men at Work, the Knack, Hall and Oates, indeed practically all the big groups of the early MTV years, were producing music that adhered tightly to the disco formula. The same steady beat, the same bpm, the same technological tricks, and the same commitment to make people dance. The biggest album of the early '80s — Michael Jackson's *Thriller*— was in every sense a disco album. The biggest new star to emerge in the '80s — Madonna — was in every sense a disco star. There were only two things that separated this new music from classic '70s disco. First, it wasn't called disco. It was called dance music, or new wave, or rock, or r&b — anything but disco. And second, it wasn't identified with urban gay men. It was mostly straight and mostly white and mostly middle class and suburban. But if you had taken an MTV dance hit from 1983 — David Bowie's "Let's Dance," for example, or Michael Jackson's "Billie Jean," or Michael Sembello's "Maniac"— and sent it back in a time machine to 1977 and played it at Flamingo, it would have fit right in.

People did not stop dancing, of course. This, to many people including me, is proof of the homophobic essence of Disco Sucks. Music did not become more varied, lyrics did not become less mindless. The beat went on. But "*dance music*," as it now came to be called, was no longer associated with gays. It was reclaimed by the same forces that had run things for decades. White, straight, mainstream, largely homophobic.

This is how it looks in retrospect. At the time, we did not realize that a revolution was taking place. After all, it was only a few months since *Rolling Stone* and *Newsweek* were proclaiming that disco was here to stay. Nobody, especially those of us riding the wave, could conceive that something as big as disco could fade from mass popularity so fast. As far as we were concerned, the Comiskey Park incident was a nasty homophobic blip, the change in radio formats a slight readjustment, the dip in disco's domination of Top Forty a momentary aberration. Clubs were still packed. Our bank accounts were still flush. Record companies, ours included, still churned out product. And of course there was no backlash whatsoever in the places that really counted, the gay clubs where disco had all begun. Gay men in big cities had paid little attention to the fact that our music had gained massive popularity out in the provinces, and we would pay little attention to the end of that popularity. For us, classic '70s disco did not die, it simply reverted back to us. I guess the best illustration of this is the fact that the glory days of the two greatest gay discos, the Paradise Garage and the Saint, lay ahead. But for those of us in the record business who concentrated on classic gay disco, the omens were bad. Our critical success may have been based on our popularity among disco cognoscenti, but our financial success was based on mass sales. Big hits with hardcore disco fans did not translate into real money until they became crossover hits and sold hundreds of thousands of records across the nation. Big hits paid for little critical successes, and without them we would be in deep trouble.

chapter twelve
A NEW
DECADE

I had high hopes for the '80s, since most people in the disco business were still convinced that our success in the '70s was just a taste of what was to come. But New Year's Eve 1980 was a mild premonition of what I would come to call the decade of hell. If nature was sending an omen, it could not have been more blunt. The whole Northeast was in the grip of a huge snowstorm, and bitter winds blew waves of snow through the canyons of Manhattan as Julio and I fought our way down to Flamingo in my brand new Buick Regal.

Flamingo's New Year's Eve party was epic, but we expected nothing less. Gay New York was at its peak at the dawn of 1980. All the wildness and abandon that had seemed refreshingly new and innocent a few years earlier had now grown into a huge, sophisticated lifestyle. We were awash in drugs, swimming in sex, and we were sure the party would go on forever. Across the city that night men crowded into discos and bars, cabarets and baths, celebrating, dancing, cruising, fucking. And Flamingo was the apex of the scene, the ultimate place to be.

Julio and I got dusted beyond belief that night, or at least beyond our usual state, which was probably already beyond belief to some people. As the party stretched into morning we decided to zoom over to the Garage in the Buick, but between the snow and the angel dust, a five-minute trip took over an hour. When we finally got to the Garage it was after 6 a.m. and they were no longer admitting. Of course this would never apply to me, but some new doorman did not know me and barred our way, and I was forced to do something I almost never do: throw my weight around. *"I own this place,"* I boasted, with apparently enough dust-inspired panache that he backed off and we flew past him. This wasn't a good sign either; it was like being barred admittance from a family gathering and having to lie to get in (I didn't own the Garage, I had loaned Michael money to help open it). There was even more madness once inside. Michael had hired Melba Moore to perform, and for her $7,000 fee she lip-synched. Michael threatened to sue. Welcome to the '80s.

From the start, the year lived up to its bad beginning. That month, I flew off to the international MIDEM convention in Cannes. Ed and I had been treated like royalty there the year before. But this time things did not go so well. We had not had any major hits in a while, the disco craze was over, and small disco labels were not exactly the toast of France. It was lonely to be stuck in a hotel room on my birthday, and I couldn't wait to get home.

Things were not exactly great on the home front either. It did not take long for the anti-disco backlash to have an effect on small labels like West End, and throughout the spring it seemed the bottom was dropping out. Disco was now a dirty word in the U.S. record industry, and since we were the famous disco label, you can just imagine the drop in business. Our bank account began to shrivel, and Ed began complaining about late-paying clients and how much time it took putting the squeeze on our distributors to keep the cash flow flowing. Not only was there no hit on the horizon, our horizon itself seemed to be slipping further and further away as disco produced fewer crossovers. It wasn't just us, either. Everybody who had bet on disco was beginning to feel the pinch. But a lot of the other labels were diversified, so as disco declined they simply pumped out more of the dance music, or rock, or new wave, whatever they had on hand. We couldn't do that. All we had was disco. That's all we knew.

I don't suppose that at this point it dawned on me that West End might eventually go down with the disco ship. I was used to success, and it just didn't seem conceivable that easy-come could just as easily-go. And of course I was high a lot of the time, during which business problems seemed a world away. I also still had plenty of money, so on my return from France on the Concorde I gave myself the birthday present of my dreams: a spectacular 50th-floor penthouse on 57th St., redone from top to bottom, mirrored, decorated, with the most spectacular views in New York. It cost a fortune to finish. Interior-designer Ed Ulrich called it the *"ultimate fuck pad,"* and I loved it. The apartment was my most visible sign of success so far, and there's no feeling like living inside your status symbol. Up there in the sky over New York, with the city glistening at my feet, I really was in heaven. I bought a telescope, and on clear days I could see the faces of airline passengers as they sat on the runway at LaGuardia.

But in a way, my extravagant new apartment was as much a denial of reality as a well-earned reward. At home in my rooftop nest I was king of the city stretched out below. But at work, I was desperate for the next big hit, and desperate that I wouldn't find it. And then, just when things were looking really bleak, it walked in the door.

Actually, Steve D'Aquisto walked in the door, the same Steve D'Aquisto I had known from the early record pool days. I always considered him a talent, but a bit of a flake, so I was not exactly chomping at the bit to work with him. But he brought along a producer named Arthur Russell, a protégé of the great John Hammond (who had first brought Billie Holiday into the recording studio and who discovered Bob Dylan and Barbra Streisand and many of the greatest talents of the past 50 years) and I was understandably impressed. Steve and Arthur wanted $15,000 to record an album, from which they promised a major hit. I knew Ed would hit the ceiling, but something convinced me they could deliver, so I dug into my own pocket and gave them the money secretly, praying that Ed wouldn't find out. It was not the first time I had done that, and it wouldn't be the last.

The first song Steve and Arthur delivered was called "Is It All Over My Face." The musicians on the record were the Ingram brothers, Patti LaBelle's extremely talented band, but they needed a new name for this project. Steve wanted to call them Loose Joints, and I told him he was nuts. Every two-bit dealer on every corner in New York was selling loose joints of marijuana, and I thought the idea was crazy. But Steve was persistent. I remember him chasing me down Broadway one day insisting that Loose Joints was a perfect name for the group, while the dealers whispered "*loose joints*" at every intersection. We'd have this free promotion I figured, if the record became a hit, so I finally gave in.

We released "Is It All Over My Face" with the male vocal on one side, and "Pop Your Funk" on the b-side, and the record bombed. Larry agreed to remix the record for free while he was in the studio working on other projects. I was afraid he'd do his usual, spending endless hours fiddling away while West End burned. But it was as if Larry sensed the urgency, because this time he went into the studio and came out in two hours with a final mix, this time using the female vocal he found on the original track. Later I found out Larry did not officially have studio time, and when the owner showed up two hours into the session, Larry had to pack up and leave. Again, nothing happens by accident. It may have been his briefest effort ever, but believe it or not, it was one of his best. We released the record with the new female vocal on one side, and the original male vocal on the b-side. The crowd at the Garage went crazy, Frankie Crocker heard it there on Saturday night, and by Monday he was playing it constantly on WBLS. Sales took off like a rocket, and Boom! We had a hit in

New York. There's no question that Loose Joints saved our collective ass in 1980, and I could finally relax a bit. But I had learned a frightening lesson. Ed and I and West End had fallen into deep financial trouble after just a short time without a hit. It was clear that no matter how well respected and seemingly successful our small record company was to outsiders, it existed on a very short shoestring. It didn't help when our L.A. distributor, Record Merchandisers, owned by Sid Talmage, a good friend of Ed's, stuck us for $48,000 when he went belly up, and then stuck us again for another $11,000. The hits would have to keep coming, or else.

If things were tense at work, they were stormy at home. My relationship with Julio continued on its zigzag course, with more fights, more break-ups, more angel dust, and in general more craziness. But by now something had been added as well, or rather someone.

carmen and gigi

Julio had a sister in Puerto Rico, and he and she were so close both physically and psychologically that they reminded me of Siamese twins. Carmen was widowed at a young age, and was left with two daughters, Lisa, a little girl, and baby daughter Gigi. Not long after Carmen was widowed Lisa died as well, and Julio was distraught that his sister was left alone with a baby girl and very little means of support. I met them on a trip to Puerto Rico and I instantly fell in love with Gigi, who was less than two at the time. But I worried about her terribly. Her mother Carmen was as erratic as Julio, and like him she had a serious substance abuse problem, except that in her case it wasn't angel dust, just good old-fashioned booze. I don't think I ever saw her without a drink in her hand, and their living conditions in that high-rise tenement were terrible. I was afraid that if Gigi grew up under those influences, her prospects would be bleak indeed — early pregnancy probably and a life of drudgery.

When Lisa died Julio reached out to try to take care of Carmen and Gigi. But he needed my help for that, and I stood by him. We brought them to New York and moved them into the downstairs apartment in my building on Warren St. in Brooklyn, where I charged a token rent. And I soon became deeply involved with little Gigi's welfare and began to think of her as my own niece, if not my daughter.

My intentions were undoubtedly good, but I now realize that I was a perfect co-dependent as far as Carmen was concerned. Her alcoholism did not improve in New York. She was drunk much of the time, and was unable and unwilling to look for any meaningful work. Now that she had Julio and me to help support her, she was perfectly willing to let things slide, realizing that my growing love for Gigi was her own safety net. Carmen was fiercely loyal to Julio, and with her fiery temper and spit-fire attitude she often took his side when we had our epic fights. But she was smart enough to know which side her bread was buttered on too, and she would be careful to smooth things over between Julio and me as quickly as possible. My growing closeness with Gigi and my entanglement with Carmen enmeshed me more tightly than ever with Julio. We now had a family to take care of, including a helpless little girl I adored. It may have been dysfunctional, but this didn't make it any less of a family. Since Julio and I broke up on a fairly regular basis, I was forever promising Carmen that no matter what happened between Julio and me, it would not change my relationship with her and Gigi. But in a sense, my relationship with Gigi probably helped to guarantee that Julio and I would not break up for a very long time.

Despite the craziness, there were rewards as well, and in the end they far out-balanced the problems. I remember one time in the spring of 1980 Julio and I fought so bitterly that he packed his bags and left town just as Carmen was about to go into the hospital for a hernia operation. I was incredibly angry that he left Carmen during what would be a frightening experience, and I was also pissed that I was left with the responsibility of getting her settled in the hospital. But after I checked her in, I took Gigi, now four, off to see her first Easter Parade and to the zoo. Sitting in the zoo that beautiful afternoon, Gigi turned to me and said something I'll never forget. *"I love you,"* she said. *"Do you know the meaning of the word love?"* I asked. *"Yes,"* she said, her eyes brimming with four-year-old innocence. *"That's when one person cares for another person."* Although I have loved and been loved in return, no one has ever loved me as unconditionally as that little girl. Today, many years later, long after my relationship with Julio ended, I am helping her through college, she often stays with me on vacations and has gone with me to Europe, I speak to her constantly at school, and consider her my own flesh and blood. She has become a lady — beautiful, articulate, poised, educated. For that alone, the occasional pain of my relationship with Julio was well worth while.

fire island

If my life with Julio in the city veered between sweet domesticity and wild arguments and drug binges, life that summer on Fire Island was over the top. No one out on the island had so much as heard about the supposed death of disco. In fact, it was the opposite: disco culture was at its very peak. People lived and breathed the latest song, argued passionately about the best DJs and clubs, built entire lives around clubbing and dressing and drugging and fucking. For me it was a total escape from the oppressive reality sweeping the music industry. Here, on this island apart, I was still in my glory days, still the very important record executive of a very important company, still at the center of my world.

And what a world. The innocent little Fire Island community I had known in the early '60s — the little beach shacks, the everybody knows everybody camaraderie — had been swept up in a tidal wave as thousands of gorgeous men poured in from all over the world, eager to participate in the myth of Fire Island Pines. You'd walk down to the beach and look out at miles of sand dunes and perfect flesh, living for nothing but pleasure. Fire Island in 1980 was Heaven.

Of course, having so much fun took a lot of work and a very demanding schedule. We slept until early afternoon, were on the beach till six, off to the Blue Whale for tea dance, back home at eight, dinner around nine or ten, then a disco nap or sex for a few hours (depending on what had happened at tea and dinner) and then by two or three it was time to go to the disco and party hearty until the sun was high in the sky. Then sleep in the late morning and early afternoon. Then the same thing all over again. It was exhausting. Friends from out of town were incredulous that we went out dancing at two or three in the morning and stayed out almost until noon. Sometimes they'd ask why we didn't simply go out in the evening, like normal people. And we'd have to tell them that they were free to go out at 10 or 11 if they wanted, but only if they didn't mind being the only people in the disco.

The big clubs that season were the Sandpiper in the Pines and the Ice Palace in Cherry Grove. Throughout the '70s developers had built huge, million-dollar houses in the Pines that made the little cottages in the Grove look seedy and pathetic. But the Ice Palace was still a very hot spot, and on weekend nights hundreds of fashionable Pines boys would float over to the Grove in water taxis, snorting poppers all the way. After hours of dancing they would stumble back to the Pines through the little stretch of forested sand dunes that separated the two communities, and it was time for sex.

That little forest was called the Meat Rack, and for good reason. Half-naked and even completely naked hunks were under every bush, behind every tree, stoned, tripping, ready for twosomes, threesomes or tensomes, whatever wandered by. It was like an open-air bathhouse, impossible to resist. But who was resisting? Certainly not me. And certainly not anybody I knew. People were having sex everywhere — on the boardwalks, on the beach, on somebody else's front lawn. Some of us just went with the flow, while others developed their own specific cruising techniques. My housemate Dick Fisher, for example, would go out jogging on the boardwalks in a skimpy, revealing little pair of shorts, and inevitably returned with some number who had crossed his path. He was nonchalant about his conquests. He'd make them wait while he made himself a sandwich. Then, sandwich and trick in hand, he would retire to the bedroom, where he would discover some other trick he had forgotten about, who was already there waiting for him. An embarrassment of riches in every sense.

In many ways we felt the world was changing in our favor. That was the summer of the Paco Rabanne cologne ad that showed a muscular stud, naked from the waist up, talking on the phone to someone he had slept with the night before. The ad copy was written in such an ambiguous way that everybody was sure the guy was talking to another guy. Although such an ad would seem unremarkable today, it was electrifying back then. We were still so underground that the idea that a major ad agency would pitch a product to a gay audience was the talk of the island.

All that was the good news. But there were omens as well. People were getting sick. So much sex with so many partners was having a fairly predictable effect, and sexually transmitted diseases were spreading like wildfire. This had been going on for several years, for most of the '70s in fact, but now it seemed to be getting worse. There was syphilis, gonorrhea, tons of intestinal parasites that were hard to get rid of, all sorts of other infections as well. A lot of people were particularly worried that hepatitis-b could actually kill in certain cases. It seemed like more and more conversations centered around the drugs people were taking to get rid of whatever they had, and people sat around swapping what amounted to war stories about infections and drugs and the latest clap doctor who could prescribe antibiotics that you could take before you got sick, to ward off whatever might be out there. The worst thing that could happen was you got the clap, which we called an *"occupational hazard,"* but a shot or two of penicillin and you were back in business.

Most of us were not particularly worried at the time. In fact, our biggest complaint was that something nasty usually meant that you were not supposed to have sex until it cleared up, which might be several weeks. When you were used to having sex with somebody new almost every day, or even several times a day, it was tough to be told that you had to take a few weeks off.

But although most infections were not that serious, I was very worried about two Fire Island friends who seemed to be getting sicker and sicker with some strange, unexplainable illness. Nick Rock and Rick Wellikoff were in and out of the hospital all summer, and no one could figure out what they had. Of course there was no reason to think it was sexually transmitted, no reason to think that it had anything to do with the way we were living, no reason to think that the two men's illnesses even had anything to do with each other. But whatever they had, it was turning them into shadows of their former selves. To this day I can remember that strange sense of foreboding I got when friends would inform me of their worsening condition. I didn't take the hepatitis vaccine that was being pushed on the gay community, because I'd had hepatitis already in 1976, but a lot of my friends did. I later came firmly to believe that the hepatitis vaccine was contaminated with the AIDS virus from blood we were buying from Haiti and Zaire.

saved by a heartbeat

Illness aside, it was still a fabulous summer for most of us. But despite the fun I was having, my troubles at West End were never far away. I had to return to the city often to deal with business, and business was far from great. Loose Joints may have saved us from disaster, but the ground was still very shaky, and Ed was now constantly breathing down my neck about cash flow and expenses and all those boring details I hated to be bothered with but now could not avoid. One hit song was hardly going to be enough to keep us going. The hits had to keep coming, and it was my job to find them. Just as I had a few months before, I now began to pray for another miracle.

One night, as we were leaving the office, the miracle appeared. Producer Kenny Nix, who had given us "Work That Body," one of our biggest hits, showed up with a rough track of a new song, a slow, sensual tribal groove layered over the thump of a heartbeat. I was mesmerized. It was like no other disco song I had ever heard — slower, dreamier, more alluring than anything on the market. We listened to it for hours that night, and my enthusiasm only grew. We decided that Taana Gardner would sing lead and Larry would do the mix, and Ed was so swept up by my enthusiasm that he agreed to clear the decks and release the song the instant it was ready.

Kenny and I agree that if it weren't for Larry's persistence in playing "Heartbeat" until his audience finally got it, nothing would have happened with it. And this took weeks. At first, they would leave the floor. This is an example of what made Larry the innovator that he was. DJs in most clubs are afraid to take risks. But Larry was the Garage.

There are certain moments in life that you cherish forever, moments that transcend the daily drudge of existence, when everything is sharp and clear and you feel utterly alive. For me, one of those moments was walking down the street in New York on a hot summer night when "Heartbeat" was being played on WBLS, pouring from every open window it seemed, every passing car, every jukebox, the world moving in rhythm to my song. "Heartbeat" caused a sensation. The pounding heart and the unusually slow tempo instantly made it one of the biggest dance hooks of all time, a classic today as when it was released. I was in heaven, saved by a heartbeat. Of course "Heartbeat" wasn't *my* song. It was Kenny's song, sung by Taana, mixed by Larry, performed by musicians I barely knew. But I had been the one that recognized it, signed it, paid for it, and carried it through. I had been the connecting link, the guy who put all the pieces together, and it was because of me that it was now out there, floating on the summer breeze all through New York, beating over the air all over the country. The high I got from that was something you could never experience on drugs. I had felt this feeling once before with "Hot Shot," and now here it was again. These were West End's biggest hits, and if you listen to them today, you can feel the excitement of those times built right into the groove.

I was peaking again a few weeks later when I took Taana to a promotional event in the Bronx and Grandmaster Flash, the father of rap, cornered me and begged for a copy of the "Heartbeat" mix. I was so flattered I would have sent him a crate. It was in this conversation that he told me about the rappers uptown rapping over our first West End release, "Sessamato," over Jimmy Stuard's reverse-tape scratch part. Grandmaster was lavishly praising "Sessamato" as the very first scratch record that rappers used before the Sugar Hill Gang made the first rap record. I floated out of the Bronx on a cloud. It seemed that despite the nationwide drop off in disco sales, things weren't so bad after all. We could still produce hits, we could still make money, we were still having an influence. Maybe everything would work out fine. After all, we were not just making disco records, we were making radio records that had a dance groove as well.

the saint

Because I was working so hard promoting "Heartbeat," I now had to spend a lot of time in the city, and one day I ran into old friend Peter Spar. Peter and Barry Lederer owned Graybar Productions, a company that installed sound systems in big discos like 12 West, and Trocadero in San Francisco. He told me he was now installing a new system in what was sure to become the ultimate gay club, and offered to take me on a walk through. That's how I first laid eyes on the club that would define our generation.

The old Fillmore East theater in the East Village had already had several lives. In the late '60s it was promoter Bill Graham's rock palace in New York, the East coast home of groups like Jefferson Airplane, Grateful Dead and the Doors. But Graham had closed it a few years before now, and it sat empty until Bruce Mailman, the owner of the St. Mark's Baths around the corner, put together a group of investors and decided to transform the Fillmore into a gay disco. Mailman hired the acclaimed architect Charles Terrel to do the renovation, and the day I saw the Saint, as he called the club, it was still under construction and looked anything but saintly. But I could immediately see that this club was going to take things as far as they could go.

Up in the air, high above the mezzanine, were the makings of a huge planetarium dome, and Peter Spar told me that Mailman was planning to create an actual working planetarium up there, under which he would build a dance floor suspended on springs. The whole construction site was vast, and it looked to me that it could easily hold several thousand people. Every other club would pale before this, including the Flamingo. The boys are going to go insane, I thought. When I returned in September to take a pre-opening tour given by one of the investors, it was obvious that Bruce Mailman indeed had the money. The place had been completely transformed, and it was unbelievable.

Even before it opened, word spread like wildfire, and Bruce began selling memberships at $250 each. To get one, you had to make an appointment and appear in person, so that the less-than-fabulous could be weeded out. I suppose it's a testimony to how big and how fabulous the gay A-list had become by 1980 that all 3000 memberships were sold out in a couple of weeks, and those who didn't make the cut were put on a waiting list and told that they might be squeezed in sometime in 1982, two years later. As a music business bigwig, I was given a free industry membership, but most of my friends sweated it out, waiting to see if they had been approved.

Opening night, September 20th, was one of the great events in the history of gay nightlife. Second Ave. was a sea of stretch limos, and the endless line on the sidewalk seemed to contain everybody who was anybody — Calvin Klein, Paul Jabara, Egon Von Furstenberg, the whole shebang. My friends Jerry Rosanbalm, Noel Garcia and Rick Snood — three of the handsomest men in New York — were pouring cocktails from Jerry's limo, which was idling at the curb. When it was time to enter, Jerry gathered everybody's coats and stashed them in the limo. People smiled at this display of disco elegance — Jerry with his own private bar and coat check in the form of a stretch limo right outside the door.

There were some people, however, who were missing that night. Namely women. In response to a member's request that he be allowed to bring Bette Midler as his guest, Mailman had issued his decree: *"Just so we can make sure that people understand, this is the line we will draw — No Women Members."* With someone as prominent as Bette Midler on the other side of that imaginary line, the message was received: this was a boy's place, and that was that.

When Mailman opened the doors at 11:30 and the boys poured in, you could actually hear the gasps of astonishment above the pounding music. The invitation had depicted the floor plan of Rome's Pantheon, and everyone assumed that this was a gross exaggeration, but it wasn't. The main lounge took up the entire space that had once held the orchestra section of the theater, and it held huge banquettes, one of which wrapped around a hydraulic system that supported the incredible tree of lights and projectors and planetarium equipment that shot up onto the dance space suspended above. The great stage of the Fillmore was now was a vast bar, and everywhere were ramps that led up, past the elaborate architectural embellishments of the old theater, to the main event: the greatest disco dance floor ever built.

The dance floor was circular and huge, and above it rose the planetarium dome, diaphanous and semi-transparent, high overhead. When lights were projected onto it the effect was unlike anything you ever saw. Up there you were in a completely other world, a world without angles and walls and restrictions, a circular world where you could whirl like a drugged dervish and swim in sound and light and beauty. Bruce had spent just as lavishly on the sound system, of course, and it shot out at you from above, below and from every side.

But things did not end there. From the grand balcony you would gaze at the constellations of stars on the immense planetarium, the dance floor pulsing below. From this vantage point the Saint reminded people of the extraterrestrial mothership from *Close Encounters of the Third Kind.* It was wonder dome filled with light and atmosphere, bursting with color and music. Most of the men on the balcony were not really there for the view, however. Bruce Mailman, also owner of the St. Mark's Baths, had decided to create a space to have sex right there in the disco, and this was it. The balcony was essentially a big orgy room, and for most guests a trip up to the balcony became almost obligatory. On a typical night you might spend a couple of hours dancing, and then, high as a kite, you'd zip up to the balcony for a quickie. Virtually everybody up there was looking for sex, and most were finding it. Then, after trysting up there in heaven, and smoking a dusted joint or snorting some coke, you'd come back down to the dance floor for another round. The balcony changed everything about the disco experience, and, in my opinion, not for the better. The definition of a good night out ceased being whether you had danced yourself into delirium, but whether you had scored. I am a romantic, and sex out in full view does not rhyme with dance and romance. For me, Bruce Mailman cheapened the whole disco experience by marketing it as a sex space with the ultimate back room. The great discos never had them. Just from the point of view of the disco esthetic, he should have left things that way. The dungeons in the Anvil and the Crisco Disco were nothing next to Mailman's bringing sex upstairs to the balcony. But no one complained. In the fall of 1980 nobody we knew was getting sick yet. However, the worst medical disaster was about to hit our community.

The appearance of the Saint illustrates the strange dichotomy that was now taking place between the music industry and gay men. Disco was rapidly dying as a national force in music, and yet in the gay world, this was the peak of disco, the era that we, the survivors, look back upon as the apex of the golden age. For many gay men today, the Saint and the Garage literally define the glory days of disco, even though historians of pop music would argue that by now, disco was as dead as a duck, at least to the polyester mentality.

What makes the death of disco even more peculiar is that straight urban people were also still going out to dance to the disco beat, and major discos were still opening that catered to that crowd as well. There was Danceteria, Bond's, Xenon, and the Red Parrot, but the most famous, and famously tacky, was the Funhouse on the west side of Manhattan. The Funhouse was the ultimate Italian Mafia horror — a 10,000 square-foot former printing shop that was now mirrored pillars, garlands of Christmas lights, a DJ booth inside a giant clown's head, cigarette girls, hot dog stands, carnival games. It was like the San Gennaro street festival on acid. And yet it was hugely popular, attracting the outer boroughs who were still in love with the *Saturday Night Fever* look: big hair, gold chains, the works. The club's most famous DJ was John "Jellybean" Benitez, who would have a major hand helping launch the career of still young, unknown Madonna, who would keep the disco flame alive throughout the '80s.

trouble in paradise

If the Saint and the Garage were two extraordinary poles to New York's dance club experience, the Saint with its sex balcony represented the pinnacle of gay white disco culture, while the Garage continued to epitomize the gay black and Hispanic sensibility. By now the Garage was well established, and there was no longer any question that it might fail. Although Michael had not succeeded in luring back the white A-list crowd, an objective now virtually impossible by the popularity of the Saint, he and Larry certainly succeeded in establishing the Garage as the ultimate tribal dance space, and it began to assume legendary status. As did Larry. People began flying in from all over the country to find out what all the talk was about, and a single visit was usually enough to send them back to wherever they came from, raving about the genius behind the turntables at the Garage. A significant group of whites more into the music than the cruising became a part of the scene as well. Every night at the Garage was a special night for me, but because so many people from the record industry were always there, I could not let myself go completely at the Garage as I did at the Saint. Still, the kind of mystical, harmonious adventure that might happen once in a blue moon at any other club was a regular Garage occurrence.

Michael went through several managers, constantly trying to find somebody who could lure the white crowd back, and several of these managers, and their agendas, clashed with La Diva Levan. There was Dennis Tomasetti, the somewhat shady character from Michael's days at Paramount, the one who had introduced him to the sleazy underside of Times Square. Dennis wasn't just sleazy, he was lazy, and his lackadaisical work habits did not endear him to Michael once Michael became his boss. Dennis was also a bit of a Mafia-type wise guy from the Bronx who had a predilection for doing things like carrying guns. Things quickly soured between Dennis and Michael. I never found out what exactly happened between them to precipitate the split, but I do know that Michael's life was threatened. Exit Dennis, and enter Larry Matarese.

Part of Larry Matarese's job was to lure the white boys back, and needless to say this did not endear him to Larry Levan. Matarese threw parties designed to appeal to the Saint crowd, and even dared to try to bring in the occasional outside DJ to spin. There were constant explosions with Larry, and exit Matarese as well. He was followed by Emilio Rubio. Emilio was a friend of Jaime's from the pre-Garage days, and he was always a gentleman with me, but he was no better from Larry's point of view, and word began to spread among insiders that Larry was seriously thinking of leaving. Larry obviously wanted Michael to believe he was serious, since he was convinced that he was utterly irreplaceable. But Michael was no dummy. Especially after the notorious biting incident, Michael realized that Larry was too erratic a foundation upon which to base his entire fortune. So as rumors spread that Larry was thinking of leaving, Michael countered by interviewing potential replacements. So it was behind the scenes at Paradise. The crowd dancing in ecstasy on a Saturday night might think they were in perfect heaven, but behind the clouds, a storm was always brewing.

jaime de la cruz

It was during this period that Michael cemented his relationship with the one person who was to have as much influence on him as I had once had, except that where my influence had been (I hope) beneficial, this new influence was to be the most deeply corrosive in Michael's life. Michael and I had once bedded the young Jaime de la Cruz on a trip to Puerto Rico, and I had a brief affair of my own with Jaime as my relationship with Michael was coming apart. Jaime was extremely handsome, blond and blue eyed. Years later, I found out that Jaime had had a crush on me, but while I certainly considered him attractive, I was in the throes of my breakup with Michael and wasn't interested. I don't think I actually rejected him, but I'm sure I didn't reciprocate his affections. He would harbor a grudge for years.

At some point after Michael and I broke up, Michael ran into Jaime again in Puerto Rico, and the two struck up a romance. Michael had already been through a couple of lovers, but now he found someone who was to be his soul mate, and his nemesis, for the rest of his life. I never could understand what Michael saw in Jaime. Some say that Jaime looked a lot like me, and that explained the attraction. I never bought that, partly because I never saw the resemblance. But their long distance love affair grew more serious, and eventually Jaime moved to New York. By now, in 1980, he was omnipresent at the Garage. Although he held no official title, he was powerful simply because he was the boyfriend of the boss, and he took advantage of that to insinuate himself into every aspect of the club, and every aspect of Michael's life, including Michael's relationship with me. Jaime's influence was so noxious, so meddling and manipulative that even if Michael and I had been on the best of terms, things would have gone downhill once Jaime entered the picture.

grace jones

If there is anyone who, for me, epitomized the untamable, anything-goes atmosphere of these last disco days before AIDS, it was Grace Jones. Born in Jamaica, raised in Syracuse, Grace had a startling, animal intensity, geometric features and a genuine star appeal and charisma that landed her top Paris modeling jobs long before her emergence as a disco diva. Nobody could ignore that striking chiseled face when it growled out at you from the covers of *Vogue* and *Elle*, but Grace had bigger dreams than success as a model. When disco hit Paris she immediately saw her chance. Although not really a singer, at least not at first, she somehow convinced people to take a chance. Her first single, "That's the Trouble," quickly climbed the charts in the U.S. and became a smash. And Grace just as quickly became an icon for gay men.

When she brought her animalistic and bizarre stage act to Studio 54 in 1978, the wild acclaim cemented her place as a true disco diva.

Tom Moulton mixed several of her records — including "I Need a Man" and "La Vie En Rose"— and was struck by the intensity of her drive. One time, early in her career, he asked her about her direction. *"I want to be a star, darling,"* she growled, which was honest enough. But she wanted stardom on her own terms, in a way that constantly raised eyebrows. People were shocked when she physically attacked London TV host Russell Harty on the air after taking offense to a question. They were shocked again when she posed nude in *Hustler,* entangled with another woman over the banner *"I have a lot of man in me."* They were shocked when she was simply being Grace. I vividly remember a time when Tom and I took her to a late-night supper at the Brasserie in New York. Even though it was 2 a.m. and the other diners were clearly night owls themselves, you could feel the ripples of amazement spreading across the restaurant as she wound her way between the tables, a panther on the prowl in nighttime New York. I adored her, but then, so did most gay men. It's hard to put your finger on exactly why. Perhaps because she, like we, defied convention at every turn. Perhaps because she rose above her roots. Because she turned the tables on society, using its own techniques and methods to transform herself into a star. Whatever the reason, when someone asks me what or who best epitomizes those wild, wacky, sexy, wonderful days, I usually think of those animal eyes, that growl, and say, if you want to know what it was like, look at Grace.

distant thunder

As is usual with gay men, things were moving in two directions at once in the waning days of 1980. Among the good news was the fact that New York's top court finally abolished the state's archaic sodomy laws; the weekly *New York Native* began publishing, giving the city a reputable (at first) source of gay news. Liberation finally seemed to be producing some tangible success. Among the bad was the fact that a study was released showing that people were being assaulted every day in America for being gay. We got a fatal reminder of that when a deranged, homophobic former transit cop drove down to the end of Christopher Street one night with a machine gun and opened fire on the crowd in front of the Ramrod, a popular gay bar. Two were killed and six were wounded in the attack, which the perpetrator later said was a result of direct orders from God. He was ultimately declared not guilty by reason of insanity.

A study by the University of Georgia had shown that violent homophobic acts are often the expression of suppressed homosexual feelings, but in retrospect, all these assaults would pale before what was going on within the bodies and blood streams of gay men themselves. Little did we know, as we danced in the discos and cruised the bars and fucked in the baths, that we were no longer safe, even in the safest of spaces. The silent invader that had entered our world several years before was about to announce itself and, in the process, blow everything away.

Throughout that summer and fall, my Fire Island friends Nick Rock and Rick Wellikoff continued to suffer one strange infection after another. They were not alone. Across the city, doctors treating gay men were puzzled by the sudden appearance of Kaposi's sarcoma, as well as an unusual type of pneumonia and several other chronic infections that were normally kept in check by the body's immune system. Nick and Rick were both suffering from several of these conditions, which totally baffled their doctors. For a while, doctors thought that Nick had been infected by his cat. My close friend Larry McDevitt was extremely worried about Rick, and I was shocked that December when Larry told me that Rick's doctors now said there was nothing they could do, that his condition was fatal, that it would worsen until the unexplained pneumonia filled his lungs and choked him to death.

On hearing his terminal diagnosis, Rick decided to check out of the hospital and go home to die. He smoked some pot and snorted the rest of his cocaine stash. He told Larry that coke was the only thing left that gave him any energy. Finally, two days before Christmas, as the country was reeling from the murder of John Lennon, Rick died. I could barely believe it, and my shock was compounded when, at a New Year's Eve party, a friend told me that Nick had just died too.

chapter thirteen
CHANGING
OF THE GUARD

All that winter into 1981 as the Saint rose, the Flamingo, its predecessor, fell. It was odd to think that a disco that had been the most exciting place in our world, the club that defined our generation, was now passé. But there it was. We had come such a long way from those early days at the Loft and the 10th Floor and the Firehouse, from the innocence of thinking that any little space, no matter how humble, could be home. Back then we had been satisfied with a decent sound system, a few spinning lights, a friend behind the DJ booth. As long as it was gay, and ours, we were happy. Then, as larger places opened, we taught ourselves to appreciate the finer points and were satisfied only with great sound, a big floor, a great DJ, a major scene. Flamingo had come along and set the standard of perfection and spoiled us rotten. And now the Saint was the ultimate stage in that evolution. You couldn't really get any bigger or better than the Saint. It was housed in one of the greatest architectural public spaces in the city, and was decorated, designed, lit and amplified to within an inch of our lives. Everything about the Saint was entirely state of the art. Where could you go from there?

The answer was away from Flamingo, which now seemed quaint in its old loft space. And so, although we still loved it, although all our memories were fond, we drifted away. In retrospect Flamingo almost surely had to close, but it didn't have to close as fast as it did. Unfortunately, just at the critical moment, owner Michael Fesco had lost his great DJs Roy Thode and Howard Merritt, and in their place he hired Wayne Scott. Like his crowd, myself included, Wayne liked playing on dust. I suppose smoking angel dust and spinning records do not mix. Sometimes the needle dropped on the record, slobbering all over the sound. *"His mixes made no sense at all to anyone, and were like listening to a lecture in Arabic,"* said Jerry Rosanbalm. Even those who had a strong nostalgic loyalty to the old place began wandering to the Saint, just a few blocks away.

As the crowd drifted away in the winter of '81, Michael Fesco announced that he was closing the club. Howard Merritt returned for the closing party, and played for 16 hours straight wearing nothing but a jockstrap amid the steam and the sweat and the poppers. Even the records were soaking. He had to towel off each one before he could play it, he remarked after. It was that kind of night. There was nostalgia in the air, but also hope. The end of Flamingo signaled a kind of new beginning. It had to die for the Saint to live.

I was thrilled at having not one but two fantastic clubs to preview West End material: the Paradise Garage and now the Saint. But my happiness was tempered by the fact that I had less and less material to preview. West End was still doing okay — on paper anyway — thanks to the success of "Heartbeat" and another Kenny Nix production, "Rap Your Heart Out" by Sweet G. But to keep going we needed solid crossover hits, and instead we now had a string of flops. Larry Levan teamed up with François Kevorkian to do a club mix for our next release, "Let's Go Dancin'" by Sparque, and the crowd at the Garage loved it, but it went nowhere outside New York City. Kenny Nix produced our next three releases, and despite his previous golden touch, they too went nowhere. I kept slipping Kenny money from my personal account to keep things going, but it was no use. Nothing connected.

Larry decided to remix the last of the three Kenny Nix songs, "Serious, Sirius Space Party" sung by Ednah Holt. But Larry was sinking deeper and deeper into a drug-induced mental haze, and each time he finished a mix he would decide that something was wrong he'd have to go back into the studio and fix. He was never satisfied, and insisted that we not release it until he was. This went on for months. We waited, the bills piled up, Ed was furious, but every time a new version arrived from the recording studio, Larry found some fault with it and insisted on going back and redoing it. By the time he decided he was finally finished it was too late. But also too early: his sci-fi mix of "Serious, Sirius Space Party" was too far ahead of its time. It hardly sold a copy.

garage on a budget

During this period the output of decent disco was rapidly declining. The record companies were moving on to other things, and many of the big labels that still produced disco were making the same mistake they always had: putting out inferior disco garbage. As a response, many of the top DJs began to create their own unique signature mixes from the available product. They would make these mixes at home, generally using synthesizers and drum machines, rather than more expensive live musicians, and they would play their mixes only in their own club, their own house. These mixes kept the hardcore discos going, and kept the fans coming back.

Necessity was mothering the invention of house music, and no one in New York was more adept at mixing for a dance floor than Larry Levan. Since many of his mixes were then placed on special tapes and distributed to fans by word of mouth, Larry's reputation began to spread beyond the Garage, and beyond New York. As his reputation grew, so did his ego, his flamboyance. The more attention he received, the more Diva he became, and the less concerned he was with the mundane matters of business and punctuality and boring things like that, and the more prone he was to unscrupulous people eager to exploit his talent.

One such person was Michael DeBenedictus who worked with him on "Serious, Sirius Space Party." Drawn to the Garage by Larry's reputation, DeBenedictus quickly ingratiated himself with Larry and they soon became inseparable. DeBenedictus seemed laid back and easygoing on the surface, but when it came to money business and control, he was unreasonable, and he saw Larry's disinterest in business as a golden opportunity. Since Larry wanted to produce his own records, Michael convinced him they join forces, and the two formed the Peech Boys, with Michael on keyboards and Larry sharing the producer's chair with Brodie Williams. I wasn't crazy about Michael DeBenedictus. Deeply suspicious was more like it. But I was crazy about their first collaboration, "Don't Make Me Wait," a great tune with a deeply infectious hook. I was sure it had the potential to become our next big hit, and I convinced Ed that we had to sign the Peech Boys to West End. We did, and it was déjà-vu all over again.

"Don't Make Me Wait" turned out to be prophetic, since once again Larry just could not settle on a final mix. He and Michael DeBenedictus would spend endless hours and endless dollars in the studio and emerge with a great mix, test it at the Garage to great acclaim, and then announce that it needed more work and refuse to let us release it. DeBenedictus was just as bad as Larry, so I got no help from that quarter. And so the same process repeated itself. Fans craved the song that they heard at the Garage, but found it was unavailable. This went on for nine months. Finally, when the initial excitement was over and the song became yesterday's news, Larry announced that the mix was finished and we could release it. But the fans had moved on to other things. Although "Don't Make Me Wait" had some success, it did not come close to its hit potential. It could have been, it should have been, as big as "Heartbeat." It could have saved us. But it was squandered by drugs, procrastination, backstage politics, ego. Instead of making us a fortune, it cost us one.

Still, Larry's innovative talent would shine through even that fiasco. During the endless remix process he asked me if he could break part of the song down to just the vocals. I thought he was crazy, since the whole point of disco is the beat, and I couldn't imagine what might happen if the beat suddenly dropped out of a song and people were left with unaccompanied vocals. It only took me a couple of moments to agree, because of my faith in him, and the result was electrifying. Esthetically, "Don't Make Me Wait" is a masterpiece. Within a month of its release, the a cappella break was being imitated everywhere by practically everybody. Larry had blazed the way for another industry standard that persists to this day. It's just too bad that he did so on a song that he waited so long to release.

I was deeply disappointed that Larry's procrastination cost us a potential hit, but I was also concerned for him. His lack of focus on his own financial welfare meant that he never saved any of the money he earned, sometimes thousands of dollars a week. This was an old story with innovators in the music business, especially African Americans. The history of pop is littered with black geniuses making fortunes for white exploiters but ending up in poverty themselves, often even while their music continues to rake in millions.

By this time I began to feel like Larry's father — Larry would introduce me as his adopted father — so I guess it was in keeping with that impulse that I decided to try to provide him with some financial security. I drew up an agreement under which he would become official producer and consultant for West End and earn a percentage of every record that he worked on in any capacity. I also set up a money market account for him, and established that upon my death he would inherit half of my interest in West End. I didn't need to do any of this, and he certainly never would have asked for it. We were already paying him for his work, and paying him quite well. But Larry was as careless with money as with everything else, and I was sure that as fast as the money came in it would go out — on drugs, on clothes, on his friends, on nothing. By now a large entourage surrounded him, and he spent like a drunken sailor. When he was working in the studio, for example, he would constantly order take-out, but not just any take-out. It had to come from Sylvia's up in Harlem, the most famous soul food restaurant in New York. He'd order a ton of food, and then when it arrived he wouldn't be hungry and wouldn't eat. On plenty of occasions he would invite his entire entourage over to his place for the after-party, stopping by Balducci's — one of the most expensive specialty gourmet shops in the city — to buy dozens of lamb chops to cook for the whole group. They'd get to his place and do a ton of drugs — usually on him — and later he'd kick everybody out. This was someone out of control, and I was afraid that if no one figured out a way to provide him with some long-term security, he'd end up someday broke and alone.

Larry seemed thrilled with the agreement and readily signed it. Then he showed it to Michael DeBenedictus, who showed it to his lawyer Michael Turock. And just as I was congratulating myself for being such a mensch, I got a call from Turock informing me that the provisions were *"inadequate,"* and that Larry deserved, and insisted on, much more. I could not understand it. This was an offering on my part, gratis, unasked for. It was like giving someone a gift and having them declare that although they didn't expect it, it simply wasn't good enough. But while I never got a decent explanation for how Larry could slap me in the face for my gesture, I did find out that at the same time he was engaged in a strange tug of war with Michael Brody. Apparently, when Larry told Michael that he was going to do occasional work for West End, Michael hit the ceiling. Michael was still angry with me, and now he decided that I was trying to horn in on the good thing he had with Larry. He took it out on Larry, and Larry, I guess, took it out on me.

I received a similar slap from Michael too, however. One that was less forgivable because Michael was far more centered and rational than Larry was. On an overseas trip, awed by the beauty of Paris, the city of lights, I decided to offer Michael and Jaime airline tickets so that they could escape some of the pressure and enjoy Paris themselves. Michael thanked me rather coldly, then asked if I could just give him the cash instead. I told him the purpose of the gift was for him to experience the beauty of Paris, and since I did not give him the cash, he never forgave me.

As the pressures built, Larry responded by erecting a sort of protective human bubble around himself through an entourage that kept him at arms'-length from those he didn't want to be bothered with. Which was practically anybody. Michael DeBenedictus was ambitious, and so was an ever-changing troupe of cute young guys who were attracted to Larry's flame. He became very temperamental, very selective, living in a rarefied atmosphere that he controlled entirely himself. I've seen it before, with stars and drug addicts and people who think they're stars or drug addicts. The holier-than-thou bubble. The 24-hour-a-day special place, so much superior to the mundane world the rest of us have to live in. I think that when Michael Turock, the lawyer, called me and complained that my offer wasn't good enough, it was his idea, not Larry's. Larry had no idea of the hurt he was causing. I was devastated though I couldn't bring myself to talk to him about it. It would have been difficult to talk to him in any case. By now he was constantly surrounded by his entourage and was high almost all the time. Turock sent us papers to redo the agreement, but nothing ever came of it. Years later I discovered that Ed, who was always playing big brother to me, had instructed our lawyer to lose those papers. Since Larry could care less about things of this nature anyway, and wasn't on his lawyer's case to settle the matter, it simply disappeared.

It wasn't long after "Don't Make Me Wait" was belatedly released that we were informed — in a chilly legal letter — that lawyers for the Beach Boys objected to our use of the name Peech Boys. The names sounded too similar, they claimed. I would have laughed at such a ridiculous objection, but since West End was the Peech Boys label, I had to take it seriously. And the Beach Boys legal team was serious. They claimed that record buyers would be confused by the similarity, and might accidentally purchase an r&b-disco record when they were instead looking to buy some tired retread by an over-the-hill '60s rock band. After much legal wrangling we were forced to change the name to the New York Citi Peech Boys. A mouthful, but one that apparently satisfied the Beach Boys.

Throughout all these problems I really grew frustrated with Michael DeBenedictus. He was consistently rude, an ungracious negotiator, and I felt he was a terrible influence on Larry. But I believed in Larry, and I gave them a personal loan to finish their next release, "Something Special." Again, the same old story. Larry and Michael insisted on dozens of different mixes. The process got bogged down and there was nothing to release. Ed expected me to reason with Larry, but it was impossible to reason with someone who was too high to care. Larry never would submit to authority figures, especially if they were friends, and as his drug habit got worse, things degenerated to the point where he would disappear for days at a time.

West End wasn't the only label having this problem with Larry, although we were probably the label that could afford it the least. He was also doing mixes for Salsoul, and I heard the same stories from them. He would reserve weeks of studio time and then disappear, or even go into hiding, leaving the meter in the studio running up huge bills. This kind of thing was all well and good when the hits were coming fast and furious and money was pouring in like crazy. The record industry has always believed in pampering artists who produce product that sells. But we were now entering very hard times, when such behavior had to answer to the bottom line. With Larry, it never did.

the party's over

By the summer of 1981, times were really beginning to look grim for labels like ours. The economy went into a recession at the beginning of Reagan's first term, and things were bad all over. But several other factors magnified this downturn for us. The Sony Corporation had just introduced the Walkman — ubiquitous today, but a major novelty back then — and suddenly the cassette format was the rage. People began building up tape collections of albums they had previously bought on vinyl, or copying records onto tape to play on their Walkman. At the same time, VCR machines finally became affordable to the average person and consumers began to pour millions into buying these devices, and buying and renting the videotapes to go with them. To make matters worse, the first generation of video games like PacMan appeared in the arcades, and kids went crazy for them.

The whole recording industry took a big nose-dive as money that previously went into the purchase of new records was suddenly diverted into these other sources of entertainment. Analysts began to speculate that perhaps, with the advent of cheap home recording devices, VCRs and video games, the record industry was about to enter a retrenchment from which it would never emerge. As if this were not bad enough, MTV appeared, and overnight the music business became the music video business. If you didn't have a photogenic star or group who could become the focus of a video — zip, no video. Without the video, you couldn't get on MTV. And without MTV, you couldn't get radio airplay. Suddenly, everything was tilted toward bankable, photogenic video stars. Studio-based groups like the Peech Boys were in trouble.

The huge glut of promotional 12-inch discs continued to flood the dance music market. This problem had first appeared back in the early record pool days, when labels began to distribute free product to DJs who then often turned around and sold these promo records to record stores. The problem had grown with the size and power of the record pools, and by now many DJs often received several copies of a record, and immediately traded the extras with record stores, either for other records, for credit or for cash. It was a great situation for the DJs, who were able to expand their own collections while skimming off any unwanted or duplicate records. It was also great for the record stores, who paid very little for these promo copies and were therefore able to set up dollar bins and attract customers with very low-priced, high-quality discs. Of course it was all completely illegal. *"For Promotional Use Only: Not For Sale Or Trade"* was stamped prominently on every label. But since this arrangement profited almost everyone — the DJs, the record stores, the record buyers — it seemed impossible to stop.

It was terrible for record labels, especially small ones like us. Our market was shrinking for a dozen reasons, from the "death of disco" to VCRs, to Walkmans and video games, the general economy, you name it. But our expenses were not declining. For all the money we spent producing and distributing product in a shrinking market, we needed to receive the maximum return. Instead, our return was steadily declining as this disco black market became the favored way for the most devoted fans to build up their collections. Then there were new entrepreneurs who started duplicating dance music without paying royalties. Somehow the dance community didn't think it was a crime when people began purchasing these bootlegs. For small labels like ours, it was the kiss of death.

friends

Times were increasingly tough. My relationship with Julio veered between love and drug madness. I was taking far too many drugs, especially angel dust. Business was bad. Friends seemed to be coming down with strange, unexplainable illnesses. In the wider world, disco was increasingly passé. Yet in many ways, these were the best of times.

The reason is friendship. Friendship has always meant a lot to gay men, I suppose because many of the things that provide meaning in other people's lives — family and children and grandchildren — we generally do not have (although this is now changing). All the way back to my earliest gay life after the army when I stumbled upon an unexpected circle of friends while cruising the parks in Boston, and then through my times in Cleveland and throughout my years in New York, I treasured my friendships. By now, if my life was lacking in other things, if there were dark clouds on the horizon, I still had my friends. And they were wonderful.

There were, of course, my long-standing relationships with Julio and Carmen and Gigi, Larry and Michael. But beyond these deep, complex attachments stretched a whole family, and I suppose the most central members of that family at the time, the ones that the rest of my circle revolved around, were Ignacio and Manolo.

Ignacio and Manolo were a couple who had escaped Castro's Cuba and landed in Puerto Rico, where Julio and I met them. Two years later they moved to Manhattan and set up an apartment and a salon of sorts on E. 54th St. We immediately became the closest of friends. Some people are magical by nature, living their lives in a sort of rare universe where harshness and ugliness are banished, where all is beauty and art and perfect taste. Such people are all too rare, sad to say, and it's even more unusual to meet a pair in which both partners are such exquisite souls. But Ignacio, who owned several successful flower shops, and Manolo, a highly sought-after architect, were such a couple. Both at work and at play, they existed in a different world from the one most of us inhabit. They could walk into a drab apartment, take a glance around, immediately move this, throw a piece of fabric over that, and the place would be transformed. They were equally at home at grand auctions as they were at cheap flea markets. They invariably found treasures where others saw only junk. It didn't matter what they did; a single stem blooming in a vase became an instant work of art.

I adored them. Simply being with them was to inhabit a wonderful, rare universe. I also came to rely on them for advice. They loved music and the fact that I was in the middle of the dance music world, and they had strong and intelligent opinions about what worked musically and what did not. Every time we did a test pressing for West End, I would deliver a copy to them. They were just as insightful about disco as everything else, and their insight came with an added advantage sometimes hard to find in friends — or anybody, for that matter — complete honesty. They never held anything back. As time passed, the salon they created on E. 54th St. became the center of my social world.

Claire Paige and her husband Marvin were two other dear friends at this time. Julio brought them into our circle. Many people, myself included, considered Claire to be Julio's female alter ego. Eccentric, wild, vivacious, she shared with Julio a deep love of opera and the arts, and she herself was a gifted artist and sculptor. If she and Julio were natural soulmates, her husband Marvin was sort of a counterpart to me. We were both, in a sense, victims of our star spouses. We were always on the phone, like two jealous husbands checking up on our wives, wondering where Claire and Julio might be. Everybody in our circle thought that Claire had a huge, unrequited crush on Julio.

In the late '70s Claire and Marvin opened a restaurant in Key West named Claire. It served great food, but Claire herself was the main draw. She was a natural hostess. She had a smile and a warm word and wild laugh for everybody, and the restaurant was a great success. In 1979 they decided to open another Claire in New York, in Chelsea, and Claire on 7th Ave. immediately became a neighborhood institution. These were wonderful nights at Claire's, all of us drinking and making toasts and carrying on. One Christmas Ignacio and Manolo and Julio and I helped decorate the restaurant for the holidays. Not even Bing Crosby's "White Christmas" was as warm and wonderful.

A striking member of our family was Chaz Goward, a tall, handsome blond from the Australian outback. When we met, Chaz had been lovers for five years with Norman Marine, another friend of Julio's. One night Norman brought Chaz along to one of my dinner parties in Brooklyn, and we became instant friends. Well, almost instant. He was completely zonked on angel dust, and my first memory of him was of this gorgeous hunk vainly struggling to wash lettuce in my bright copper sink, so stoned he could barely function. But Chaz was not always as zonked-out as the way he appeared that first night. Even though he had never learned to read or write in the wilds of Australia, he moved to New York determined to try to make something of himself, and it didn't take long. He soon became manager of one of the city's most prestigious catering companies, and we were all amazed that this gorgeous matey could turn out lavish events for the likes of the Kennedys and the Javits. Chaz was a real dynamo — organized, focused, and naturally brilliant. (He did learn to read eventually.)

There was something else that made Chaz special, at least in our circle. He was an openly gay dad. He wanted a green card, and a lesbian friend, Jay, wanted a baby, so it was a match made in heaven. They married and not long afterwards Jay produced Jason, who looked exactly like his father — blond, blue-eyed and bright as can be. Chaz and Jay both took care of the baby, and as he grew up he spent considerable time with Chaz and his lover Norman. Everyone in our circle was in love with Jason, and everyone was very impressed that Chaz — one of our crowd — could be such a great father.

Still another new friend at this time — one of the few who would survive the coming holocaust, and help me write this book — was photographer Brent Nicholson Earle. Ignacio had met Brent, and at some point Brent offered to photograph Ignacio's sculptures. Ignacio was so impressed with the result that he sent Brent over to my penthouse to talk about photographing my canvasses. I was playing with little Gigi that day, and Brent and I immediately hit it off. Even though I am not particularly astrologically inclined, I thought there must be some astrological connection. He asked me when my birthday was. The connection was stronger than I had guessed. We shared the same birthday. We became friends and he began helping me write this book.

In addition to these newer friends, I still had my old circle of Fire Island buddies. There's nothing in the world like old friends, those who knew you way back when, who know all the ins and outs of your personality and your history, who can call you on your bullshit, tell you the truth, support you when it counts. I realize this today more than ever, since almost all of these friends are now ghosts lost to the plague. Back then, of course, I had no idea that our time on Earth together would be so short. I thought they would always be with me: my "therapists" Ray Ford and Dick Fisher, who knew me better than anyone, and never let me forget it; my disco friends David Lynn and the handsome Mark Rosenfeld; my soulmate Larry McDevitt, who was now the successful and public-spirited head of all the STD clinics in New York; Brian Wallach, Lou Malkin and Dino Georgiou. These were the guys who knew me back when Michael and I were lovers, even before. They were my sounding board and my support, people who did not have to lecture me when I was out of line, who could just shoot me a dirty look or a barbed comment for me to get the message. These guys had loved and accepted Michael when we were a couple, and now they loved and accepted Julio just as much. Between these old friends and my circle of new friends, I could face any obstacle, survive any disappointment, weather any downturn. When we would gather at Ignacio and Manolo's for one of our many dinner parties, I was in the bosom of a home as real, as meaningful, as any blood family's. The only thing I could not survive was losing them. And yet unbeknownst to me in the summer of 1981, that was the very thing I was about to face.

One good thing emerged from that summer of tremors and warnings. Ignacio had been nagging me for a while to do something with the five-story SRO that Michael and I had bought in Chelsea in 1973. I now owned the building independent of Michael, and if it had been left to me to decide, I would have let it sit there and rot. It was a hellhole, a stinking nest of cockroaches and pathetic, drunken tenants, and there was nothing I could do about it. The city's rules about rent-controlled tenants were a nightmare of red tape that would have given Kafka the chills. I had some vague notion that at some distant time in the future I might fix it up and make it my home. I'd have an apartment there, the plan went, Julio would have another, Carmen and Gigi would have their own, and we'd rent out the rest. But this was a pipe dream, and I rarely gave it a thought. I loved my penthouse, and with my mounting problems at West End I had absolutely no energy to confront the horrible mess on 22nd St.

But once Ignacio saw the place, it was a different story. He thought it was *"magnificent," "fabulous," "brilliant."* It was a *"treasure,"* with *"unlimited possibilities."* I thought he was nuts, and more or less told him so. The fact was that even if I had wanted to do something to fix the place up, it was impossible, since city law did not allow me to evict even the worst tenants, those who were a physical danger to others, or who were months derelict with the rent. In those days SROs (single-room occupancy) were the city's housing of last resort for the poor, the addicted, the mentally ill, the alcoholic, anyone who had no place else to go. In other words, my tenants. I suppose such an arrangement made sense from the point of view of a compassionate but skinflint society. People who, for whatever reason had no control of their lives, still had to live somewhere, and it was a hell of a lot cheaper to warehouse them in rundown rooming houses than build them decent, affordable housing. In any case, the strict rules governing rent-controlled housing made rehabilitation impossible. Any building that became an SRO seemed destined to remain one forever.

But then a tenant died, I paid others several thousand dollars to move, hired an architect named Earl Coombs to draw up some plans, and Ignacio sprang into action. I gave him permission to do whatever he wanted, thinking that nothing much would come of it. After all, what motivation could he have? He was successful, had plenty of money. He and Manolo lived in a fabulous place on chic Upper East Side. But now he announced that he intended to fulfill his fantasy of becoming a sculptor, and that he had found his ideal studio. Suddenly this refined, elegant creature was like a demon possessed. Carpets were ripped up, walls were scrapped, garbage flew everywhere, dumpsters were filled and carted away. And I suddenly realized that Ignacio was serious. He was indeed going to carve an elegant sculptor's studio out of a corner of my ruin. I was so thrilled that I made him a deal. I'd give him the space for free if he would agree to act as superintendent of the building, dealing with the tenants and perhaps overseeing the renovation of any other units that might become vacant. It was the perfect arrangement, and soon I had a working artist as a tenant and building superintendent.

my garage family

I also had a pretty fabulous family over at the Paradise Garage. But my relationship with them was completely different. They treated me not only with the utmost respect, but also sometimes with trepidation and fear. And therein lies a tale about the secret of Michael Brody's success.

One thing I'll say for Michael: he certainly knew how to build a staff that was efficient and loyal. His group of workers felt they were part of something more than just a workforce. Michael created an environment of mutual respect, of love. People who worked for him adored him, and they tended to like each other as well. Sure, there were inevitable tensions and rivalries, but the overriding feeling was of belonging to a big, crazy, happy family. And to most of that family, I was the undisputed, slightly scary, godfather. For years I couldn't understand why they thought of me in such a way. My proprietary interest in the Garage had never been that great after all, and lasted only until Michael paid back his loan, which he eventually did. For most of the Garage's history, I actually had no financial stake in the business to speak of, not even as a part owner. And yet everyone there always treated me like Mr. Big, the real owner, the power behind the throne. I just couldn't understand it. The only time I remember ever implying I owned the Garage was that New Year's Eve when I was dusted all the way to the moon and that clueless doorman wouldn't admit my entourage. That was the only time. I have always had a visceral dislike of executives and owners who throw their weight around. Yet people would fall silent when I walked in, and would practically bow and scrape to Mr. Cheren. I eventually found out why, and the reason illustrates Michael's very intelligent way with people.

Michael's management style was extremely laid back. People would adore him because he was kind, generous and easy going, but of course they tended to take advantage of that. There would be constant little incidents where people would fail to follow orders, or would challenge his authority. So Michael simply invented a sinister higher up — me — and let it be known that I had the final say. He darkly hinted that I was some kind of Jewish Mafioso, and that you really didn't want to fuck with me. Then, whenever the staff was giving him a hard time, he'd simply announce that Mel Cheren was on his way over. Boom, they would all fall in line. I wasn't that crazy about what Michael was doing when I finally found out about it years later. But even though I struck a certain amount of fear in their hearts, I grew to love the wacky crew at the Garage as a second family. Anybody who went there felt the same.

There was Kenny Eubanks, who ran the food concessions and made sure everybody always had wonderful food and drink.

There was Noel Garcia the doorman, a smoldering, handsome Colombian who handled the difficult door job with total grace and kindness. There was Bobby Falace, an old friend of Michael's, who faithfully ran the coat check for years. There was Willy Gonzalez, a Puerto Rican bodybuilder, who ran the even more difficult job of security. Willy was straight, and Michael offered him the job one day out of the blue, when he saw Willy working out at the gym. Willy thought Michael was really trying to get him into bed — which Michael probably was — but he took the job anyway, and became one of the club's most valuable employees. Michael never did get him into the sack however.

Of course there were a few bad apples in a staff as large as that one, but they generally didn't last long. Especially once Jaime de la Cruz began throwing his weight around. One employee I really did not like was a security guard named Benny. His attitude was so rough that one time I pulled him aside and told him to lighten up, but even I, Mel Cheren, didn't seem to scare him. Benny was straight, as were several of the Garage employees. But unlike most of them, he had an attitude about it. Most of the straight guys were incredibly handsome, and they kind of liked all the attention they got from the gay staff and the members. The looks and the cruising stares and the occasional little pats on the behind. But Benny only went for that when he was calling the shots. So one night when Jaime put his hand on Benny's bod without permission, he was rewarded with a fist in the mouth. Jaime wanted Benny fired immediately, and he insisted that Michael return from vacation immediately to do the dirty work, which Michael did. End of Benny.

Like all great discos, the psychic center of the Garage was the DJ booth, which had its own staff and operated by its own rules, Larry Levan's. DJ booths formed a whole culture all their own. The Garage had the ultimate booth, with one area reserved for the

DJ himself, and another more spacious area with couches and tables where the DJ's entourage would gather. The whole thing was generally tightly guarded by a security man, and for many disco fans the ultimate sign that you had arrived was the day you were invited, or allowed, into the booth. Like any hierarchy, booths had a source of supreme power — the DJ — surrounded by a court and an entourage as serious in its own way as the royal courts of old, with its own etiquette, including rewards for the faithful and punishment for the disloyal. Usually banishment. Larry's space was the envy of every DJ.

DJ booths were social places, the ultimate spot in the disco to meet and greet. But serious business went on up there, too, since it was the place where record promoters usually went to present their latest releases to the DJ. A booth could be pretty schizophrenic — men in suits intent on conducting important business and rubbing their padded shoulders with the wildest, druggiest people in the world. The DJ booth was also the ultimate VIP room, since this is where stars like Madonna and Diana Ross inevitably wound up when they came to the club. And in the middle of it all was the mad king who ruled this strange court: La Diva Levan.

Larry needed trusted employees to help him keep things together in the booth, people who could read his mind and know who he wanted around and, just as important, who he did not. Mostly he wanted to be surrounded by the incredible, ever-changing entourage of gorgeous boys he seemed to collect wherever he went. He could more or less live without everybody else. His most valuable employee in that regard was David DePino, the booth doorman. Larry and David were great friends — I first met David when Larry brought him along to one of my dinner parties unannounced — and I suppose because of their closeness, David instinctively knew who was okay and who was not. Up in the booth Robert DaSilva worked the lights, and to round things off there was Lydia the boothie, a self-proclaimed witch who was forever sprinkling magical powders over Larry and chanting and doing her voodoo. Lydia was madly in love with Larry, and eventually began telling everyone that she had borne his baby. She was convinced that this was true, but so far as I know, she and Larry produced no children, either by witchcraft or more traditional methods.

Finally, there were DJs who came from all over the country to check out what Larry was doing, and pay their respects. For many of them, a trip up to the booth at the Garage was like a pilgrimage. Larry had a small band of famous fellow DJs who were regular members of his retinue. There was Frankie Crocker, who constantly informed his thousands of daily listeners on WBLS about the goings on in the booth. There was Frankie Knuckles, Larry's old friend who was now the top DJ in Chicago, where he was helping to invent house music at his famous club, the Warehouse. There was Richard Vasquez, a former graphics designer who was deeply influenced by Larry's style and went on to become one of dance music's most highly regarded spinners. There was also Larry Patterson, handsome, well groomed, and able to kick Larry in the ass when he needed it. And there was Tee Scott.

Tee was a shy, reserved young man who had become a DJ almost by accident, and quickly became a legend in his own right. His quiet personality was a perfect foil for Larry's out-going craziness, and the two became great friends. Eventually, they both became studio remixers, and often competed for the same jobs. But that never interfered with their friendship. Tee tells a story about how once, when black rubber wristbands were all the rage, he had searched for some and couldn't find any. One day he noticed that Larry was wearing an entire armful, and casually asked where he might get some. Larry immediately removed his entire arm's worth and put them on Tee's arm. Tee never took them off after that, even for surgery. Larry could be the ultimate diva bitch, but he constantly did little things that made people love him all the more.

But there could be major flare-ups as well, and one of the most legendary concerned Frankie Crocker. The Garage frequently put on shows by the top disco artists — all of our West End acts performed there — and one day in 1981 Michael had scheduled a performance by Gwen McCrae. Suddenly, the day before the show, Gwen's record company called and canceled, claiming that Frankie Crocker had forced their hand. It seems that Frankie and WBLS had booked Gwen for a show the following month, and Frankie thought that Gwen's earlier appearance at the Garage might take the luster off of her WBLS appearance. This was ridiculous of course, since the Garage did not advertise and the general public would never even know about the Garage show.

Michael was beyond furious. After all, Frankie Crocker had practically built a career picking up on the latest hits and hottest trends at the Garage. He and his entourage always had carte blanche there. Michael called him, and to his shock Frankie gave no ground, pointing out that his radio station was much more important to a singer like Gwen than a mere appearance at a downtown disco. So Michael shut himself up in his office and composed a letter from hell. He railed at Frankie Crocker, pointed out all the ways that Frankie had benefited from his close association with the Garage, told Frankie that he and WBLS had nothing to do with the Garage's success, informed him that he was going to announce the reason for Gwen's cancellation from the stage that night, and ended by banning Frankie Crocker and his entire WBLS staff from the club, effective immediately. He then sent the letter not only to Frankie, but to the station's management and owners, to Larry Levan, and to the entire

Garage membership as well. It was an explosive moment, but it didn't end there. Frankie was banished for almost a year. I thought the whole thing was a bit much, but there was no talking to Michael when he was in his never forgive mode. At some point months later Frankie apparently figured his banishment must be over, and showed up at the door. Joey Llanos didn't know about the banishment, and admitted him as one of Larry's guests. Michael completely lost it, screamed in Frankie's face and had him thrown out, and then for good measure, fired Joey, one of his best employees. Joey was only fired for a few hours, though. Once Michael had let off enough steam, he forgave Joey. But the story illustrates something I had learned about Michael years before. He never ever forgave a slight. And the more powerful he got, the less he forgave.

chapter fourteen
IT WAS CALLED GRID...
AND THEN AIDS

The *New York Native* published an article on May 18, 1981 that announced the beginning of the end of our lives, although we didn't know it at the time. The headline, "Disease Rumors Largely Unfounded," seemed reassuring. The text, however, was less so. Dr. Larry Mass reported that many people were getting sick, and it wasn't just a few isolated cases like my friends Rick and Nick, who had died a few months before. It was a lot of us.

The Center of Disease Control's newsletter made it official the next month. A strange outbreak of pneumonia was spreading in the gay population on both coasts, striking down otherwise healthy men in the prime of their lives, filling their lungs with fluid and smothering them to death. A few weeks later a new report linked these cases to an even more mysterious skin cancer, the strange and rare Kaposi sarcoma, which generally affected only elderly Sephardic jews, in whom it was usually fairly benign. But in its gay victims this cancer was fulminate, spreading not only over their skin but also throughout their internal organs. Some gay men who had the cancer also had the pneumonia, indicating that the two diseases — so seemingly different — were being spread by, or caused by, the same thing. Whatever it was, I was fairly oblivious to all this at first. True, my friends Rick and Nick had already died of something strange, but I had no clue that what they died of was linked to some larger threat. Julio and I were smoking angel dust on such a regular basis by now that I could blot out anything. Bad business. Bad personal problems. Bad anything.

But I was in the middle of a cluster of people who were already being deeply affected by this new disease, and who were not about to ignore it in a haze of angel dust or a blizzard of cocaine. There had been so much VD in the past several years among gay men — syphilis, gonorrhea, intestinal parasites, hepatitis — that quite a few public-spirited men in my circle had become involved in efforts to monitor what was going on and warn gay men about the dangers. So when this new syndrome appeared, they were right on top of things. My good friend Larry McDevitt was in charge of all the STD clinics in New York, and even though no one had any idea at first whether this thing was sexually transmitted, he found himself at the center of a lot of information, and none of it was good. At the same time, two other friends from the disco world, promoter Ed Anthony and DJ Michael Jorba (who was also a public health advisor on sexually transmitted diseases) were concerned that the cancer might be a new sexually transmitted disease. They wanted to use the Chelsea clinic, one of the city's STD testing sites, as a headquarters to monitor new cases and provide treatment. There, they wanted to set up a separate staff that would focus exclusively on this problem. But this would cost money. Michael Jorba wrote up a funding proposal and sent it to the health commissioner, who passed it on to Larry McDevitt. I first heard about the whole problem one night while sitting with Larry in the balcony of the Saint, surrounded by men having casual sex as they always did in the balcony of the Saint. Larry told me about Ed Anthony and Michael Jorba trying to raise money for their plan, and he thought I might be able to help out. In retrospect, it's hard to remember what I thought as I first heard about what would later become AIDS. We had no idea, of course, that this was to be the defining event in our lives. Sitting there in the balcony of the Saint, gazing at the crush of bodies undulating in the flashing lights and the pounding music way down below on the dance floor, how could we possibly have known that many of those beautiful men, perhaps most of them, would eventually die of a disease that as yet had no name? We could not know; we did not know. But whatever this was, I knew it was serious and I wanted to help.

Since Ed Anthony and Michael Jorba were planning a benefit for the Chelsea clinic at the Saint, I volunteered to provide the live entertainment at no cost. I knew I could get almost any major disco star for free, since some of them owed me something, and they all owed their careers to the gay men who were now in trouble. It was to be my first attempt at AIDS fundraising, and it was a sad learning experience. Despite my promise to provide the entertainment for free, Ed Anthony insisted on booking Tina Turner for the benefit. Her career was undergoing a major renovation, and her $15,000 fee would eat up much of the money we would raise. I could not understand why anybody would want to pay fifteen grand when I could get equivalent stars for nothing, but I was to learn that there were hidden agendas beneath even the most altruistic-seeming gestures. Even then, at the start.

To make matters worse, Bruce Mailman decided to erect a huge stage for the event, and I was told by Peter Spar that Bruce had decided to charge building costs to the Chelsea clinic organizers. Since the stage would also cost around fifteen grand, the upshot was that although the benefit party was a success, it hardly raised any money for the clinic. Tina Turner got her fifteen grand, Bruce Mailman got this massive stage (which he was then able to make pay for subsequent events). The clinic got bupkis. I suppose the two subsequent decades of waste and mismanagement in AIDS organizations can be traced back to that sorry attempt.

But the silent invader was not about to wait for us to get our act together. Very rapidly now, men began getting sick, and what had begun as a rumor of illness and swollen glands and fatigue, now emerged as a looming presence in our lives. The medical establishment announced that underlying both the cancer and the pneumonia was a deeper problem, the breakdown of the immune system, which made the body susceptible to infections it could otherwise fight off. Doctors began to notice stranger and stranger symptoms: weird parasites that almost never affect humans, rare funguses, unusual viruses, mycobacterium. Since all these symptoms stemmed from the underlying immune system breakdown, the new syndrome was baptized GRID — Gay Related Immune Deficiency. Nobody was happy about the name, since it seemed to demonize gay men further.

But there was no denying that gay men were the main victims, and no denying that society was totally ignoring the issue. So a pioneering group of gay men began to meet on a regular basis to plot some kind of strategy: Edmund White, Nathan Fain, Arthur Bell, Larry Kramer, Paul Rapaport, Paul Popham and Larry Mass. We met at different members' apartments, including Ignacio and Manolo's, as well as Larry Kramer's and Paul Popham's. One day at Paul's the group decided that the best way to proceed was to set up a tax-exempt group, which required officers and a formal organization. Edmund White sat there on the hassock, crossed-legged, and simply decided, then and there, what was what. *"Everybody listens to Paul Popham,"* Edmund said,

> so he should be president. Larry McDevitt follows orders fine from Paul, so he should be vice president. Joe Pachek owns a company and has lots of money. He should be treasurer. And Brad Fransden. He takes good notes. He should be secretary. Everybody agreed?

They all agreed, and that was it. The Gay Men's Health Crisis was born. The new organization had no funds and no headquarters. We were traveling from living room to living room, and this could not continue for long. A permanent group was going to need a permanent home, and I realized that my building on 22nd St. was such a home. Ever since I had turned the management over to Ignacio, the building had been transformed. An old tenant would leave or pass away, and Ignacio and Manolo would go to work fixing up and moving their eccentric artist friends into the newly reclaimed spaces. By now the 22nd St. inhabitants included a snake collector, a Cuban santero, a fan dancer from 12 West and the Garage, two of Robert Mapplethorpe's black models, and an old friend of Ignacio's from Puerto Rico. The building was still far from a desirable address, but where there had once been only pathos, there was now pathos mixed with the glorious nuttiness of disco.

Just as GMHC was getting under way, an empty room became available underneath Ignacio's studio, which I offered to the new group rent-free. It took them a split second to accept, and within a few days the all-volunteer GMHC was open for business. Who would have thought that this rag-tag group, holed up in a borrowed Chelsea rooming house, would grow into one of the nation's largest medical service organizations, with hundreds of employees, thousands of volunteers, and a budget in the tens of millions? A lot of us probably thought that whatever this disease was, it would be fixed in a few months. That's always the way it is at the beginning of a war, when the men march off to battle. I'll be home by Christmas.

But we quickly realized that GMHC was going to have to grow fast to keep pace with the immediate demand for services and information and referrals. As the weeks went by, demand grew tremendous. The government was doing nothing, panic was setting in, people were desperate for information, those who were sick had no idea where to turn and needed referrals to doctors who had no inkling of how to treat them. There was never any question — we simply had to do it all for ourselves. Suddenly, my place on 22nd St. was a beehive of activity, with the sick and the volunteers and the worried-well streaming in and out almost 24-hours a day.

Ignacio's art studio, just above the GMHC offices, quickly became a sort of staff lounge. Ignacio himself became a sort of unofficial counselor. Sitting there amid his fabulous sculptures and his beautiful art, he offered support and therapy — and the occasional joint — to beleaguered volunteers. It might seem strange that those who were the first in the fight against AIDS took little drug breaks from their volunteer activity, but for many, it was the only way to handle the horror of caring for the dying, who were often their friends and disco buddies. As the suffering and terror increased, Ignacio was inspired to produce absolutely magnificent art — his best ever. We would see often in the years ahead, how so many gay men would transmute a nightmare into art.

The crisis grew worse. GMHC needed a lot more money. At this point, everyone was a volunteer, and every bit of material was donated, from the chairs to the phones to the paper for the copiers. But there were mounting expenses that good will alone could not cover, and we needed a source of cash. Since most of our friends were disco bunnies, it made sense to throw a disco benefit. After our unhappy experience at the Saint, the next logical place was the Garage. Michael readily agreed and also agreed to charge us only what it cost to throw the party.

We set the date, April 10, 1982, and decided to call the event "Showers." We also decided (for some reason I can't recall) to make it a red party. Ignacio persuaded a businessman friend to donate hundreds of strips of lightweight wood. He and his friends painted the wood red and hung it from the ceiling of the Garage. This was a massive undertaking, but we had no trouble finding people to help. It seemed that after an initial period of denial towards the end of 1981, when it had been hard to motivate people to get off their butts and do something, people were now eager to get involved. Larry McDevitt had the feeling that many of our friends were literally sitting by their phones, waiting for someone to call and ask them do something. Anything.

I was in charge of finding entertainment, so after getting no response from some, I called Bob Schwaid, Evelyn "Champagne" King's manager. I didn't even finish asking before he said yes, Evelyn would be glad to do it. I had a much harder time with Jacques Morali, who managed the Ritchie Family. Morali was the kind of guy who used to keep a bowl filled with cocaine on his coffee table, but now he was suddenly a born-again Christian. He said that the Ritchie Family could only appear if someone made a speech from the stage denouncing drug use, unsafe sex and other *"immoral things."* That kind of moralizing was out of the question back then. No one knew what was causing this new disease, whether it was sex or drugs or a virus or none of the above, and it certainly would not have pleased the audience — who had paid a lot of money to help the cause — to be lectured about *"immorality"* from the stage of the Paradise Garage. I urged Morali not to impose his moral agenda, and assured him that the GMHC representatives would take care of educational messages in their speeches. He finally agreed, and it seemed like everything was falling into place.

I began to get nervous, though, when we had still only sold 500 tickets just two days before the event. Then New York was hit with a rare April blizzard and was buried in ten inches of snow, and we got hysterical. After all this work, all this planning, the benefit was going to be a bomb. I made my way down to the Garage that night filled with foreboding. It wasn't just that we desperately needed the money, or that we had worked so hard. It was that gay men needed to show that they cared about whatever it was that was striking us down. If only 500 guys showed up, it might mean that most of us didn't care, that we couldn't get our heads out of the disco cloud long enough to save our own lives. Larry Kramer and a few others had tried to raise money already, with practically no luck. If that continued, where would we be?

But when my cab turned the corner onto King St. that night, all my fears vanished in a second. Despite the awful weather people were pouring into the Garage in droves. Gay men had finally got the message, and it was a fabulous night. Evelyn "Champagne" King was wonderful, thanking us over and over again for inviting her, as if we were doing her the favor. She sang "Shame" and "I Don't Know If It's Right," her established hits, and she debuted "Love Come Down," the song that would secure her lasting place in disco's hall of fame. The New York City Gay Men's Chorus performed, still on a high from their Carnegie Hall debut just a few months before. Everything was wonderful — the art auction, the spirit of the crowd, the entertainment.

But for me the highlight of the evening was Paul Popham's speech. Here was a man whom we had considered another disco friend — handsome, suave and intelligent — to be sure, but simply one of us. A party guy. And now he was onstage, giving this rousing call to arms, displaying the most remarkable leadership and insight and ability to inspire. I sat with Ignacio and director Jose Quintero, and we all had tears in our eyes as Paul told us how we were going to have to fight this battle ourselves if we were going to survive. It was the beginning of the gay community's fight against AIDS — which had not even been named yet — and when Paul finished, the crowd went absolutely wild.

There were only a few minor glitches that night, but I suppose they were telling. I was in the office when the VIP buzzer rang, indicating that some celebrity was at the door. It turned out that

Calvin Klein and Ian Schrager, two of the wealthiest men in New York, were asking to be admitted for free. I've always been disgusted by arrogance, and I told the guy in the office to make them go around to the front and pay like anybody else.

A similar issue arose later. Ray Caviano, the head of RFC Records, had promised me that he would donate $2,000. After the party I reminded Larry Kramer about this and asked him to call Ray and collect the pledge. But it turned out that Ray thought that we were going to announce his gift from the stage, and since we didn't, he forgot about it. Apparently, contributing to the sick and dying was not enough of a motivation for him. He wanted everybody to know how generous he was.

Still another glitch had to do with the invitation. It turned out that some people were upset about the April showers theme. Some thought it referred to *"golden showers,"* which was about as far from our intention as you could get (although I suppose some people were probably disappointed that it did not refer to golden showers.) In any case, we raised over $50,000 that fabulous night. And aside from Michael's minimal expenses, every cent went to GMHC. In later years we would raise millions, but to me, that first fifty grand was the best. It meant that people cared, that we could pull together and save our friends. Whatever happened in the future, we would all be in this together. As we have been.

hits and misses

Aside from worries about our health crisis, I had plenty of business problems the rest of 1982 and well into 1983. West End was teetering down a rocky road; I had to keep finding hits to keep the ball rolling, and it wasn't getting any easier. Luckily, we scored again with *"Do It to the Music"* by Raw Silk. The lead singer was Sybil Thomas, daughter of Rufus Thomas, the famous soul singer from Memphis whose signature song was "Walkin' the Dog," and sister of Carla Thomas, who had a huge hit in the '60s with "Gee Whiz." Now it was Sybil's turn. Her performance on "Do It to the Music" was great, the song was infectious, and I hoped against hope that it would make it with the fans.

The night we debuted the song at the Garage, Larry played it six times. If I had any doubts about the song's potential, they were dispelled by Larry and by the crowd's reaction. Frankie Crocker was being allowed back into the club, and he went into a state when he heard it. By next Monday it was in heavy rotation on WBLS, which guaranteed sales of at least 20,000 copies, even if the song otherwise went nowhere. But this song had legs. It entered the Top Ten, and stayed No. 1 on WBLS for five consecutive weeks. Once again, West End had been saved by a timely hit.

Unfortunately, we needed a continuous string of hits to stay viable, and "Do It to the Music" proved to be the exception. Our next release was Nick Martinelli and David Todd's remix of two songs, "You Can't Have Your Cake and Eat It Too" by Brenda Taylor, and "Ride on the Rhythm" by Mahogany. Both songs were popular with DJs and dance floors across the country, but they were only moderately successful in the record stores. Then Jacques Morali approached me and I agreed to release several of his next productions. Jacques had become very full of himself following his spectacular success with the Village People, but he had for the time being lost his touch. His material sounded more and more like pale imitations of earlier hits, and by the time he got to West End, he was becoming increasingly desperate to duplicate his initial success.

The first Jacques Morali production we released was "Party" by Julius Brown. It was a huge hit at the Saint, but by now we realized that having a hit at the Saint meant virtually nothing for record sales. At the Garage, when people loved a song they went out and bought the record, and radio DJs like Frankie Crocker put it into heavy rotation. In general, a Garage hit translated into a record store hit almost overnight. Not so at the Saint. The radio jocks didn't hang out there, and moreover, the Saint's DJs had a practice of taping their mixes and selling the tapes. As a result, the Saint fans could get all the current hits on a single tape, instead of having to buy them one record at a time. When Jacque Morali's "Party" was poorly received at the Garage and a smash at the Saint, I knew we were in trouble. Sure enough, the song did only moderately well.

But this was just the beginning of our troubles with Jacques Morali. His next record, "Stay with Me," was written and sung by the talented Steve Dunne, who performed under the name India. Unfortunately, Steve chafed under Morali's overblown production style, and that song, too, went nowhere (although it was another crowd-pleaser at the Saint). Although our production deal would continue with Morali for another year, all he was producing were flops. His last release with us was "Diana," a tribute to Diana Ross. But even though it was mixed by Jellybean Benitez, who was about to have great success mixing Madonna, this one sounded like a knockoff of Laura Branigan's "Gloria," and it was Jacques Morali's biggest bomb yet. I don't think anyone played it.

We weren't having problems just with Jacques Morali. Nothing much was working at all, and West End began sinking under a mountain of debt. The one bright spot was our album of Taana Gardner songs. Our friend Diane Strafaci designed the album cover, and it featured a photo of Julio, Willy Gonzalez and Steve Williams in all their muscle glory. The album may have been designed by a woman, but it definitely appealed to gay men, and it did well. But our relationship with Taana, one of our biggest stars, was disintegrating. Taana had a new boyfriend and manager, an 18-year-old hoodlum, who not only carried a gun, but let everybody know it. He would accompany Taana to her performances and threaten club owners: unless Taana was paid up front, and paid better money, she wouldn't go on. There's a long, sleazy tradition of that kind of thing in the lower echelons of the music business. It amounts to extortion, and it was exactly the kind of business practice that I did not want West End to be associated with. So even though Taana was one of our few remaining successes, our relationship began to grow distant, and Taana began to grow apart from her producer Kenny Nix as well. Things were not looking good, and Ed was constantly complaining about cash flow. I didn't want to hear about it, and it began to become a drag just to go into the office every day.

To make matters worse, Ed and I found ourselves in the midst of an ugly lawsuit in the spring of 1983, and our adversaries were none other than Larry Levan and his nasty sidekick Michael DeBenedictus. The two of them had produced a song called "Something Special," which was meant as a follow up to "Don't Make Me Wait." Ed and I had paid them plenty of money to finish this production, and as usual it had taken forever. But now that it was done, Michael DeBenedictus refused to release it unless West End agreed to pay them even more money. Ed and I considered this blackmail, and we refused. DeBenedictus convinced Larry that they should take the song to a bigger label and get a more lucrative deal. They trooped over to Chris Blackwell at Island Records and, without telling him that they were under contract to us and that West End had already financed the song, proceeded to sell it to him. We had no choice but to sue.

It was traumatic. For one thing, Larry was my old and cherished friend, my surrogate son. I could hardly believe that he could do such a thing, even under the influence of DeBenedictus and all the drugs he was taking. For another thing, West End wasn't doing well, and we really needed another hit. Luckily, Chris Blackwell was reasonable. When he found out that we had paid for the production of the song, he agreed to reimburse us $50,000, and we didn't have to drag things out in court.

I'll never forget the day we all met in Chris's office to sign the final papers. Larry was extremely upset about the whole situation, pacing around, snarling in the corner, whispering with DeBenedictus. Even though it was obvious that Ed and I were the wronged party, DeBenedictus had convinced Larry that we were somehow taking advantage of him. To get back at me, Larry made a point of mentioning that Jaime was throwing a surprise birthday party for Michael and that I had not been invited. He knew that this would upset me even more than the lawsuit — and it did. I have long forgotten the business details of that meeting but I vividly remember that snub. When mutual friends confronted Jaime about it later, he pretended that he had simply forgotten to invite me. But I knew better.

jaime takes over

Jaime and I had not been getting along for quite some time. To put it simply, I loathed him and thought he was a terrible influence on Michael. He could be a charmer when he wanted, and plenty of people were taken in by his snaky little smiles and his glamorous lifestyle and lines of cocaine. But I saw him for what he was: money grubbing, egotistical, over-bearing, social climbing, superficial, callous toward others, an asshole. I tried to hide these feelings and quietly hoped that Michael would eventually realize just how nasty his boyfriend was. I thought that this had finally happened the time Michael went on a trip to

Puerto Rico and, while he was gone, Jaime completely redecorated Michael's apartment. Tore down walls, put in new carpeting, the works. Michael was furious when he returned. He hated what Jaime had done. He took it as a blatant put down, a comment by Jaime on Michael's own plebeian taste. I really thought Jaime had gone too far, and that this would be the end of their relationship.

But no. If anything, Jaime's hold over Michael, and his influence at the Garage, only grew. Before the apartment fiasco, Jaime was satisfied being the power behind the throne. Now, he took a more open role in running the place, even taking over directly when Michael went on trips. And he was not exactly beloved by the staff, even by many of his purported friends.

One such friend was Eduardo, who collected tickets at the door. One night, right in front of Eduardo, Jaime pointed to him and said, *"Mel, what do you think of this big fat slob?"* It was the mean kind of thing he did knowing he could get away with it because he controlled the purse strings and slept with the boss. I wouldn't say something like that to a stranger, but insults were the least of Jaime's sins. Another time he developed some grudge against David DePino, and when Michael left town Jaime stopped paying David's salary. David kept quiet, and kept working, biding his time until Michael returned, at which point he quietly told Michael what Jaime had done.

Michael at first refused to believe it, because the records showed that the money for David's salary had been faithfully withdrawn each week — in cash. Then it became obvious that Jaime was not only ripping off David, he was pocketing the money himself. But although Michael was ashamed of Jaime, and although he immediately reinstated David's salary, he did nothing to discipline Jaime. It was almost as though Jaime had some strange power over Michael, that he was the custodian of some secret, and that Michael was powerless to challenge him. Years later we would find out that it was in fact this. But for now, having gotten away with the David DePino rip-off, Jaime was, if anything, emboldened, and moved to take even more control.

He now set about to ensure that his intrigues would never again be exposed to Michael. First, he maneuvered to have his ex-lover Emilio Rubio hired as manager. Emilio was extremely capable and likable, and I'm sure that Michael agreed to hire him for these qualities alone, not simply because he was Jaime's ex. But the fact that Emilio owed his new position to Jaime made Jaime's position practically unassailable. Jaime's next move was to have his extremely close friend Elida Carazo placed in the position where Jaime wanted the most direct control — where the money was. Elida was made club cashier, and even though she was close to Michael, her ultimate loyalty was to Jaime. When she needed a green card to stay in the U.S., Jaime married her.

Jaime had now filled the two most important positions in the club with his own close friends. It's hard to imagine why Michael fell for this, since he had been very clever about easing Larry's close friends out of those same positions just a few years before, realizing that in such pivotal jobs he needed people who were loyal to him alone. But now he surrendered more and more power to Jaime, and it was very clear to the rest of us that Jaime was planning to be around for the long haul. Most of the staff who had long-established relationships with Michael disliked Jaime. And more often these friends suddenly found themselves on the outs with Michael. Jaime would whisper something into Michael's ear, some exaggeration, some incriminating lie, some intrigue, and the next thing you know, somebody would be demoted or fired. I'll never forget when Michael called Joey Llanos, one of his oldest and most loyal employees, and fired him over the phone after Joey had had some harsh words with Jaime. Others were tired of refusing Jaime's sexual advances. And as far as women were concerned, Jaime had a deep animosity and was constantly trying to get rid of Michael's female friends. Judy Weinstein, because she is female, found herself increasingly excluded from Michael's confidence after Jaime began to consolidate his position. The club's original, family atmosphere began to dissipate. Slowly but surely, the well was poisoned.

jaime and me

Because of my long and deep relationship with Michael, Jaime viewed me as the greatest potential threat to his power: Public Enemy No. 1. In retrospect I have never been sure whether I actually cautioned Michael about Jaime at the outset of their relationship, or whether Michael used my "Mr. Big" reputation to try to intimidate Jaime the way he used it with other employees. Whatever the case, Jaime once confronted me in a moment of rare candor — I'm sure he was massively high on coke at the time, since he usually was — and said *"I've hated you for years, because you once said to Michael, 'Be careful of Jaime and his friends, they're going to screw you.'"* I told him that I didn't remember ever actually saying that to Michael (Lord knows I thought it to myself often enough), but I didn't deny it. I told Jaime that I might have said it, and that if so, it was wrong of Michael to tell him. Needless to say, this hardly endeared me to Jaime. As long as he remained in the picture, my relationship with Michael was headed for more trouble than ever. And Jaime would remain in the picture for life.

As 1983 began, Ignacio and Manolo threw a big surprise 50th birthday party for me at their apartment on 54th St. Michael was in rare form that night, laughing and carrying on, acting as if all the tension and bad vibes were a bad dream. We tore the house up that night, and everything was great until Carmen's loser boyfriend Louie got wasted and fell onto a glass coffee table and shattered it. Then Louie got belligerent and challenged Julio to step outside and fight. Someone intervened and got Louie out of there, thank god, and good spirits were restored.

Louie aside, it was a great night. I felt surrounded by love, and was showered with thoughtful gifts. A bonsai from Claire. A tiny TV from Michael that could fit on your wrist. "A Book of Memories" from Brent, filled with poems and songs and pictures he had taken of our friends and my paintings. I was deeply moved by this outpouring of affection, and I was particularly happy that Michael was in such rare form. It was one of the best evenings I had spent with him in ages, and it was made more special since he was there with Jaime and I was there with Julio and we were all getting along.

Ignacio and Manolo had created an enormous card in the form of a record, and everybody signed it. I was touched that Michael wrote, *"Mel, you are a star. I love you."* To my surprise, Jaime also wrote *"I love you."* Perhaps we could come together after all. But later that night, Jaime pointed out his message on the card, turned to me and said, with his usual ice, *"Since Michael loves you, I guess I have to too."* It was the last time Jaime would ever use the word love and my name together in the same sentence.

the greatest show on earth

Over 1983, GMHC had slowly spread out on 22nd St., so that by now they occupied three-quarters of the building. I had never charged them rent, but with the group now occupying most of the building, we signed an agreement in which they would pay a token rent of $200 for however much space they needed. Still, even though they were getting their headquarters virtually for free, the expenses mounted as the caseload grew, and something clearly had to give. By January 1983 they were stumbling from crisis to crisis. Cases of AIDS — it had now been officially named Acquired Immunodeficiency Syndrome — were doubling almost every month, and no matter how much money we raised, it was never enough. AIDS was now the number one topic of gay life. It seemed that people were getting sick everywhere, but nowhere more so than in our circle. At this point, none of my closest friends — Michael, Julio, Ignacio, Larry Levan or McDevitt, Brent — were affected. Yet. But I now knew tons of acquaintances and friends of friends who were suffering and dying, and the organization we had founded to battle this horrible disease looked as though it would never be able to handle the increase in demand. Fifty grand had been a windfall the year before. Now we needed a million. Even more.

It was at this point that Paul Popham came up with the idea of booking an entire night of the Ringling Bros. Circus at Madison Square Garden for a benefit. It was an audacious idea. The Garden is huge, GMHC was small, and the idea of filling up such a gigantic space was breathtaking. Merely to make the down payment to reserve the evening was going to cost $100,000 — more money than we had ever raised up to that point. But Larry McDevitt came up with an ingenious plan. He pointed out that we all had plenty of friends who could afford to lend the group $1,000 each. If we simply approached 100 people and got each one to lend us a thousand dollars, we'd have the down payment. It worked so well that within a few days we had loans from 135 people, and actually had to start sending money back. We booked the circus, and began to sell tickets. By March 15th, advance ticket sales were going so well that we were able to return the money borrowed from our friends. But the board came up with a clever plan. They decided that we would wait until after the circus was over and everyone had seen what a fabulous event it was. Then we would write to our donors offering to return their loans, but we would word the letter in such a way as to encourage them to forget about it. It worked brilliantly. Many never asked to be repaid, and we raised significant extra cash from that little scheme.

But amid all the planning for the circus, there was major trouble behind the scenes. Larry Kramer had been baiting Mayor Koch for his inaction about AIDS, and baiting the board of GMHC for not baiting Koch as strongly as Larry himself was. He was convinced that AIDS required political action as much as caregiving and service-providing. He argued that we had to scream and yell to get society to help us. And his number one target was Mayor Koch. Larry finally confronted and embarrassed the mayor at Lenox Hill Hospital; the confrontation made the network news, and Koch reluctantly agreed to meet with a delegation from GMHC. But even though the meeting was a direct result of Larry's actions, he was not picked to be part of the delegation. Board members thought he was too confrontational, and that he would probably just antagonize the mayor. They chose Mel Rosen and Paul Popham to represent the group instead. This pushed Larry over the limit, and he offered his resignation to Paul Popham on the spot. To his surprise, Paul accepted it, and later that night the board voted to accept it as well. They had gotten tired of constantly fighting with Larry over what he thought was their timidity, which he usually phrased as their "chickenshit" attitude. Most of the guys on the board were just not the screaming type. They felt that they had their hands full simply trying to care for the afflicted and provide services and that kind of thing. Many of them, like me, were still more closeted than out, including Paul Popham. It would take a few more years, and a lot more death, before Larry Kramer would be able to found a second group — ACT-UP — which would finally take to the streets.

Larry almost immediately regretted his resignation and wanted back in. But the board refused to reinstate him, which prompted him to write a series of passionate letters. *"You guys simply must be pushed into more action,"* he wrote.

> One of the saddest things for me has been to find out how enormously disappointing each and every one of you has been as a friend. But one of my problems is that I expect too much. Or perhaps we weren't really friends. FIGHT HARDER. AND FASTER.

It was against this background of strife that the planning for the circus proceeded, and finally the big night finally arrived. The circus was billed as "The Biggest Gay Event of All Time," and it surely was. Madison Square Garden was completely sold out. In the gorgeous souvenir program, which was designed by Enno Poersch, West End took out a full page ad: *"Through our crisis we have found unity. Since the cost is so high, let us use it wisely."*

The night began with Shirley Verrett of the Metropolitan Opera singing the national anthem as Leonard Bernstein conducted the orchestra. It was electric, and when it was done all 15,000 of us were screaming at the top of our lungs. Then the circus began and everybody went wild. I'm sure that none of those jugglers and lion tamers had ever heard ovations like that before, or since. But perhaps the most bittersweet moment of all came during Paul Popham's speech. He asked Larry Kramer to stand up and be acknowledged with the rest of the founders of GMHC, and the applause was deafening. Larry was always controversial and he remains so to this day. But people understood his contribution, and that was their way of thanking him for it.

I was thrilled with the success of the circus, and by the fabulous post-circus party that Michael threw at the Garage later that night. The wonderful Sharon Redd sang her hits "Beat the Street" and

"In the Name of Love," and Michael promised to donate all of the liquor proceeds from the evening to GMHC. But like everything else back then, backstage backstabbing marred even that success. A couple of months later GMHC had still not received the proceeds from the Garage party, and the producer of the circus event, Harry Diaz, wrote to Michael asking where the money was. Unfortunately, Harry decided to copy the letter to me, saying later that he believed that since Michael and I were close, it might help if Michael knew that I was aware of the situation. But since Jaime was now in the picture, it did not help. In fact, it was a disaster.

Michael wrote back that Jaime had a friend from Puerto Rico who had arrived in New York sick with AIDS and penniless, and that this friend had gone to GMHC for help. Since GMHC had simply referred Jaime's friend to welfare and food stamps, Jaime and Michael, furious, decided that instead of donating the benefit money to GMHC, they would give it directly to Jaime's friend instead, to help pay doctors, food, and living expenses. But with that Michael wasn't finished. *"I question why a copy of your letter was sent to Mel Cheren,"* he wrote.

> Mr. Cheren is a volunteer in this crisis, and not an official of GMHC, nor does he have anything to do with me or Paradise Garage. Mr. Cheren has used the information contained in the letter in a negative manner with the intent of embarrassing me and discrediting the Paradise Garage.

I had done nothing of the sort, but I wasn't really that surprised. Michael's letter had Jaime written all over it. I could just see him whispering lies into Michael's ear, and then probably dictating the letter to Michael, or even writing it up himself.

Jaime's hold over Michael was not only a drain on his friends and his business, it was also a drain on Michael himself. As hard as Jaime pushed him away from his old circle, something always pulled him back, some memory of better times. Jaime would inspire Michael to an outburst of vindictiveness, like the letter to Harry Diaz, and then Michael would turn around and try to make things up, usually when Jaime wasn't around. Nothing better illustrates this than another incident, which happened the summer Michael wrote that nasty letter.

Michael invited me out to his house on Fire Island. This, by itself, wasn't so unusual. With Michael, nasty incidents often happened amid friendly gestures. But this weekend was different. One afternoon we sat on the deck and he suddenly began pouring his heart out to me. As he talked about his many complex business problems, the problems of a successful entrepreneur, it reminded me of the old days, when he often cried on my shoulder. I thought about the day we met on the island when he was a 19-year-old messenger boy with everything to look forward to. I thought about our dream on the steps of the Loft of a disco democracy where gay men could celebrate themselves in all their diversity, and how wonderful it was that Michael had actually made that dream come true, but how strange it was as well: Nothing turns out the way you envision it when you're young. Even success.

Gay life had lost its innocence since those early days. I had lost mine, and Michael had lost his. And we had lost each other. As he spoke, he reminded me of the boy he once was, alone and insecure, an anger deep down inside, the hurt of his childhood still festering under the skin of a budding millionaire. Suddenly, without any prompting from me, he began speaking of Jaime, and I was startled by what he said. *"I hate him,"* Michael spat out. *"I hate him because he hates my friends, hates the island, hates everything. And he's always either drunk or high on coke. He makes me totally miserable."* I said nothing. There didn't seem any need. Michael knew what he was doing. If things with Jaime were so bad that he could actually speak of hate, then nothing I could say could change things. For once, Michael would have to work out his destiny without any help from me. I didn't press him for specifics that afternoon. I wish now that I had. I only found out much later from Joey Llanos of a conversation he'd had with Michael that did get specific. Michael told Joey that he had caught Jaime in bed with so many different people on so many different occasions, including right in Michael's own home, that his feelings for Jaime had completely evaporated. He confided that they no longer slept together, since the very idea of physical intimacy with Jaime disgusted him. And yet they stayed together, tied by some bond that no one understood.

It was touching that I could still have such moments with Michael, that we could briefly revert to our old roles, me the mentor, he the kid needing a shoulder to cry on. But such moments didn't last long. That same summer Michael offered me his Fire Island house for an entire wonderful week, which I spent with Julio, Ignacio, Manolo and a new friend from the Garage, Ricky Willock. It seemed like another example of the old Michael — generous, giving, wanting to do something nice for the people he loved — except that he charged me a thousand bucks for the week.

chapter fifteen
THE BUBBLE
BURST

The year 1983 was a disaster for West End. We weren't on top of things anymore but I couldn't really blame the music industry. In fact, dance music was booming, it simply wasn't booming for us. It was the year of Michael Jackson's *Thriller*, the second biggest selling album of all time, and its signature hits, "Billy Jean" and "Beat It," were disco in every sense. This was also the breakout year for Culture Club, whose cross-dressing lead singer Boy George would be at home on any gay dance floor.

But while the public kept on dancing, the whole context had changed. MTV now ruled the music business and new wave was the music of the moment. With the help of flashy videos, groups like Men at Work, Eurythmics, and Duran Duran sold millions. Michael Jackson and Boy George were photogenic, charismatic video celebrities, as famous for their looks, their style, their moves, their personalities, as for their music. The old Svengali days, when producers concocted hits with near-anonymous singers, building them up in exclusive dance clubs, creating a buzz among the disco glitterati that filtered down to mall girls in Duluth — those days were gone in a world ruled by MTV.

And yet that is what we did, Ed and I, at West End. We were known for the old-style gay and black club music that was the mainstay of our business, and as far as the general public was concerned, that style was now as dead as... well, as dead as disco. By now the biggest groups and artists from our era — the Village People, Gloria Gaynor, Sister Sledge — were practically oldies acts. *"Video,"* as the lyrics said, *"killed the radio star,"* and styles passed us by. I could have tried to keep up with things and change with the times, but with drugs and AIDS closing in, I had enough problems just making it from day to day. A major effort to change professionally, to branch out in new directions, to reinvigorate a dying business, was just beyond me. I felt increasingly like a dinosaur facing extinction. From a business perspective, I was.

For a while I nursed hopes that the setbacks of 1983 could be reversed. We worked out a deal to license and sell our records in Britain through Arista Records, and the deal looked great on paper. The West End logo would be prominently displayed on the top of the record labels, with a small mention of Arista at the bottom. We'd burst into the hot British market backed by one of the biggest record companies around, and they'd get a toehold in the hardcore dance music and black music market. When our first Arista release, Raw Silk's "Do It to the Music," did very well in London, I thought our problems were over. But there was a reason why Arista had never been successful marketing our kind of music. They had no feel for it, didn't understand it, didn't really like it. And ultimately, that meant they couldn't sell it. So after our first success, nothing much came of the deal, and it soon became clear that Arista was not going to save us.

As '84 progressed, the setbacks of '83 turned into debacle. Money leached out of the company, debts piled up, and somebody had to fork over cash to keep us afloat. Somehow, that somebody was always me. Ed argued that he had no cash reserves, or that his wife controlled the family finances and wouldn't let him throw good money after bad, or argued that I owned real estate and I could afford it. While he piled up excuses, I poured in the cash. He was simply unwilling to help bail out West End, so it was either me or bankruptcy, and I couldn't accept that my record company was doomed. When we released Forrrce's "Keep On

Dancin'" (which did not sell very well), I took another puff of angel dust and made it my theme song. I was going to keep on dancing even if the whole world fell apart.

my angel carolina

It was at this point that I teamed up with Carol Kohlreiter, an ambitious businesswoman with big connections and big ideas for West End. She was pals with all sorts of stars and executives, she seemed to be bulging with money, and she saw me as her next project. I fell for her, hook, line and sinker.

I thought Carol was a dream come true. A born optimist was just what I needed at a time in my life when things were falling apart, when death and illness and failure seemed to be closing in around me. She gave me the promise of better days. If I had been straight, I probably would have fallen in love with her. In a way, I suppose I did. Ed couldn't stand her from the start. He had seen these types before, he said, too many times. Phonies. Leeches. And usually when he saw them, they were feeding off of me. It was a pattern, he said, and it was getting worse. I suppose I should have listened, but by now Ed and I were on different planets and I didn't take his advice seriously, or really take it at all. What did sour old Ed know about Carol or anybody else? He wasn't on angel dust practically every night. He didn't know that feeling when that extra hit of cocaine kicks in and the ideas and plans start flowing and the music is lifting you into some better place and everything seems possible. He didn't understand that Carol could make things happen. Ed was Mr. Business, Mr. No. And Carol was Miss Right. Miss Hope. Miss Fun. I went with her.

Her first big project was to open a West End office in London, which she was going to call Other End. It went nowhere. Next she found a group she wanted to produce, a rock/dance act called Sensus. They seemed thoroughly average, but Carol had huge plans for them. She could guarantee heavy rotation on MTV, she said. She had the contacts, was plugged into the hit-making machinery. If West End agreed to release the product, we were headed for the big time again.

Ed was having none of it. He insisted that if Carol was so fucking confident, she could invest thirty grand of her own money into West End to show her commitment. We fought like trapped animals. I thought it was an insult to Carol, making her pay for the privilege of working with us. I was embarrassed that Ed would stoop so low, and make us look so cheap. So when he continued to insist that Carol put up or shut up, I secretly offered to advance the thirty grand to Carol myself as a gesture of good faith. We would let Ed think that the money came from her, and perhaps he'd begin to believe in her.

We shot the Sensus video on the same day that West End had a meeting with singer Lola Falana, who was interested in breaking into the dance music market and was shopping for a new label. I was terribly impressed with Lola Falana, who was not only poised and beautiful but seemed incredibly classy and professional. Things were looking up. Then the Sensus video was released, I held my breath, and everything fell apart. The video was a resounding dud. Ed never believed in Carol's connections to MTV, but even if she did have them, it didn't matter in the end. The video never got airtime, was never really in contention. It was all a pipe dream, a lost cause.

Then the other shoe dropped. Ed found out that I had actually loaned Carol the thirty grand and pretended it came from her, to deceive him and show him I had been right about Carol all along. I had seen Ed plenty mad before, but never anything like this. He was beyond furious. He'd go speechless, then explode in rants that cut me to the bone. He dredged up every mistake I ever made in my life, and there was plenty to choose from, especially when it came to being a bad judge of character and being taken for a ride. I had increasingly involved myself, and sometimes Ed, with a stream of bad prospects, flop songs, professional slackers like Larry Levan and Michael DeBenedictus, ego cases like Jacques Morali, cockeyed optimists like Carol, bad investments every one. Worse, as he saw it, I was constantly supporting gold diggers, gigolos, slick operators like Michael, hard-luck cases like Carmen, hot young guys whom I hired mainly for their looks. I was out of control, spending money I didn't have and failing to seek out and find the genuine talent that would have kept the money coming in. Ed forced me to demand the thirty grand back from Carol. When she initially hesitated, I panicked and wrote her a sharp note threatening legal action. She quickly repaid me, but we terminated our relationship, and I was back to square one.

The whole business with Carol depressed me tremendously. Ed continued to attack me relentlessly, and going into the office became a nightmare. Then the deal with Lola Falana fell through, mainly because things were so financially tight at West End. For the first time, I questioned not whether West End would survive, but whether I wanted it to. And under the circumstances, the answer seemed to be no. Music was no longer fun. Nothing, for that matter, was much fun. But music was becoming a serious negative, an emotional and financial drain. With all my other problems, it didn't seem worth it anymore.

a pile of problems

I certainly had plenty of other problems. My own drug taking was already out of control, and as things got worse, it did too. I suppose that raises the old addict's question: how much were drugs causing my other problems and how much were drugs a reaction to them? In my case, the answer was both. I had been in training for my addiction long before AIDS and long before business began to go sour, but while things were going well all the dust, pot, coke and booze seemed under control, harmless, even liberating. As trouble gathered, as AIDS swelled into a nightmare, as business went south, drugs took more control, clouding my judgment about everything — business, friends, relationships, life — and contributing to bad decisions, important mistakes, failures. As these multiplied, there was only one thing to do: take more drugs. And so I spiraled down, locked in an addict's embrace with Julio. He was already at rock bottom and seemed to like it there.

His sister Carmen and her boyfriend Louie seemed to like it there too, although their poison was plain old booze. One day drunk as a skunk, Louie turned on the gas stove in the apartment, but passed out without lighting it. The gas fumes overwhelmed the building and almost blew it up, and the landlord, fed up with Carmen and Louie's drunken brawls, moved to evict them. Now it's very hard to evict someone in Manhattan for any reason, as I well know, and in this case the judge was Latina herself and seemed to side with Carmen at first. But on her crucial day in court, Carmen barged in like a boozed-up bat out of hell, surly and argumentative and itching for a fight. She was too charged up to understand that the judge was taking her side. The judge would ask her a simple question, and she'd spit out things like, *"If they don't want me in the building, I don't want to live there!"* Within a few minutes the judge was fed up and said fine, you want out, baby, you're out. Case closed.

By this time I was so locked into the grid of what we now call co-dependency that there was no question that I wouldn't run to the rescue once again. Julio descended from the dusted heavens long enough to decide that the only way to make sure that Carmen was safe from eviction was for me to buy a co-op and rent it back to her. I agreed wholeheartedly, mostly because of my concern for little Gigi, who had enough problems just trying to grow up in that atmosphere. I knew that with Carmen's reputation she could never find a place that required references, so I eventually managed to find a decent little one-bedroom in Chelsea, bought it and they settled in.

Just when I was getting all this straightened out the IRS came to call. I had never been audited before, and for years I had entrusted my finances to a character named Jack Webber, who seemed comical enough, with his ten chins and his stutter. But I soon found out that my books were a total mess, Jack was a so-and-so (my lawyer demands I curb my true words for Jack), and I had to find a new accountant — not a happy prospect when you're in a major audit by the IRS. Luckily, I found Alan Landzberg, a great attorney specializing in tax law. He managed to straighten everything out, and in the process became a valued friend.

It just seemed like the world was coming unstuck. Even good things turned bad. In February Michael closed the Garage for the staff trip to Rio, and it turned into a minor international fiasco. Some of them got in trouble with drugs and the law (no small trick in laid-back Rio). Michael spent half his time bribing authorities and bailing people out and spiriting them out of the country. Everyone managed to get back to New York in one piece, but there was a strange feeling in the air after that, as though things were slightly out of control.

The Garage lumbered on with huge parties and some great performances, and it was now transformed by an incredible new sound system that Larry designed, featuring his bass-heavy speakers, the Levans. Michael added the fabulous Crystal Room and a Visuals Room where films were shown, and he made sure the place kept growing and the changes kept coming. Between the tension and the extravagance and illness and the heroin that now seemed to float through the crowd like a dark haze, the Garage had a whole new edge.

There was an invasion of sorts by the House of Extravaganza, one of the great snapping, voguing *"houses"* of young drag queens that were a fixture of black gay New York. Larry knew all about houses. He had met Frankie Knuckles years before when the two of them tagged along with a house in Harlem. In a way the Garage was like a giant house itself, the House of Levan. But the 'Ganzas were something else. Years before they charmed movie audiences in the documentary *Paris Is Burning,* they were smoking the Paradise Garage. I think Larry was wary of them at first. They were highly competitive and they were determined to rule and snap and outshine in every way. Their chief approach to life was summed up by the phrase *"giving shade,"* which loosely translates into *"not taking any shit,"* and if Larry was not on their wavelength, they were perfectly happy to throw Miss Levan a whole bucketful of shade. But great minds think alike, and pretty soon Larry and the 'Ganzas were thick as thieves, and the combination injected a major dose of mad drag queen energy into the Garage. The place became their second home, and they seemed wiser in a sense than other Garage regulars who centered their lives on the club. After all, on Mondays, after the party was over, the 'Ganzas still had each other.

Graffiti artist Keith Haring became a major fixture on the Garage scene, and he and Larry became close friends. Together they co-hosted the first "Party of Life" in April, a fabulous, star-filled event. Madonna debuted her new song "Like a Virgin," and the super A-list people (Andy Warhol, Halston and Diane Von

Furstenberg) swarmed all over the Garage, not their usual haunt. David DePino was entertaining Diana Ross in the DJ booth when Grace Jones walked in, done up as only Grace can be. *"The Queen is here,"* David announced. Diana Ross shot him a look of daggers. There was only one queen where she was concerned.

That summer the edge got sharper. A drug dealer named John-Boy had been passing off baking powder for cocaine, which didn't sit well with somebody. One night outside the club a limo pulled up, a window rolled down, a gun appeared, and John-Boy was lying in a pool of his own blood. Needless to say, the neighborhood association was in an uproar over a drive-by shooting in artsy, middle class downtown Greenwich Village. The Garage was blamed, naturally, and pressure intensified to shut it down.

casa '84

I couldn't take much more, and it was with great relief that I rented a house on Fire Island that summer from my old friend Bill Klein. We called it Casa '84. By this time a lot of friends were visibly sick but never spoke about it, and Bill was one of these. AIDS was such a terror that many chose to suffer in silence rather than deal with pity or ostracism. A typical way to find out that a friend was sick was to look at him one day and see, with a sudden sense of dread, that he had that look. That gaunt broken look, like a medieval artist's rendition of incarnate death: hollow eyes, bulging cheekbones, a gray pallor. Bill had that look.

I put it all behind me once I got out to the Island. Bill's house was a total dream, two huge glass octagons on stilts with views of both the ocean and the bay side. It was airy and open, a vessel of brightness in the gathering gloom. I filled it with old and new friends mixed — Ignacio and Manolo, Brent, Chaz, — and tried to fill in the void with good company, tons of drugs, and painting. I painted like a maniac all summer. I was trying to lose myself in a dream of escape. Not that I could really escape anymore. Ed's constant, demanding calls from West End did not stop just because I was 60 miles away; and Fire Island was ground zero of the AIDS epidemic, sickness and reminders everywhere, sometimes terrifying reminders. Larry Basile, a new friend that summer who was soon to become a best friend, returned to the house with a horror story.

Larry had met a handsome guy on the dance floor of the Pavilion and they went back to the guy's house for sex, which happened to be unprotected, and unsafe. Afterwards, the guy casually showed Larry a lesion and told him it was Kaposi's sarcoma, with a little hint that perhaps Larry might now get it too. Larry was blown away, and we urged him to speak to the guy's housemates. When he did, they informed him that they all knew what he was doing — he was apparently doing it all the time — and that they had been begging him to desist, but to no avail. A couple of years later, when Randy Shilts published *And the Band Played On*, he related the story of Patient Zero. A Canadian airline steward who had done the same kind of thing all over the country, including at a famous house on Ocean Walk in the Pines, which would be considered the first epicenter of the epidemic. I knew everybody in that house, and I remember thinking that the Patient Zero story was pretty farfetched. Not because it wasn't true, but because there must have been lots of Patient Zeros. Tons of them, including the guy who had sex with Larry Basile.

Chaz came out to the Island. After his stint as a successful caterer Chaz was now maitre d' at Claire's restaurant, and he was the model of hard work and sobriety, at least compared to me. He was horrified about the condition I was in, fiddling on Fire Island while New York burned. With his typical outback honesty, he told me point blank that I was squandering precious time painting and partying and taking drugs. *"Ya should be back in the city, mate, fighting to save West End and working on your building on 22nd St. Ya gotta fight."*

He was right. Even if I couldn't save West End, I could save the building on 22nd St. The '80s real estate boom in New York had finally caught up with Chelsea, the neighborhood of my building was suddenly hot. Whole blocks were being renovated, rents were going higher; my gritty old street was showing unmistakable signs of elegance. With the proper investment, a building like mine could become a gold mine as a co-op or rental apartments, or as a guesthouse. It certainly was big enough to be a small hotel. And I could now do something with the place, now that GMHC was beginning to move out.

Despite all my other troubles, at least I had this valuable piece of real estate, Chaz pointed out, my remnant of my years with Michael. Doing something with it wasn't going to be easy since the city had just announced a moratorium on converting SRO rooming houses into co-ops. (My building technically remained an SRO, even though there were only a couple of intransigent tenants left.) But however easy or however difficult, I wasn't doing anything for anybody by drugging myself into a Fire Island dreamland out there and painting myself into a corner. If my finances continued their downward spiral and I did nothing, Chaz pointed out that I could end up losing 22nd St. as well. But I just wasn't into it. I wasn't into doing anything about West End. I knew Chaz was right, but it was easier to light up some more angel dust and plow my hands into my paints, and trust in a providence that had clearly deserted me.

This summer was the last of my life before AIDS. True, it wasn't really life before AIDS, since AIDS had already happened. But it hadn't really happened to my immediate circle yet. Not to Michael and Julio and Larry Levan and Larry McDevitt and Chaz and Brent and Ignacio and Ray Ford and Dick Fisher and new friends like Larry Basile. It hadn't happened to me. It was everywhere around us now, but it wasn't in us. I could push it away if I really tried, and I feared that there wasn't much time, that it would find a way in.

This summer was also the swan song of my record business, the business I had devoted my whole career to. Everything was connected, and everything was about to wither, and I didn't want to know that it was true. And so I imploded under a mountain of drugs, and exploded in a burst of creativity, and blew the nightmare away for one last time. And amazingly enough, I was happy. It's one of the paradoxes of my life. That summer was one of the happiest and most productive seasons of my life. As it drew to a close, Bill Klein came out and asked me if I wanted to buy the house. He was franker now. His illness could no longer be hidden, and he didn't try. He was dying, he said. He would not be needing the house anymore, and wanted me to have it, since it agreed with me so well. He had *"bought a mountaintop"* somewhere, he said, and was going off to be in peace. I would have loved to buy Bill's house, if for no other reason than that he wanted me to have it. But I was in no position to buy anything. I was this close, but also about to begin losing things. It broke my heart to pack up the summer's odds and ends and say goodbye to Bill, and plunge back into the plague. But there was no way out.

back to reality

Brent had suffered a nasty summer breakup with his lover Al. I offered him a space on 22nd St. in exchange for his services as superintendent. So at least the building was being well managed.

Ignacio and Manolo helped Brent with the design of his rooms on the top floor, and Brent did most of the work himself, clearing away rubble from GMHC and long departed tenants. One day a huge refrigerator he was hauling broke loose and tumbled down a flight of stairs after Brent just two steps ahead. He landed at the bottom of the stairs and was about to be crushed, just when this huge tumbling refrigerator got wedged-in between the wall and the banister. Sometimes we realize how lucky we are, even in the midst of general desolation. Nothing happens by accident, not even accidents. Things can always get worse.

By mid-September Brent was finished with his room, and I was impressed. The room was beautiful, spare and elegant, and it demonstrated the building's potential. It wasn't that 22nd St. was really a wreck, it was just a mess. Intrinsic beauty was lurking just under the fading facade. I finally became serious about renovating the whole building, and I began planning an apartment for myself there as well. I loved my uptown penthouse and had no desire to move, but I knew in the back of my mind that if things got much worse it might have to go, and so I got Manolo to design a nice garden duplex for the ground floor, and hoped I would never have to move in.

But I still had a seemingly insurmountable problem: the city's moratorium on turning SROs into apartments. I begged the bureaucracy to cut me some slack, arguing that I had donated the building to GMHC for several crucial years. But try begging any bureaucracy for anything, especially in New York. No new co-ops, they said, period. Then my old friend Alberto Cintron, who had originally introduced me to Ignacio and Manolo, proposed a simple solution. If the city won't let you convert the building into co-ops, he said, then don't. Convert it into a guesthouse instead. A gay guesthouse. There was no decent gay bed-and-breakfast in the entire city, and since Chelsea was rapidly turning into a gay neighborhood, the place was perfectly located. My new friend Larry Basile operated a gay guesthouse in Boston, and he seemed prosperous enough. It made perfect sense, and so I began.

departure

Just as this huge project was getting underway, the other major project of my life, West End, finally fell apart. At the end of October I received a particularly unsettling call from Ed telling me to come into the office. From the tone in his voice, I could guess that this was it, and it was.

Ed told me we were going bankrupt and that we had to shut down the office and cope with the consequences: the creditors, the legal issues, the unpaid bills. He said that he knew that I didn't want to have to deal with all that, and so he offered to let me out. Our back catalogue was still selling, he said, and he could make enough money off of that to make it worth his while to do all the odious paperwork involved in bankruptcy. In effect, the company would continue as a remnant of its former self. He would pay off old bills from the sale of old product, and I would be released from any further involvement and any further hassles. It made sense to me. I never had a sense for business, and I certainly didn't have a head for the complexities of bankruptcy, which is truly all work and no play. And so I agreed. I handed over all of my stock certificates in West End Music Industries to Ed, assuming he'd need them for the bankruptcy proceedings, and that was that.

In retrospect, I believe Ed never intended to close the company, and probably never intended to file for bankruptcy either. He realized he could probably make a hundred grand a year for many years, simply licensing our old product, but to do that he needed me out of his hair. By telling me we were effectively finished and that we had to shut down, and by nobly offering to take care of the details, he seemed to be doing me a favor .

Of course, it was a terrible mistake to hand over my stock and walk away from West End, leaving its remnants in his hands, but I would only slowly come to realize this over the next several years. I had no idea at the time. Between the friends I was losing and the angel dust I was smoking, I wasn't thinking rationally, or even trying to. All I knew was that I hated the pressure of trying to save a dying business, and now that Ed had declared that the battle was lost, I was almost happy to escape.

We packed everything up — the master tapes, contracts, files, the whole detritus of a dream — and moved the cartons downtown to W. 22nd St. and stored them in the basement, where they remain to this day. It was like the death of a family member who has been sick a very long time: pain at the loss, mingled with relief that the suffering was finally over. I didn't know what I felt, really, but the demise of West End seemed to fit in with everything else that was going on around me. The great Before was really over. Disco, success, optimism, all were all slipping away. The terrible days were now upon me.

halloween

Claire and Marvin threw a Halloween bash at their restaurant, and asked the children in our circle, Gigi and Jason (Chaz's six-year-old son) to get dressed up and hand out party favors. It was all in good fun, and Jay, Jason's mom, created a fantastic costume, dressing him up in a bird outfit made of feathers. Julio and I were late for the party, having another of our epic arguments, but Chaz was there, working as maitre d'. Seeing his son romping around in feathers in a restaurant filled with lighted candles gave him a funny feeling, and he asked the busboy Danny Luna to blow the candles out. Danny went to Bobby Rinaldi, the assistant manager, who refused, and the party went on.

Suddenly, horrible screams and total pandemonium. Jason had reached over a lighted candle, and in an instant his whole body was in flames. Not just an arm or a leg, but everything. Chaz jumped on his son in a vain effort to put out the fire, and burned himself in the process, but Jason was burned practically beyond recognition. They finally got the fire out and covered him in ice until the paramedics arrived and rushed him to the hospital, but the fire's horrible damage had been done.

That same evening, Julio and I rushed to St. Vincent's hospital the second we heard the news, and it was simply beyond belief. Jason was in such extreme pain that there are no words to describe it, and Chaz was past all consolation. As the days went by he held a constant vigil by his son's bedside, wracked with guilt that he was somehow responsible for the tragedy by not insisting that the candles be blown out. But since he had made that request and it had been denied, he decided to resign from his job at the restaurant and sue Claire's for damages.

It eventually became clear that Jason would survive, at the terrible cost of being scarred and disfigured for life. But Chaz and Jay were emotionally scarred as well, and for that matter, we all were. As gay men, there were few children in our lives. Amid the growing fears of AIDS and the sickness looming around us, these kids were like a lifeline, little vessels of hope and light. And now suddenly, this impossible, unbelievable thing. We all felt guilty, all felt that there was something we should have done, or could have done. Any last shred of optimism seemed to be extinguished that night. Jason received a multi-million dollar settlement — small consolation for his shattered childhood and ruined beauty — but there was never an emotional settlement, either for him or for Chaz or Jay, or for the rest of us.

Then, just as I was reeling from this, AIDS finally reached into the center of my life. Ray Ford, one of my oldest and dearest friends, my Bruise partner, was suddenly stricken with toxoplasmosis, a brain infection that destroyed most of his motor functions. It was sudden. One day he was fine, the next he was in the hospital practically unable to do anything for himself, even fasten the snaps on his pajamas. I sewed him a new pair that he did not have to fasten, and brought them to the hospital as a Christmas gift, but the only gift he wanted was to get out and be well again.

AIDS had also struck Emilio Rubio, the former manager of the Garage. He and Ray were in the same hospital. Thus began the ritual that was to become so common in the years ahead. We would go from hospital room to hospital room to be with our friends, just as we had once gone from disco to disco with them. Ray's state of mind was very different from Emilio's. Ray just wanted to get out of the hospital. Emilio just wanted to die. He was ash gray, skin and bones, and he asked if anyone could bring him some pills to end it all. I tried to put a good face on things and be reassuring. *"You've got to keep on living,"* I said, *"and get well and get out of here."* But he just turned his head away. *"This is not living,"* he whispered. And he was right.

Julio and I went to Ignacio and Manolo's for Christmas dinner, and suddenly it seemed like AIDS was everywhere. Herb Walker, one of their other dinner guests, had just been released from the hospital. He seemed confident he was going to beat AIDS. But I was so filled with dread that I could barely eat. A few days later Bob Marshall, an old friend from Fire Island, died, and on January 2nd Dick Fisher and I trooped off to his funeral. Then, that same night, Dick called me with horrendous news.

Ray Ford had been released from the hospital a few days before, and was determined to pick up his life and go back to work. But when he tried to go to his office on the first working day of the new year, he found he couldn't so much as button his shirt. Ray was always extremely proud and had a horror of being a burden to anybody, and so he did what he felt he had to do. He taped the door to his bedroom closed, took dozens of sleeping pills, and lay down to die. Unfortunately, Ray's lover Bob Golden arrived while Ray was still breathing. Bob panicked, called a doctor friend who was nearby, and called 911. The doctor dragged Ray into the shower to revive him, the Emergency Medical Services rushed in right after that, and between them they worked on Ray for a full 45 minutes of pointless agony. Dick and our other close friend Larry McDevitt arrived while all this was going on and they were horrified, not only that Ray had decided to commit suicide, but that he was being put through this final indignity. You couldn't really blame Bob. He couldn't bear losing his partner, the man he loved. In the end, it was useless to try to keep him alive. Ray was dead. And AIDS had finally struck my inner-most circle of friends.

"If I loved you any more, it would be too mushy" was what Ray used to say to me when we'd be out dancing, or walking on Fire Island, or when he'd listen with endless patience as I droned on about my problems. I relied on him so much that I called him my therapist, and banked on the fact that no matter how hard things got, he'd always be there to listen and help. And now he was the first to go, and we never got to say goodbye. I was numb. The aftermath — the arrangements, the funeral, all of it — passed like a dream. Things could simply not get worse.

a shoulder to lean on

Throughout the past year I had become good friends with Larry Basile, and had come to trust and admire him tremendously.

Larry had once studied to become a Catholic priest, but in the years since dropping that calling he turned into a very successful businessman. He owns the Chandler Inn, a thriving gay guesthouse in Boston, as well as a bar and some other businesses, and he also has a highly developed sense of community responsibility. He supports many gay charities, and that quality drew me even closer towards him. Despite the fact that he could dance and drug with the best of us, he is far more organized and focused than most of my friends. It was his success with the Chandler Inn that convinced me that I might have a shot at creating a similar place in New York.

Now, in the aftermath of Ray's death, as I was wandering around in a daze, Larry Basile came to my rescue. As I told him about my problems, he offered to look at my books and help me come up with a workable plan. He realized that I was in very dire straits, and that major changes were going to be necessary if I was going to survive financially. He took out a piece of paper and made a list of those changes, and they were breathtaking. According to Larry, I was going to have to consolidate all my holdings into the building on 22nd St. I would have to sell the building in Brooklyn and the co-op apartment that I was subletting to Carmen. I would have to move out of my penthouse and sublet that as well. I was going to have to move into 22nd St. myself, even though my apartment there was still only in the planning stages and wouldn't be ready in the foreseeable future.

These were hardly minor changes. They meant giving up my whole style of life, and making a million sacrifices and suffering a million indignities in order to try to salvage a future from the ruins of my recent past. The cash flow just wasn't there, and I was supporting people like Carmen when I really could no longer afford to. But despite the fact that Larry convinced me, even terrified me, I just could not bring myself to act on his advice, at least not yet. All I agreed to do was continue to work on the plans for turning 22nd St. into a guesthouse, and I put off everything else. Perhaps these changes wouldn't be necessary. Perhaps there was some other way out.

That winter we made enough progress with the renovations that I was able to open and take in my first guests. The name Colonial House Inn seemed apt, even if the place was not a colonial style building. The words Colonial House had been etched over the front door when I bought the place, and my very first job had been at the Colonial Paint Brush Company. The Colonial House was quite disorganized at first, and hardly luxurious or comfortable. There were only two or three rooms, and none had phones or private baths. But they were very cheap — only $25 dollars a night at first — and Larry Basile sent a lot of business our way from Boston, young gay guys flying down to the city to attend the big disco parties. At least it was a start.

As much as I tried to throw myself into fundraising, it became increasingly clear that I wasn't doing what I really needed to do. Namely, fundraising for myself. My financial condition continued to deteriorate until it finally became obvious — even to me — that I was going to have to bite the bullet and take Larry Basile's advice. It was immensely difficult. That penthouse was the tangible proof that I had made it in life. Leaving it was proof that I had blown it. Since I still nursed hopes that I might be able to move back in someday (the building might eventually go co-op and if I retained the lease I could buy it at an insider's price), I decided to sublet it rather than give it up altogether, and I happened to have a friend who was looking for a place to set up his mistress. This wasn't easy, since the building refused my request. I had to sneak my belongings past the doorman one piece at a time, like a thief, but eventually it was done, and I was out. Moving to Colonial House was like plunging into ice water.

I felt that I was retracing my youthful ascent from rags to riches, but in reverse. I was going from a stunning penthouse to a single shabby room with cockroaches. The conditions were so bad that Julio suggested I move in with him, which was another disaster. We'd have our usual, operatic fights and he'd work himself into some dusted rage and order me out, digging the knife in further by yelling, *"How dare you shout at me in MY apartment."* I'd find myself trooping alone up 8th Ave. with a few shopping bags, like a bag person, back to my crummy little room.

And so I found myself at the lowest point of my life. I remember one particularly stifling summer night, cockroaches crawling up the walls, my shorts sticking to me in the unairconditioned swelter, unable to sleep, in a deep depression, furiously painting a picture of the building as it looked then, with its shabby, peeling facade, a mirror of my soul. I cried so much I could barely see what I was painting, and all the while I kept repeating to myself, *"My life is drech, shit, nothing. After all the success, this is where I have ended up and who I am. Nothing."* The irony was delicious, although I couldn't appreciate it at the time. I had been the sole support of dozens of people. Carmen was at that moment living in a beautiful apartment I was subsidizing. Julio was in his own comfy pad. Ed was living off of the proceeds of our record company. Michael was a multimillionaire, largely thanks to my advice and my help, and here was I, alone in an SRO flophouse, broke, sweltering, ruined. Yes, it was the drugs. Yes, I had made mistakes. Yes, AIDS and the approaching illness of so many friends, and the death of Ray, had thrown me off balance. But it was also my generosity, and the fact that I had given and given and given for years without ever taking for myself. Ed had been right about that. I had been a sucker, too much of a mensch, and this was the price I now had to pay, and it seemed more than I could bear. I seethed with rage, both at myself and at everyone around me who was leeching off me.

There is this to be said for hitting bottom. There's no place to go but up. From that night in hell I made a decision. If I was going to have to live like this, to give up almost everything simply to try to survive, then those around me were going to have to cut themselves loose. No more Mr. Nice Guy. And the first thing that was going to have to go was Carmen's co-op. I figured that she could move into Julio's apartment, and that he could move into the Colonial House with me. It seemed simple and eminently fair, since I had been subsidizing her for years, which not only helped her, but also helped Julio. When I approached her with the idea she was incredulous. *"Oh no,"* she said, *"I could never do anything that would disturb my brother's life."* I couldn't afford to subsidize her anymore and absolutely had to sell the co-op, I told her. *"That's your problem,"* she spat. *"I'm not going anywhere. And if you want to force me, you'll have to pay me ten grand, minimum."* In the process of our argument it all came out — her resentment of me, her long-standing dislike of me — the works. It was a little Latino class war right in the bosom of what I thought was my extended family. *"We have nothing,"* she hissed at one point, *"and you have everything."*

In the old days I would have folded right then and there, but there's nothing like the specter of total ruin to focus the mind. So for perhaps the first time in my life, I said no. I insisted. She was moving, end of story. And to my surprise, she found a place fairly quickly, in a half-sister's apartment not far away, and for less rent. Then I put my Brooklyn building on the market and got lucky. The New York real estate market was booming, and a bidding war broke out between two interested parties. I walked off with a decent profit. Suddenly, things were not so bleak. Just as Larry Basile had predicted, the money from the two sales could accelerate the renovations on Colonial House, including my own apartment there, and pretty soon the place would be a beehive of activity.

Seeing that I had come into some money, even Julio began treating me better. I was heartened also that Michael would come to me for help with the Garage. The city was really cracking down on the club, trying to prove that it was financed by organized crime. This is often the case with nightclubs in New York, but it certainly wasn't the case with the Garage. Michael needed me to sign some documents verifying that I had lent him money to start the place, and I agreed. I was happy to do this, since in my straightened circumstances it somehow felt good to be back in the position of helping Michael.

Then, a few weeks later, I was advancing Ignacio and Manolo a short-term loan to help them buy their co-op apartment, and thanks to a glitch at the bank I was going to be short ten thousand dollars for a single day. I needed a one-day loan for that amount, and I thought it was only natural to go to Michael, for whom a one-day loan of ten grand was tantamount to petty cash. Just to be gracious about it, I offered him a thousand dollars in interest, knowing he would refuse. After all, even a loan shark doesn't get ten percent a day. Michael agreed to lend me the cash and then, to my total astonishment, just as instantly agreed to accept the thousand dollars in interest. A thousand bucks for a single day's loan. I couldn't believe it, and I couldn't do anything about it, since I had made the offer myself. I suppose that as far as my new assertiveness was concerned, it was two steps forward and one step back. That ten grand was jinxed, since it managed not only to strain my always edgy relations with Michael further, but also helped end my old friendship with Dennis Lasker.

Dennis, you recall, was that supremely beautiful boy who had picked me up at Ty's and bought me a drink and with whom I had an affair shortly after Michael and I broke up. We never actually became lovers, partly because he wanted to move to LA to try his hand in the movie business. He had indeed become a successful movie executive, thanks in sum to his love affair with a famous director. I was still a bit in love with him myself, and very impressed by the fact that he hung around with Diana Ross and Jack Nicholson. He was actually the person who first brought Diana to the Garage, a visit that began her long love affair with the club. But on subsequent trips to New York he seemed different, and it occurred to me that, as with so many other friends, drugs were not doing him any good.

Recently Dennis had called me from LA with the news. He had lost his job at Paramount, broken up with his director/lover, lost his apartment, contracted hepatitis, and was in overall bad shape. I flew him to New York and put him up in a room at the Colonial House so he could recover. And by chance, the day I borrowed the $10,000 from Michael and needed a place to stash it for the night, I happened to put it under a mattress in the same room Dennis was staying in, and I told Dennis. The next day, I found it was short eighty dollars. I began to grill Dennis and the truth came out. He had become a serious addict, was shooting drugs, and needed money for a fix. So everything suddenly made sense: the lost job and lost apartment, the end of his relationship, the hepatitis, his overall decline. My beautiful, hopeful, ambitious golden boy was a stone cold junkie.

I suppose that should have been it. If my newfound assertiveness meant anything, it should have meant that when friends rip you off, they cease to be friends. But old habits die hard, and I rationalized that he was simply desperate. A real thief would have taken the whole ten grand and vanished. I chewed him out and let him off the hook. Shortly afterward, I got a call from jail. Dennis had been busted in a shooting gallery, a seedy downtown building where people paid money to stick their arm through a hole in a wall to be injected with their drug of choice — in his case, heroin. He had actually been arrested with the needle still in his arm. This, aside from being disgusting, was particularly criminal in his case; the needles were shared with other users and Dennis had a wicked case of hepatitis. I reluctantly went down to bail him out, and when I got there I also chewed him out. To my surprise, he tried to justify himself by telling me that he had actually gone up to the gallery to score some cocaine for me. Right. This was finally too much, and I booted him out.

the american run for end of aids fiasco

As the AIDS crisis grew, so did my desire to do something to fight it. Sometimes it seemed like the helplessness, that horrible feeling that the world was falling apart and there was nothing you could do, was as bad as the disease itself. Since Brent was busy promoting his AREA run, and since I was on its board of directors, I more or less adopted that as my pet project, and in the process learned some bitter lessons about human nature. Now that I was getting my own financial house in order, I transferred some of my old gullibility, a part of my nature that had hurt me so much in business, into this new pursuit. It didn't serve me any better there.

That summer my Colonial House manager, Alberto Cintron, introduced me to a couple of guys who were working on something called the Spirit Project to raise money for AIDS. Mark Manetti and Mark DeAngelis didn't have any references to speak of. Manetti had worked as a waiter, and they both claimed to have run some big events at the Saint, so I took them at their word and trusted them. They seemed smart and eager and responsible. How bad could people be who were working to fight this horrible plague? I explained to them about Brent's plan to run around America, and they loved it and agreed to join forces. Their idea was to have Brent do a preliminary run around the five boroughs of Manhattan on Halloween, which we'd call the Spirit

Run. A taxicab would follow him with its meter running, and we'd get people to agree to match the amount that was on the meter at the end of the run. We could raise a fortune if enough people agreed to be sponsors, and we'd also get a ton of publicity, which would energize everybody and help publicize the much larger run to come. Mark and Mark agreed to do all the promotion through their Spirit Project — such a scheme would never work unless it was heavily promoted — and I agreed to come up with the ten thousand dollars seed money they would need to do their promotional work. I quickly found nine friends to donate a thousand dollars each, with the last thousand coming from me. It was relatively easy. I promised my friends that if anything went wrong, I would pay them back from my own pocket.

I had become much closer to Paul Popham, the head of GMHC. I truly admired him as the man who had everything — looks, talent, leadership, brains, and a great, giving heart. He was an idol to many people, and I was proud that he had become a friend to me. One day during a meeting for the Spirit Run (Paul had contributed a thousand dollars of his own to the effort, and sat on the advisory board), I noticed some odd make-up on his face. Paul was no drag queen, and makeup looked very incongruous on his face. A few minutes later, when he wasn't looking, I stole a closer look. Under the make-up were the purple spots, the lesions, the Kaposi. Paul, who had done more than anybody to fight the plague, had AIDS himself. I was so devastated I could barely finish the meeting, could barely breathe. For some reason, I had always thought that those who were the first in the fight against AIDS would somehow themselves be spared. It just didn't seem possible that these selfless men, who had taken up the banner to save their stricken friends, could possibly become stricken themselves. Now, in one instant, I felt the true impersonality of nature. AIDS was going to kill Paul. I began to think, when I could think again, that it was going to kill us all.

If anything, this made me even more determined to press ahead with the Spirit Run. I thought it was in excellent hands, but soon I began to hear disquieting rumors from people on our board that the Spirit guys did not seem to be following through on their promises. I was so busy with the renovations at Colonial House that I didn't pay much attention at first, but the rumors became more persistent. Finally, three weeks before Halloween, I decided to take a look into their operations, and discovered the awful truth.

Mark DeAngelis and Mark Manetti had spent almost the entire ten thousand dollars on anything and everything except promoting Spirit Run. It had gone to their other projects, gone to pay the rent on Manetti's apartment, been squandered in little shell games, whatever. They were, in effect, AIDS profiteers, a breed that would become depressingly familiar as the years rolled along. They were living high on the hog, basking in their reputations as noble fund raisers and altruists, when in effect AIDS had provided them with the goose that laid the golden egg. This was a disaster for Brent and his run, and I really let them have it. I just could not believe that people could be that callous. But the only result of my ranting was that they became indignant and obstructionist. And now Halloween was approaching, the run was scheduled, virtually no promotion had been done, and practically nobody knew about it. We were faced with a terrible decision: to run or not to run. We decided to go through with it anyway, simply to try to save face for AREA and the much bigger run around America that Brent was going to attempt. But it was clear that without promotion and publicity, the likelihood of attracting the media and sponsors was vastly diminished. I feared the worst, and the worst happened.

Brent began his Halloween run at four that afternoon in front of City Hall, and finished at four the next morning in Union Square. I know that long-distance running is a metaphor for loneliness, but in this case the loneliness was more than symbolic. It cut to the bone, just like the cold wind that blew all night. Instead of cheering crowds and the glare of TV news lights, there were empty streets and a silence only broken by the occasional anti-gay slur. A few onlookers threw eggs. The rest were indifferent, since most people had no idea who this runner was being followed through the canyons of Manhattan and the tidy streets of Queens by a lone taxi cab, an old lady in a Buick, and a few friends.

It was not only a devastating embarrassment but a financial disaster. We raised nothing, and since I had personally guaranteed that if anything went wrong I would reimburse those who donated the initial seed money, I paid back the entire nine thousand dollars to my friends. All in all, I was out ten grand, and had not succeeded in raising a dime for AIDS.

For some reason, the failure of the Spirit Run made me even more determined to make the AREA run a success, and I was not about to give up on Brent's larger plans. So one day as winter approached I brought Brent down to the Garage to meet with Michael and Jaime, hoping to convince them to contribute something to the cause. I wasn't really surprised that Jaime showed no interest — for him, charity definitely began at home. But I was surprised and upset that Michael seemed to give in to everything Jaime said. He just sat there quietly throughout the pitch, saying nothing, allowing Jaime to do the dirty work of turning us down.

By this time Jaime was practically running the club. Michael, who almost used to live there, was now coming in less and less, to the point where he generally came in only once or twice a week and stayed away entirely on weekends. The place was still hopping — indeed it was now more popular than ever — and most members probably did not even realize that a quiet revolution was taking place at the top.

It was hard to figure. On the one hand, the Paradise Garage had been Michael's dream and obsession, and the fact that he now barely paid attention to his creation made no sense. In addition, it was increasingly clear that Michael loathed Jaime. He had said as much to me and to others, and it was glaringly apparent every time I saw them together. They no longer lived as a couple, were no longer lovers — Michael had been through two additional boyfriends by this time — and he had even told the staff on several occasions that Jaime was to be ignored, that he was out. But then he never followed through, and it almost seemed that the more distance Michael put between himself and Jaime, the more powerful Jaime became. I wondered whether the AIDS crisis had simply taken the wind out of Michael's sails — that he now had so many stricken friends that he just couldn't cope. Or perhaps his increasing troubles with Larry made him want to withdraw.

Larry was now completely over the top drugwise, and even though we had that in common, his addiction, combined with his mercurial temperament and egotism and wildness, made him simply too hot to handle. During this period I saw him less and less, mainly out of choice, and I could understand why Michael might feel the same. After all, despite the fact that Michael had initiated a roster of additional DJs, Larry Levan was still the main draw. It must have been frightening and extremely annoying to have your business based on an out-of-control addict. Still, Larry had always been hard to handle, and that had never stopped Michael from paying the closest attention to every detail of his business. His growing distance and remoteness, and his increasing reliance on the person he feared, simply made no sense.

One New Year's Eve I hosted several friends from out of town, and everybody wanted to go to the Garage. I called ahead and Jaime — uncharacteristically — told me to come on down with my whole party. But when we got there we were stopped at the door. The doorman called up to Michael, who sent word down that Julio and I were to be admitted free, but that the rest of my party had to pay. I was extremely hurt. New Year's Eve was a time Michael and I had always spent together, and on this particular night many people were being admitted free. It seemed like a deliberate slap in the face, and I was so embarrassed that I paid for my whole party to get in. When I finally found Michael at his usual place beside the soundboard, I was too embarrassed to say anything about the incident. But as I stood there looking at him, it suddenly struck me that he didn't look well. I mentioned this to Julio, but he assured me that Michael was fine, that he had just lost weight.

a columbia university study

As 1986 began, my anxiety about my own health began to gnaw away at me. So many friends were sick that it seemed prudent to find out about myself, so when I heard that a study of gay men was being conducted at Columbia, I enrolled. I could find out about my own health status, and do something for the community at the same time. Since most AIDS research was being conducted by straight doctors, I thought it important that they understand gay men. The people administering the study were kind and compassionate and careful not to judge, but the study itself was complex and a little frightening. In addition to giving blood and all sorts of other samples, I had to fill out a huge questionnaire about personal sexual practices, reliving what I did, when and with whom. They then gave me a coded card to present when I returned for my HIV test results.

It may sound strange, given my checkered past and all my previous worries, but on the day I was scheduled to get my test results I was filled with an odd confidence. It just did not seem possible that I could be infected, and I walked over to the clinic with a little bounce in my step. When the attendant came out with my results, I experienced only a second of trepidation and took a deep breath. And then the good news — I was not infected. The rest of the meeting passed in a haze; I hardly heard what she said. I had escaped, and since nothing happens by accident, I knew there had to be a reason. I was here to do something: to bear witness, help the dying, to find a cure, sound a warning. A thousand feelings washed over me, but elation was strangely not among them, nor was any desire to celebrate. Too many friends were sick and dying. This good fortune was for me alone, and under the circumstances I felt that I could not even share it with anybody. Like a well-fed man amid the starving, it seemed impolite even to feel happy.

Of course, I had to tell Julio, and of course I expected he would be happy, both for me and for himself. After all, we were still sexually intimate, and although we had both been practicing safe sex for quite awhile, the fact that I was HIV negative could only increase the odds that he was too. But Julio seemed indifferent to my news, almost hostile. I realized that under his macho exterior he was absolutely terrified for himself, and the fact that I had been tested simply raised an issue he was more comfortable ignoring. When I took the opportunity to urge him to get tested and even join the study, he got furious. He would not get tested, he said, and he would not discuss it further, end of story. It would be a long time before we talked about it again.

A few weeks later Ignacio and Manolo threw me a birthday bash, and it was the first time in quite a while that I had felt like celebrating anything. Things were not nearly as gloomy as they had been the year before. My financial situation was looking at least a bit better. I was out from under the oppressive weight of West End. The renovations at Colonial House were proceeding well. I was uninfected. Ray's death was now a year behind me, and although I still missed him terribly, time was doing what time always does. Brent's Spirit Run had been a disaster, but his much larger run was only six weeks away, and we were consumed with all the work we had to do. That night he brought Dr. Tom Waddell as his date, and the example of this man, the founder of the Gay Games, gave me hope that perhaps I was making a difference too. Perhaps things weren't so bad after all.

Practically all my closest friends were there, and the only person I really missed was Michael. When I called him a few days later, he apologized profusely. He said he had been overwhelmed with things, including the new apartment he had just about finished renovating. I asked when I could see it, and to my pleasant surprise he invited me over the following week.

As the sun was setting on an icy cold Saturday afternoon, I headed down to Canal Street to see his new place. It was spectacular. The view of the Hudson River, its state-of-the-art technology, exquisite furnishings, Michael's apartment bespoke of someone who had made it in life. Michael had created a millionaire's home, and I couldn't help thinking that this is what he had wanted all along. The poor messenger boy, the striving student, the dreamer who had once lovingly tended his only possession, his little car — and now here he was, the rich man, the success, surrounded by the fruits of his labors. Best of all, he was still young enough to enjoy it. Still a kid really. As much as I had been depressed by my own problems over the past year, Michael's triumph lifted me up. After all, I had set him on this road, and now here he was, troubles behind him, ready for the good times.

It seemed like all the old tensions between us unwound that winter afternoon. He opened a good bottle of wine and poured freely, savoring my approval. He spoke of his new young lover,

Sammy Nunez, with whom he seemed to get along. He spoke of how he had finally managed to extricate Jaime from his personal life, even as he increasingly relied on Jaime to run the business. I realized that despite appearances, despite everyone's bewilderment at Jaime's role in running the Garage, Michael knew what he was doing. He had finally arranged life the way he wanted it. He was moving on, and Jaime's management of the business was allowing him.

As the sun set over the Hudson, Michael lit candles and poured more wine. We talked and laughed, and I continued to marvel at the apartment, and at him. Then, in the flickering candlelight, I noticed something odd, and without thinking, with no forethought, no sense of impending doom whatsoever, I blurted out *"Michael, what's that spot on your chin?"*

He didn't answer, and in the silence I could hear a clock ticking. Only that. No answer or offhand, *"Oh, it's nothing, just a spot."* Plain silence, punctuated by a clock ticking away dreams and hopes that will never come again, ticking out the time now, AIDS...AIDS...AIDS. I thought I would faint. I saw the waves wash against the Fire Island beach the night we met. I saw a beautiful boy in the moonlight. I saw my beautiful boy, my only love, his smile flashing in the darkness. I saw us on the stairway of the Loft, planting a seed in his soul. I saw us at Stonewall, swept up by hope. I saw us at the Garage, amid the spectacle he had created. I saw Larry spinning, thousands dancing to our dream. And to those moments, and all our other moments, would now be added this: something rose up out of my heart and flew away and has never returned. In that silence, in the ticking of Michael's clock, I turned old.

Oh, Michael. The universe is cold, and we are just little specks of dust, drawn together by some strange gravity we call love, and it cannot save us. We think it can, we hope it can, but it cannot. You could not save me, and I could not save you, and in those silent seconds when hope died, I finally realized the depth of our aloneness. We sat there in the candlelight together, but we were alone, you with the mark of death on your chin, me with an old man's tired heart, unable to speak. Not because our tongues were tied, but because, facing the void, there was nothing to say.

You finally broke the silence, Michael, but what you said was not true. It was an echo from your wounded childhood, and mine, the childhoods of all the little gay boys alone in their rooms at night, believing that the love that wells up within us is our fault, believing that we are guilty, when all we are is human. *"I guess I brought it on myself,"* you said. In some small way I suppose you may be right. Many people were infected and died through no fault of their own, but not all of them got sick as fast as you, or died as quickly. We have to want to live, we have to hope. A year earlier you said something to me that struck ice in my bones. You had opened yourself to a poverty and a want and vulnerability that none of your worldly successes and fancy apartments and expensive trips could balance out. *"Mel, there is no such thing as real happiness,"* you said, when I asked if you were happy. What a sad thing to say, Michael. How untrue. I was happy with you. No such thing as happiness. That belief alone is worse than a virus, worse than a plague. It lets plagues in. And so, while you did not bring AIDS on yourself — you were as innocent of that as we all were — perhaps you knew what you were talking about. If you abandon hope, you abandon life.

chapter sixteen
DECADE
OF HELL

Work can be a great liberator. In normal times it can help give
purpose to our lives. In the worst of times, it, like drugs, can help
us forget. And so, as the truth finally sank in that from now on our
existence was to be defined by a plague, I threw myself into the
destructive passion of drugs, which I consumed with an almost
unconscious dedication, and the constructive passion of work. In
transforming the Colonial House into both a thriving business
and a permanent home, I was helped tremendously by Chaz.

His relationship with Jay, Jason's mother, became so strained in
the aftermath of Jason's tragic accident that they separated. He
moved out to California to get away from the bad memories.
When I initially offered him the job of managing the Colonial
House he was reluctant, since he had no desire to return to New
York. But work wasn't easy to come by in California, and Chaz
eventually found himself taking out an ad in the Advocate and
offering himself as a male escort. I'm sure he was excellent at this
line of work, given his personality and his stunning looks, but it
was a staggering waste of talent, his own way of hitting bottom.
So, after much pleading, and even a trip out to California to
convince him, he finally agreed to pack up his stuff and drive
back to New York to my rescue.

Colonial House had been moving forward too slowly. My first
manager, Alberto Cintron, turned out to be unsuited for the job.
He ran the place like a disorganized disco — showed up to work
late, left early, and lacked the kind of initiative that the project

really needed. The final straw came when I discovered that one of the employees he hired — he had my habit of always hiring gorgeous boys who looked great but didn't do much — was ripping off our guests. Alberto knew about this but did nothing. He was afraid I'd get angry, he said, had he told me. Clearly, I needed someone a lot more organized, and honest.

Chaz arrived in February '86, and it was like a cyclone had struck the moment he walked in the door. He was almost too good to be true. There was, for example, the case of the door. Our front office was cut in two by a wall, and you had to walk out into the hallway to get from the front of the office to the back. Clearly, a door was needed, but even something this simple required negotiating a maze of bureaucratic permits and red tape, which had completely defeated Alberto. But Chaz cut through it like the Gordian knot. The day he arrived he took stock of the situation and decided — right, mate — we need a door here. Out came a sledge hammer. Within a few hours, there was a door and all the electrical rewiring that went with it. I couldn't decide if I was ecstatic that things were getting done or petrified that Chaz was going to bring down the wrath of the city bureaucracy. I hired him to be manager, but it quickly became clear that a far better plan would be to put him in charge of renovations. He was a natural born contractor and could do much of the work himself. I agreed to run the front desk myself and give him free reign with the renovations. More progress was made in a week than had been made in months, and pretty soon Colonial House was really moving forward.

But Chaz's arrival put a major strain on my already strained relationship with Julio. Julio was jealous. He and I had spent a thousand dusted evenings together making grandiose plans about what we would do with the Colonial House, and they always came to nothing. Half the time we wouldn't even remember our aspirations the next morning. This was fine with Julio. He'd roll another joint of angel dust and come up with another pipe dream. But dreams were coming true now, and they weren't Julio's. He saw Chaz actually do things: transforming Colonial House and making it work, organizing my personal life, trying to make me comfortable, helping me get my act together. Although I had no romantic ideas about Chaz, Julio came to regard him as a major threat.

At first it was just little things. Julio would find fault with something Chaz did, criticize his plans, nag at him. But it soon escalated into open warfare. At one point Chaz hired Julio's sister Carmen to do some housekeeping, and Julio exploded when he saw his pampered sister cleaning bathrooms. *"My sister can't clean toilets,"* he practically screamed at Chaz, to which Chaz calmly replied, *"If I'm cleaning them, she's gonna have to clean them too."* Carmen didn't last long at that particular job, but the tensions only grew.

Things had been going downhill with Julio and me for ages, and with Chaz now in the picture, Julio began to fear that we were on our last legs as a couple. So one day he announced that we should go to couple's therapy to work on our problems. I thought it was a pretty good idea, but unfortunately neither of us was really ready to do the one thing that was necessary for us to get our acts together — namely, quit taking drugs. By this time our very personalities were shaped by angel dust. It permeated our relationship and poisoned everything. Julio, however, did not even want to tell the therapist about that aspect of our lives. I insisted, and the therapist sent Julio to a doctor to wean him off the dust with some other drug. He went — he seemed genuinely determined to do what was necessary to get our relationship back on track — but his addiction was just too strong. He would return from the doctor and light up another joint.

I wasn't much better. I told the therapist that I had to smoke dust simply to deal with Julio, a rationale, which she patiently explained, was a classic cop out. I had to quit, she told me, and she was right. But I couldn't. We continued in therapy for a few more months, but I eventually realized it was a waste of money. We were not ready to face up to our addictions, and without doing that, nothing else was going to do much good. Things quickly degenerated between Julio and Chaz until the tension was more than Chaz could bear, and one day it finally came to a head. Chaz had long pestered Julio to help him pick out a color for the hallways, and Julio had done his usual waffling number, unable to make up his mind. So finally Chaz simply picked out a color on his own and painted the halls. It looked great.

Julio said nothing until one afternoon when he was working the front desk. I had an absolute rule for both of us — no angel dust when we're on duty. But this particular day Julio disappeared into a back room and emerged completely wasted and itching for a fight. Sitting there facing the results of his indecisiveness and Chaz's enterprise, he freaked. I heard the screaming and yelling, and came out to find Julio lashing out at Chaz in the most insane, hysterical terms. I took over the front desk and begged Chaz just to throw Julio in the car and drive him home. When they had gone a few blocks Julio grabbed the steering wheel and almost caused an accident, and kept screaming at Chaz: *"You finally did it. You finally pushed me out and fucked me over."* Somehow Chaz managed to get Julio home in one piece, but he was completely shaken and didn't return to Colonial House for the rest of the day.

The next morning he came in and handed me his letter of resignation. He was tired, he said, of watching us destroy ourselves with drugs. He said that he believed that my own drug problem was a direct result of Julio. *"He's always keeping you fucked up on dust*" was how he put it, and that whenever he tried to talk to Julio about it, Julio would just tell him to mind his own business and leave us alone. I was beside myself with despair, and spent the rest of the day begging him to reconsider. He finally agreed to stay, but the tensions never dissipated. If anything should have convinced me to get help with my addiction it should have been that — the possibility of losing the one person who was turning my life around. But it didn't. I got used to the tension and lit up another joint.

One reason that quitting seemed so impossible was that by now it seemed that almost every day brought news of another friend sick. One of my worst memories was the day Manolo called and told me that Ignacio had it. They had been vacationing in Puerto Rico, and one day on the beach Manolo noticed one of the spots on Ignacio's body. They returned immediately to New York, Ignacio went into the hospital, and when I raced over to visit, he was fairly upbeat. He was an immensely strong person, and he seemed determined to take control of this thing and not let it defeat him. After his release from the hospital he immediately built up a support network of doctors and healers, and he seemed almost to be turning the whole thing into the same kind of work of art he turned everything into. But Manolo was devastated, and so was I. The fact that Ignacio had just had a triumphant art exhibition at a major gallery a few months earlier made this thing seem ironic and even more pathetic. After working so hard on his art and finally achieving the recognition he deserved, to be struck like this. I simply couldn't believe it.

Next to all this, drugs were a welcome relief. When things got too tough, I could smoke dust and disappear into a fantasy where these things weren't happening. But in my sober moments — and I still had plenty of sober moments — I was even more determined to do what I could. The best way to fight back, I figured, was to make sure that Brent's AREA run across America was a success. After the Manetti/DeAngelis disaster we had finally hired a competent full-time administrator. Bill Konkoy was everything Manetti and DeAngelis were not. Bill put the run together, raised money, organized it, and finally the big day arrived. On a cold Sunday in March, several hundred people rallied on the steps of City Hall to send Brent and Marion off. With Gigi by my side, I presented Bill with a check for a thousand dollars that I prayed would be a tiny drop in what I hoped would be the ocean of money we would raise.

Brent dedicated the run to Paul Popham, and presented Paul with a humanitarian award, a beautiful glass statuette of a runner. But when Paul emerged from the crowd to accept it, I was stunned. He had kept very much to himself over the past few months while on chemotherapy (I suppose he realized that his disease and its treatments were doing terrible things to him), and ours had become a telephone relationship. Only speaking to him on a regular basis, I still imagined him handsome and vibrant, the way he always was, the most beautiful man in our circle, the idol of the dance floor. And now Brent announced his name, and a gaunt, white-haired old man uncertain of his footing struggled up the steps of City Hall, thin as a rail. So it was in the spring of 1986. From a community of life we went to a shrinking circle of death.

One unexpected consequence of AIDS was that it brought people together. There's something about the intensity of illness and the specter of death that focuses us on the important things in life, and makes the petty things seem truly petty. In the months following my discovery that Michael was sick, a lot of our little quarrels and disputes faded into the background and we became closer than we had been in years. We began spending a lot of time together, and since I wanted to distract him from his fears, I tried to engage him in all sorts of plans and future projects.

Pretty soon we fell into a familiar rhythm, hatching schemes to buy buildings, open new clubs, start an art gallery, renovate apartments. It was wonderful to spend so much time with him again, and wonderful to see him engaged in life. Occasionally I would see the old flicker in his eyes, when it almost looked as though he thought he might drum up the energy to beat this death sentence. I wanted to instill hope — it was the one thing Michael really needed — and I think sometimes I did.

That summer he was particularly happy with the float that the Garage mounted in the Gay Pride parade. Since I was marching with AREA — Brent had run all the way to Chicago but flew back for the parade — I didn't get to see the Paradise Garage float boogying down Broadway. But that was all right. Michael could describe it to me. The float was covered with dancers and glitter and half-naked bodies, and a huge sound system blasted out Larry's Garage classics. A thousand people danced their way down Fifth Avenue with the float, and as they passed St. Patrick's Cathedral, the Cardinal came out and made a point of condemning this shocking blasphemy. Michael cranked up the volume even louder. He had a gleeful twinkle in his eye describing to me how he was trying to drown out the homophobes with Larry's music. Michael, it definitely seemed to me, was trying to fight back. Fighting back with music reminded me of the old Michael.

That summer he actually began to claim that he was happy, especially with his new boyfriend Sammy Nunez. Sammy had originally been a member of Larry's entourage at the Garage, and in the process had got to know Jaime. When Jaime realized that his romantic relationship with Michael was permanently on the rocks, he did what he always did. He would keep himself in the picture by finding someone for Michael who would remain loyal to him, Jaime. And so he introduced Sammy to Michael and played matchmaker, and it worked. Michael fell for Sammy, and pretty soon they were deeply involved.

I liked Sammy at first. He was a welcome change from Jaime. While Jaime was sly, scheming and evil, Sammy was honest and completely friendly. I would soon learn otherwise, but at the time I fully supported their relationship. When I was looking for a new receptionist for the Colonial House and Michael recommended Sammy, I hired him on the spot. I was concerned that this arrangement might strain my renewed closeness to Michael, especially if things didn't work out with Sammy. How do you fire the lover of one of your best friends? But Michael assured me that nothing that happened with Sammy at work would threaten our friendship. I arranged Sammy's schedule so that he could spend as much time as possible with Michael. It seemed the least I could do, considering how much Michael depended on his new lover.

I suppose that in trying to distract Michael from AIDS, I was trying to distract myself from it as well. In general, I succeeded. There's practically no limit to our ability to deny, especially when what we're trying to deny is death itself. But sometimes the truth breaks through like a sledge hammer.

Michael hardly ever went into the Garage anymore, and I knew he must miss it, so one night when Larry was on a particularly amazing roll, he made a tape of his music that I could bring to Michael out in Fire Island. Julio and I took the seaplane out and showed up unannounced to surprise Michael. We caught him and Sammy sitting down to dinner, and since they were not expecting us, Michael was wearing shorts. I stopped dead in my tracks: Michael's legs were a mass of lesions, great purple blotches that ran like ink stains all over his once beautiful skin. It was worse than I had dared imagine. Michael ran into the bedroom and emerged wearing long pants. He obviously did not want me to see him in that condition, and I was devastated. I don't know what upset me more, the fact that I had invaded his privacy, or the fact that I had to face how bad things were. He very graciously invited Julio and me to stay for dinner, but I was too upset. I mumbled something about having to get back to the city, and we ran for the boat. I cried all the way home on the train. I cried and cried. My denial was finally denied me, and I just couldn't bear the thought of Michael going through that pain.

blackmail

That summer and fall I began to realize that it might have been a mistake to hire Sammy. Not because of anything to do with Michael — things were fine in that regard. But Sammy was firmly in Jaime's pocket, and I soon discovered that anytime I discussed Jaime around Sammy — usually to criticize him — Sammy would leap to Jaime's defense. It seemed as though I had what amounted to a spy right under my own roof for one of my least favorite people. Jaime, who was constantly trying to poison my relationship with Michael, was now constantly stopping by the Colonial House to see Sammy, which made me very edgy. My own apartment was now finished, largely thanks to Chaz's amazing efforts, and one day without knocking Jaime walked right in on me sitting there. He said hello, but I was so startled by this apparition that I didn't answer. It gave me the creeps.

The flip side to this, however, was that because of Sammy, Michael stopped by very often as well. This made me very happy. It was great to show off my new duplex apartment with state-of-the-art everything, and a beautiful backyard and hot tub. I liked being with Michael. One afternoon that fall he seemed weighed down by everything. I offered to have him come live with me. I wanted to cook for him and take care of him and try to bring back his health. He was very touched, but he declined. He didn't give a reason, but I knew why. He didn't want me to watch him deteriorate. Michael was vain about his looks, he always loved being the beautiful golden boy, and he knew that the spreading Kaposi was turning him into something less than beautiful. It seemed obvious. If this went on, he would soon be covered with lesions from head to foot. When this happened, he wanted to be able to hide from the world, especially from me. At one point that afternoon he repeated what he had said the day I found out about his illness: *"I'm responsible for what is happening to me."* *"Don't say that,"* I protested. I told him how much he had upset me the time he said that there is no such thing as real happiness. I told him there was still hope. If he could just beat this, the rest of his life could be beautiful. He had everything going for him. But he knew that none of this was to be, and so he didn't reply. He just looked wistful.

I only partly knew why. Later, I was to find out the whole story. It was, of course, Jaime. For one thing, Michael suspected Jaime of infecting him. He had grown so disgusted by Jaime's sexual appetites that he stopped having sex with him a few years before. At the time, I remember him saying that Jaime was *"such a pig. I'm afraid he'll give me something."* But Michael was still connected with Jaime in a thousand ways. If anything, even more now that he relied on Jaime almost exclusively to run the Garage, not a healthy relationship as business relationships go.

Michael frankly hated Jaime, and the feeling was mutual. Our friend Bobby Falace had traveled with Jaime to Mexico to buy Michael AIDS drugs that were illegal in the U.S., and one day on the beach, Jaime confided in Bobby. Jaime hated Michael's guts. *"He humiliated me,"* Jaime said, referring to an incident long ago at the Garage, when he and Michael were quarreling and Michael made a staff announcement that Jaime no longer had any official capacity at the club. Bobby Falace told me that he was taken aback by the venom in Jaime's voice. Jaime seemed to be speaking about his very worst enemy rather than his former lover and current meal ticket. Bobby and I were struck by the inexplicable weirdness and the obvious danger of the situation: Michael had a fundamental mistrust of Jaime, and Jaime loathed Michael, yet here was Michael sending Jaime off to Mexico to buy drugs Michael prayed would save his life. This did not seem wise on Michael's part. We all assumed that Jaime was a major beneficiary of Michael's will, since Michael feared that if he didn't take care of Jaime in his will, Jaime would do all sorts of evil things after he was gone. It all seemed so crazy: If Michael and Jaime hated each other so much, why was Jaime still around? Why was he running the club? Why was he in Michael's will?

Michael was unable to answer any of my questions, but I eventually found out the truth, and it was pretty chilling. Like many club owners, Michael had been skimming money from his own business for years and having Jaime deposit it for him in bank accounts in South America. Cheating the taxman is obviously a major temptation for people like Michael, whose business is largely conducted in cash. Millions flow into a club like the Paradise Garage, and it's relatively easy to report most of it and simply spirit the remainder away. Such a scheme was the undoing of Steve Rubell and Ian Schrager at Studio 54, and it's been the downfall of plenty of others as well. But Michael never got caught by the feds. He got caught by himself instead. By letting Jaime into the scheme and using Jaime to launder his money, he opened himself up to blackmail. After Jaime had figured out the whole scam and become an integral part of it, he turned around and coolly informed Michael that if he didn't get what he wanted — and he always wanted something — he would blow the whistle on Michael. The consequences were unthinkable, years in jail probably, so Michael was stuck with Jaime. He couldn't get rid of him, quite the opposite. As the years went by, Jaime would demand more and more. He got more money, power, control, his name in the will, what have you. Michael would either have to give in to Jaime's demands or face the possibility that everything he'd worked for would be taken away.

In fact, once Jaime's noose tightened, Michael was unable to defend himself against Jaime's direct thievery. As Michael began to spend less time at the Garage, Jaime instituted a skimming system of his own. He instructed his doorman to return a certain percentage of the tickets sold to the cashier who was then instructed to resell them a second time and turn this cash over to Jaime. This scheme enabled him to skim off an incredible $15,000 a week Michael suspected, but any confrontation with Jaime risked the danger that Jaime would make good on his threats.

The fact is, Michael could have become immensely rich without ever skimming a single dime. Even run legitimately, the Paradise Garage was a gold mine. Michael had spent his early years always going short, never having enough, and he was determined that once he made it, he would never be poor again. But his determination to strike it rich made him greedy, and drawing a sleazy number like Jaime into the scheme sowed the seeds of his own undoing. None of us knew that this was the situation Michael was in before he found out he was infected. AIDS could only complicate things. Michael needed someone to run the club in his increasing absences, and the one person who insisted on grabbing that power and control was the person he hated the most in the world, and who hated him the most. They were stuck with each other, and Michael resigned himself to the fact, which, in the end, I truly believe sapped him of the will to fight back and try to go on living.

As the horrible year 1986 drew to a close, Michael began to sequester himself more and more, and I saw him less and less. The Kaposi was spreading, and he didn't want anyone to see him this way except Sammy, who quit his job at the Colonial House to devote himself full time to Michael. As I was attempting to somehow deal with all this, word came from Puerto Rico that Alberto Cintron, my first manager at Colonial House, had suddenly died. This news hit Manolo and Ignacio particularly hard, not only because they were old and dear friends of Alberto's, but also because Ignacio's own health was beginning to decline, and he was starting to lose hope. Alberto's death, and particularly the fact that he had gone so extremely quickly, seemed to take the wind out of Ignacio's sails.

Then, just before New Year's, as if to cap off the year with one more final nightmare, Chaz came to me with the news that he too had AIDS. But he was confident that he would beat it, and he had a new lover, and that gave him hope for the future and made him want to keep on living and fighting. This kind of attitude is vitally important, and I did everything I could to encourage Chaz, but I was beginning to have a harder time convincing myself that any of these men, my vital and vibrant friends, were going to survive. Looking at Chaz, so healthy and handsome and energetic, it seemed almost impossible to believe that he held within him this ticking time bomb. And yet by now, I knew that this is how it begins — health, optimism, strength — and then, little by little, the long decline. The occasional infections. The lost weight. That look. And finally, the doctors and hospitals and desperate searches for cures, the respirators, the emergencies, the AIDS wards and lost hope. The call in the middle of the night. The memorials. The ashes of a life held in a little urn. How could we go on like this? How could I go on, with Michael, Ignacio, Paul, Chaz, so many others? And with Ray already gone? It seemed like the end, but it was only the beginning.

Brent ran on across America. His journey halfway through had been buffeted by wind, rain and indifference, and the news that his good friend and mentor, Tom Waddell, was now also battling with AIDS. Brent ran on into the new year, the torchbearer lighting the way, darkness all around. When night fell over Manhattan, I could almost see Brent's tiny flame in the distance, a specter of hope running for our lives somewhere out there.

The horrible year 1987 began. For the first time in my life, I paid no attention to my birthday. What was there to celebrate? Julio and I were fighting again, and at times barely speaking to one other. I began to withdraw from my friends and spend more time alone with my worries. Alone seemed safer. Reminders of AIDS were everywhere, signs and omens of what was happening, and I found even basic social functions excruciating. There was always someone who was sick visibly or someone whose lover had just died, or someone who had just found out he was infected.

When I was with friends, I could not even talk about the anxieties that were eating me up. Since I was uninfected, my own problems seemed minor. So many others were going through hell, and I felt selfish and petty burdening my friends with my own problems. As the number of friends who were infected increased, there were fewer and fewer I felt I could confide in, until it seemed there was no one left at all. It's odd. Anyone going through what I was going though would be considered, by almost any objective person, to be in the midst of a great, pivotal crisis, and to need all the help and support he could muster from his friends and family. Yet the very nature of my crisis — that my friends were dying, my world was dying — not only made getting help and support an impossibility, but also made me feel guilty even looking to find support. I was supposed to be the strong shoulder everybody could cry on. There was no shoulder for me.

My father called with more bad news. My parents were now in their 80s, and there had been signs for a long time that my mother's memory was not what it once was. My father called to say that Mom was beginning to act very erratically, and that he was frightened. I flew up to Boston to assess the situation, and was horrified. It was much worse than my father had let on. Mom had Alzheimer's disease that was advancing rapidly. She would forget where she was, suddenly shout out *"Daddy! Daddy!"* at the top of her lungs. Her mind was wandering off. She had all the depressing signs of a mind being destroyed. Dad was distraught and completely incapable of dealing with this himself, so I moved them to New York, and put them in Colonial House in a large room with private bath that had just been renovated on the ground floor, right next to my own apartment. Now, in addition to my other problems, I had my parents' nightmare under my roof as well. And believe it or not, I had still never come out to them. How I would maintain my secret, with my friends dying everywhere around me and my father and mother living in the next room, was beyond me.

As winter wore on, I was glad to see that Michael's health did not seem much worse. But I was shocked by the change in his attitude. He began to seem thoroughly defeated and defeatist, as though all his best days were now behind him and all he had to look forward to was decline and death. One day he came by, and as we talked he reflected sadly on the parade float that the Garage had mounted in last year's Gay Pride. He had enjoyed it, but there would be no float this year. It was too much work and he didn't have the energy, he said, his voice cracking.

I was very moved that he was taking me into his confidence about such a sensitive thing. But I was also sad at what he was saying and what it meant for him. And then, a light went on. If Michael didn't have the energy to put together a float, I would do it for him. I did have the energy and the time, and I could enlist plenty of people to help. Of course, the first people I would have to enlist would be Jaime and Sammy, since Jaime was now in charge of the Garage and Sammy was now Michael's lover. This wasn't a happy prospect, but I bit the bullet and asked them for a meeting. I now found myself Saturday night at the Garage, face-to-face with the person who had become, by now, my nemesis. I started off trying to clear the air. *"Jaime,"* I said as he stared at me coldly,

> What you are to Michael, Sammy and I can't be. What Sammy is to Michael, you and I can't be. And what I am, you two can't be. So let's just try to work together and surprise him with this float.

I told them I could probably get several record companies to pay for it, since they owed so much to Michael and the Garage. And I promised that if I wasn't successful, I would pay for it myself. They acted as though they thought the float was a good idea, and I left with the impression that we had a deal, the most important aspect of which was that we would keep it a secret from Michael. It would be a surprise, something to lift his spirits.

The next Monday morning, the phone rang and it was Michael. He was extremely angry and hostile. *"What the hell are you trying to do?"* he demanded. Before I could say anything, he launched into a tirade. *"You're getting in my way and stepping on my toes, and I don't like it one bit. Please stay the hell out of my business."* All I could do was mumble, *"Okay, Michael, whatever you say,"* before he hung up. I was devastated and, at first anyway, dumbfounded. Why was he angry that I was trying to give him a beautiful surprise? But how did he even know about it?

Jaime went to Michael immediately after our meeting and told him of our secret plan, twisting it so that, in Jaime's version, I was trying to elbow my way into the business, and that this idea of a float is the first part of my evil plot to begin my takeover of the Garage! Of course, Jaime's version made perfect sense on its face, and I realized what an idiot I had been going to him in the first place. Jaime was determined to isolate Michael from anyone and everyone who might threaten his own strong hold over Michael. If the float had come off successfully, and especially if I had paid for it, Michael would have seen that at least someone was devoted to him, that someone did care and wanted nothing in return except to make him happy. This, Jaime could never allow. It would make him, who never did anything without an ulterior motive, look bad by comparison. And he was devious enough to figure out how to stop it. I do have to hand it to Jaime. Not only was he devious, he was very successful at it.

What disturbed me more than Jaime, however, was the role that Sammy played in all this. Clearly Sammy must have known what I was trying to do, and clearly he could have communicated that to Michael if he had wanted to, and just as clearly, he had not. The fact that Sammy must have gone along with Jaime's version of my plan, and confirmed it to Michael, made me, in turn, suspect the worst, that Sammy was an active participant in Jaime's plot to isolate Michael from his genuine friends. Sammy and Jaime were in cahoots. Michael needed all the true friends he could get, and if he were being actively poisoned from his true friends by the two people who were not —his lover and his business manager — what chance did he have? From that point on, my relationship with Michael again became strained and, thanks to Jaime and Sammy, would never heal.

As Michael sank into despondency and isolation, something crucial happened that would change everything. For years, Michael had been fighting a war of attrition with the city government and the neighborhood association. They were constantly trying to close the Garage as a public nuisance and disturber of the peace. Their attacks had been draining but had never succeeded. The landlord must have been the person most unhappy throughout all of this, however. He was under this constant pressure to get rid of the place.

Now he had his chance and could finally dispose of the club and all its headaches. Michael's ten-year lease was soon up. When New York Telephone agreed to rent the entire building as a facility to store and repair its vehicles, Michael was informed that the lease would not be renewed in September when it expired. Michael offered a pile of money, but the landlord adamantly refused to change his mind. Although Michael could have fought this and won, it became clear that his choices were move the club or close it. Under normal circumstances, moving would not pose too big a problem. The major asset of the club was its extraordinary sound system, which could easily be relocated. There were, in addition, plenty of club spaces on the market. AIDS had knocked the wind out of many gay discos and much of gay nightlife in general. What the changes in the music industry had not been able to do to gay disco, AIDS was, and with a vengeance.

Gay nightlife was dying because gay men were dying, and attendance at virtually all the major clubs was dwindling, although this wasn't nearly as noticeable at the Garage as it was at most of the other clubs. AIDS really began in New York as a disease of white gay men, and the very forms of promiscuity practiced at places like the Saint, with its notorious sex balcony, must certainly have contributed to the demise of its clientele. The Garage was sexually mixed, and more racially mixed than the Saint, and the Garage had no sex rooms. Although AIDS was certainly having an impact at the Garage, and ultimately the epidemic would cut as wide a swath through the Garage as through the rest of the gay world, that would take longer. While the other clubs faded, teetered, and closed, the Garage was booming, and was a regular gold mine for Michael.

Moving to a new space would have been relatively easy, but Michael had AIDS, and this, of course, made all the difference. If his clientele wasn't dying, he was, and as for the immense project of moving, his heart simply wasn't in it. When it began sinking in that he really was losing his lease, he made a few fitful attempts to scout around for a new location, and even met with Bruce Mailman about taking over the Saint's spectacular space. It would have been a dream come true — a physical space to match the energy and vitality of Larry Levan's musical vision and the Garage's loving crowd. But Michael knew that the job of moving was too much for him. And I suspect, and others suspect as well, that, in the end, Michael wanted his Paradise Garage to die with him. It was his legacy, his life's work, and for it to die with him would make him missed as deeply as his creation. If he died and the Garage continued, the passing of Michael Brody would just be another tragic blip on the radar screen. People would remember him and shed a tear, and they would keep on dancing. If he died after moving the Garage, Jaime and Sammy would soon run it into the ground. (By now he knew what he was dealing with in those two.) So the Paradise Garage would have to close forever in September. Michael told virtually no one, not even Larry, just as he had told virtually no one that he was sick. Then one week in April, when he was sure his decision was final and irrevocable, he announced that there would be a meeting of the entire staff that Friday night in his office.

A tremor went through the club. No one seemed to know what this meeting was about, but rumors flew, and no one had a good feeling about it. When the appointed time came, the staff trooped into his office as though they were going to their own execution, and Michael began by announcing that he had AIDS. Only a very small circle knew, and they had been sworn to silence, so this came as a shock. Michael then announced that he was losing his lease in September, and that he had scouted for other locations but did not think it would be possible to move the operation anywhere else. As a result, he expected that the Paradise Garage would close permanently in September, and he wanted them to know well in advance, so that they could begin looking for other jobs. He asked them to remain at their posts until the closing, and promised important bonuses to everyone who did, the size of the bonus depending upon how long the person had worked there.

The room was in complete silence, as though someone had announced that the world was coming to an end. Then Larry stood up, shaking and furious with tears in his eyes, and stormed out of the office slamming the door behind him. As everybody sat there stunned, unable to say anything, they could hear Larry starting to play out in the empty club. His music got louder and louder until it was deafening. The sound system drivers blew out. Pushed past their limits the whole thing just exploded, and it was silent again. It took hours of frantic work to fix the damage before the club could open that night, but the damage to the staff's morale could not be fixed. The Garage was the ultimate expression of the whole fabric of gay night, and it could not be fixed. Michael's death announcement took the very breath out of it.

We were all so used to denial, for a while many people simply could not accept the news. Some began dissecting Michael's words for any clue that the end might not be final. He had said he would update them. Perhaps this meant that he was still looking for a new space. He was no longer coming into the club, so perhaps this meant that he was wheeling and dealing and scouting out new locations. Maybe the doctor's diagnosis isn't that bad. Maybe there's hope. But at the same time, most of us knew deep inside that we were just fooling ourselves.

Of everyone who was affected by the closing of the Garage, none was as furious, grief-stricken or bereft as Larry Levan. The Garage was his palace, his court and universe. He was a legend because of the Garage, and he knew that there was only a slim chance that he would ever again find a club that would be built around him the way the Garage had been, or find a club owner as tolerant of his foibles and fuck-ups. Most DJs never get one such opportunity in their entire careers. It was highly unlikely that Larry would get two. The end of the Garage was going to mean the end of his security, and I worried about him most of all. His drug taking was totally out of control, he was wilder than ever, his reputation among club goers as a genius was easily matched by his reputation among club owners as trouble. Unless he got his act together, his future did not look secure at all.

Dealing with all this, I now received disturbing news about Paul Popham. His condition was worsening, and he had to go back into the hospital. When I called him, he sounded like the same old Paul. All he cared about was how I was doing, how things were at Colonial House, how my parents were. Just the tone of his voice made me feel better, and I thought I could relax a bit. It was probably just some minor infection, I thought. Then a day or two later I got a call from his lover Richard Dulong telling me that if I wanted to say goodbye to Paul I had better hurry over to the hospital immediately, since the end had arrived.

Julio, with whom I was barely speaking, offered to take me over. I have seen the horrible damage that AIDS can do more times than I care to remember, but nothing prepared me for what it had done to Paul. He was a sunken human skeleton, ancient and ashen, a vacant ghost with glassy eyes that did not see. It was impossible to tell whether he even knew we were there. I fumbled for something to say to Richard, some word of comfort or wisdom, anything to communicate my pain and horror at what was happening, but I couldn't say anything at all. This was Paul Popham, the man who had devoted his life to fighting the plague and saving his friends long before he knew he was infected himself. Paul was the fighter who was going to lead us out of the battlefield by the sheer force of his personality, his hero charisma, his competence and intelligence. He was the most golden of the golden boys, the charmer, the disco idol, our leader, and he was my friend. If AIDS could do this to him, what chance did anyone have? I stumbled from the room in shock, my mind reeling, speechless. I went home and sat there in silence for four days, until the phone rang with the news that it was over.

Paul's memorial service reflected the immense impact he had made on all of us. The president of the American Foundation for Aids Research (AmFar), Dr. Mathilde Krim called him *"a giant amongst men,"* and other people spoke movingly about his life and what it meant to them, but the person whose words affected me most was Dan Bailey, who was a member of the board of GMHC then. *"Paul did many things in life that he was proud of,"* Dan said,

> but his stewardship of Gay Men's Health Crisis was the thing he was most proud and positive about. In a very real way, GMHC would not exist had it not been for Paul Popham. It was his leadership qualities, intelligence and determination that encouraged the rest of us to dig in and go on even when things looked bleak and we were bone tired. It was his ability to steer us forward and keep us focused on the real goals while some were caressing their egos — and criticizing him in the process.

This was Dan's pointed dig at Larry Kramer, whose famous fights with the leaders of GMHC had been particularly painful for Paul. Larry had attacked Paul mercilessly, and they stayed estranged for years. But now, after Paul's death, Larry let it be known that he and Paul had made up at the very end. I suppose this made Larry feel better, or less guilty, but the truth was that there had been no reconciliation whatsoever. Richard Dulong, Paul's lover, hardly left Paul's side, and he knew this and told me so. *"Paul has become a metaphor for strength, courage and ethics,"* Dan said, and the entire room seemed to echo in assent. I sat there with Bart Flanagan, Paul's first lover, and reflected on the incredible importance of what Paul had tried to do, and what he had meant to all of us. A measure of that importance, and a source of deep sadness, is that within a few years Paul would be followed by Bart Flanagan, Dan Bailey and Richard Dulong.

Bart and I went over to Paul's apartment the day after the funeral, and Paul's mother and his brother David were there packing up Paul's things. This visit began my lifelong friendship with Paul's mother Muriel. She regaled me with stories about Paul's life. He was a Green Beret in Vietnam, and on the front lines he couldn't receive packages, only letters. But in those letters Muriel would slip little packets of Kool Aid and Lipton Soup mix. Once, when Paul's platoon was surrounded for days and days, those packets multiplied like a miracle and kept everyone from starving. If saving us from AIDS had been as simple as that. Paul received the Bronze Star for Vietnam, and it seemed to me that if there were any justice in the world, he would receive a Purple Heart from some higher authority for fighting AIDS. Maybe he has.

Paul's crushing death made me even more desperate to do something effective to fight AIDS, and it finally occurred to me that many people in the music industry were deeply affected by what was happening, and the industry itself should get involved. After all, musicians are often great fundraisers for charity, and all the way back to George Harrison's famous concert for Bangladesh there had been a flurry of major benefits for causes through the '80s — Band-Aid, Live-Aid, Farm-Aid. Why not an Aid for AIDS?

I approached my old partner Ed, who was still running what remained of West End, and Ed thought it was a great idea. The best approach would be to concentrate all our efforts on getting radio stations, nightclubs and record companies to designate a single day to the cause. All their programs that day would be concentrated on AIDS fundraising and awareness. Since the project was to be focused on a single 24-hour period, we would call it *24-Hours-For-Life*. I went to Keith Haring with the idea, and he came up with a beautiful logo — two blue figures carrying a yellow and orange clock, its hands a few minutes shy of twelve. Keith put in his black signature marks as accents, and he put *24-Hours* in yellow, and *For-Life* in orange, at the bottom. He donated the logo and said we could use it without any restrictions. This gave a huge boost to our efforts, and soon t-shirts, posters, and buttons with his logo were all over the country.

We planned to introduce the concept at the New Music Seminar, an international conference of progressive music that's held each year in New York, and we secured several prominent music industry honchos to participate in the press conference. March 12, 1988 would be the date for the nationwide fundraiser, we announced, and it seemed like the wheels were in motion. Unfortunately, the press conference wasn't as well attended as I had hoped, and there was speculation that the music industry as a whole didn't really care about AIDS, which was still perceived to be a gay disease. I was sitting on the dais, with my friends and my father in the audience, when Ed brought this up. *"I think the straight community is aware, and ready to deal with this plague,"* he said.

> The money for 24-Hours-For-Life is going to have to come from the straight community, since the gay community is tapped out. I know this is possible. My partner is a gay man, and I am straight. We have had a good working relationship for many years.

A lightning bolt went through me, and I felt like I was going into shock. There was my father sitting right there in the audience, and Ed had just said I was gay. When it was my turn at the microphone, I recovered enough to be able to say,

> I'd just like to thank my partner for helping me to come out to my father after 54 years. And to my peers in the industry, I can't think of a better place to come out than at a forum discussing plans for an AIDS benefit.

This got laughs and a big round of applause, but I was still reeling. Afterwards I asked Ed, *"Why in the world did you do that?"* and he replied, very casually, *"Don't worry about it. Your father was sleeping through the whole thing."* *"Bullshit,"* I replied, and then I had to face my father. He seemed thoroughly unfazed. *"Did you hear what Ed said?"* I asked. *"Sure,"* he replied. *"Did you know that before?"* *"Well,"* he answered, *"I kind of thought so, but it really doesn't matter. You know I love you anyway."*

After decades of hiding one of the most important aspects of my life from my parents, after a lifetime of quiet shame and dissembling, in a roomful of industry executives and journalists and my father, taped and broadcast on the Gay Cable Network, my straight business partner outs me. Talk about nothing happening by accident. It was a tribute to dad's warm and accepting character that he didn't seem to care one bit. It made me wonder why I had spent so much of my life in hiding.

Now that I was at last out of the closet seemed to put me in sync with a lot of what was happening in the gay world in 1987. This year was a turning point in the way we dealt with AIDS and, in consequence, the way we dealt with ourselves. There was finally a sense of defiance in the air. In the spring Larry Kramer gave a speech at the gay community center that resulted in the formation of ACT-UP. The new group immediately took to the streets. Out in San Francisco, activist Cleve Jones began to plan an enormous AIDS memorial quilt that would be unveiled on the Mall during the massive March on Washington to be held in October. I was proudly planning to attend. People were now fighting back, and soon that fight would begin to bear fruit, not only in the battle against AIDS, but in a new attitude of gay awareness we had of ourselves. ACT-UP's slogan *"Silence=Death"* about summed it up. Victimization was out; militancy was in.

Unfortunately, this new attitude alone could not save the people I loved, and I was afraid it was coming too late for many of my friends. I was particularly worried about Ignacio. He and Manolo had always been private, but now they became so private that I had not seen them in a long time, and therefore couldn't really tell how Ignacio was getting along. I would call and offer to do something, or just to stop by, but my offers were politely but firmly declined. The first week of August, I got a horrible call from Ignacio. He sounded terrible. He was in constant pain; his condition was deteriorating rapidly. He asked if I could find him a gun. When things became too unbearable he wanted to be able to spare himself and Manolo any more misery and put an end to it all. His desperate tone shocked me beyond belief, and his final request was extremely difficult for me. I would have done anything for Ignacio, but I just couldn't do that. I could not bring myself to participate in his suicide.

I had another idea. Ignacio had always worshipped the great artist Louise Nevelson, who was now in her 80s and living in Little Italy. She was also a very private person, almost reclusive, so these two kindred spirits had never met. But Ignacio adored her so much that he would wait outside her studio for hours in hopes of catching a glimpse of her. A few times he had even followed her around Little Italy like a distant admirer. Once, he sent her a copy of the catalogue when a prominent gallery mounted a major exhibition of his work, hoping she might recognize a disciple and come to the show. She never responded, but he seemed content worshipping her from afar.

Now, desperate for some gesture that might ease his suffering, I called Keith Haring. He then called dancers Bill T. Jones and Arnie Zane, who traveled in Nevelson's circles. They got Ignacio's catalogue to her through mutual friends. A few days later a messenger arrived at Ignacio and Manolo's apartment bearing Ignacio a beautiful bonsai tree and a hand-painted card. Louise Nevelson had had drawn a charming picture of a cat on the card, with the message *"To Ignacio Zuazo from Louise N."* Manolo said that a wonderful sense of peace came over Ignacio when he got Nevelson's gift. The person who was his greatest inspiration had at last acknowledged him. He told Manolo that he felt that her gesture meant that his art would live on, and that it would one day be recognized after he was gone. He seemed to achieve some sort of release, and two days later he died quietly. The world lost a great artist when Ignacio left us, and I lost another great friend. But I was grateful that I was able to do something to ease his final days, and I was equally grateful to Keith Haring, Bill T. Jones and Arnie Zane for helping someone they barely knew. Arnie died shortly thereafter, and Keith a few years later. Bill dances and choreographs and has become one of the world's great artists, and his positive HIV-positive message has been an inspiration to millions. But while my attempt to make some gesture to Ignacio succeeded and seemed to bring him a certain solace, another gift I was working on backfired horribly, and served only to drive Michael and me farther apart, just when he needed me the most.

Inspired by our new AIDS organization, I began to paint a large canvas called *24-Hours-For-Life*. Against a pastel blue background

I placed two radio towers. They symbolized my hope that we would be able to use the media and the music industry to transmit the message of our event around the world. At the top of the canvas I began to place dedications to the many friends, living and dead, who had taught me or helped me or in some way changed my life or assisted in the fight against AIDS. I planned to include lots of these dedications by the time the picture would be finished, and many of them were going to be friends who were still very much alive. But I began with only three — Ignacio, Paul Popham and Michael. Ignacio and Paul were both, of course, dead and gone, and it simply never occurred to me that if Michael should happen to see the picture while it was still in this unfinished state, he would think that I had already consigned him to the dead, and was memorializing him before he died. But this is exactly what happened.

Michael had been back in the hospital for blood transfusions, and one day, after he had been home for a few weeks, he stopped by. I was thrilled to see him, especially after all the unpleasantness a few months before about my attempt to build a float for the Paradise Garage. By coming to see me, even though he was still very weak, he seemed to be letting me know that he had put that behind us, and that our friendship was back on track. I don't know what I was thinking, or if I just wasn't thinking at all, but I impulsively decided to show him the unfinished picture. As he looked at it, a dark expression suddenly came over his face. At first I didn't understand, but he looked at me with real pain in his eyes. *"What are you trying to do, Mel, bury me?"* I immediately grasped what he saw, and I was horrified. I was planning to add many more people to the painting, I tried to explain to Michael. It was still unfinished. My painting had only the best intentions, but somehow all my explanations made us even more uncomfortable together. It felt as though all the good feelings between us were evaporating, and that from now on there would be almost nothing we could do to prevent us from drifting further apart. And in this case I could not fault Jaime. Jaime had done nothing.

I could not have known that this was the last time I would ever see Michael. Our first meeting years before had been the beginning of hope. This last one left me with nothing but regrets. Shortly afterward, I received an invitation. The cover displayed a reproduction of a painting of a nude woman lying on her side, dropping grains of sand from her hand. Inside, it said this:

> THE SANDS OF TIME
>
> Every so often, something beautiful in our lives passes on. We find sadness in this because we can no longer see it or feel it, or be near it. However, we must remember that these things live on in our memory, and in spirit.
>
> We have sad news to share with you. The lease of the Paradise Garage officially ends October 1st 1987. Paradise Garage will come to an end at that time.

It contained the dates of the last three weekends in September, and ended with these words:

> There is not a moment of regret.
> The spirit of the Paradise Garage will always be there,
> and possibly one day in the future,
> we'll be partying again.
>
> In love and hope,
> Michael Brody and
> The Staff of the Paradise Garage

I held it in my hands like a bill of execution. I had known that the Garage was ending since the day Michael made the announcement months before, but somehow I had always hoped for a reprieve. Now, here was the tangible evidence that it was indeed over, and that the end was just a few weeks away. That final invitation was somehow a symbol of everything that was happening: Michael was dying, so many friends were dying, and disco was dead. The sands of time indeed.

chapter seventeen
THE END

As word spread through our circle that the Garage was closing in just a few weeks, a funeral atmosphere seemed to envelop us. Although the official reason was that the club had lost its lease, we felt that the real reason was another bitter example of how AIDS was reaching its poisonous tentacles into our lives and snuffing us out.

It was particularly painful for me for so many reasons. The Paradise Garage, in a very real sense, had grown from the baby that I helped conceive and Michael had carried to term long ago. Who could have guessed back then in the glory days of disco before the world had even embraced our music, that a plague would rise up in our midst and kill us, and kill the very form of expression that sustained us? We had been so optimistic, the future had seemed so limitless, our true liberation had seemed so possible and imminent. We were going to change the world, and now the world had turned its back on us. We were going to show the world how to live, and now we were dying. We were going to dance our way to happiness, and now our dance was ending in a flurry of obituaries and closings and angry demonstrations. Worse, the world was blaming us, saying that we had brought this disaster upon ourselves.

I have always believed in the transforming power of dancing. From my earliest days in the music industry, I had seen how dancing brings people together, how the drudgery of daily life can be erased and pain transmuted when the music plays. Now, as we faced the greatest pain of all, the worst drudgery, we needed to dance more than ever. Physically needed it, since so many people were in such grave danger, their health breaking down, their immune systems gone. Dancing gave us hope, strengthened us in a way no drug or therapy could possibly do, especially in 1987, when there were no drugs or therapies at all, other than the newly prescribed AZT, which wasn't much. It was a vicious circle. AIDS was depriving us of hope and strength, and now, just when we needed the added strength dancing can give, AIDS was depriving us of that as well. The Paradise Garage closing was like a great metaphor for everything that was going wrong, and now, as September began, the end was here and there was no return. Michael's condition worsened the first of the three final weekends, and he had to go back into the hospital. It was as though he and the Garage were tethered in some psychic link, and since he was going to die, the Garage was going to die with him.

I went down the first Saturday night of the three closing weekends, and it was like walking into a funeral parlor. Larry was up in the booth playing what amounted to dirge after dirge. Nothing up-tempo, nothing to remind us of better days, just one depressing, tragic song after another. I was outraged. We all had enough of dirges in our daily lives. If the Garage had to go, it should go out the way it came in, celebrating the joy of life, the power of dance. I marched up to the booth and confronted Larry. *"Don't blame them for what's happening to us. It's not their fault. It's not anybody's fault."* Larry looked at me with tears in his eyes and looked out at the sea of unhappy faces. He was losing his everything, and he was speechless. I reminded him of why we were here in the first place, why we needed an ecstatic last few weeks before our refuge went dark. It was his duty to make these weeks a time to remember. There would be enough sadness and silence later on. Still without saying a word, he motioned me back down to the dance floor. I didn't know what was going to happen — his gesture was like the ghost of Christmas future, pointing the way to the grave. But from that moment on, Larry's music suddenly went magic. A light came on and we were back in the glory days. He blended Garage classics with the hottest sounds of the moment. He played a stream of West End hits, maybe for my sake, maybe for nostalgia's sake. The crowd, which had been milling around in a funk, suddenly jumped up to dance, and from that moment on, until the last night three weeks later, the crowd was in a state of euphoria, and Larry played the greatest, most inspired sets of his life.

Backstage it was anything but euphoric. The staff was in a state of grief over what they were losing and high anxiety for their future. Many had not found jobs at other clubs. Since other clubs were either closing or cutting back, virtually all the staff feared that even if they did find another job, they would never find one at a place like this. There was no other place like the Paradise Garage, and there might never be again.

Long-festering hostilities and problems were coming to a head, and there were petty skirmishes everywhere. Jaime and Sammy were by now as thick as thieves and seemed determined to clean the club out of whatever wasn't nailed down. Michael had given instructions about who was to get what — furniture, art, and so on was to be distributed to various friends and staff and supporters. But Jaime and Sammy ignored Michael's instructions, and soon a steady stream of valuable objects began flowing out of the club and into their own hot hands. I was particularly appalled to see them walk out with a number of sentimental things that I had given Michael over the years, including a beautiful table and several valuable paintings I had given him after we split up. It was very clear that Jaime and Sammy didn't care a whit about their meaning or value as mementos to anyone. Joey Llanos watched all this with disgust, and got to the hospital to tell Michael about it. But it didn't seem to matter to Michael anymore. He was facing his own extinction and pulling away from the cares of the world, and I suppose he had a lot more on his mind than the earthly possessions he was leaving behind. Long after the ordeal was over and done with, Michael's mother confided to me that Michael's only comment had been a quip about Jaime probably opening a junk shop with all the things he purloined from the Garage. Joey was so appalled that he put up a *"Vultures Beware"* sign over the office door when he returned to the club.

I went over to see my parents. A few months earlier, it had become clear that my mother needed round-the-clock care, and this was not practical in the room they were living in at the Colonial House, so I got them an apartment on 23rd St. Blinded by my other problems I could barely stand to see what was happening to my mom and dad. My mother lay there vacant, remembering nothing of her life, not knowing who she was or where she was or who we were. She responded to my father, but did not recognize him as her husband, and the pain of this in his eyes was heartbreaking. I left them and wandered the streets of Chelsea in utter despair, and I found myself talking to God. Bargaining, actually. I asked God to please take my mother in exchange for Michael. My mother had already lived a full and happy life, and she had nothing to live for but continued pain and emptiness. Michael was young and had everything to live for if only he could be spared this horror. It would be better for everybody around. I begged God to do this one thing. I begged him to listen. My mother would be at peace. Michael would live.

I returned to the Garage the next weekend, and went in to see Elida in the office. I wanted news about Michael. I had not spoken to him since our last meeting when he had been so upset about my painting, and I was desperate for any word on his condition. I told Elida about my bargain with God. I hoped she would understand but she stared at me with cold disbelief. Jaime had been working on her as well, it was obvious, telling her whatever he told her to turn her against me. Everyone and everything it seemed was turning against me, and there was no one to turn to, no one to talk to, except Michael himself.

I could not go to him in person since he was by now completely isolated from me and almost everyone. So I decided to write him a letter. I wanted to clear the air, to get everything out on the table, to touch his soul. I couldn't bear to think of him dying without our ever being able to achieve some kind of closure. I realized that any letter I wrote would, if it were honest, be painful. Some people might not understand how I could write a painfully honest letter to someone who was dying; it is the time we are supposed to forget honesty, forget closure, and just offer support. But I had already lost too many friends without really saying what must be said, and I knew from painful experience that once a loved one is gone, there's no way to clear the air for good. With Michael I couldn't let this happen. He had been the most important person in my life. So much had been left unspoken between us. Now he was being poisoned against me, and if he died under these circumstances I didn't think I could go on. And so right there in the Paradise Garage at 8:30 on a Sunday morning I began writing to him, and it all came pouring out.

I admitted my mistakes. I apologized for pushing him away after we broke up. I reminded him that he had once written me *"Our Love, Forever,"* but it seemed that now, when he needed me most, our love was turning to distrust and hate. I admitted that I had been wrong when I refused to join him in starting the Garage — *"You became the rich one, not me,"* I wrote, but I was immensely proud of him. *"We all made so many mistakes,"* I wrote, *"and in spite of it I love you and pray you get well. I hope you get so angry at what I'm saying that you will fight to stay alive."* Then I brought up the issue of the end of the Garage, which I did not believe had to happen. It was a mistake to ever stop dancing, and a mistake to let the Garage die when it really didn't have to. I reminded him of how I had offered to try and keep the club alive, but that Jaime had twisted my offer to make it sound as if I was trying to get my hands on a good thing for my own personal gain.

> You know that's not so. I want to save the space for those "dancing victims" and the people who will lose their jobs, and all the rest would go to fight AIDS — I would write and sign that in blood.

> I love you so very much, and I'm sorry for all the hurt I put you through, my baby. I wish I could push back the time. I would do it differently. I only wish for you to get well.

Then I told him about my bargain with God and how Elida had acted when I told her. *"Oh, Michael,"* I wrote, *"I asked Him to take my mother and keep you alive. And I love my mother very much."*

When I was finished I had second thoughts, so I showed the letter to Noel Garcia, who had known us both from the beginning and knew all the ins and outs of our relationship. I asked him if I should send it. Noel looked at me with the sadness of experience. *"Yes, Papi, send it,"* he replied. I was heartened but still unsure, so I asked Elida. She begged me not to send it. *"Michael's too sensitive,"* she said. *"He won't take it well."* On leaving the club, I shared a cab with Sammy, and told him about it too. He also asked me not to send it. Now I didn't know what to do, so for the moment I did nothing. But by telling Sammy and Elida, I had tipped my hand to Michael. They went to him immediately and told him what I was contemplating. That night the phone rang, and it was a weak but raging Michael, calling from his hospital bed.

He was as cold as ice, all the resentment and bitterness of our troubled years and all our fights just barely contained beneath the rancor in his voice. It was a brief, terrible conversation, like a business call from an estranged partner. *"Please stay away,"* he said. *"Stay out of the office and stay out of the DJ booth."* And he hung up. Jaime was standing by his side when he made that call I know, and I know that Jaime wanted him also to say, *"And stay out of the club altogether."* But Michael could not go that far. He could not cut me off from the very thing that had come from me, the very thing that tied the successful adult to the boy he had been with me. He couldn't go that far, but he went as far as he could, and I was shattered. The thought suddenly struck me that this cold, hostile call might very well be the last time I would speak to Michael. I prayed it wouldn't. As it turned out, it was.

In the turmoil of these emotions, I completely forgot, and suddenly remembered late that night, that it was my father's birthday, and I called to wish him well and apologize. As usual, he was totally understanding, and I got into bed torn with a thousand fears and regrets. I drifted into a fitful sleep and I was myself years before standing over Ben Brody, Michael's father, as he lay dying of cancer. He grabbed my arm again as he did that day, and again he told me, *"I'm glad you're Michael's friend."*

I continued working on my letter over the weekend, and I must have written and rewritten a thousand times. I woke at 6:30 Monday morning and feverishly went back to work writing again. It was turning into an epic, alternatively loving, bitter, nostalgic, angry. Everything I felt about Michael and everything I felt for him flowed out through the ink onto the paper. When my letter was finished, I was still uncertain whether I should send it. I called my old friend Bill Scott in Houston who was a therapist and one of the smartest people I knew, and who was also privy to my whole Michael history. To my surprise, Bill insisted that I send the letter. You must have closure with Michael before he dies, Bill said, and he with you. My mind made up, I took the letter to a florist friend, and he made up a beautiful floral arrangement and then personally delivered the letter and the flowers to Michael's hospital room. Jaime was there and angrily took the letter and the flowers and closed the door in his face. I can only imagine what happened next.

It was the week before the final closing of the Garage, and it seemed that everything was going wrong. Julio and I were on the outs again, having huge fights about everything and nothing. Almost all of my Garage friends were beside themselves wondering what we were going to do and how we were going to keep our extended family together. Then, at the bleakest moment, I received a phone call that seemed to promise a way out.

Since the Flamingo, Michael Fesco had become a promoter and had recently started a Saturday night event at the Palladium, a mammoth, mostly hetero disco operated by Steve Rubell. Fesco's party was thrown in the Michael Todd Room, a sort of club-within-a-club that sat high above the Palladium's main dance floor. He had tried to attract the Saint crowd to his new Saturday night event, but that his strategy was not working, and he wanted to know if I was interested in getting involved.

Here was my unexpected opportunity to create something that could hold the Garage family together. If I could convince Larry to DJ, we could move the crowd over from the Garage and keep things going at the Palladium. I was pretty sure that the main problem wasn't going to be convincing Larry to spin. The problem was going to be getting him to show up. He was erratic, and so devastated by the Garage closing that his presence could never be guaranteed.

Larry Basile agreed to co-promote, and we decided to hold our opening night the weekend after the Garage closed. We named the event "Upstairs," and hired George Morel as second DJ. I had heard him at Tracks and knew he was a rising star. We printed up flyers advertising that this was to be the next big thing. I know it seems odd. The world was falling apart around us, Michael was dying, the Garage was closing, and here I was going into the nightclub business on a few days' notice. I was desperate to try to salvage some of the magic that Michael and Larry had created at the Garage, and I always say that nothing happens by accident. The call from Michael Fesco was proof.

Friday, the first night of the closing weekend arrived. I stopped by the printer's to pick up the flyers that I could hand out at the Garage and start to create a buzz for the new Upstairs event. The crowd outside the Garage was the largest I had ever seen outside a club. The whole world seemed to be gathering to pay its last respects. The Paradise Garage was a big club, but not big enough to handle a crowd that size, and precedence would go to members and their guests. The sheer mechanics of crowd control at the door looked colossal, and eventually, since so many people were unable to get in, things got out of control. Violence heightened the smell of doom and unreality that permeated the whole weekend. In the night's frenzy and frustration, someone outside in the crowd got stabbed.

I left most of the flyers in the coatroom and took a handful to give out. Larry looked pleased to see his name prominently displayed, but he remained noncommittal over whether he would actually show up and spin. He was too involved in the Garage closing drama, and I left him and spent the rest of the night dancing.

The next night, Saturday, the closing of the Paradise Garage had mutated into a large media event. It had been a big story in New York for some time, but the stabbing the previous night was all over the papers and TV the next day, and the final night turned into a circus. If anything, there were more people outside than the evening before. Many of them came down with no thought of actually getting in the club. They just wanted to be in on it this very last night, and they were literally camping out in front on King St. There were film crews; reporters were poking around interviewing people, die-hard fans screaming and crying, some of them threatening suicide.

Inside in the midst of all these feathers and tears and fabulousness, drab plainclothes police stood out like sore thumbs investigating the stabbing. I took one of them on a little tour, trying to explain the difference between the people inside (members) and the people outside, but he seemed supremely unimpressed by my analysis and left me at the coat room where I went to pick up the flyers I had left the night before. But the flyers were gone. They had not been distributed, Jaime had confiscated them and taken them straight to Michael, and from the looks I was getting, Michael was not pleased about my plan.

I didn't realize this at the time, although I suppose I should have. I should have guessed. Jaime and Sammy had decided long before that after the Garage closed, after Michael died, they were going to start their own club to cater to the Garage family. With their inheritance from Michael, the two of them had it made. (And if they had been decent businessmen, they probably would have.) They saw my plans for the Palladium party as a direct threat to their own plans for a post-Garage club (even though they had not yet announced those plans), and they were frightened and furious. They went immediately to Michael to once again depict me as the one attempting to rip off the Garage crowd and cash in on its demise.

Nothing could have been further from the truth. I had no desire to go into the club business, and no need to try to make a financial killing, since by now Colonial House was doing nicely. Indeed, if I did have any aspirations in terms of clubs, it would be to back a non-profit disco that would channel its proceeds back into the community to fight AIDS. I had tried to convince Michael that he should do this with the Garage, and if I'd had any long-term plans for my Upstairs event (which I didn't really), they would have been that. But of course this is not what Jaime and Sammy believed, and this is not the picture they painted for Michael. I was portrayed as the devil, trying to steal their crowd, their money, and their cushy future.

Still, I was unaware of all this. In the emotions of the moment, I wanted nothing more than to be the white knight in shining armor who had figured out a way, at least in the interim, to hold the whole family together. My ignorance made me think that even Jaime and Sammy would be happy with my plan, and I still had a few flyers I was determined to hand out, and had written a special one out for Sammy: *"To Sammy, my favorite lover-in-law, this one is for you — until you can get something going. Never stop dancing!"* I found him standing beneath the DJ booth and went over to give him his invitation. He turned on me like an ice queen. *"You're not wanted here,"* he snarled. *"Get out!"*

I was stunned. Here, on our very last night at the Garage, I was being ordered out by a young man I had employed and done everything I could to help. I was so shocked that it didn't really register. I just assumed that it was Jaime, of course, who had turned Sammy against me, and that he didn't really mean what he was doing. So I just walked away into the sanctuary of Larry's DJ booth. Larry was spinning away in a frenzy of good spirits and he didn't seem to be aware of the fact that this was his last night on Mount Olympus. He was outdoing himself with every mix, the crowd was wild into it, and I quickly forgot the ugly scene with Sammy in all the excitement. Suddenly a security guard lumbered into the booth. *"I'm embarrassed about this because I know who you are,"* he said, *"but I've been ordered to ask you to leave. Jaime wants you out."*

I didn't want to bother Larry with this on his last night and figured I could handle it myself. As I went down the stairs with the guard, two more guards were waiting for me with arms crossed Mafia style. In a gesture out of an old gangster movie, Jaime beckoned them bring me over. I stood my ground. *"Let him come over to me if he wants to talk to me,"* I told them. *"It's gonna take someone a lot bigger than him to throw me out of here,"* I told a friend of David Depino's and ducked into the kitchen. Not knowing what to do, or whether I was about to be forcibly ejected, I told my friend Matty Novak what was going on. He rushed up to the DJ booth, and Larry picked up the phone that instant and called Jaime in the office: *"If you do not stop fucking around with Mel immediately, I'm going to stop the music and end the night right here and now."*

Larry meant business. Jaime knew that the alternate DJs were so loyal to Larry that none of them would ever play if Larry instructed them not to. Larry did, in fact, immediately announce to everyone in the booth: *"If I walk away, don't anybody go near the turntables."* So that was that. Saved by Larry Levan. I retreated up to the booth and stayed there for the rest of the night. Jaime and Sammy danced below us like vultures, shooting up nasty looks every time they caught my eye. Larry saved me from the ultimate humiliation.

It was the strangest, most nostalgic night ever. Larry took us on a musical journey that encapsulated the whole history of disco. Gwen Guthrie and Liz Torres gave scorching performances; divas on the order of Grace Jones were on the dance floor. Garage regulars were now in ecstasy, now sobbing out in the open on the dance floor and in dark corners all around the club. Many members brought guests — husbands, wives, lovers, sometimes even children — so that in the future when the greatest disco in history was described, they would know. The party went on into the next day, and by afternoon it reminded me of a dance marathon. People were drooping and dropping in place, passing out and getting back up, fighting to stay awake.

Being introduced to many of the lovers and spouses and children of friends — many of whom I had never met — moved me to the point that later that afternoon I called Julio and asked him to bring my father and Gigi down to the club for us to experience this final night together. Julio and I had been on the outs again for some time, so it surprised me when he said he would. But it was a mistake I realized the moment he arrived. He showed up dusted out of his mind, itching for a fight. My father had decided not to come, but Gigi and a little friend of hers were with Julio, and he was so abusive to those two little girls that Gigi was reduced to tears. He created a totally disgraceful ranting and raving and threatening scene. When he finally gathered up the girls and stormed out I shuddered with relief. I wanted them with me on this extraordinary emotional occasion, but in the spirit of the moment I guess I had forgotten how crazy Julio had become. Now that Julio had gone, I could continue on with my real family, the sea of friends and friendly faces I had grown to love so much over the years. They understood.

Larry's mother Minnie arrived early in the evening with a mountain of her succulent soul food — roast pork and collard greens and corn bread — and I accompanied her up to the booth where we ate with Larry and Keith Haring. We began to get very emotional, reminiscing about the years we had spent in this place, and worrying about what would become of us all. We were that little family within a family, the parents eating and drinking and laughing and crying upstairs in the DJ booth, while the children were downstairs swirling below us, dancing their last dances. I suddenly felt completely wiped out. After so many hours of drugs and dancing, and all the tensions and confrontations with Sammy and Jaime and then Julio, and Minnie's soul food on top, my spirit wanted to dance forever, but my body had to shut down. I was cramping up and shaky but I could not force myself to leave just yet, and I found myself down on the dance floor for one last round.

The dance floor had now been going non-stop since the night before, and many of the people were in a trance, almost immobile, really like marathon dancers from the old days. I took up my favorite spot on the dance floor, right below Larry, and went into a trance of my own. Suddenly all the lights went dark except for a single spotlight, which I suddenly realized was fixed on me. The Trammps classic "Where Do We Go from Here?" came on. Just as he had used his music so many times in the past to send me a greeting or a rebuke, Larry was sending me his final message from the DJ booth, and in this case his final question. I stood alone in the spotlight and everything I had been holding inside for so long — Michael's illness, Larry, Julio, the end of the Garage, Jaime and Sammy — welled up to the surface and burst. I cried like a baby. All eyes were on me in the spotlight, but many of them were crying too. It was only about nine in the evening and the party was scheduled to keep going on until one or two in the morning, but this, for me, was the real end of the Paradise Garage. *Where do we go from here?*

With the Trammps resounding and receding from the speakers, I knew it was time for me to go, at least take a break. Not counting Friday night, I had now been here almost 20 hours straight, and if I was going to witness the final moments I had to have a shower and a nap. I went up to tell Larry that I'd be back for the very end.

I was cramping up so terribly I couldn't leave without assistance. Someone had to help me into a cab.

A friend from Boston, Kendall Morrison, was staying with me that weekend, and as soon as I got home and jumped into the shower and passed out on my bed, Kendall called down to tell me that Julio was on the phone. I was too exhausted, had a terrible case of laryngitis, there was no way I was going to deal with Julio again. I'd speak with him the next day. A few minutes later there was a commotion and Kendall was shaking me awake. *"You'd better come quick,"* he said. *"Julio's trying to break down the door."* I raced upstairs in a bedsheet, and to my astonishment Julio was at the door screaming and ranting, trying to smash our beautiful carved doors in with his boots. He was disturbing the whole house, but rather than allow him destroy the doors, I let him in.

I had seen him in hysterics more times than I cared to remember, but never like this. He was foaming at the mouth. He was violent and frightening, on the verge of murder, and the guy working the front desk was so terrified he called 911. Three police cars and six officers came in, and they could see that Julio was past all reasoning. Trying to calm him down and get him to leave only enraged him more. *"Why don't you tell them I've been your lover for ten years?"* he screamed. *"I don't think they really care,"* I answered. Frankly, at this point neither did I. It was totally humiliating, being berated and screamed at in front of my friend from Boston and my staff, the police, everybody. The police escorted Julio out, and I collapsed.

My plan was to take a quick disco nap and return to the club for the final moments, but after all this, I fell into a deep sleep and didn't wake up until well into the next day. By that time, it was all over. For better or worse, I had missed the final moments of the Paradise Garage. Later, I discovered that I wasn't the only Garage regular who wasn't there for the finale. They couldn't bear the tears and emotion of those last seconds, and by midnight many of the old-timers bid Larry farewell and slipped off into the night.

But Larry was determined to keep the party going a full 24-hours, and he continued spinning until two in the morning. He spun his nostalgic favorites — Jocelyn Brown's "Make It Last Forever" and Sister Sledge's "We Are Family" — as the last weeping revelers gathered in a circle and lit candles. He then played a taped message from Michael, expressing his regret that he could not be there and wishing everyone well. This was followed by Diana Ross and the Supremes, "Someday We'll Be Together," and Larry's Two Tons of Fun classic, "Just Us." As the closing chords of "Are You For Real" echoed in the cavernous garage, the famous sound system went silent, I was told. The lights came up on the tears, the litter, the wet confetti, and the last remaining members straggled out into the street for the very last time.

In the weeks following the closing, Mickey Smolar had to deal almost single-handedly with the difficult task of dismantling the club. Single-handedly because staff members had not received the bonuses Michael had promised them if they remained on the job until the end and most of them were furious and not willing to lift a finger. The money that Michael had set aside for them had disappeared, and Mickey had to pay a few loyal staffers an hourly wage to help him. Everything had to be removed and dispersed before the new tenants could move in. He had a lot of trouble trying to get Larry to come in and help dismantle the sound system and pack up his records. Larry just couldn't be bothered with such mundane details. On the final day before the new tenants were scheduled to take possession, Larry showed up. By this time, very little remained of the club, but the sound system was still intact there waiting for him, and the people helping Larry cried when they cut the wires and took the sound apart.

Sadder was the fate of Larry's records packed up and put in storage in a warehouse in Chelsea. The storage fee was about a hundred dollars a month, but Larry would never pay. The person in charge of the space called Larry after a few months. If he didn't come through with the fee, his records would be sold at auction. Larry's response was yeah, yeah, you'll get your money, and then he forgot about it. He could have paid or got them out of storage, I offered him the money, but he kept putting it off, and the most famous record collection in the history of disco was sold off at auction. Larry's friend Danny Tenaglia was so distraught that he bought some of the most irreplaceable records and gave them back to Larry, but most of Larry's records were gone.

Ricky Willock happened to be walking past Jaime's apartment building shortly after the Garage had been completely dismantled and the new tenants moved in, and there in the garbage waiting to be picked up, was the famous black metal Paradise Garage sign that used to hang on the building. Ricky retrieved it and immediately brought it to me. We couldn't believe that Jaime had been so callous, and disrespectful, to discard it. I was terribly grateful that Ricky brought it to me, and to this day it resides on the sun deck of the Colonial House. Someday I hope to donate it to a disco archive, if one is ever established.

Sometimes when I'm down in the Village I wander over to King St. and stare up at the old building. It's odd to see it today. There's no plaque, no sign, nothing to remind passersby that this was the best disco in the world. It's just any ordinary garage once again, an oil-splashed wreck of a building with New York Telephone utility trucks inside. The ramp leading into the club is just a ramp again, now and then disgorging a truck or a car. A weary guard sits in a little booth on the main floor, where thousands lined up clamoring to get in. The street is desolate and quiet but there are ghosts. I can still hear the music on that dingy street, and one particular song is always playing:

> Someday we'll be together.
> Someday, sometime in the future
> You will turn around
> And see there's nothing to be found,
> And you'll come running back to me.
> Someday
> We'll be together.

chapter eighteen
PIECES
OF A DREAM

My life has been a series of mornings after, but none was so dark as the morning after the Garage closed. The lights were out, the music was over, and it seemed likely that our Garage family was going to be dispersed forever. In a lot of ways, what happened to the Garage was a metaphor for what was happening to our lives. A whole world based on love and joy, the idea that you can dance your way through adversity, was dying or seemed to be in those horrible years.

Thankfully I was too busy to mope. My new Upstairs event at the Palladium was to begin the next weekend, and I allowed myself the hope that if we did it right we might be able to keep the Garage family together, at least for the time being, and keep Larry busy. I worried about him. If nothing else, all the work organizing this event kept me busy and prevented me from dwelling too much on the way things were turning out. Friday before our opening I went over to Tracks, a new club, to hand out flyers and Julio was there. Though I tried to avoid him, he was determined to seek me out and try to patch things up. But after his last horrendous episode I told myself that this time was it. Life with him was chaos and it was never going to change. I had to make my final break. Just as I was about to walk away, Jaime sauntered up, drunk and visibly stoned and more or less out of his mind. *"You son of a bitch,"* he hissed. *"You want Michael to die so you can get your hands on all of his money."* I suppose this was the first time I had actually heard him say out loud to my face that there was a money thing between Michael and me. I wanted Michael to die, Jaime said, so that I could inherit his estate and be rich. Hearing this from his own lips was a shock, but it shouldn't have been. It was the basis of Jaime's whole twisted scheme to drive a wedge between Michael and me. Having planted that lie in Michael's always-suspicious mind, he could reinterpret everything I did as a part of some sinister master plan.

I had no expectation of inheriting a thing from Michael, of course. Back when we were lovers I was a beneficiary in his will, as he was in mine. But I had long ago rewritten my will and so had he, several times. Although he never told me its contents, there was no question in my mind that if he left me anything at all it would be some token, at most, a painting or something to remember him by. But Jaime's charge was more than completely baseless. It was almost as if he needed to transfer to me the very thing he himself was doing. After all, he had arranged things so that he and Sammy, his best friend, were going to be Michael's main beneficiaries. Maybe he felt guilty and his way of dealing with it was by putting it on me. What better sucker?

I was rattled by his accusation, but I took the opportunity to ask Jaime something I wanted to know since I'd sent my letter to Michael. *"Did I make Michael cry?"* I asked him. Yes, Michael cried when he read my letter, Jaime sneered. Good. *"That's what I wanted him to do, you asshole."* The whole point of my letter was to get Michael to achieve some sort of catharsis about his relationship with me so that he would be able to cut loose from the built-up hurt he'd kept inside him. Reading the letter and snorting disgust would have meant that he was still refusing to deal with this central thing in our lives, repressing it and refusing still to feel it. But Michael had cried. Maybe he could achieve lasting peace; maybe I could, knowing that the circle was now complete and nothing had been left unsaid. Jaime could not be expected to understand this, of course, so I asked him if he really truly believed that I wanted to get my hands on Michael's fortune, did he think I would have written him such a letter? Was that good strategy to get on somebody's good side, by making him cry? This started a new argument. Jaime was often capable of saying the nastiest things with a smile on his face, but this night he was absolutely vile. I don't remember most of what he said, only that the reason Michael and I are so alike is that we're both Jews and love money. It looked like Julio was about to punch Jaime, he was so riled up. I couldn't believe how odd, about to be fought over by the two people in the world I was most angry with. I pulled them apart and dragged Julio away.

The next morning fuming over the scene with Jaime I wrote Michael another letter. This one was not about Michael and me. It was about Jaime. I berated myself for having allowed Michael to fall into Jaime's clutches. It never would have happened had I not pushed Michael away. Again I repeated my love for him, and again I begged him not to give up. I had come across a button that said *"God forgives, I don't,"* and remembering how it was always such a joke between us that Michael never forgave anybody the slightest thing, I stuck the button in the envelope with a little note. *"I thought this button was perfect for you. I hope it gives you a smile."* I sent the letter again with flowers and the sinking feeling that this might be the very last communication I would ever have with Michael, and it was.

The weekend arrived with the debut of our Upstairs party. Several hundred people showed up, nowhere near the crowd we were expecting. Many of the Garage regulars were in such mourning that they couldn't bear to go to a different place, at least for a while. Many of them thought it would be betraying the memory of the Garage to go out dancing the very next weekend, and others never went out dancing ever again. One good thing came out of that first night though. I met my next boyfriend, a beautiful young Puerto Rican named Willy Marquez. Willy had been a Garage regular, but somehow I had never met him. I looked him over now and could hardly believe I had ever missed him. We spent half the night on the stairs outside reminiscing about the Garage, and by the end of the night we were the best of friends. Larry didn't show up, but that didn't cause a major problem. We had George Morel as back-up just in case.

The next week I didn't make it to the Upstairs party myself, but to the march in Washington instead. The gigantic gay and lesbian march was organized to protest the Supreme Court's Hardwick decision affirming states the right to ban consensual same-sex activity. The march was gigantic, and it made me feel better surrounded by so many hundreds of thousands of other gay men and lesbians fighting for our rights and our lives. Brent's AREA run, which had traveled around the country for 20 months, pulled into Washington that weekend, and he was joined by 300 runners from around the country. They ran around the Capitol and down the whole length of the Mall, and we had a great ceremony on the grounds behind the White House. The next day the AIDS quilt was unveiled spread out on the Mall. The quilt had 1,920 panels and was moving beyond belief. When Brent, Marion and I finally found the panels for Ignacio and Paul Popham, we were in tears. Who could have imagined at that time that in less than a decade this same quilt would have grown to 40,000 panels?

Back in New York I was busy promoting our Upstairs party, which was beginning to take off. Larry came by the second week stoned almost incoherent, and it became obvious that he was not going to work out as the DJ. The closing of the Garage had completely unhinged him, and I really began to worry about what would happen to him now.

As it turned out, the success of the Upstairs party was its own undoing. The Palladium had always taken a dim view of parties that attracted an interracial crowd. The owners, and Steve Rubell in particular, desperately wanted to avoid their club being associated with blacks or latinos, exactly the crowd we were trying to attract. Our crowd grew, our favor fell. We were informed after a few more weeks that the party was being canceled. No one came right out and said that the ethnic mix of the crowd was the reason of course, which would have been discriminatory and illegal. But we were given excuse after excuse, anything they could think of, and in such an atmosphere we did not want to continue. It all reminded me of the very reason why the Paradise Garage had been so important to begin with, how little New York nightlife had changed from the time when we had dreamed of a place without prejudice or harassment, and it made me miss the Garage all the more.

I heard nothing from Michael as the weeks went by. Jaime was guarding him jealously, and except for Jaime, Sammy and Elida, no one could see him. I kept hearing rumors that he was not doing well and was in and out of the hospital, but I received no call, no letter, just a long silence, during which life went on. Willy Marquez moved in with me in November. Our friendship had grown into a sort of romance, not really love, but a lot of fun. Willy's innocence was like a breath of fresh air, and having him around prevented me from falling back in with Julio. I began to think that this time I had finally broken that circle of mutual destruction.

Michael's illness became a thing that lurked in the background: never really present, never far away. Every time the phone rang, every time a mutual friend visited, it was always in the back of my mind that this could be it. A few days after Christmas, it came. Ricky Willock stopped by the Colonial House, and from the terrible look on his face standing in the hall, I knew. Michael had died at home the day before. I thought I was prepared. (Along with the reports that Michael wasn't doing well, there were lots of people with AIDS not doing well, but many of them just kept going.) For some reason, I was consumed with a desire to know about Michael's final days. I asked Ricky to call the apartment and ask Jaime for details, not telling Jaime, of course, that he was with me. Jaime was not too communicative, but in the course of the conversation he informed Ricky that I was not welcome at the funeral.

I suppose I should have been insulted, but in fact I was relieved. I could not have delivered some fake eulogy. I don't think I could have tolerated sitting there watching Jaime shed tears as he was counting his new-found riches. In my opinion, then and now, Jaime was very much responsible for Michael's death. Not because he may have been the person who infected Michael, and not because he was traveling to places like Mexico to procure all sorts of highly questionable drugs; we'll never know the truth about either of those things. He was culpable because he blackmailed Michael, and psychologically tortured him and isolated him, and made his life so miserable that he finally gave up and wanted to die. The grave was Michael's only escape from Jaime.

I woke up crying the morning of Michael's funeral. Willy went in my place. He reported to me afterwards that it was a very small gathering for such an important person. David DePino, Joey Llanos, Noel Garcia, a few on the Garage staff were there and a couple of close friends like Diane. But Larry was conspicuously absent, as were most of the staff. Most of them did not know that Michael had died. After the funeral a small group returned to Michael's apartment, and they were appalled that Jaime and Sammy were doing cocaine in the bedroom and laughing and bragging about what a fortune they had inherited. Infuriated, Noel Garcia was ready to kill Jaime, and it surely would have come to blows if Michael's mother had not intervened. Hearing all this from Willy, I was glad that I hadn't been there.

Three days later Jaime and Sammy showed up at the World to celebrate New Year's Eve and their newfound fortune, dressed to the gills in white outfits that belonged to Michael. The World had recently opened in an old ballroom on the Lower East Side, and Larry was spinning for the New Year's party. This, I'm sure, is what led Jaime and Sammy to this particular club. What better and more morbid way to flaunt their ascendancy over Larry than to show up in Michael's white finery on New Year's at a club where Larry had to work? Michael Sampson was running the lights that night in the booth with Larry, and a mutual friend came up and told them that Jaime and Sammy were down on the dance floor bragging about all the things they planned to do with their inheritance. This, believe it or not, is how Larry Levan found out about the death of Michael Brody. Even though Jaime and Michael Sampson lived in the same building a floor apart, Jaime had not bothered to tell him, and by extension, Larry.

Larry and Michael were stunned beyond words, and I heard from Larry later how horrible the circumstances were. Here he is in a DJ booth spinning for a thousand people on New Year's Eve. His job is to keep things going and keep the spirit festive and happy. Suddenly he is told that his mentor, the man most responsible for his career, his employer for the past 13 years, is dead and buried, and nobody has thought to come and tell him. The best that Larry and Michael Sampson could do with this belated news was a moment outside on the fire escape in the cold winter air. They stood there and hugged each other and then returned to the booth and to the party that must go on.

Thinking back, I wish that Larry had been with me that night, at the New Year's Eve party I was giving at home. Bill Scott, Chaz, Brent and Al, Dick Fisher, Larry McDevitt, and a few other old and dear friends had been invited, and I decided not to cancel after I heard about Michael. I needed to be around friends at a time like this. We spent the time reminiscing, and at midnight, when they played the song about old acquaintances not being forgot, I looked around and realized how many were already gone, and wondered how many more would be gone by the next new year.

After everyone else drifted home, Willy, Brent, and Al and I talked about where to go dancing. The Saint was now filled with ghosts; we couldn't go there. The Garage was gone. For the first time in almost 20 years, there was no center of gravity, no obvious place to go dancing on New Year's Eve in New York City. For a population that had made dancing and partying a lifestyle, that's saying a lot. We finally decided on Baseline, a new little underground club where Junior Vasquez was spinning. Junior was making a name for himself as one of the most influential DJs of the new generation who had learned at the feet of the masters like Larry Levan, and I wanted to support him. At first I wasn't sure we had made the right decision going to Baseline. It was small, dark and claustrophobic, and I couldn't help thinking what a letdown it was after the energy of so many incredible New Years at the Saint and the Garage, and the Flamingo and the Loft before them. As the night progressed I began seeing more and more people from the Garage. Pretty soon I realized that many familiar faces surrounded me and there was comfort in that.

Although I didn't know Junior Vasquez well, and he didn't know Michael well, I went up to the booth and told him. He stopped the music and announced to the crowd that Michael had died, and asked for a moment of silence. A hush fell over the room, and one by one people began removing candles from tables and placing them in the center of the dance floor. As the floor became a mass of flickering candles and the room grew brighter, I saw that many of us were in tears and crying. I had been barred from Michael's empty, cold funeral, but now here in this small club in the wee hours of New Year's Eve, I was having my own memorial. Michael would be pleased.

Heading for a major depression the next day I booked a flight to St. Thomas. Michael and I had been happy there many years before. Every place reminded me of Michael, but instead of making me sad, I found it comforting. All comfort vanished upon my return to New York, however. Michael's will had been read: 65% of his estate went to Sammy (35%) and Jaime (30%). Michael's mother Jean received 25%, and Elida, the remaining 10%. I was appalled. This is what it said on paper, but the reality was that a huge portion of Michael's estate was in cash, squirreled away in safety deposit boxes here and there, foreign bank accounts and so on, hidden money that was Jaime's needless to say, since he was the only one who knew where it all was. For example, I remembered Michael telling me that he had $450,000 in a safety deposit box in New York. His mother went to the bank and the box was empty. God knows how many other boxes were empty.

But far worse than this is the fact that Larry, the person most responsible for Michael's success, received nothing. I was flabbergasted, and so was everyone else. Even those who normally stuck up for Michael through thick and thin, good friends like Diane Strafaci, were outraged. Perhaps the meanest thing in the will was that although there had always been a verbal agreement that the Garage's spectacular and valuable sound and light systems would go to Larry, Michael left them to his mother, a woman who could not possibly have the slightest use for them. It seemed as though Michael was deliberately cutting Larry off from everything, even things that seemed unquestionably to be his.

I was so outraged that I hired an attorney to see if there was anything that could be done for Larry, but unfortunately there was not. For one thing, although the attorney uncovered all sorts of questionable dealings around the will, most of them were merely unethical rather than strictly illegal. For another, Larry was not a blood relative, and so had no solid legal claim to anything. During our first meeting with the lawyer, he showed up high on heroin. I'm usually blind to that kind of thing, but the lawyer realized it and she really let Larry have it. I continued to pay her for awhile, hoping she would figure out some way for Larry to get something, but because he was now so zonked-out on drugs that he was in no shape to vigorously pursue the matter, in the end it was hopeless. Jaime and Sammy became lovers soon after Michael's death, and they rode off into the sunset with his fortune. Larry, who was at least half of that fortune, never received a cent.

I was upset when Jean ignored Michael's wishes to be cremated and have his ashes scattered at the place we first met, off the beach on Fire Island. She took the ashes home with instructions that they be buried with her. I wanted to protest, but couldn't. Jean and I were not on the best of terms at the time. We had been friends for years until she saw my last letter to Michael, in which I had included the button, *God forgives, I don't.* She assumed that this meant that I did not forgive Michael. She was terribly hurt that I would make such a gesture, and I certainly understand how she felt. When I eventually had the opportunity to explain that the button was a private joke between Michael and me (Michael's famous tendency never to forgive a slight), Jean and I became better friends than ever. A year later, on the day that would have been Michael's 44th birthday, she gave me a gift that means more to me than anything else I possess, an old photo of Michael and me that Jaime was about to throw away. Jean told him that she wanted it for herself, and she kept it for me for Michael's birthday. It is a picture of us in the early '70s on Fire Island, two skinny guys in bathing trunks and tans, our arms around each other smiling in the sun, over which Michael has inscribed:

"Nothing is more important than friendship. Not fame, not money, not death." Michael had this photo framed and matted, I have no idea when he wrote those words. Was it when he was diagnosed with AIDS and was reflecting on his life and death? Was it many years before? I'll never know. All I know is that it is the most precious thing I own.

As winter turned into spring, I fell back into my old patterns. Willy moved out after it became clear that someone so young and energetic was not the best companion for me. Not long after that, Julio began calling me every day, begging for reconciliation. At first I resisted, but I was very vulnerable and unsettled and filled with regrets about how I had messed up my relationship with Michael, and I guess all these feelings made me susceptible to Julio's constant pleas. Pretty soon we were back together, and back to the drugs and fights and the whole routine. Around the same time, my mother's Alzheimer's progressed to the point where she had to go into a nursing home. It was better for her in the end, but it was hell on my father and me.

I kept myself halfway together by continuing my work on *24-Hours-For-Life*, the music industry AIDS fundraising group we were struggling to get off the ground. I considered it a genuine scandal that the music industry had done so little to fight a disease that had taken so many people from our profession. I was sure that if we worked harder, we could turn *24-Hours* into the industry's major AIDS organization, and I was willing to work and wanted to do something useful to fight back. Then, a few months after the Garage closed we heard the news that seemed to seal the end of our era. The Saint was closing at the end of April, and the reason was the same. In the case of the Paradise Garage, AIDS had killed its creator. In the case of the Saint, AIDS killed its clientele (and would eventually kill its creator as well).

The Saint was so huge that it could comfortably hold several thousand, and for years it was crammed every Saturday night. But by 1988, it was lucky if it drew a few hundred souls, even on a good night. The rest were either dead or mourning or dying, or taking care of someone who was. At one point the club sent out its annual membership renewals and over 700 came back marked: Return to Sender — Occupant Deceased. The spirit had completely gone out of the place. When a realty company offered Bruce Mailman more than six million dollars to buy the building and turn it into a cineplex, he jumped at the chance. I had approached Bruce with the same idea that I had urged on Michael, to turn his club non-profit with proceeds to fight AIDS, but Bruce, the ultimate gay capitalist, looked at me as though I were on another planet. He eventually did contribute a lot of money to AIDS, but my original idea was apparently too far out for him.

The final Saint party was set for April 30, and it was to be a great marathon, ten DJs spinning nonstop for almost two days. The announcement seemed to galvanize everyone who was left, and when the closing weekend finally arrived, people from all over had flown in to New York. For the Boston crowd, including a lot of old friends like Larry Basile, the Colonial House became a sort of rendezvous, and we were booked solid. We all trooped over to the Saint, not sure whether we were going to one of the historic parties of all time, or our own funeral. In a way, it was both.

The Saint had always been my second favorite place, since I preferred first the eclectic mix and family feeling of the Garage crowd. But there was no question that the Saint was the apex of our whole dance culture, and we all knew what it's closing meant. That first night we danced like demons to Mark Thomas's opening set, and at eight in the morning we went wild when the dome rose up to reveal the great Thelma Houston singing her classic — and now eerily timely — "Don't Leave Me This Way."

When she closed with "Saturday Night is Shining on My Monday Morning Face," you could see the most macho of macho men in tears. Then came DJs Michael Fierman and Paul Jabara, who had the audacity and also the good sense to play his brilliant mix of Donna Summer's "Last Dance." Donna Summer had denounced the gay community in a fit of fundamentalist Christian bigotry, and although her music was consequently banned from most gay clubs, "Last Dance" was one of the true signature songs of our era and under the circumstances couldn't have been more appropriate.

Julio and I left on Sunday for a breather, and returned at seven that evening for the final push which would take us through Sunday night and climax at noon on Monday. We got there in time for Howard Merritt's set, only to find that Howard had bowed out when he discovered that Bruce Mailman was paying each DJ only two hundred bucks, although this historic party was raking in a fortune. Warren Gluck took over the booth at eight that night and his set concluded hours later with an amazing performance by Sharon Redd who sang "Beat the Street" and "Love Insurance." *"Thank you for giving me my career,"* she called out to the audience, many of whom were in tears. *"You are my history."* She concluded with "In the Name of Love," and the place exploded.

Jim Burgess came out of retirement to play the penultimate set at 4 a.m. Monday morning. Jim was very ill and this was his swan song; he died shortly thereafter. But AIDS didn't stop him from pushing the envelope one more time. At one point he dared bring the energy to a complete halt. He played ten minutes of Bette Davis dialogue from her old tearjerker, "Dark Victory." The crowd hooted their disappointment. He finally put them out of their misery with Candi Staton's jubilant "Young Hearts Run Free." It was that kind of event, a true marathon — the good, the bad, and the ugly all mixed up with love and nostalgia and regrets, and death hung over the dome.

After 36 hours non-stop music, it was Robbie Leslie's turn for the final stretch to noon. Being the last DJ on the last party was the undeniable star position, and it was a great affirmation for Robbie, who had moved back home to Florida two years before amid rumors that he, too, was dying. Thank God it was not true. He made the best of it. As noon approached, my friends and I gravitated toward our regular spot on the dance floor, drawn together at this last moment as though we were waiting for the world to end. In a way, we were. Surrounded by all this love and emotion, I couldn't stop feeling the presence of all those who were not with us whose spirits were floating above us in the Saint's famous dome. Outside our world was dying, and we were about to be thrown out of our sanctuary back out into that world. We were about to be deprived of our beautiful escape for a place from which there was no escape. It was almost unbearable.

For me, and I think for many that night, this was the true end of disco. Not that moment years before when the outside world turned its back on our music. We never really cared about that anyway. We created our music and our culture on our own, and we remained true to it even when everyone else decided that disco sucked, and went on to other things. But disco sucks did not end it for us. What ended it for us was AIDS. It was the true finish to the trajectory that had taken us from little underground clubs in out-of-the-way lofts to the apex of the music industry and, for a moment, the axis of popular culture. Now was the end of the path that had taken me from a wide-eyed kid who arrived in New York decades before filled with ideas about changing the world. It led me through all the magical revolutions, the glory and all the grief and, surrounded by friends about to die, deposited me here on a dance floor about to go silent. This was the end.

With Jimmy Ruffin's "Hold Onto My Love," Robbie Leslie bid us farewell. This was his signature song that he'd remixed into a classic back when the Saint was the Saint. As the stars blinked out in the famous dome forever, as we stood in the darkness wondering what to do next, suddenly Marlena Shaw's voice rang out — *"Now I am strong enough to accept change"* — and a spotlight went just on her face on stage. She broke into her beloved "September" song medley. It begins with "It Was a Very Good Year" and ends with "Touch Me In the Morning," and when the familiar sad trumpet cried over the weeping crowd and Marlena sang *"We don't have tomorrow, but we had yesterday,"* the circle was complete: she performed this same medley the night the Saint opened, already from a different era, when we were young and going to live forever.

The final chord, the last beat echoed and faded, and it was all over beneath the cavernous dome. Small groups huddled together, young men looked old with grief and loss. Nobody wanted to leave, leaving meant never returning, but slowly we stumbled out into the street onto high noon on an overcast regular Monday workday in New York. People were going about their business rushing around, walking dogs, shopping, hailing cabs. Someone had spray painted *"Hold Onto My Love"* over the entrance to the Saint, but most pedestrians walked by oblivious. A world had just come to an end and now we were going to have to find our way in a new world, to survive if we could or, like most of my friends, even many of those who were there that final night, die.

chapter nineteen
LIFE

The years after the closing of the Garage and the Saint were not easy. A new community built on activism instead of escape, on protest instead of partying, was struggling to rise up out of the ashes of AIDS, and I wanted to be a part of this community as well. There were groups to organize, money to raise, demonstrations to attend. And so many funerals.

I spent a good deal of the next couple of years struggling to make a success out of our group *24-Hours-For-Life*. The music industry, with its deeply ingrained homophobia, continued to resist playing a major role in AIDS fundraising, and our efforts were constantly thwarted by failure to secure big names and major industry endorsements. We continued with our plan to create a one-day event in which nightclubs, radio stations, concert halls and stadiums would turn over their profits to AIDS, and we got help from cutting-edge performers like Michelle Shocked and Billy Bragg. But in 1988 our main assistance came from pop star Dionne Warwick, the singer who had been a star in Florence's stable two decades before.

Dionne had started the Warwick Foundation to provide health care for people with AIDS and promote awareness of the disease, and when I heard about it I got the idea of teaming up with her. I enlisted Florence Greenberg, who had remained in contact with Dionne, in this effort, and Florence arranged a meeting with Dionne's manager Guy Draper. I had a very bad feeling about Draper from the start. He seemed to me to care nothing about AIDS, but he agreed to have Dionne team up with *24-Hours-For-Life* for the big AIDS charitable weekend they were planning in June of 1989. Florence became the honorary chairwoman, and it seemed like our efforts were moving in the right direction. Dionne announced a joint fundraising concert that would lead up to the big weekend, and she enlisted all sorts of big names, from Rosalyn Carter and Betty Ford to Muhammad Ali, Bob Mackie and Luther Vandross. My dream of a huge AIDS event seemed to be coming true, and I could hardly contain my feelings of gratitude for Dionne.

Our first joint venture was *"In Loving Memory of Sylvester,"* a trip down disco memory lane. AIDS had claimed the mighty real Sylvester, the biggest star of disco, the year before, and turnout at this concert and party was great. Linda Clifford, Carol Douglas, Loleatta Holloway, Vicki Sue Robinson, Sharon Redd — a slew of top disco stars performed their hits. Tears came to my eyes when our own wonderful Taana Gardner sang her West End hits "Work that Body" and "Heartbeat." But this was just a prelude to the main event.

Months were spent organizing our big weekend in New York: six major nightclubs were to hold events in line with our *24-Hours* theme. Gladys Knight was a major supporter. She conducted a press event for us at Studio 54 and agreed to be the official chairperson for our events, which were timed to coincide with her own mega-events. The whole thing was billed as the *"That's What Friends Are For"* weekend, and the plan was for the Warwick Foundation to hold a lavish, star-studded dinner on Thursday night on the U.S.S. Intrepid with performances by Dionne, Frank Sinatra, Gladys Knight and Sammy Davis, Jr. This would be followed with an incredible concert at Lincoln Center on Saturday night, featuring Gregory Hines, Rita Coolidge, Patti LaBelle, Cyndi Lauper, Stephanie Mills, Mary Wilson, Whitney Houston and a ton of other celebrities. Then, on Sunday night, the six clubs would hold their own theme events, and all proceeds were going to *24-Hours-For-Life* and were to be disbursed to various AIDS charities.

Club impresario Stanley Burke was instrumental in convincing the six big clubs to get involved. Stanley really threw his heart into the project, and I don't know how we could ever have organized it without him or Jeanne Gianas. The whole weekend would be punctuated by press conferences, speeches and dedications. Dionne's events were guaranteed to raise a fortune, and ours were expected to raise $100,000. But glitches occurred almost immediately. Perhaps the most damaging was that GMHC announced that it would hold its annual Thank You party on the same night as our events. GMHC's was a free event to thank those who participated in their enormous AIDS Walk. This, we knew, was inevitably going to cut into our turnout, since the party was free and was bound to attract a lot of people who cared both about AIDS and about dancing. Since a portion of our proceeds was to go in fact to GMHC, we were faced with a major conflict. But our pleas that GMHC reschedule its party were rejected by the group's director Richard Dunne. This was particularly frustrating. (Later Geoffrey Braff, who became GMHC's next executive director, wrote me a letter apologizing and promised that such a thing would never be repeated.)

Dionne also wanted to throw a thank you party for our volunteers but didn't have the money. Since I was already planning a dedication that Sunday at Colonial House to honor the founders of GMHC, which had been born in my building, I offered to expand the dedication into a thank you party for our volunteers as well, and to pay for it all. In the end, I spent a fortune of my own on the whole effort, taking out lines of credit and stretching myself to the limit. My friends thought I was crazy, but it was something I had to do. It turned out to be a huge sad disaster.

Although Dionne's events seemed spectacular successes at first, they were eventually engulfed in a scandal that seriously damaged her reputation and destroyed her foundation. A few years later, newspapers were full of stories claiming gross mismanagement, ineptitude, and extravagance. Guy Draper, whom I had so disliked when I encountered him, was reported to have spent a fortune on all sorts of luxuries for the stars. In the end Dionne's foundation closed having raised 2.1 million dollars and having spent 2.8 million — in expensive programs for the events, limos and first-class airline tickets and hotels, and so on — meaning that nothing in effect actually went to AIDS, and that the foundation actually owed $700,000. The whole mess made headlines, was the subject of an ABC News *Day One* investigation and became a huge scandal. My most vivid memory of it was at a taping of the *Geraldo Show*. Dionne tried to defend herself and was on the verge of tears. I was in the audience, and spoke bitterly about Guy Draper. Florence came on the show as well, but she was no longer at the top of her game and her appearance didn't do much good. (That sad afternoon was to be the last time I would ever see my old mentor. Soon after the *Geraldo* taping Florence suffered a stroke and then a heart attack, and died not long after that). Of course, this whole scandal would not come out until several years after the event. At the time, we didn't have a clue that Dionne's events were anything but glittering successes, and I was filled with anticipation about how great our own club events were going to turn out.

That Sunday afternoon we held a moving ceremony in front of Colonial House to dedicate a plaque for the six founders of GMHC. We invited the three living co-founders to the ceremony (Larry Kramer, Larry Mass, Edmund White), and Larry Mass came and gave a very moving speech. He talked about the three co-founders who had died (Nathan Fain, Paul Popham, Paul Rapoport), and he was particularly eloquent about Paul Popham.

Even many people who had never met Paul were deeply moved by Larry's speech. Then Brent accompanied Paul Popham's mother and Michael's mother to unveil the plaque on the façade of the building:

FIRST PERMANENT HOME
GAY MEN'S HEALTH CRISIS
1982-1984
CO-FOUNDED 1981 BY:
NATHAN FAIN
LARRY KRAMER
DR. LAWRENCE MASS
PAUL POPHAM
PAUL RAPOPORT
EDMUND WHITE

FIRST PRESIDENT OF THE BOARD
PAUL POPHAM
1947-1987

After everyone was invited into Colonial House for the reception, I lingered outside gazing at the plaque. It was a little piece of history, a representation of a moment in time when gay men had come together to save our brothers and ourselves. It was both sad and glorious, and it suddenly struck me how important it is to preserve the memory of our time, the good and the bad, so that future generations of gay people would know who had come before, and know that they had both a community and a history. I lived a good chunk of this history, and I had long toyed with the idea of writing a book about the Paradise Garage and my life in the disco business. But now I made up my mind. Standing there looking at the plaque, I came to the decision that resulted in this book while standing there looking at the plaque. Several years later, Larry Kramer would bring Barbra Streisand around to see my building for the movie that she was planning to make of Larry's play, *The Normal Heart,* which was about the formation of GMHC. We make muffins every morning for our hotel guests

I told her, and when she asked if I had any extra I was so nervous I forgot to get her one. She was very charming.

Dionne Warwick, however, was hours late to the dedication reception that Sunday afternoon. Earlier, Guy Draper had called to say she was canceling, but I chewed him out so badly that he finally brought her down. She immediately lit up the room, and I had a good feeling about the coming night of parties, the culmination of all my work for almost two years. When the time came, a star-studded entourage piled into the three limos I had rented, and we were off to a night of what promised to be great events all over town. Aside from me, Jeanne Gianas and Stanley Burke, the entourage included Dionne, Gladys Knight, Mary Wilson, Tony Orlando, Rita Coolidge, the actor Dustin Nguyan from the then-popular *21 Jump Street*, and the famous Dallas Cowboy Duane Thomas. We made quite an impression when we entered a room.

Our first stop was the Village Gate, where Rosie O'Donnell was doing a stand-up show. She greeted us from the stage when we entered and everything seemed fine, but I was disturbed by the size of the crowd. It wasn't exactly embarrassing, but it wasn't very good either, and the Village Gate was not a large space. Next we zipped over to Heartbreak, which had scheduled an evening of music headlined by Paul Shaffer, the musical director of the *David Letterman Show* (and who also wrote with Paul Jabara, the Two Tons of Fun classic, "It's Raining Men"). By now it was 10 p.m., and I began to worry in earnest. Hardly anybody was there. We tried to reassure ourselves that it was still early, and that more people would surely show up, but I was getting tense.

Then we hustled everybody back into the limos for the ride up to the Red Zone. Gwen Guthrie and Brenda K. Starr were performing. This huge club would be packed I was sure, and the earlier disappointing turnouts would be forgotten. But when we entered, the Red Zone looked completely empty. A person here, a person there, and otherwise nothing but vast empty space. By now reality was impossible to deny. Our event was turning into a disaster, and I couldn't believe it was happening. I hardly knew where to look, and to make matters worse, I had to put a good face on this all-star entourage witnessing our failure.

I apologized to Dionne and Gladys, and suggested that they didn't have to feel obligated to continue making the rounds. They hardly had to be asked twice, and a limo took them back to their hotels while the rest of us went on to the Tunnel for an event billed as a House Music Jamboree, featuring India and several other up-and-coming performers. Practically no one was there either, and the rest of the night was just as bad. Larry Levan was spinning a "Remember the Garage" event to a slightly bigger crowd at Choice, but by then I was devastated, and so were Jeanne and Stanley Burke. We passed by the Palladium where GMHC's party was underway, and it was jammed with over 5,000 people and it was free, which was probably the main cause of our failure.

Back home that night, I was tortured by self-doubt. The whole weekend had been my idea, and it was a total bomb. Not only did I feel disgraced, I was also broke. In the past week alone I had spent over $20,000 on the Colonial House reception, the limos, the tickets to the Dionne Warwick events, plus all the additional, unforeseen expenses. Over the past two years I had spent over $100,000 constantly digging into my pocket for *24-Hours-For-Life*. And all of it went for nothing. The Warwick Foundation would later send us a check for our portion of the proceeds from the six club events, but after the event costs, $5,000 was all that was left. It would have been far better if I had made my contributions directly to the various AIDS charities. As a result of this experience, *24-Hours-For-Life* became largely inactive. We still had our board of directors and our legal status, but we no longer had much spirit, and I really began to despair that anybody would ever be able to galvanize the music industry into the fight against AIDS. It seemed as though no matter how hard I tried, I was powerless against this thing that was killing us.

My attempts all along seemed ground in the dirt, but I did not give up and in the end finally came to fruition. Bob Caviano had been a manager for many major acts back in the glory days of disco, but I never remembered him as an activist. In fact, when I approached him to secure some of his acts for early AIDS benefits, I always came away empty handed. But Bob contracted AIDS in 1990, and in December of 1991 he wrote a commentary in *Billboard* that put out the call to the music industry. He enlisted Tim Rosta, a tireless AIDS activist, as his director, and Daniel Glass, the general manager of EMI Records in North America, as well as several expert fundraisers. Then he came to me.

Bob and Tim explaining to me what they were trying to put together was like hearing myself recorded years before making the same pitch. They needed a bona fide non-profit organization to be their fiscal sponsor, and they asked me if *24-Hours* could help. After polling our board, we agreed to make our organization the fiscal sponsor of Bob's group. We became LIFEbeat. I was thrilled that after all my struggle and effort, and all our failure, I was finally able to realize my dream. I joined the LIFEbeat board, and today I'm happy to say that LIFEbeat has galvanized the music industry's fight against AIDS and raises a fortune. Bob Caviano died shortly afterwards of the disease he did so much to fight, but the organization he started lives on, and I'm proud of the role I was able to play in helping to get it off the ground.

There are a lot of loose ends to tie up in this story of my life in disco, and sadly, most of them end in death. The years after the closing of the Garage and the Saint were years of almost unbearable loss. AIDS virtually wiped out the acquaintances of a generation, and in the process also took most of my remaining close friends.

One day I got a frantic call from Larry McDevitt telling me that Dick Fisher had just come down with PCP, and I had to race up to Roosevelt Hospital to help him get admitted. Larry and Dick were my two oldest friends, and so far the three of us had escaped the horror, or so I thought. Finding Dick gasping for air in the emergency room was a total shock. I tried to remain calm on the outside and give him all the support I could, but I was screaming on the inside that one of my two oldest and dearest friends was suffering the same fate as so many others. Larry finally arrived at the hospital and we got Dick settled into a room. I watched him fall asleep and noticed how sunken his cheeks were, and I wondered how I could have refused to admit his condition for so long. Yet even as I was thinking this and looking over at how drawn and spent Larry also looked, I still thought to myself just that he was only tired because he'd been through a lot.

Dick survived his first bout with PCP, but he never regained his health. He was deeply depressed that he could not go out to Fire Island that summer, where he had been a fixture for 30 years. We had all been Fire Island housemates in an earlier era, and Dick remained faithful to the Island ever since, but this year he was simply too weak to go out. He had several more bouts with PCP, and then he was struck with toxoplasmosis. AIDS began to destroy his brain. He suddenly became incapable of distinguishing what was real and what was not, and he drifted off into wild flights of fancy, lost in fantasies and reveries that he was convinced were real. Seeing him lose his health was horrible enough, but it was worse to watch him lose his mind. I visited him constantly during those six final weeks in the hospital, and from time to time he would have moments of absolute clarity and realize what was happening to him, and manage to make some sort of joke about it. But those times became fewer and farther between. There was nothing more the hospital could do for him, and in one of his lucid moments he let us know that he wanted to go home, and not long after that he died there. I shut down emotionally when I heard the news. I wanted to cry but I couldn't. Dick was my oldest friend, the brother I never had, yet I did not shed a single tear for months. I didn't have any more left I guess.

The very same day Dick died, Brent's wonderful mother Marion had a heart attack in her home upstate in Lockport. Brent had recently lost his lover Al to AIDS, and he was beside himself that Marion had fallen critically ill. Those few days unfolded like a bad dream. There was Dick's funeral, at which I could not speak I was so choked with grief. There was Brent helping me with the reception even as he made frantic plans to go home to be by his mother's side, and then, as the reception was ending, the long-distance call that Marion, too, had died. The day was a compound nightmare.

No one helped me through those dark years as much as Chaz. Although his own health was declining precipitously by the end of the '80s and he'd had several close calls that sent him to the hospital, he always fought back and always ended up back at work at the Colonial House and often taking care of me. He constantly stood guard over my finances and fought to get me to toe some kind of responsible line. Early in 1991 his health declined to the point where he and his lover Raphael decided that it was time to relocate to Florida, and they found a place near Raphael's family in Miami.

His one final gesture before he left New York changed my outlook completely as well as my life. He came to me one day and told me that he was very worried about the amount of time I spent isolated in my apartment. Since we were ending our lives together, without him to draw me out he didn't know what would happen to me. *"You're not meant to be alone,"* he said, and then added rather cryptically that he had *"taken the liberty of doing something I hope you won't be mad about."* With that he left the room. I stood there, wondering what in heavens he was talking about, when suddenly two gray schnauzers came bursting into the apartment and practically knocked me over with their energy. Chaz explained that the dogs were brothers who had belonged to Bob LaSenna, a mutual friend, who was too sick to take care of them any more, and Chaz figured that they were just what I needed to lift me out of the doldrums. I was instantly won over, and amazed at how quickly they caused a change in me. It became virtually impossible to remain cut off and shut down with these little bundles of dynamo always demanding my time and attention, and showering me with unconditional love and affection.

Chaz departed a few weeks later, off to his new life in Florida. I think it was a good life. I hope it was. We stayed in touch, and a couple of years later, when the end was near, I went down to say good-bye. His ex-wife Jay and son Jason were there along with his lover Raphael, and he was surrounded by the love that he had cultivated all his beautiful life. When we were alone I told him all that he had done for me, and how I could never really express how much it meant. He had saved me, quite literally. Saved the Colonial House when I didn't remotely have it together. Saved me from myself. I told him my life would have turned out much differently if it weren't for him, and it would have turned out much worse. How can you thank somebody for that? He didn't need to say anything. There was nothing to say. He died peacefully not long after. His monument is all around me, this home and guest house which he, more than anyone else, built.

My nemesis Jaime died as well, but not before he and Sammy made a hopeless attempt to revive the Paradise Garage. About a year after the Garage closed, they sent out invitations to the whole Garage family announcing that they were opening a place called the Paradise Ballroom in Times Square. Jaime had somehow conned Michael's mother Jean Brody out of most of the Garage sound and light equipment, but in time Jean realized what Jaime was using it for: to capitalize on the Garage name. Her son Gerry, Michael's brother, sent out a letter to the old mailing list announcing that this new venture was *"unauthorized"* by the Brody estate, and that the use of the Garage logo *"in no way associates, affiliates or connects the Paradise Garage with any other club either opened or about to open in the New York City area."* Jean sent a letter herself to Jaime, in which she wrote: *"I rue the day my son met you because you are the one person responsible for his death."* But it was no use. Jaime and Sammy had the money and now they decided to use the name.

Needless to say, I was beyond furious, and so was Larry Levan. I didn't think I could bear it if Jaime succeeded in his final scheme — to take what Michael and Larry and I had created to use for his own enrichment. There was no point in approaching him with my idea of using such a space as a non-profit source of funding to channel the power of disco to battle the AIDS plague. Jaime was in it for the money, there was no question about that. It seemed that everyone I knew felt the same: this was the worst irony, a despicable trick, the ultimate degradation of Michael's memory.

Instead of allowing myself to go overboard getting angry and obsessed, I decided to have a little fun instead. I rented three limos on opening night and invited a whole group of friends and former Garage employees to accompany Larry and me to the event, knowing that I, at the very least, would probably not be admitted. That day Jeffrey Stokes and I went shopping for an appropriate opening-night gift for Jaime. I went to the fish market and bought the largest, most disgusting fish head I could find. I put it under a hot light until it really stank. I wrapped it in a beautiful gift box and finished it off with a great big bow. That evening when my guests arrived — Larry Levan, Dick Fisher and Larry McDevitt, Kenny Eubanks, Ricky Willock, Jeanne Gianas and several others — everybody went into hysterics. Kenny, who had suffered for years under Jaime at the Garage, begged for the honor of delivering the present himself, and I happily agreed. Life may have been grim, but this was fun. We proceeded up to the club in our limo motorcade, and were pleased to find very few people waiting outside. For an opening night, it hardly seemed like a smashing success. We hung out in our limousines for awhile, laughing and whooping it up, until I finally decided the time had come to make my entrance — or at least try. Everyone else wished me luck and waited in the limos as Jeanne and I ventured forth into the unknown.

The invitation promised that anyone with an old Garage membership pass would be admitted, and since I was VIP Member #1, with my pass to prove it, I was immediately given two complimentary passes. But as soon as we entered the lobby, two looming security goons strode up to me, looked me down and said, *"Sammy says you can't come in."* I told them to tell Sammy that was fine with me, and Jeanne and I returned to the limo like veterans. As we sat there laughing and fuming, Kenny decided it was time to deliver the present. He told me later that when he found Jaime inside, Jaime immediately saw the package and went all gushy and cooed, *"Oooh, is that for me?"* *"But of course,"* Kenny replied, and Jaime took it and put it aside unopened in the office for later.

In the meantime, as we sat outside in the cars, one of Jaime's assistants came running up with a message for Larry. *"Oh Larry,"* he said, *"Jaime says it's ok for you to come in, and you can bring as many people as you want."* Larry drew himself up into full diva mode, and with the iciest, bitchiest tone he could muster — and believe me, it was pretty bitchy — said, *"Tell Jaime two things: That I'm with Mel Cheren. And that he can go fuck himself."* The poor kid, who trembled before this Larry Levan, just stood there in a blank, as Miss Levan put her diva's finger on the window button and zipped it up in his face, and away went the three limos rollicking into the night.

Later, we heard the story of what happened with my gift. It seems that during three days the smell in the club's office got worse and worse, and when it finally became unbearable, Jaime realized it was coming from the pretty little gift box in the corner. *"This had to have come from Mel Cheren!"* he reportedly screamed when he finally opened it. Larry and I giggled like Lucy and Ethel over this. Of course, my practical joke was a pale reflection of the real malice I felt toward Jaime for what had happened in Michael's last years and the fact that he, Jaime, instead of Larry, had ended up with most of Michael's money. But in the end it hardly mattered whether I wished him well or ill in his new endeavor, since it managed to go completely bust without any assistance from me. It was a total flop from day one. Even Judy Weinstein, a die-hard Garage loyalist who had been rooting for it, called it *"tacky and tasteless."* Jaime just didn't have Michael's touch, and almost everybody realized that he and Sammy did not embody the real spirit of the Paradise Garage.

Their efforts collapsed and the place shut down in a couple of months, taking a decent chunk of their inheritance with it. They'd brought in co-investors, and they were forced to put up as collateral two large apartments they had inherited as well as the entire Garage sound and light system. They lost it all to their co-investors and disappeared to Puerto Rico, their tails between their legs. Of course, there was still plenty of money left, and in due course I heard they had opened some sort of club in Puerto Rico. This was the last I heard of them, at least directly. Years later, when I was discussing with friends my plans to write this book, I got a strange, disturbing letter at Colonial House that had to have come from Jaime. It said, among other things, that I made all Jews look bad, that I was a thief, and I was warned not to *"try to write a book about the club or a lot more dirt will come out."* Included was a gift certificate for a visit to Dr. Jack Kevorkian. That was the last I heard until 1997, when a mutual friend told me that Jaime had died from AIDS. Sammy was reportedly still going strong, working in the nightclub business in Miami, at least until the summer of 1998 when I ran into Diana Strafaci with the news that Sammy had committed suicide.

There were so many deaths that sometimes it seems my entire circle was wiped out. AIDS took away so many friends and acquaintances that it's difficult to keep count. My dear friend Larry McDevitt. My friend the therapist Bill Scott, who had become a gay leader in Houston. Richard Long, the supreme sound designer. Singers and musicians like Michael Callen who had given so much to the cause. Wade Benjamin, my lover after Michael. Party promoter Steven Cohn and Bruce Mailman, owner of the Saint. Michael Wilkinson, who started Disconet, the company that produced dance remixes and compilations. Marc Paul Simon, who practically invented disco promotion. Danny Luna, who went home to Colorado to die. We also lost most of the people from the early days of GMHC: Dick Gross, his lover Dick Failla, Dan Bailey, Roland Blackway, Raymond Jacobs, the list goes on forever. Mark Rosenfeld died the same day as Tom Waddell, who founded the Gay Games. Keith Haring died after becoming a very effective AIDS activist, tirelessly working for the cause and donating a huge amount of his priceless art to various groups. The night my mother died, I knew the only medicine for my grief was a night of dancing, and, as nothing happens by accident, the first song I heard Junior Vasquez playing when I walked in the door of the Sound Factory was "I'll Always Love My Mama," the early classic by the Intruders. I was holding back tears but then Junior stopped the music and made the announcement and played her unforgettable "In the Name of Love," and all I could think of was Sharon Redd, dead. It can't be. Brent, Larry Basile, Julio and others became ill but have managed to hang on, though not without a lot of pain and difficulty. Julio and I continued our on-again off-again relationship for several years after the end of the Garage and the Saint. He finally took the HIV test in 1990, tested positive, and took it very badly. Among other things, he decided that I was the one who had infected him. When I pointed out that his theory was impossible, since I tested negative, he accused me of being a sort of HIV Typhoid Mary who could infect others though uninfected himself. Julio retreated more and more into his cloud of angel dust, and life between us became, if possible, even more strained and bizarre, and degenerated to the point of violence.

There was a terrible scene when he punched me in the head so hard that my ears rang for several days. I saw him the next day in the Gay Pride Parade. He grabbed our *24-Hours-For-Life* banner out of a friend's hand, then turned to me and said, *"What I did Friday night I've been wanting to do for the past 15 years. And the next time, I'm going to kill you."* I believed him and every feeling that I ever had felt for my one-time fantasy totally drained out of me. The shock of this was so strong that it made me do what I had never been capable of before — end it with Julio once and for all. I pulled the banner away from him, left the march and never looked back. I have not spoken to him since. And I quit smoking angel dust, the drug that had had such a terrible effect on my life ever since Julio and I became lovers. I haven't smoked it since.

chapter twenty
FINALLY,
THERE IS
LARRY LEVAN

The bottom fell out of Larry's life after the Paradise Garage closed, as was to be expected and understood. He lost his empire, his good friend Keith Haring died, as did many of his closest friends, but over time, he somehow managed to pick up the pieces of his career. As I already mentioned, he found the occasional gig like spinning at the World on New Year's Eve. He also began working at Studio 54, and in 1989 he became DJ at Richard Vasquez's new club Choice on the Lower East Side.

Choice was certainly on a smaller scale than the Garage, but Larry began to draw his old, loyal following, and soon the club was thriving. He even began to toy with the idea of singing his own material. At one point he announced that he would sing "Real Love" (a song he had written and produced himself), and do so while rising out of a coffin as the vampire Lestat. He was so nervous about singing that he put off the performance until nine in the morning, when there were only about two hundred people left in the club. Still, it was a stellar performance.

Unfortunately, Choice closed the following February, shortly after Keith Haring died, and Larry was bereft. His heroin problem was worse, his spinning had grown more erratic, and it became increasingly difficult to find gigs. Many people began to notice that Larry was losing touch with his crowd, something that often happens when a DJ is too high to really connect with what's happening on the dance floor. At the same time, the careers of several of his contemporaries were really beginning to skyrocket.

Junior Vasquez, who was a disciple of Larry's, had now become a major star at the new Sound Factory. Larry's old friend Frankie Knuckles, the guy with whom he first began his DJ career years before, was back from Chicago and a regular at the Red Zone, and was being hailed everywhere as the founder of House music. Frankie was also having extraordinary success as a studio producer and remixer. He and several other top DJs were managed by the indefatigable Judy Weinstein, but when Judy tried to help Larry, as he had helped her, she ran into a wall of apathy and disorganization.

"He didn't want what I was trying to give," Judy says.

> I had to focus on guys like Frankie and David Morales, because these guys had a future, a vision. They knew where they wanted to go, but Larry simply became too caught up in drugs.

Everybody knew about Larry's drug problem. What we did not know — what none of us knew — was that Larry may have been dealing with HIV as well. He made a cryptic comment about it once, but we never knew for sure.

As time passed, I found that I was virtually supporting Larry — paying his rent and forking over money for all sorts of things, especially drugs. It got so extreme that sometimes he would show up at Colonial House and walk straight to the front desk and ask the attendant for money from petty cash. Even though I was supporting him, I was constantly bickering with him, both about money and drugs and also about the way he abused his long-suffering mother Minnie. He would often treat her like dirt, showing up at her apartment strung out and broke, finagling money out of her, then disappearing for weeks at a time until he was down and out again, at which point he'd suddenly reappear. Throughout it all, Minnie was the salt of the earth, enduring

Larry's abuse and neglect without complaint, cooking for him, being there for him, always without judgment and blame. She and I would spend hours on the phone, commiserating over his behavior, and she would often kid me that she and I should get married in order to make legal my unofficial adoption of her son. But beneath the banter was a sense of mutual desperation. Both of us knew that there was little we could do to stop, or even moderate, Larry's self-destruction.

In the summer of 1991 Larry came to me and demanded that I return a Keith Haring painting that Keith had given Larry years before. Larry had always asked me to keep it safe, afraid that in a moment of weakness he might sell it for drug money. Now he wanted it back, to do exactly that. I didn't want to return it, but figured that I had no right to say no, since it was his. Later that summer, when he suddenly found himself homeless, he moved in with me. This caused mutual friends to accuse me of being co-dependent with Larry, which in a way I suppose I was.

Desperate to find a reason for Larry to get it together, I began planning a new record label called the Sound of Garage that would produce the kind of music that Larry had popularized at the Garage. The plan was that Larry, I and Florence Greenberg would be at the helm, and the product would be distributed by Ed Kushins using West End Records, which still existed on paper, and which was still providing a decent income for Ed. But there was no love lost between Ed and Florence, or for that matter between Ed and Larry. Ed well remembered how irresponsible Larry had been in the old days, and he correctly suspected that things were even worse now. So Florence, Larry and I decided to go it alone, and for a while we were taken up in the excitement of planning and dreaming about a reentry into the business. But soon Florence's health declined and she could no longer make the trip into New York for our meetings. Then Larry lost interest as well. He also began to tire of living with me, since it was cramping his style, especially in terms of drugs. By the end of the summer he had moved in with one of his drug cronies, and was sinking back into his old habits. Our plans lost momentum, and I eventually had to abandon my dream of the triumphant return of Larry Levan.

But despite all these problems, Larry had a resilience that kept him going through the worst of times. And then times began to improve. He went into drug detox, tried on several occasions to get his act together, and seemed to be making progress, although it was always two steps forward and one step back. But the thing that really changed his fortunes was the fact that although his star was definitely tarnished in New York, he had become a legendary figure in Europe and Japan. Legendary and in popular demand. Europeans and Japanese knew nothing of his drug problems, they only knew that Larry Levan was widely considered the greatest DJ of all time, the star of Paradise Garage, and they wanted him. He began to get invitations to spin at places like the Ministry of Sound in London, and found that he was wildly popular there. He helped design their sound, which was virtually a carbon copy of his sound system at the Paradise Garage. He also discovered that he was a huge star in Japan. The Japanese actually seemed obsessed with Larry Levan and anything to do with him, and he began traveling there regularly as well.

It was a shock to him, a great, wonderful, empowering electric shock. The moment he stepped off the plane in London or Tokyo, he was treated like a superstar. So as the early '90s progressed, things improved for Larry. I began to hope that he might actually have a golden future. He was back in the studio with François Kevorkian, producing and remixing. The result of these sessions is "Strong Enough," a soaring antidote to doom and despair, with celestial flutes and thundering baselines, and the magnificent voice of Loleatta Holloway. It is cosmic dance floor gospel, a supreme synthesis of Larry's particular genius. It would be his last time in the studio, and is all the more remarkable for that. "Strong Enough" was Larry's final message of love.

One day he informed me that he was planning a triumphant tour of Japan for his birthday in July, and wanted me to accompany him. I thought it was just a pipe dream, and when I told him I'd be glad to go, I was almost kidding, since I had no expectation that he would actually follow through. When the birthday tour came and went without me, I was hardly surprised. But shortly after his return, he stopped by to tell me that he was returning to Japan almost immediately for a Harmony Tour in August with François Kevorkian, and this time I really was going with him. Sure enough, a few days later he stopped by again, this time with my airline ticket. I couldn't believe it.

Minnie explained this as Larry's way of repaying me for all I had done for him, and I suppose he also wanted me to see for myself the way he was treated in a country where he was still revered as a star. Sure enough, the minute I got off the plane in Tokyo, it was like a dream. There were posters everywhere advertising the tour, and I was fascinated by the way the Japanese described it. A typical poster, with all its errors and misspellings, went like this:

> INGREDIENTS, FACTORS, ELEMENTS AND
> RESULTING PRODUCT AND BYPRODUCTS OF
> DANCE MUSIC AS WE KNOW IT.
> INGREDIENTS: R&B, Disco, R&R, Reggae, Classics, Jazz,
> International.
> FACTORS: Sound Effects, A Cappella, Atmosphere.
> ELEMENTS: Sound System, Lighting.
> PRODUCT: Dance Music, Pop Music.
> BYPRODUCTS: House Music, Rap.
> Schemed by LARRY LEVAN
> Directed by FRANÇOIS KEVORKIAN

The Japanese, it seemed, were very organized and methodical about one of the most disorganized, least methodical movements in popular culture. The tour was managed by a Japanese fellow named Taka, who seemed to idolize Larry. But Taka hardly knew what he was in for when he signed on. It seems that Larry was very concerned that his drug supply was not going to last the tour, and threatened to return to New York unless sufficient drugs could be procured. Taka took all this in stride, and neither François nor I had any idea that he was being forced to scramble around trying to find drugs for Larry, something which is not easy to do in Japan.

A few days into the tour when I arrived in Tokyo, Larry floated down the wide staircase of the fabulous Ana Hotel on a cloud, and greeted me like the only superstar. Larry and François played two nights at Endmax, and they were treated like gods. The last night at Endmax, which was my first night in Tokyo, Larry left the club in the morning and was mobbed. Kids clamoring for his autograph, begging him to sign t-shirts and records, showering him with praise, so filled with wonder at Larry Levan.

Throughout the tour Larry and I shared a room, and we had perhaps the best times we had ever had together in our lives. We spent a few days r&r at a very lavish resort in Okinawa. We talked about our hopes and dreams for the future, about this book, about my plans of establishing a record label as a source of funds for LIFEbeat. One night I asked him to promise me that I would have the pleasure of seeing him on top of things again in New York. He promised me I would, and said that this time, he would not mess it up.

But all was not well. He never did drugs in front of me, but he was doing them constantly. He was trying to do what he had always tried to do with me: show me he was all right, giving back to me some of what I had given to him, making an effort to show that he cared, that he loved me. One way he did that was to send me messages through his music. I was planning to leave Japan several days before Larry left, and on our last night at Gold, one of Tokyo's most popular clubs, he played a stream of West End classics. That night was our ultimate high together, the apex of our whole stormy, chaotic, exasperating, exhilarating years together. The crowd went crazy, screaming and chanting his name long after he left the turntables. But it seemed to me that almost every song Larry was playing was for me, a message of love from the king of DJs to the godfather of disco. It would be the last time I would hear Larry play.

He accompanied me back to the hotel while I packed and got ready to leave. Suddenly, a black cloud seemed to descend over him. I figured that he was depressed that I was leaving, and that soon he'd also have to leave and go back to face his diminished popularity in New York, so I tried to cheer him up. But just as I was about to leave there was a knock at the door, and one of his drug buddies came in and hovered around us, like the angel of death. I didn't want to stay another minute, and got ready to go. I gave him a hug, and then, with a withering look at his friend, said *"Have fun, Larry, but please don't overdo it."* He replied, *"Oh, right,"* as if to say, please don't preach to me dad. And I left. All the way to the airport I was torn between my ecstatic memories of the night before and my fears of what would happen to him.

He seemed to fall apart after I left. On the day he and François were scheduled to fly back to New York, he announced that he was terribly sick with some sort of flu, and couldn't make the plane. François reminded him that the tour promoters would stop paying the five-hundred-dollar a day hotel room as of that day, and that if Larry stayed, he'd be spending a fortune that he didn't have. But Larry could not be convinced, and François flew off to New York without him. He called Larry every day after that, and Larry reported that he was terribly sick, with a raging fever that left his bed soaked with sweat.

Five days later Larry arrived in New York in a wheelchair, broke and still terribly ill. François and I went out to the airport, but a slight traffic accident detained us and by the time we got there he had disappeared. He finally showed up at Minnie's without a dime. Soon he was back in the hospital, where he stayed for several weeks in rehab — this time I could not reach him. When he got out, it was back to the same old thing.

One day I got a call from Diane Stafaci, who said she had just run into Larry in the East Village. She was talking to some young friends in front of her gym when along came Larry, stoned completely out of his head. She introduced him to her friends, who were awed to meet him, but Larry just mumbled something and staggered away. Diane was so overcome by this apparition that she immediately burst into tears. Suddenly, she felt someone tapping on her head. She turned, and there was Larry. *"Don't cry, Dee,"* he said quietly. *"I'm okay."* And then he walked away.

I promised Diane that I would check up on him, and finally managed to track him down. He came by a few days later, Wednesday night, November 4, the last time I saw him. He told me he was going into the hospital again, that he was still very sick. I showed him my new facelift and told him I was also having chest implants, and he told me, *"Mel, your face looks great, but please don't do anything else. Please don't put anything in your body."* I told him that I was glad that he was going back into the hospital, where he'd be taken care of. Four days later, November 8, the hospital called. A lady doctor quietly informed me that I was listed as the next of kin of one Lawrence Philpot, and that she was very sorry to inform me that he had just passed away.

Lawrence Philpot was Larry Levan. I was utterly shocked. The doctor explained that Larry had been suffering from cardio endocariditis, a fluid build-up around the heart, and that in his weakened condition, he had simply died. That was it, the end of a life, the end of the greatest talent in disco. Alone in a hospital, addicted, broken, a lost legend.

I called Larry's sister in Philadelphia. A childhood friend went to Minnie and broke the news. Minnie was absolutely beside herself with grief. Brent and I traveled out to Queens that night to see her, and we stayed up to the wee hours talking and crying and reminiscing. Minnie was filled with memories. Larry as a baby. Larry as a young kid who dreamed of being a DJ. Larry with his famous Dobermans. Larry at his peak, ruling the Garage. When the Garage closed, Larry had told François that something in him was dying, that his life, his fame, were over, all going up in smoke. About six months before, Larry had announced to Minnie that he was going to die. He told her that he had had a good life, a good time, made plenty of money, but now he was simply going to die. Minnie asked him to pray, but he was convinced of it. I tried to assure her how much Larry loved her, but Minnie cut me off. She had a more realistic view of things than I had ever suspected. *"He knew I was a sucker,"* she said.

> He used to tell me to mind my own business. I cried many nights, many nights. Maybe God took him from me to save me. He's probably better off dead and free from that drug. He's better off because now they won't find him in the street, with a needle in his arm all cold. I'm glad I didn't see that.

The next day I plunged into the funeral arrangements. We needed a huge space, and managed to secure St. Peter's Church beneath the Citicorp building. It was lucky we did — over a thousand people showed up. François prepared a tape of Larry's classics to play before the service, and we suspended an angel holding a little mirrored ball over the box that held Larry's ashes. After the scheduled service, people were invited to come up and offer their own personal remembrances and memories, and the service went on for two hours.

I was the last to speak. *"I really don't know how to begin to summarize the incredible difference Larry made in my life,"* I said.

> I was deeply touched that he thought of himself as my adopted son. Like most families, we had our ins and outs. I'm sure that those who know us well would agree that most of my gray hair can be attributed to Larry. But in Japan, he said that he wanted to come back to New York and make amends with people. I'm sorry that he never got the chance. But looking back, I'd have to say that it was well worth it.

And it was well worth it. We gave something to the world. Larry gave something that resonates to this day. Yes there are ghosts, yes there are many regrets. There were mistakes. But there is music, and joy, and acceptance, and love. And today all over the world people remember. Young people, who were never there in person, are there today in spirit, dancing and singing, expressing their own hopes and dreams. That's what we gave. Dreams and hope. We could have done better. But then, we could have done much worse.

Larry! When I got the call from the hospital, I cried so much I almost ruined my facelift. And you know you're not supposed to cry after a facelift. Remember when you warned me not to have those implants? Your advice was, as always, right on the mark. The doctor, who turned out to be a quack, intimidated me and said it was too late to change my mind, although I did try to back out. Like a fool I went through with it. Your last bit of advice could have saved me much pain and suffering having those implants removed if I would have listened to you. I know you and Michael are getting Paradise ready for us, Larry. So save a place on the dance floor for me. And, Larry, this time please don't bite Michael — again!

epilogue

Larry Levan had an extraordinary perceptive sense, and these past few years would have been so much easier having him here with me, but now I'm on my own. Since Larry passed away I have lost many more dear friends: Dick Fisher, Larry McDevitt, Bill Scott, Chaz Goward, Bart Flanagan, Noël Garcia, Dennis Lasker, Jackie Yordan, Willy Marquez, Gene Haviland, and Richard Sabala. Richard, a lighting genius, was supportive of my artwork. At a Saint-at-Large White Party he used ten of my oil/fluorescent paintings above the Roseland dance floor. This book is dedicated to these men and to all the other wonderful men who left us much too soon.

I wanted to write this book for two very specific reasons. First, so that these wonderful friends, who made the '70s and '80s so memorable, would not be forgotten. Second, because so many of these men were mentors to so many young men. Most importantly, a whole generation is now without enough mentors, since so many of my generation have passed away. The book you have just read has taken longer to write than to have lived, so it seems. It is a project that has taken its toll, even destroyed a friendship or two. The story of my life is both good and bad, but if I can get even a few young people to learn something from my experience then the whole project will definitely have been worthwhile.

Early in the book I let you know that nothing happens by accident. A casual trick in the park changed my whole life. Sincerely thinking about everything that happens to you each and every day just might prevent you from missing the one situation that would make a positive difference in your life, as it did in mine. Keeping some form of a diary, if only a few words each day or week, can help jog your memory in years to come.

Studies have sought to show whether a specific gene structure determines a person's sexuality. I believe this to be true, even though it has not been proven. But whatever your sexual orientation, the point is to be proud of who you are. Just as God didn't run out of black paint and so started painting white (or was it the other way around?). I believe that in God's infinite wisdom He created gay people as a guarantee that a certain part of the population would not reproduce. (Multiply the 20,000 sexual experiences I've had over the years, for example, by the millions my partners have been with and you'll see. It all adds up!) If Gay is good enough for God then it is good enough for me. I believe God said, "Leave the changing of diapers to your heterosexual mothers and fathers. Your legacy is your creativity and sensitivity, and your art." God created heterosexuals to get married and have children, giving Gays time to do the decorating. Mothers and fathers who are creative are so preoccupied working to raise a family they simply don't have as much time to create. And it is sad to see parents discourage adolescent males from creative pursuits. Dad would rather see son toss a ball than paint, draw, or make music. While I'm on the subject, since society requires us to obtain licenses for so many things, I hope that in the future a license will be required to become a parent, with mental and physical tests before granting permission.

A study on homophobia by the University of Georgia illustrates a very important point: Men driven to commit violent homophobic acts may have suppressed homosexual desires themselves. Gay spokespeople, unfortunately, have not made this study known through the media. If it were, it might force violent homophobes to retreat so far back in their closets that they would be afraid of exposure if they got caught. Exposed to society as repressed homosexuals, they would not be the heroes they are now thought to be in some circles.

There is a very important point I would like to make for gay history. Every major city in this country has at one time or another been revitalized by gay men and women: never has this important contribution ever been mentioned and applauded. Its time to accentuate the positive, and eliminate the negative: Back Bay in Boston, Center City in Philadelphia, Dupont Circle and Adams Morgan in Washington DC, Chelsea, Brooklyn Heights, Boerum Hill, Cobble Hill, Park Slope, West Village in New York, South Beach in Miami, West Hollywood in Los Angeles, Castro and Mission Hill in San Francisco, Montrose in Houston, and countless other neighborhoods where gay people are building communities.

If we are to have peace and equality we have to get involved, even if getting involved means only getting out and voting. Your rights are something you have to fight for. The more that Gay people come out to family and friends, the sooner we can achieve our goals. Rather than the media's interpretation, a national Gay and Lesbian cable network, for instance, is one way to send out the right message about who we are.

Many people try to blame my generation for the AIDS epidemic without taking into account the prospect that in the 1970s we did not know that what brings life can also bring death. When our community realized what was happening to us in 1981 we took charge. We let the world know that there was a crisis. Since we were a close-knit group it was self-evident that there was an epidemic at hand, years before the government would listen and act to prevent so many unnecessary deaths. I hope that science can someday give us back the sexual freedom we once knew, but until then when I hear people bragging about having unsafe sex, it sounds suicidal to me. It's like drugs: use if you must, but don't abuse. Easy to say, perhaps, but if you think you have an addictive personality you should stay away completely.

I have never spent any time envying what others have. Friends' successes are my success, and my success is theirs. In what I call the Pyramid of Life, God says, I can't take care of everyone on earth so I'm going to make good things happen for you and in turn you take care of a little flock and they in turn do the same for others. I feel it is a true blessing that God has given me the opportunity to give rather than to be in need.

The longer I live the more I believe that we were each put here with a definite purpose in mind. For a number of years, I've had three fantasies. My first two have become a reality: publishing this book and bringing back West End records and creating Garage records (for charity). I hope and pray to become associated with a distribution company that will embrace the concept I have for Garage Records. With profits after taxes and expenses going to charity, the distributor would get a percentage for distribution, not to mention the respect being involved in a non-profit charity project. As I write this, Paul Newman has quietly raised over $100 million on salad dressing and popcorn. Can you imagine what could be raised with music? Music with a purpose?

Since the Godfather is entitled to ask for a payback for his helping others, this brings me to my third fantasy. The world today needs a place where black and white, straight and gay can come together and party as one. I've been told that my book would make a great script for a movie. Movies need a set. The only possible set is the original Paradise Garage building. My fantasy is to buy back the Garage building and put it back to what it was. With new technology, it could be made even better. The reconstructed Paradise Garage would be turned over to a community chest of charities and be run as Paul Newman does with food products, all profits after taxes and expenses going to these charities. The club would be open seven days a week. The downstairs space never used before would be turned into a Disco Diner like the Hard Rock Café. I would have Larry's ashes placed in the entrance of the club and someday, hopefully not too soon, I would like my ashes to be with his.

Sometimes when I find myself feeling regret about the absence of a major relationship over the last ten years, I reflect on the past and realize that, in fact, I've had more than my share. The best of the best. I have been blessed with many great memories and two very wonderful relationships. Affairs with some of the most desired sex fantasies. I'll name just two. Chad Douglas, whom *HX* magazine called the hottest male porn star, once told me that I was one of his fantasies. A few years after he passed I saw one of his videos and I realized that he used the same technique on others that I used on him. He knew how good it made him feel. I would place Cole Tucker in the same desirable category as Chad, and Cole is a very dear friend as well. The lesson here is that growing older is not something to fear. Feelings and desires do not diminish, and although a lot of your priorities do change, you never stop looking for a meaningful relationship. I still am. Life is so much more rewarding if you can share it with someone.

I'm very happy to write that that after ten years of not speaking to one another, Julio and I finally broke the ice at Gigi's graduation from University of New Hampshire this summer. We have since made an effort to rekindle our friendship, it has been a lot easier now, since we are both no longer in a cloud of dust. We've come full circle.

Before this goes to print there is one last story I would like to share with you. A gay man, 33-years old, living in New York, received a copy of this manuscript. He called to thank me last night, saying that this book, my life story, has empowered him to deal with his family back home who have over the years berated and abused him because he is gay. After hanging up, I realized that this seven year labor of love has already made a difference. I know that all my hetereosexual friends who read this book are gay friendly, and I hope they will understand my emphasis on empowering gay, lesbian, and transgendered youth to love themselves and not let anyone tell them that they are less than equal.

Nothing happens by accident, and if you have been blessed with a good life, giving back to others is the ultimate high. I pray that the true spirit of the Paradise Garage will return for a new generation. A place where black, white, straight, and gay people from all over the world can come together to celebrate life as one.

dedicated in loving memory

ED ANTHONY - I met Ed through Larry McDevitt when they were planning a health clinic fundraiser. That was how I first got involved with what later was to become the most important AIDS organization, GMHC (Gay Men's Health Crisis).

A.J. ANTOON - A Broadway producer and songwriter. He was a very close friend of Brent Nicholson Earle. They co-wrote a song from an idea that I suggested.

ED APREA* - Part of my Fire Island family. His life was cut short not only because of AIDS, but by being burned with too much radiation.

DAN BAILEY - A good friend. Early member of GMHC. A real gentleman.

STEVE BAKER - I met Steve through Michael Brody early on in our relationship. He was a schoolteacher.

WAY BANDY - Famous makeup artist to the stars. I met him through Claire Paige, former owner of the restaurant, Claire.

URBANO BARRERA - A very close friend of Ignacio Zuazo. He lived at 318 W. 22nd St. before it was Colonial House Inn. A very talented floral designer.

GREG BAUER - Julio used to cut his hair. One of the A-list.

LLOYD BEARDSLEY - Superstud bartender at the Fire Island Boatel for many seasons. Opened his own bar in Palm Springs.

REV. WADE BENJAMIN* - My live-in lover for over a year, 1977-79. An Episcopalian minister.

MARK BERGEN - Another one of Julio's customers. He was the light man at the Saint for a long time.

STANLEY BERKE - Club 1018 promoter, and as a volunteer ran the 24 Hours For Life portion of the "That's What Friends are For" weekend with the Dionne Warwick Foundation.

ERIC BERNARD - An old friend of Michael and me. A well-known interior designer.

PETER BESSI* - Friend and sexual partner, before I met Michael. Took over ownership of Arcos Blancos Guest House in Puerto Rico.

COLIN BIRCH* - A friend from the Island.

BILL BLACK - Friend of Brent Nicholson Earle.

ROLAND BLACKWAY - A very honorable man. The lover of my former manager at Colonial House Inn, Fernan Royo.

JOEL BLOCK* - One of my housemates at Camp Tommy at Fire Island.

BOB BORLAND - Friend from Flamingo.

BOBBY BRESLAU - Friend of Julio Velez. Garage devotee. Managed Pop Shop for Keith Haring, and was also a talented designer.

MICHAEL BRODY* - My lover and business partner for 10 years. Played one of the most important roles in my life.

JACK BRUSCA - A very talented painter. A friend of both Michael Brody and me.

SHAUN BUCHANAN - Saint DJ, a real nice guy.

JIM BURGESS - One of the early legendary DJs. He came to New York via Atlanta, where I met him. He played at 12 West. He mixed one of Karen Young's records for West End.

MICHAEL CALLEN - A gay hero. I was honored to have him stay at the Colonial House Inn as my guest while he was completing his musical memoirs.

PETER CAMINITI - Part of the Flamingo crowd.

DAVID CAMPBELL - He was a Pines fixture playing his tambourine at Fire Island Boatel tea dance. He designed the West End 12-inch jacket.

PAUL CARO - Early volunteer at GMHC at 318 W. 22nd St.

DON CASTELLANOS - A good friend for many years. One day he called me, told me to come over to his place where he gave me his whole vinyl collection.

BOB CAVIANO - He managed Grace Jones and Larry Levan. I gave him the use of my 501-C3 from 24 Hours For Life so that he could start LIFEbeat, of which I am on the board. Bob put a face to the AIDS crisis for the music industry.

AL CAVUTO* - One of the first *Playgirl* centerfolds. Looked like a handsome, hunky version of Burt Reynolds.

DON CIABATTARI - Ex-boyfriend of Julio Velez. We visited Don in California.

ALBERTO CINTRON* - Part-time art dealer, became close friend and helped run early stages of Colonial House Inn.

FRANK CIOFFI - One of my Fire Island roommates at Camp Tommy 2. He was a schoolteacher, a real nice guy.

STEVE COHN - Club promoter/owner of River Club, credited me for helping him get started when I gave him entertainment for his first successful party.

STUART COLBY - A friend from Fire Island. He was a rabbi, and conducted services at Fire Island.

DAVID COLE - A very talented music producer. Part of Clivilles and Cole, and also a very kind person.

DUANE COLGLAZER*- He and his lover Bill Rifkin were the founders of the Pleasure Chest.

DENNIS COLWAITE* - A friend from Flamingo days. He did a show of my paintings at his art gallery.

JOE CONCILIO - My accountant. He was part of the Fire Island/Flamingo crowd, a real class act.

JOHN CONGER - Friend from Flamingo.

EARL BURNS COOMBS - I never got to use the plans he designed for my building. After turning the building over to the GMHC for two years I changed my plans when they moved out and decided to start my bed and breakfast, Colonial House Inn.

GLEN COOPER - A gifted pianist, my dear friend and Lupe Flores's lover.

PATRICK COWLEY - Talented producer, mixed Michele's "Disco Dance" for West End.

MARTIN COX (a.k.a. CHAD DOUGLAS)* - One of the memories I'll never forget. Pure great sex.

JEFFREY CROWLAND - Owner of the restaurant, Company. He said that I was his personnel manager because I sent him so many people for jobs.

WES CRONK - Designed and made 78 quilts for me at the Lesbian and Gay Community Center.

CAL CULVER* - Star of *Boys in the Sand*. He also owned Big Ruby's in Key West.

JACK CUSTER - Friend of Julio. He owned first gay messenger service, On Route.

MITCHELL CUTLER - One of the first GMHC volunteers, he started the Buddy System.

TONY DALY - Volunteer for the 24 Hours For Life "That's What Friends Are For" weekend, produced by Stanley Berke.

KEN DAWSON - First Director at S.A.G.E.

OVIDIO DeARMAS - Bill Guncet's lover. He was in the travel business, a real gentleman.

MARK DeANGELIS - Was a promoter for Spirit Project.

LARRY DEASON - A beautiful, sweet person. A flight attendant.

RICHARD DeLONG - Paul Popham's lover, started first art auction for AIDS.

ED DEL VECCHIO * - A good friend and much more. He aspired to an acting career.

TED DEWES - A hot, charming, funny Englishman. Told some great stories of his friendship with Elton John and the Queen Mother.

HARRY DIAZ - A friend. He headed the GMHC circus fundraiser.

RON DOWD - A very talented gentleman, part of the Flamingo crowd.

LARRY DOWNS - A Flamingo friend, a doctor to many friends.

JUAN DUBOIS - Keith Haring's lover.

JOHN DUKA - A very successful journalist. One of Julio's customers.

KEN DUNCAN - A very successful photographer.

RICHARD DUNNE - Headed GMHC for a period of time.

HARVEY EINMAN - A friend of Mike Brody and part of Fire Island crowd.

JERRY ESPOSITO - Harvey Einman's lover, part of the Fire Island crowd.

RICHARD FAILLA - A good friend. He was the first openly gay judge to be appointed to the Criminal Court by his good friend Mayor Ed Koch.

NATHAN FAIN - One of the founders of GMHC, A very caring individual.

MEL FANTE - Worked for America Airlines before opening a very successful gift shop at Fire Island Pines.

JONATHAN FEARING - A talented, handsome DJ.

JOHN FINELLO - Part of our crowd.

JIM FIORE - A housemate one season at the house on Ozone.

JOHN "DICK" FISHER - My best friend for 35 years.

BART FLANAGAN* - Paul Popham's first lover. We became very close friends for many years. A real Mensch.

RAY FORD* - Body, Heart and Soul by God. Like Dick Fisher, one of my best friends.

BOB FOSCINA - A sweet wonderful kid, a close friend of Paul Popham.

GARY FRANCE - A frequent guest at Colonial House Inn.

BRAD FRANSDEN - Secretary of original GMHC board of directors.

MANUEL FRIERE - Airline steward, a very attractive gentleman.

CARLTON FULLER* - One of the Fire Island hunks, and a frequent playmate of mine.

GARY GALANTE - A good friend of Larry Basile from Boston. I met him when he stayed at the Colonial House Inn. He was an anthropologist.

CURTIS GALLOWAY - A customer of Julio.

ARMANDO GALVEZ - Helped Michael Fesco create special parties at Flamingo.

HECTOR GARCIA* - Willie Marquez's lover, a very attractive man.

NOEL GARCIA - I knew Noel for many years. He worked the door for Michael at the Garage. He was one of the most popular employees, and was one of the most easygoing and handsome men. Was Winston cigarette model; his face was on all the uptown buses.

WALTER GIBBONS - One of the best legendary DJs. He mixed one of West End's big hits, "Doin' The Best I Can'" by Bettye Lavette.

MORT GINDI - We sat at the same table at one of the political dinners, a nice man.

TOM GLANTZ - I met Tom through his very close friend and mine, Lorenzo Ramos. We spent a lot of fun times together. A loyal friend.

BOBBY GOLDBERG - Started and owned In-Service Catering.

BOB GOLDEN - Paul Popham's roommate and Ray Ford's last lover, a very gentle man.

FEDERICO GONZALEZ - Early GMHC volunteer. A real Latin gentleman.

DONNY GONZALO - Donny was part of the Boston crowd that would come to New York on weekends to go to the Saint. This crowd loyally supported Colonial House in its early days.

BOBBY GORSHEN - Was part of the music industry. He worked for Ray Caviano at RFC Records.

CHAZ GOWARD - My first hotel manager, made my life better. He was one of a kind. If it weren't for him I would not have what I have now.

HERB GOWER - A very handsome man, Phil Patrick's lover.

BRUCE GRANOVETTER - David Lynn's lover. He was a psychiatrist.

PETER GRIMES* - Was someone I was very fond of. Very nice. A real hunk. Many fond memories.

BILL GUNCET - Body, Heart & Soul by God. Was a very handsome man, once Mr. Cuba.

BOBBY "DJ" GUTTADERO - One of the most famous of the legendary DJs. A real nice guy. He was a pioneer DJ who worked in film scoring.

SAM HADDAD* - Very interesting person, a real wheeler-dealer. He took over 12 West and called it the River Club.

JIM HALL - Nice man, Julio used to cut his hair.

DAVID HANKERMEYER - David Landay's lover. David H had to be special to be with David L . . . and he was.

KEITH HARING - Designed 24-Hours-For-Life logo. A great artist and humanitarian.

DAN HARTMAN - A legendary writer, producer and performer of many dance classics. Dan presented the *Billboard* award, one of several, that the Paradise Garage won for best sound and lighting. I accepted for Michael Brody. Dan also did a benefit for the Manhattan Center for the Living; we called the party Miracle.

MICHAEL HATOFF - The last lover of Enno Poersch. A friend for several years.

GENE HAVILAND* - I met him at his 40th birthday party in L.A., while Julio and I were vacationing there in 1974. We became good friends and much more. He was a Jesuit priest at one time. A very brilliant man and someone who enjoyed life.

DR. JACK HEFTON* - NY Hospital Cornell Medical's burn unit lost an important doctor. He was also one of the most handsome and hot men.

HELMUT - One of the Fire Island hunks.

JEFF HENRY* - Someone I knew back in Boston many years ago.

FRANK HOULIHAN - Frank was a DJ at the Ice Palace on W. 57th St. I used to bring him records when I was promoting for West End.

CARLOS HUNTER - A partner in the restaurant Claire. A Latin gentleman.

GERRY IAVANNI - Part of the Boston crowd who stayed at the Colonial House. I believe he was a social worker. He was in the seminary with Larry Basile.

JOHN IOZIA - Used to call me his rabbi. Someone whose wisdom I greatly miss.

CRAIG LOGAN JACKSON - I didn't know him for a long time. He was a close friend of Manuel Fernandez. He was very active with the Hetrick Martin School.

ARTIE JACOBS - A friend from the dance community. One of the early DJs who became a producer.

RAYMOND JACOBS - Raymond was one of the first people to handle the GMHC crisis hotline. He was also a teacher and extremely respected by all who knew him.

JAMES JESSOP - One of the owners of the 10TH Floor, an intimate club in the early '70s.

DENNIS JOHNSEN* - Many fond memories of times spent with Dennis.

GIL JOHNSON - One half of Bayside 6, my first rental on Fire Island. Gil loved and lived life to the fullest. He and John Robinson had a very special, more than 40-year relationship.

JIM JOHNSON - Jimmy Peters' lover. Talented with flowers and throwing parties.

JOHN KAPPAS - John worked for Michael Fesco at Flamingo. He was a good friend of Julio's.

RICHIE KACZOR - Another of the legendary DJs. He was the DJ at Studio 54 at the height of its popularity.

PATRICK KELLY - A wonderful designer, a very nice person and a close friend of Ricky Willock.

LARRY KERT - The original Tony in West Side Story, he dated my best friend Dick Fisher.

NATHAN KOLODNER - A very fine gentleman, one of the executive directors of GMHC. He wrote to the city on my behalf concerning the problem with my building.

BILL KONKOY - A dynamic personality; ran A.R.E.A.

DAVID KRAVITSKY* - A beautiful young man. A gymnast. Many fond memories.

SAL LANZA - A friend from Fire Island, a man's man.

PHIL LANZARATTA - One of the early GMHC volunteers.

BOB LASENNA - When Bob got too sick to take care of his dogs, I adopted Danny and Josh when they were one year old. They have brought me so much joy and peace.

LARRY LAVORGNA - A doctor, part of the Flamingo crowd.

RICHARD LEACH* - A very kind, wonderful young man. He worked at the Saint parties and later for me at Colonial House.

KEVIN LECLAIR - Part of the Boston (Larry Basile) crowd. Kevin managed the Chandler Inn for Larry. He was a very intelligent and kind person; lots of fond memories.

LARRY LEVAN - If you read the book, what else is there to say?

THEO LIST - A doctor. Part of the Fire Island friends, a real nice guy.

RICHARD LONG - The Rolls Royce maker of sound systems: the Garage, the Palladium, Studio 54, and many others.

DIEGO LOPEZ - A wonderful, kind man. Early GMHC volunteer.

DANNY LORD* - I met Danny at a college dance. He was a beautiful young man — I invited him to come to New York. This was after Michael Brody and I had split up. When Danny showed up in New York I took him out to the Island and he became an instant star. The last time I had dinner with him was when I was in San Francisco. He was very special.

BOB LOWE* - Body, Heart & Soul by God, did publicity for West End for a while, and took my advice and became a lawyer, specialized in adoption law.

MICHAEL LUCARELLI* - Very intelligent, did not realize his own worth. Beautiful young man.

DANNY LUNA* - He became like a son. If he'd had the time he could have developed into a fine natural artist.

DAVID LYNN* - A friend from the early '60s. He bought real estate after seeing what Michael and I did. He created Big Ruby's in Key West.

JOSE LYNN - Worked in the office at the Garage. He was very loyal to Michael.

JIMMY MACK* - A Flamingo and Pines friend.

BRUCE MAILMAN - Owner of the Saint, St. Mark's Baths.

MICHAEL MALETTA - Cut my hair until he moved to San Francisco. This prompted me to go to Julio. The rest is history.

NORMAN MARINE - I met Norman and his twin brother, Ralph, through Chaz Goward, who was Norman's lover. Norman and I grew very close when we became housemates in Camp Tommy II, as we called it.

ROYAL MARKS - Part of the Flamingo/Pines crowd. Well-known art dealer.

BOB MARSHALL - A long-time Fire Island friend; a nice man.

FRANK MARSHALL* - Good friend of both Michael and me. Later worked for Michael at the Garage.

WILLY MARQUEZ* - Was a regular at the Garage, but I met him at the first Upstairs party at the Palladium after the Garage closed. Body, Heart & Soul by God, even though he grew up without the advantages most of us take for granted. His mother Carmen has taken care of my father for over ten years. My father's love for Carmen is what has kept him going since my mother passed away.

BRUCE MATIRE - A friend.

STEPHEN MATZA - Long-time friend and housemate on Fire Island.

JIM McDERMOTT - Did promotion for me at West End Records in the early '80s.

LARRY McDEVITT* - We were housemates on Fire Island for several years. Larry was the first secretary for GMHC. He worked at the New York City Health Dept. He became one of my closest and dearest friends. He asked me to spread some of his ashes on the dance floor, which I did at the Sound Factory (now Twilo). He was on the board of 24 Hours For Life.

JOE McDONALD - Model and customer of Julio.

JOSEPH McEARTHY - I knew Joseph for years; a very wise and caring individual. He became a valuable 24 Hours For Life board member.

KEN MEEKS - A friend from Fire Island.

BILL MERCADO* - Very sexy guy that Michael and I met who became a friend over the years.

RICHARD MESSINGER*- Flamingo/Island friend.

GREGORY MEYERS - Boyfriend of John Iozia, a fine DJ. He played one of our parties at the Upstairs after the Garage closed. He and Nicky Siano played together.

FRANCOIS MILLET - Flamingo/Fire Island friend.

STEVE MOLLETT* - Met in Puerto Rico and had a fling. He was an attorney in the Nixon White House. We kept in touch.

MICHAEL MONTE - My good friend Les Ross's lover. After they broke up Michael and I started seeing one another. He was a very nice, wonderful man.

BOB MORRIS - An East Side New York dentist. I knew him from E. 47th St. YMCA in the '60s.

PHILLIP MOYSON - Dated my manager Chaz. He cut hair.

SERGIO MUNZABAI - DJ with WBLS, mixed a number of club records.

AL MURPHY - Lover of DJ Larry Patterson. He managed Club Zanzibar in New Jersey.

BILLY NACHMAN - Bruce Mailman's Saint partner.

DAVID NAPOLI - Part of the Island crowd.

JACK NAU - A friend of Paul Popham.

HUGO NIEHAUS* - A friend of Michael and me, and a playmate.

BUDDY NORE - I got to know Buddy when he was doing fund raising for God's Love We Deliver.

ALAN NOSEWORTHY - A customer and friend of Julio Velez.

BOB OLIVERI - Part of the Island crowd.

JOE PACHEK - One of the owners of Sterling Sound Mastering Lab. First treasurer of GMHC.

BURT PALMANDORA* - A very sexy man, "Big" Burt. Fond memories of Burt in L.A.

AL PAPALLARDO* - A very dear friend, a fine loving person. He tried to bring N.Y. nightlife to L.A.

JOHN PAPPAS - Part of the Flamingo/Island crowd.

DENNIS PASSER - My doctor. A real nice guy. He once told me that I was one of the sexiest guys he knew. It's nice to hear that once in a while.

PHIL PATRICK* - A man's man, part of my Top Ten list, a real gentleman.

LARRY PATTERSON - A great DJ, a good friend of Larry Levan. He worked for Prelude Records.

BOBBY PAZZULI* - A friend of Julio.

DAVID PELLIGRINO - When I first met David he was the Dance music buyer for Strawberries record store in Boston. He also was a talented DJ, playing at the Loft in Boston.

LARRY PERRON - Once a top model, a Fire Island housemate on Ozone.

JIMMY PETERS - A close friend of Larry McDevitt. He knew how to throw great parties.

ENNO POERSCH - A dear friend. Talented artist, created GMHC Circus/Rodeo logos.

KENNY POLSKY - Kenny was part of the Fire Island family. He was a good friend of my good friends Louis Malkin and Dino Georgiou whom I have known for over 35 years.

PAUL POPHAM* - A close friend, founder and first president of GMHC. Captain in Green Berets, he received the Bronze Star for saving his platoon in Vietnam.

SHELDON POST* - A very close friend, owner of Chelsea Pines.

STEVEN POWSNER - Being a long-standing member of the Founder's Circle at the

Gay and Lesbian Community Center, I had the privilege to meet and know Steven when he was president of the center. A kind and gentle man.

BOB RAFSKY - I met Bob through Brent Nicholson Earle. Bob was a major AIDS activist.

PAUL RAPOPORT - One of the founders of GMHC.

DON REITER - A friend.

NAZIH RICHANI - Another person I met through Brent. I did not know him for long. What I knew of him I liked.

BILL RIFKIN* - A friend in many ways. Founder of Pleasure Chest.

MICHAEL RILEY* - A friend.

BOBBY RINALDI - A good friend of Julio Velez and me. He was manager of the restaurant Claire.

EDDIE RIVERA - Eddie started and ran the second DJ record pool called IDRC. He was a very passionate music person.

JOHN RIZZUTO - A very talented executive, a good friend.

NICK ROCK - A friend, lover of Enno Poersch.

DAVID RODRIGUEZ - A great DJ.

GIL RODRIGUEZ - A DJ. A teacher. A good friend.

JOSE RODRIGUEZ - Jose was a very talented individual. He was the man who made Tom Moulton realize that if you mastered a song on a 12" disc instead of a 45rpm you would get a much hotter sound. Thus the 12" single was born.

RAUL ROSAS - Jack Brusca's lover. Raul was a very talented architect. He did some work for me at the Colonial House. He conducted business in a very professional manner. He was one of the handsomest men in our community.

ED ROSENBERG - A friend from the Islanders Club.

MARK ROSENFELD* - A very dear friend.

LESS ROSS - A good friend. We used to hang out and party.

GARY ROVERANA - A friend from the Island.

STEVE RUBELL - Owner of the infamous Studio 54. I used to run into him when he hung out at the Garage. He had great respect for Larry Levan's talent.

EMILIO RUBEN - Manager of Paradise Garage, always a gentleman.

RICHARD RUSKAY* - Owner of the famous and very successful eatery, the Empire Diner. A real nice guy.

ARTHUR RUSSELL - I met Arthur through Steve D'Aquisto. I learned that Arthur was a protégé of John Hammond, who discovered Bob Dylan, Barbra Streisand, and Aretha Franklin. Arthur produced several songs for me. His music is more popular today than when it first came out. His song, "Is It All Over My Face," by Loose Joints was just sampled by Nellie Hooper for the movie, *The Big Tease*.

VITO RUSSO - A gay activist.

RICHARD SABALA - Richard was one of the most intensely passionate people when it came to his work. He was a lighting genius. I always told him that if a movie was ever made from my book, I wanted him to be part of the creative process. He was one of my biggest fans when it came to my artwork.

FRED SACKETT - A long-time friend.

BOB SIDDONS - Buzz Hoff's ex-lover. He was a fireman, a friend.

MARC PAUL SIMON - One of the best promotion men, instrumental in Donna Summer's career.

MICHAEL SKLAR* - Actor, friend.

DAN SKOLIS - Managed my building in the late '70s.

DAVID SKRIVANEK - Famous porn star, lover of one of my dearest friends, Buzz Hoff.

RICK SMITH* - Called to make a reservation at Colonial House, we met and became good friends. He was a professional golf instructor. He met the Boston crowd and moved to Boston until he got sick. He was a fun-loving guy.

ALLAN SOBEK - Former lover of Brent Nicholson Earle.

DAVID SPADA - Designed the Rainbow rings. Created costumes for Grace Jones and many other artists. Absolut Vodka did Absolute Spada. We worked on Party of Life V together.

PETER SPAR - Part owner of Graybar Sound with Barry Lederer. They were responsible for sound at 12 West, the Saint, and Trocadero.

BOB SPIEGEL - Schoolteacher, nice man.

GEORGE STAVRINOS* - Great artist, friend, and a lot more.

STEVE STEGMAN - A good friend. We once competed for the same person's affections. Steve won.

JOHN STERN* - A photographer. We spent a few memorable nights.

TOM STODDARD - A GMHC friend.

JEFF SWENTON - Part of the Boston group that stayed at the Colonial House during the Saint era.

SYLVESTER - A great artist, he once told me the Garage was his favorite club to perform in.

TOM SZALKEWICZ - A very talented writer. Part of the Fire Island crowd.

BRIAN TADESCO - A Fire Island friend.

SNOOKY TATE - A close friend of Ricky Willock. A true renaissance man.

MARTY TAUB - A friend.

ROY THODE - A wonderful DJ, a good friend. Many wonderful evenings dancing to his music. I gave him his first mix to do. Sesame Street asked me to have a remix done for the Cookie Monster, "C is for Cookie." I had Roy do one mix and Larry Levan do another.

KARL TILLOTSON* - Worked for me, a real beautiful man.

MICHAEL TOBIN - A DJ in Boston.

GARY TOMLINS* - A friend in more than one way.

ANDY TSIKLIS - Andy was from Boston. One of his jobs was handling the door at the Loft, the only after hours club at the time in Boston.

LARRY VanPARIS - A very close friend of my dear friend Bill Scott.

JOHN VASON* - A fond memory of some evenings spent together in L.A.

VAN VICKERS* - A very handsome caring young man.

PETER VOGEL - Worked for Gov. Cuomo. A friend. He was Don Castellano's long-time lover.

DR. TOM WADDELL - Started Gay Games. He was a boyfriend of Brent Nicholson Earle.

CRAIG WARDRUFF* - A friend, Fire Island house mate.

WES WEIDNER - A good friend.

RICK WELLIKOFF - A good friend.

WYN WELPIN - Worked on the *Today Show*, a good friend of Shelly Post.

RICHARD WENDRUFF - Mike Brody's cousin, he ran 24-Hours-For-Life,

STEVEN WIDUP - Julio and I used to be house guests of Steven and his lover Robert at their beautiful home in Key West. He later became a real estate agent.

MIKE WILKINSON – Started Disconet.

GEORGE WILSON * – Helped Blue Fletridge create the original Islanders Club at Fire Island, a bus service to and from the Island. George and I had a brief affair.

HENRY WINSLOW – DJ, a friend.

RAY YATES – Ray was definitely one of the early legendary DJs. I spent many memorable nights at the 10TH Floor where Ray played. He was one of the first DJs to make tapes for fashion shows.

JACK YORDAN* – Jackie was a close friend since the middle '70s. I threw Jackie his 21st birthday party on the beach in Puerto Rico. He was the younger brother of Dino whom I was seeing. Jackie was one of the most likeable people I have known. He had one of the most incredible speaking voices. I will never forget him.

BART ZOCCANO – A beautiful man, great taste in art. He bought one of my paintings.

IGNACIO ZUAZO – A very dear friend, someone who inspired me, a true friend, a great artist.

*sex partner.

disc-o-la fortune 500
discothèque songs of the '70s

Compiled by Ed Rothschild, with assistance from Johnny Tripp and Chipper McKearnin

1.	Shame - Evelyn "Champagne" King (RCA) '78
2.	Le Freak - Chic (Atlantic) '78-'79
3.	Try Me I Know We Can Make It - Donna Summer (Oasis) '76
4.	San Francisco / Hollywood - Village People (Casablanca) '77
5.	Honey Bee / Never Can Say Goodbye / Reach Out - Gloria Gaynor (MGM) '75
6.	Boogie Oogie Oogie - Taste Of Honey (Capitol) '78
7.	I Found Love - Love & Kisses (Casablanca) '77
8.	I Will Survive - Gloria Gaynor (Polydor) '78
9.	Love Hangover - Diana Ross (Motown) '76
10.	Disco Inferno / Where the Happy People Go - Trammps (Atlantic) '77, '76
11.	Don't Leave Me This Way - Thelma Houston (Tamla) '76
12.	Born to be Alive - Patrick Hernandez (Columbia) '79
13.	I'll Always Love My Mama - Intruders (Gamble) '73
14.	Mighty Real / Dance (Disco Heat) - Sylvester (Fantasy) '78
15.	Date With the Rain / Girl You Need a Change of Heart - Eddie Kendricks (Tamla) '72
16.	Contact - Edwin Starr (20th Century) '79
17.	This Time Baby - Jackie Moore (Columbia) '79
18.	Devil's Gun - C. J. & Co. (Westbound) '77
19.	Last Dance- Donna Summer (Casablanca) '78
20.	Woman / Wild Safari - Barrabas (RCA) '73
21.	Macho Man - Village People (Casablanca) '78
22.	Where Do We Go From Here - Trammps (Golden Fleece) '73-'74
23.	Let's All Chant - Michael Zager (Private Stock) '78
24.	Ask Me / Good Things Don't Last Forever - Ecstasy, Passion & Pain (Roulette) '74
25.	Stayin' Alive / Night Fever - Bee Gees (RSO) '78
26.	The Love I Lost - Harold Melvin & Blue Notes (Philadelphia International) '73
27.	La La Peace Song - O. C. Smith (Columbia) '73
28.	Hot Stuff / Bad Girls - Donna Summer (Casablanca) '79
29.	Come to Me / Don't Stop Dancing - France Joli (Prelude) '79
30.	Down to Love Town - Originals (Motown) '77
31.	Bad Luck - Harold Melvin & Blue Notes (Philadelphia International) '75
32.	I Feel Love - Donna Summer (Casablanca) '77
33.	Sugar Pie Guy / Hey Babe - Joneses (Mercury) '74
34.	I Love Music - O'Jays (Philadelphia International) '75
35.	First, Last, My Everything / Can't Get Enough - Barry White (20th Century) '74

36. Ten Percent / My Love is Free - Double Exposure (Salsoul) '76
37. Zing Went the Strings of My Heart - Trammps (Buddha) '72
38. The Hustle - Van McCoy (Avco) '75
39. Sex Machine / Give It Up Turn It Loose - James Brown (King) '70
40. T.S.O.P. / Love is the Message - MFSB (Philadelphia International) '74
41. When the Fuel Runs Out - Executive Suite (Babylon) '73
42. Do What You Wanna Do - T. Connection (TK) '77
43. Under the Influence of Love / Love s Theme - Love Unlimited Orchestra
    (20th Century) '73
44. Love Train - O'Jays (Philadelphia International) '73
45. Hot Shot - Karen Young (West End) '78
46. Black Skin Blue Blue-Eyed Boys - Equals (Shout) '71
47. Life and Death in G & A - Abaco Dream (A&M) '69
48. Sultana / Rain 2000 - Titanic (Epic) '71, '74
49. Think (About It) - Lyn Collins (People) '72
50. Rock the Boat - Hues Corporation (RCA) '74
51. In the Bush / Keep on Jumping - Musique (Prelude) '78
52. Get Down Tonight / That's the Way - K.C. & Sunshine Band (TK) '75
53. Don't Stop Til You Get Enough / Rock With Me - Michael Jackson (Epic) '79
54. We're on the Right Track - Ultra High Frequency (Wand) '73
55. Love to Love You Baby - Donna Summer (Oasis) '75
56. Fly Robin Fly / Save Me - Silver Convention (Midsong) '75
57. There But For the Grace of God - Machine (RCA) '79
58. Where There is Love / Once More with Feeling - Whispers (Janus) '74
59. It Only Takes a Minute - Tavares (Capitol) '75
60. I Can Understand It - New Birth (RCA) '73
61. Dirty Old Man - 3 Degrees (Philadelphia International) '75
62. I Don't Love You Anymore / You Can't Hide - Teddy Pendergrass (Phila Inter) '77
63. Enough is Enough - Barbra Streisand & Donna Summer (Casablanca) '79
64. Swearin' to God - Franki Valli (Private Stock) '75
65. MacArthur Park / Heaven Knows - Donna Summer (Casablanca) '79
66. It's a Shame - Spinners (V.I.P.) '70
67. Soul Makossa - Manu Dibango (Atlantic) '73
68. Ring My Bell / Don't Drop My Love - Anita Ward (TK) '79
69. Dance Dance Dance - Chic (Atlantic) '77
70. Turn the Beat Around - Vicki Sue Robinson (RCA) '76
71. Lady Marmalade - La Belle (Epic) '75
72. Do You Think I'm Sexy - Rod Stewart (Warner Bros) '79
73. Brazil - Ritchie Family (20th Century) '75
74. Rock Your Baby - George McCrae (TK) '74
75. I'll Bake Me a Man - Barbara Acklin (Brunswick) '73
76. Got to Get You Back - Sons of Robin Stone (Atco) '75
77. Shake Your Body Down to the Ground - Jacksons (Epic) '79

78. Hit and Run - Loleatta Holloway (Gold Mind) '77
79. Dreaming a Dream / Every Beat - Crown Heights (De-Lite) '75
80. Heaven Must Have Sent You - Bonnie Pointer (Motown) '79
81. More More More - Andrea True Connection (Buddha) '75
82. Love In C-Minor - Cerrone (Cotillion) '77
83. Runaway Love / If My Friends Could See Me - Linda Clifford (Curtom) '78
84. Dance With Me / Do You Want to Get Funky With Me - Peter Brown (TK) '78,'77
85. I Am Somebody / I ll Go - Jimmy James & Vagabonds (Pye) '75
86. Shake Your Groove Thing / Reunited - Peaches & Herb (Polydor) '79
87. Peace & Love - Ron Butler & Ramblers (Play Boy) '75
88. I've Got the Next Dance - Denise Williams (Columbia) '79
89. Hey Girl Come and Get It - Stylistics (Avco) '75
90. Get Dancin' - Disco Tex & Sex-o-lettes (Chelsea) '75
91. Hollywood Swinging - Kool & the Gang (De-Lite) '75
92. You Should Be Dancin' - Bee Gees (RSO) '76
93. Star Wars - Meco (Mill) '77
94. Pop Muzik - M (Sire) '79
95. Magic Bird of Fire / Runaway - Salsoul Orchestra (Salsoul) '77
96. Knock on Wood - Amii Stewart (Ariola) '79
97. Makes You Blind - Glitter Band (Arista) '76
98. Good Times - Chic (Atlantic) '79
99. Do It Any Way You Wanna - Peoples Choice (TSOP) '75
100. Happiness is Just Around the Bend - Main Ingredient (RCA) '74
101. I Don't Wanna Lose Your Love - Emotions (Columbia) '76
102. Cherchez La Femme / Sour & Sweet - Dr. Buzzard's Savannah Band (RCA) '76
103. Girls - Moments & Whatnauts (All Platinum) '75
104. Don't Le Me Be Misunderstood - Santa Esmeralda (Casablanca) '77
105. Instant Replay / Countdown - Dan Hartman (Blue Sky) '78
106. The Bottle - Gil Scott Heron (Strata East) '74
107. Ain't No Stoppin' Us Now - McFadden & Whitehead (Phil. Int.) '79
108. Harmony - Suzi Lane (Elektra) '79
109. I Love You / Rumor Has It - Donna Summer (Casablanca) '77
110. We are Family / Greatest Dancer - Sister Sledge (Cotillion) '79
111. Dr. Love - First Choice (Gold Mind) '77
112. Christmas Medley - Salsoul Orchestra (Salsoul) '77
113. Happy Radio - Edwin Starr (20th Century) '79
114. East to West / Lady America - Voyage (TK) '78
115. Heaven / Don't Take Away the Music - Tavares (Capitol) '76
116. Romeo & Juliet - Alec R. Constandinos (Casablanca) '78
117. Come Into My Heart / Love's Coming - USA - European Connection (TK) '78
118. Ladies Night - Kool & the Gang (De-Lite) '79
119. Native New Yorker - Odyssey (RCA) '77
120. Mighty High / Mighty Clouds - Mighty Clouds of Joy (ABC) '75

121. Brother's Gonna Work It Out - Willie Hutch (Motown) '73
122. Free Man / Right Track - South Shore Commission (Wand) '75
123. Little Bit of Love - Brenda & the Tabulations (Epic) '72
124. 4 Seasons of Love - Donna Summer (Casablanca) '76
125. Do It ('Til You're Satisfied) / Express / Peace Pipe - B.T. Express (Road Show / Scepter) '74, '75
126. Doing It to Death - J.B.'s (People) '73
127. Get On the Funk Train - Munich Machine (Casablanca) '77
128. Honey Please - Barry White (20th Century) '75
129. Give Me Love / Super Nature - Cerrone (Cot) '77
130. I Believe in Miracles - Jackson Sisters (Prophesy) '73
131. Uptown Festival - Shalimar (Soul Train) '77
132. It's a New Day - James Brown (King) '70
133. Risky Changes - Bionic Boogie (Polydor) '78
134. Year of Decision / When Will I See You Again - 3 Degrees (Phil. Int.) '74
135. My Mistake Was to Love You - Diana Ross & Marvin Gaye (Motown) '74
136. Keep on Dancing / Do It At the Disco - Gary's Gang (Columbia) '79
137. Where Are All My Friends - Harold Melvin & Blue Notes (Phil. Int.) '74
138. The Boss / No One Gets the Prize - Diana Ross (Motown) '79
139. You and I - Rick James (Motown) '78
140. Who's That Lady - Isley Bros. (T-Neck) '73
141. Don't Bring Back Memories - Four Tops (Motown) '69
142. Hang On In There Baby - Jimmy Bristol (MGM) '74
143. Cuba - Gibson Bros. (Island) '79
144. K-Jee - Nite Liters (RCA) '71
145. Midnight Love Affair - Carol Douglas (Midsong) '76
146. Casanova Brown / Do It Yourself - Gloria Gaynor (MGM) '75
147. Can We Come Together / Disco Party - Trammps (Atlantic) '76
148. I Caught Your Act - Hues Corporation (WB) '77
149. YMCA - Village People (Casablanca) '78
150. Kung Fu Fighting / Blue-Eyed Soul - Carl Douglas (20th Century) '74
151. Crank It Up - Peter Brown (TK) '79
152. Love Epidemic / Stop & Think - Trammps (Golden Fleece) '75
153. Hi Jack - Herbie Mann / Barrabas (Atco) '75
154. Theme from Shaft / The Men - Isaac Hayes (Stax) '72
155. Touch and Go - Ecstasy Passion & Pain (Roulette) '76
156. I Got to Have Your Love - Fantastic 4 (Westbound) '77
157. You'll Never Find Another Love - Lou Rawls (Philadelphia International) '76
158. Coco Motion - El Coco (AVI) '77
159. Two Hot for Love - THP Orchestra (Butterfly) '78
160. Could This Be the Magic / Come With Me - Donna Summer (Oasis) '76
161. Who Is He - Creative Source (Sussex) '74
162. Could It Be I'm Falling In Love / I'll Be Around - Spinners (Atlantic) '72

163. You Want It You Got It / Feel the Need - Detroit Emeralds (Westbound) '72
164. Love Is the Answer - Van McCoy / Stylistics (Avco) '74
165. Welcome to the Club / Look Me Up - Blue Magic (Atco) '74
166. Nice & Slow - Jesse Green (Scepter) '76
167. Rio de Janeiro - Gary Criss (Salsoul) '78
168. Newsy Neighbors / The Player - First Choice (Philly Groove) '74
169. Got to Have Lovin' - Don Ray (Polydor) '78
170. Shame, Shame, Shame - Shirley & Co. (All Platinum) '74
171. Ain't That Enough for You - John Davis & Monster Orchestra (SAM) '78
172. Love Don't Go Through No Changes - Sister Sledge (Atco) '74
173. Dim All the Lights / On the Radio - Donna Summer (Casablanca) '79
174. Here Comes That Sound - Love De Lux (WB) '79
175. Young Hearts Run Free / Run to Me - Candi Staton (WB) '76
176. Just Look What You Have Done - Brenda Holloway (Tamla) '67
177. Pow Wow / Green Light - Cory Daye (RCA) '79
178. Galaxy - War (MCA) '78
179. You + Me = Love - Undisputed Truth (Whitfield) '76
180. I Got Ants In My Pants / Good Foot - James Brown (Polydor) '72
181. Miss You - Rolling Stones (Rolling Stone) '78
182. Rapper's Delight - Sugar Hill Gang (Sugar Hill) '79
183. Armed & Extremely Dangerous / Smarty Pants - First Choice (Philly Groove) '73
184. Victim - Candi Staton (WB) '78
185. Float On - Floaters (ABC) '77
186. Found A Cure / Nobody Knows - Ashford & Simpson (WB) '79
187. Doin Fine Now - New York City (Chelsea) '73
188. Lovin is Really My Game - Brainstorm (Tabu) '77
189. Another Star / Isn't She Lovely / Sir Duke - Steve Wonder (Tamla) '76
190. Where Is the Love - Betty Wright (Alston) '75
191. I Need A Man / La Vie en Rose - Grace Jones (Island) '77
192. Disco Nights (Rock Freak) G.Q. (Arista) '79
193. I Gotta Keep Dancing - Carrie Lucas (Soul Train) '77
194. Tangerine / Right Size / Salsoul Hustle - Salsoul Orchestra (Salsoul) '75
195. Rough Diamond - Madleen Kane (WB) '78
196. It's Better Than Walking Out - Marlena Shaw (Blue Note) '76
197. Vertigo / Relight My Fire - Dan Hartman (Blue Sky) '79
198. Let's Start the Dance - Bohannon (Mercury) '78
199. Doctor's Orders - Carol Douglas (Midsong) '74
200. Got My Mind Made Up - Instant Funk (Salsoul) '79
201. Haven't Stopped Dancing - Gonzalez (Capitol) '79
202. I Got It - Gloria Spencer (Jay Walk) '72
203. Hot Pants / I'm Coming - Bobby Byrd (Brown Stone) '71
204. Freedom to Express Yourself - Denise La Salle (ABC) '77
205. Chains / Cream Always Rises - Bionic Boogie (Polydor) '78

206. Put Your Body In It - Stephanie Mills (20th Century) '79
207. Dance to the Music - Sly & Family Stone (Epic) '69, '79
208. El Bimbo - Bimbo Jet (Scepter) '75
209. Superman - Celi Bee & Buzzy Bunch (TK) '77
210. Move On Up / My #1 Request - Destination (Butterfly) '79
211. Keep On Truckin' / Boogie Down - Eddie Kendricks (Tamla) '73
212. What a Difference a Day Makes - Esther Phillips (Kudu) '73
213. Satisfaction / I'm Weak - Harold Melvin & Blue Notes (Phil. Int.) '74
214. Sing a Song - Earth, Wind & Fire (Columbia) '75
215. Love Machine - Miracles (Tamla) '75
216. Love and Desire - Arpeggio (Polydor) '79
217. Sure Know How to Love Your Man - Willie Hutch (Motown) '74
218. After Dark - Pattie Brooks (Casablanca) '78
219. Trouble Maker - Roberta Kelly (Oasis) '76
220. Lady Bump - Penny McLean (Atco) '75
221. The Chase - Giorgio (Casablanca) '78
222. You Little Trust Maker - Tymes (RCA) '74
223. Everlasting Love - Carl Carlton (Back Beat) '74
224. You Can Do It - Al Hudson & Partners (MCA) '79
225. Flashlight - Parliament (Casablanca) '78
226. Stoned Out of My Mind - Chi Lites (Brunswick) '73
227. Love Insurance - Front Page (RCA) '79
228. She's a Winner (Win, Place or Show) - Intruders (Gamble) '72
229. I Wouldn't Give You Up - Ecstasy, Passion & Pain (Roulette) '74
230. How Can I Forget - Realistics (Brunswick) '73
231. Come On Dance, Dance - Saturday Nite Band (Prelude) '78
232. I'm Your Boogie Man / Keep It Comin' - K.C. & Sunshine Band (TK) '77
233. Let's Groove - Archie Bell & the Drells (TSOP) '76
234. I Love You, Yes I Do - Independents (Wand) '72
235. Feed the Flame - Lorraine Johnson (Prelude) '78
236. Mighty, Mighty / Evil - Earth, Wind & Fire (Columbia) '74
237. Car Wash - Rose Royce (MCA) '76
238. Dynamite Explodes - Gentle Persuasion (Soul Dimension) '73
239. Dance and Hum Along - Jackson 5 (Motown) '73
240. Crystal World / Taj Mahal - Crystal Grass (Polydor / Private Stock) '75
241. Stop to Start - Blue Magic (Atco) '74
242. Ain't No Mountain High Enough - Diana Ross (Motown) '70
243. You Keep Me Hangin' On - Supremes (Motown) '66
244. I'll Be Holding On - Al Downing (Chess) '74
245. Ease On Down the Road - Consumer Rapport (Atlantic) '75
246. Star Love / Got to be Real - Cheryl Lynn (Columbia) '79
247. Reasons / Way of the World - Earth, Wind & Fire (Columbia) '76
248. Can't Fight Your Love - Modulations (Buddah) '74

249.	Superstition - Stevie Wonder (Tamla) '73
250.	Slow Down - John Miles (London) '77
251.	Dancer - Gino Soccio (WB) '79
252.	Find My Way - Cameo (Casablanca) '75
253.	Rock Me Again & Again - Lyn Collins (People) '74
254.	At the Copa - Barry Manilow (Arista) '78
255.	Spanish Hustle / Bus Stop - Fatback Band (Event) '75
256.	Back Stabbers - O'Jays (Phil. Int.) '72
257.	Don't Send Nobody Else / If You Were There - Ace Spectrum (Atlantic) '74
258.	Shake Your Booty - K.C. & Sunshine Band (TK) '76
259.	Move On Up / Superfly - Curtis Mayfield (Curtom) '72
260.	Dreamworld - Don Downing (Scepter) '74
261.	Up Jumped the Devil / Magic is You - John Davis & Monster Orchestra (Sam) '77
262.	Thank God It's Friday - Love and Kisses (Casablanca) '78
263.	Young and In Love - Ralph Carter (Mercury) '75
264.	Bongo Rock - Incredible Bongo Band (MGM) '73
265.	The Break - Kat Mandu (TK) '79
266.	From Here to Eternity - Giorgio (Casablanca) '77
267.	Main Line - Ashford & Simpson (WB) '74
268.	Show and Tell - Al Wilson (Bell) '74
269.	Groove Me - Fern Kinney (TK) '79
270.	Gut Level / Walking in Rhythm - Blackbyrds (Fantasy) '75
271.	The Best Disco in Town - Ritchie Family (TK) '76
272.	Running Back and Forth - Edwin Starr (Motown) '72
273.	Back In Love Again - LTD (A&M) '77
274.	Looking for a Brand New Game - 8 Minutes (Precep) '73
275.	Welcome to My World - Mass Production (Atlantic) '76
276.	You're the One - Little Sister (Stone Flower) '70
277.	This Is It - Melba Moore (Buddah) '76
278.	One Night Affair - Jerry Butler (Mercury) '72
279.	I Know I'm in Love - Chee-Chee & Peppy (Buddah) '72
280.	Sinner Man - Sarah Dash (Kirsh) '78
281.	Got to Give It Up - Marvin Gaye (Tamla) '77
282.	Shoot Me (With Your Love) - Tasha Thomas (Atlantic) '78
283.	Ask Me What You Want / My Man is a Sweet Man - Millie Jackson (Spring) '72
284.	It's a Miracle - Barry Manilow (Arista) '75
285.	Rock & Roll - Gary Glitter (Bell) '72
286.	Gimme Some Lovin' - Kongas (Polydor) '78
287.	I'm a Man - Macho (Prelude) '78
288.	After You Had Your Fling - Intrepids (Columbia) '75
289.	That's the Trouble / Sorry - Grace Jones (Beam Junction) '76
290.	Sentimentally It's You / No Romance - Theo Vaness (Prelude) '79
291.	Party Girl - Pattie Brooks (Casablanca) '77

292. What Goes Up (Must Come Down) - Tyrone Davis (Dakar) '73
293. Changes / Frame of Mind - Vernon Burch (UA) '75
294. You Got to be the One - Chi Lites (Brunswick) '74
295. Soul Power - Maceo & the Macks (People) '74
296. Kool & the Gang - Kool and the Gang (De Lite) '72
297. Let's Get Together - Aristocrats (WB) '73
298. Boogie Wonderland - Earth, Wind, Fire & the Emotions (Columbia) '79
299. Best of My Love - Emotions (Columbia) '77
300. Love Magic - John Davis & Monster Orchestra (Columbia) '79
301. Have a Cigar - Rose Bud (WB) '79
302. I've Got to Use My Imagination - Gladys Knight (Buddah) '74
303. Pick Up the Pieces / Work to Do - Average White Band (Atlantic) '74
304. I Do Love You / Sitting in the Park - Billy Stewart (Chess) '65
305. Hooked for Life - Trammps (Atlantic) '75
306. Sweet Dynamite - Claudja Barry (Salsoul) '77
307. Tell Me What You Want - Jimmy Ruffin (Chess) '74
308. I Love the Nightlife - Alicia Bridges (Polydor) '78
309. I Like What I Like - Everyday People (Paramount) '71
310. Dancin' - Crown Heights Affair (De Lite) '76
311. Too Late - Tavares (Capitol) '74
312. I'm in Heaven - Touch of Class (Mid Song) '76
313. Just Begun - Jimmy Castor (RCA) '72
314. Calypso Breakdown - Ralph McDonald (TK) '76
315. Pursuit of the Pimpmobile - Isaac Hayes (Stax) '74
316. Lady, Lady, Lady - Boogie Man Orchestra (Boogie Man) '75
317. Chicago Theme - Hubert Laws (CTI) '75
318. Beautiful Bend - Boris Midney (TK) '78
319. What's a Heart Good For - Miracles (Tamla) '73
320. Heart Be Still - Carl Graves (A&M) '76
321. Makin' It - David Naughton (RSO) '79
322. Foot Stompin' Music - Bohannon (Brunswick) '75
323. Rise / Rotation - Herb Alpert (A&M) '79
324. I Can't Stand the Rain / One Way Ticket - Eruption (Ariola) '78,'79
325. Sweet Charlie Babe / Precious, Precious - Jackie Moore (Atlantic) '73
326. To Each His Own - Faith, Hope & Charity (RCA) '75
327. Forbidden Love - Madleen Kane (WB) '79
328. Bananaticoco - Max B (Virgo) '71
329. Block Party - Anthony White (Salsoul) '77
330. Helplessly - Moment of Truth (Roulette) '75
331. Stop, I Don't Need No Sympathy - Lyn Roman (Brunswick) '74
332. Cathedrals - D.C. LaRue (Pyramid) '76
333. The Bull - Mike Theodore Orchestra (Westbound) '77
334. Fly Away / Souvenirs - Voyage (TK) '79

335. Dance, Dance, Dance - Calhoon (WB) '75
336. Don t Knock My Love (pts. 1&2) - Wilson Pickett (Atlantic) '71
337. Crazy About My Baby - Bonnie Bramlett (Columbia) '73
338. Low Down / It's Over - Boz Scaggs (Columbia) '76
339. Have You Seen Her - Chi Lites (Brunswick) '72
340. Movin' On / Change - Brass Construction (United Artists) '76
341. Machine Gun - Commodores (Motown) '74
342. Action 78 / Love Disco Style - Erotic Drum Band (Prism) '78
343. I Just Can't Say Goodbye - Philly Devotions (Don De) '74
344. Choosing You - Lenny Williams (ABC) '77
345. Hold Your Horses - First Choice (Salsoul) '78
346. Sisters and Brothers - Rita Fortune (Columbia) '74
347. Tell the World - Harold Melvin & Blue Notes (Phil. Int.) '76
348. I Get Lifted / Sweet Music (Wand) '76
349. We Can't Get Enough - Bingo (S. Blue) '73
350. Nowhere - Hocus Pocus (Shield) '75
351. Njia Walk / Street Dance - Fatback Band (Percep) '72
352. Take Me Home - Cher (Casablanca) '79
353. X Rated Symphony / Chico & the Man - Joe Bataan (Fania) '75
354. Come Get to This - Marvin Gaye (Tamla) '73
355. I Told You So - Delfonics (Philly Groove) '72
356. Funky Nassau - Beginning of the End (Alston) '71
357. Fight the Power / Live it Up - Isley Brothers (T-Neck) '75
358. Jungle Fever - Chakachas (Polydor) '72
359. My Love Supreme - Milton Hamilton (TR) '76
360. Deputy of Love - Don Armando's 2nd Ave. Rhumba Band (ZE) '79
361. Each Morning I Wake Up / Love Won't Let Me Wait - Major Harris (Atlantic) '75
362. I'm Gonna Let My Heart Do the Walking - Supremes (Motown) '76
363. One More Minute - St. Tropez (Butterfly) '79
364. Summer of 42 / Exodus - Biddu Orchestra (Epic) '75
365. Kiss and Say Goodbye - Manhattans (Columbia) '76
366. Don't Stop the Music - Bay City Rollers (Arista) '76
367. Heart of Glass - Blondie (Chrysalis) '79
368. I Love to Love / Fire - Tina Charles (Columbia) '76
369. You Stepped Into My Life - Melba Moore (Epic) '79
370. Brickhouse - Commodores (Motown) '77
371. Happiness - Pointer Sisters (Planet) '79
372. Play That Funky Music - Wild Cherry (Epic) '79
373. Happy 'Bout the Whole Thing - Dee Dee Sharp (TSOP) '74
374. If You Love Me Like You Say You Love Me - Betty Wright (Atco) '72
375. You've Broken My Heart - Sound Experience (Bell) '74
376. Music is My Way of Life - Patti LaBelle (Epic) '79
377. Only You - Teddy Pendergrass (Philadelphia International) '78

378. Outa-Space - Billy Preston (A&M) '73
379. Drive My Car / Blow Your Whistle - Gary Toms Empire (Brunswick) '75
380. Dance With Me - Carrie Lucas (Solar) '79
381. Once You Get Started - Rufus (ABC) '75
382. Night Rider -Venus Dodson (Warner Bros) '79
383. Think Before You Stop - Notations (Gemico) '75
384. Think It Over - Cissy Houston (Private Stock) '78
385. Don't You Want My Love - Debbie Jacobs (MCA) '79
386. Undecided Love - Chequers (Scepter) '75
387. Daddy Cool - Boney M (Atco) '76
388. Get Up and Boogie / Hollywood - Freddie James (Warner Bros) '79
389. Love is the Ultimate - Ultimate (Casablanca) '79
390. Wishing on a Star - Rose Royce (Whitfield) '77
391. Papa was a Rolling Stone / Law of the Land - Temptations (Motown) '73
392. Could Heaven Ever Be Like This - Idris Muhammad (Kudu) '77
393. Disco Lady - Johnny Taylor (Columbia) '76
394. Take That to the Bank / Second Time Around - Shalamar (Solar) '78,'79
395. Melting Pot - Boris Gardiner Dynamic (Jaguar) '74
396. Get Down - Gene Chandler (20th Century) '79
397. Long Train Running - Doobie Brothers (Warner Bros) '73
398. My Claim to Fame - James Wells (AVI) '78
399. Baby Face / Old Time Medley - Wings & Prayer (Atlantic) '75
400. Do or Die - Grace Jones (Island) '78
401. Je Suis Music - Cerrone (Cotillion) '78
402. Work That Body / When You Touch Me - Taana Gardner (West End) '79
403. Le Spank - La Pamplemousse (AVI) '77
404. If You Can't Beat 'Em - Mark Radice (United Artists) '76
405. Get Off - Foxy (TK) '78
406. Wear It Out - Stargard (Warner Bros) '79
407. Whatcha See is Whatcha Get - Dramatics (Volt) '71
408. Let's Get It Together - El Coco (AVI) '76
409. You Gonna Make Me Love You - Jones Girls (Philadelphia International) '79
410. A Little Lovin' - Raes (A&M) '78
411. Black Water Gold - African Music Machine (Soul Power) '73
412. Open Sesame - Kool & the Gang (De Lite) '77
413. Somebody's Gotta Go - Mike & Bill (Arista) '75
414. Don't Stop Me - David Christie (Salsoul) '78
415. It's a Disco Night - Isley Brothers (T-Neck) '79
416. Praying for a Miracle - Soul Generation (Ebony) '74
417. Whistle Bump - Deodato (Warner Bros) '78
418. Rain Forest / Jump for Joy - Biddu Orchestra (Epic) '76
419. Music - Montreal Sound (TK) '77
420. Sun Sun Sun - Jakki (Pyramid) '76

421. (Everybody) Get Dancin' - Bombers (West End) 79
422. Getting Together - Brothers Guiding Light (Mercury) 73
423. Sweet Summer Suite - Love Unlimited (20th Century) 76
424. Let's Do the Latin Hustle - Eddie Drennon (Friends) 75
425. I Love America - Patrick Juvet (Casablanca) 78
426. That Old Black Magic - Softones (H&L) 75
427. Give It To Me - J. Giles (Atlantic) 73
428. Beyond the Clouds - Quartz (TK) 78
429. Los Conquistadores Chocolates - Johnny Hammond (Mile) 76
430. Beat of the Night / Pump It Up - Fever (Fantasy) 79
431. I Don't Know What It Is - Ripples (CRC) 73
432. Spring Rain - Silvetti (Salsoul) 77
433. You Haven't Seen My Love - Ones (Motown) 67
434. Free Love - Jean Carn (Philadelphia International) 77
435. Superstar Revue - Ventures (United Artists) 75
436. Baby Blue / I Wanna Rock You - Georgio (Casablanca) 79
437. Sunny - Yambu (Montuno) 76
438. Pagliacci - Maynard Ferguson (Columbia) 76
439. Tom the Peeper - Act One (Spring) 74
440. No. I Dee Jay - Goody Goody (Atlantic) 78
441. Come On and Do It - Poussez (Van) 79
442. Just Keep Thinking About You - Tata Vega (Motown) 79
443. Dance a Little Bit Closer - Charo (Salsoul) 77
444. Nobody Loves Me - Jeanne Burton (Cotton) 75
445. When You Wake Up Tomorrow / Chance / Rock - Candi Staton (Warner Bros) 79
446. Stubborn Kind of Fellow - Buffalo Smoke (RCA) 77
447. I Don't Know What I'd Do - Sweat Cream (Shady) 78
448. Erotic Soul - Larry Page (London) 77
449. Lost Time / Georgia After Hours - Richard "Popcorn" Wylie (ABC) 74
450. Boogie Woogie Dancin' Shoes - Claudja Barry (Chrysalis) 79
451. Land of Make Believe - Champs Boys (Vogue Imp.) 77
452. One Monkey Don't Stop No Show - Honey Cone (Hot Wax) 71
453. My Baby's Baby - Liquid Gold (Parachute) 79
454. One More Try - Ashford & Simpson (Warner Bros) 76
455. Skin Tight / Fire - Ohio Players (Mercury) 74
456. Street Talk - BCG (20th Century) 76
457. Pillow Talk - Sylvia (All Platinum) 73
458. Rain - Dorothy Morrison (Elektra) 71
459. Disco Connection - Isaac Hayes (ABC) 76
460. A.I.W. (Amwana) / Chicano - Black Blood (Main) 75
461. Running Away - Roy Ayers (Polydor) 77
462. I Shot the Sheriff - Eric Clapton (RSO) 74
463. Never Get Enough of Your Love - Street People (Vigor) 75

464. One Day of Peace - Love Committee (Golden Fleece) '74
465. Je T'Aime Moi Non Plus - Jane Birkin & Serge Gainsbourg (Fontana) '69
466. Na Na Hey Hey Kiss Him Goodbye - Steam (Fontana) '69
467. Music for the Gong / Fire - Osibisa (Decca / Warner Bros) '72, '73
468. Stars / Body Strong / I Can't Stop Dancing - Sylvester (Fantasy) '79
469. Love, Love, Love - Donny Hathaway (Atco) '73
470. Wow - Andre Gagnon (London) '76
471. Kung Fu Man - Ultra Funk (Contempo) '74
472. Elusive - Babe Ruth (Capitol) '76
473. Get Up Offa That Thing - James Brown (Polydor) '76
474. African Symphony - Henry Mancini (RCA) '76
475. Love Do Me Right - Rockin' Horse (RCA) '75
476. Corazon / Water Bed - LTG Exchange (Scepter / Wand) '74
477. Take a Little Love - Liquid Pleasure (Midsong) '76
478. Hold Tight - Vickie Sue Robinson (RCA) '77
479. Angel Face / Gimme Some Lovin' - Glitter Band (Bell) '74
480. I Got Your Love - Stratavarius (Roulette) '76
481. Burning - Carol Douglas (Midsong) '78
482. Only Your Love - Tymes (RCA) '76
483. Savage Lover - The Ring (Van) '79
484. Journey Into Love (Magic Fly) - Kebekeletrik (TK) '77
485. Let Them Dance - D.C. La Rue (Casablanca) '78
486. Zodiac Lady - Roberta Kelly (Casablanca) '77
487. Ain't Nothing Gonna Keep Me - Teri DeSario (Casablanca) '79
488. Who Loves You / Dec. 63 - 4 Seasons (Warner Bros) '75,'76
489. Brazilia Carnaval - Chocolate Boys (Imp) '75
490. Get Into Something - Isley Bros. (T-Neck) '70
491. Show Me What You're Made Of - Mista Charge (Target) '77
492. Hello It's Me - Nazz (SGC) '69
493. Forever Came Today - Jackson 5 (Motown) '75
494. Follow the Wind - Midnight Movers (Benee) '73
495. Beggin' - Timebox (Deram) '68
496. Cloud Nine - Mongo Santa Maria (Columbia) '69
497. Up In a Puff of Smoke - Polly Brown (GTO) '74
498. Track In A - Cat Mother (Polydor) '69
499. Mongoose - Elephants Memory (Metro) '71
500. I'm On Fire - 5,000 Volts (Featuring Tina Charles) (Philips) '75

discography

Selected Scepter Records

Banzaii – Chinese Kung Fu
Bimbo Jet – El Bimbo
BT Express – Do It ('Til You're Satisfied) / Express / Peace Pipe
Ernie Bush – Breakaway
The Chequers – Undecided Love
Don Downing – Dreamworld
Jesse Green – Nice and Slow (mixed by Mel Cheren)
The Independents – Arise and Shine / I Love You, Yes I Do
Clara Lewis – Needing You
L.T.G. Exchange – Corazon / Waterbed
Bobby Moore – (Call Me Your) Anything Man
Patti Jo – Ain't No Love Lost / Make Me Believe In You
The Secrets – (Baby) Save Me
South Shore Commission – Free Man
South Side Movement – Mud Wind
Sweet Music – I Get Lifted (mixed by Mel Cheren)
George Tindley – Pity the Poor Man / Wan Tu Wah Zuree
Ultra High Frequency – We're On the Right Track

Larry Levan Productions/Remixes

Steve Arrington – Summertime Lovin' (Salsoul)
Patti Austin – Honey for the Bees (Qwest, '85)
Dee Dee Bridgewater – Bad for Me (Elektra)
Bumblebee Unlimited – Lady Bug
Central Line – Walking Into Sunshine (Mercury, '81) / Heat Stroke (Supertronics, '86)
Class Action feat. Christine Wiltshire – Weekend (Sleeping Bag)
Cognac – How High (Salsoul, '80)

Convention - Let's Do It (SAM)
The Cookie Monster - C is for Cookie (Sesame Street, '76)
The Cut - Kindness for Weakness (Supertronics, '86)
Dinosaur L - Corn Belt (Sleeping Bag)
East Village People - Love's Gonna Get You (SAM, '82)
Eastside Kid - Love is Gonna Get You (Too) (SAM)
First Choice - Double Cross (Salsoul)
Aretha Franklin - Jimmy Lee (Manhattan)
Frontline Orchestra - Don't Turn Your Back (RFC)
Taana Gardner - Heartbeat ('81) / No Frills ('81) / Paradise Express ('79) / When You Touch Me ('79) / Work That Body ('79) (West End)
Glass - Let Me Feel Your Heartbeat
Gwen Guthrie - It Should've Been You (Island, '82) / Padlock mini-LP (Garage/Island, '83): Hopscotch, Seventh Heaven, Getting Hot, Padlock, Peanut Butter / Ain't Nothin' Goin' on But the Rent ('86) / Close to You (Polydor, '87) / Ticket to Ride (4th & B'Way, '87)
Hanson & Davis - I'll Take You On (Fresh, '86)
Dan Hartman - I Can Dream About You / We Are the Young   (MCA, '84)
Loleatta Holloway - Greatest Performance of My Life (Salsoul) / Strong Enough (Active, '92)*
Ednah Holt - Serious, Sirius Space Party (West End, '81)
Imagination - Changes (MCA, '83)
Inner Life - Ain't No Mountain High Enough / Make it Last Forever [feat. Jocelyn Brown] (Salsoul)
Instant Funk - Everybody / I Got My Mind Made Up ('78) / Body Shine / Slip Slap Lickedy Lap (Salsoul, '79)
Jamaica Girls - Need Somebody New (Sleeping Bag, '83)
Grace Jones - Feel Up (Island, '82)
David Joseph - Can't Hide Your Love (Mango/Island, '83)
Chaka Khan - Tearing It Up (Warner Brothers)
Lace - You Can't Play Around (Atlantic, '82)
Larry Levan's Greatest Hits Vol. 2 - Various Artists (Salsoul)
Logg - I Know You Will (Salsoul, '81)
Loose Joints - Is It All Over My Face (West End, '80)
Man Friday - Jump / Love Honey, Love Heartache (Vinyl Mania, '86) / Winners (Warner Bros.)
Janice McClain - Smack Dab in the Middle (Warner/RFC, '80)
Merc & Monk - I Get Carried Away (EMI, '85)
New York Citi Peech Boys - Come On, Come On / Dance Sister / Life is Something Special/ On a Journey (Island, '84)
Billy Nichols - Give Your Body Up to the Music (West End)

Jeffrey Osborne - Borderlines / Plain Love (A & M, '83)
Tony Paris - Electric Automan (Vanguard, '85)
Peech Boys - Don't Make Me Wait (Garage/West End, '82)
Plunky & the Oneness of Juju - Every Way But Loose (Sutra, '82)
Bert Reid - Groovin' with You (Next Plateau, '84)
Smokey Robinson - And I Don't Love You (Motown, '84)
The Rock - Tramaine (A & M)
Nile Rodgers - State Your Mind/Stay Out of the Light (Warner Bros, '85)**
Jimmy Ross - First True Love Affair (Quality, '81)
Jimmy Ruffin - Falling in Love (RFC)
Bunny Sigler - By the Way You Dance (Salsoul)
Skyy - First Time Around / Skyyzoo (Salsoul, '80)
Sparkle - Handsome Man (Salsoul)
Sparque - Let's Go Dancin' (West End, '81)*
Strikers - Body Music (Prelude, '81)*
Sylvester - Someone Like You (Megatone/Warner Bros)
Third World - One More Time (CBS Columbia)
Vicious - Black Mamba (Garage/Island, '84)
Narada Michael Warden - Nature of Things (Warner Bros, '85)
Tracy Weber - Sure Shot (Quality, '81)
Karyn White - Facts of Life (Warner, '86)
Esther Williams - I'll be Your Pleasure (RCA)

*with François Kevorkian.
**with Judy Weinstein.

West End Records catalog (out of print)

WE100	Black Emanuel - Motion picture soundtrack (album) 1976
WE101	How Funny Can Sex Be - Motion picture soundtrack (album) 1976
WE102	The Magic Pony - Motion picture soundtrack (album) 1977
WE103	Michele - Magic Love (album) 1977
WE104	The Bombers - (album) 1978
WE105	Karen Young - Hot Shot (album) 1978
WE106	The Bombers - Bombers 2 (album) 1979
WE107	Taana Gardner - Work That Body (album) 1979

discography

WEI08	Colleen Heather - Heartbreaker (album) 1979
WEI09	Tony Humphries/ Various Artists - Master Mix Medley 1982
WESI2100	Sessomatto - Sessomatto 1976
WESI2102	Dick Lee Sound of Inner City - Mary Hartman Mary Hartman 1976
WESI2103	Jakki - You Are the Star 1976
WESI2104	Garrett Scott - Nah Nah Kiss Him Goodbye 1976
WESI2105	The Chuck Davis Orchestra - Spirit of Sunshine 1977
WESI2106	Philly U.S.A. - Speak Well 1977
WESI2109	Dawn Robertson - With All My Heart 1977
WESI2110	Michele - Disco Dance 1977
WESI2111	Karen Young - Hot Shot 1978
WESI2112	The Bombers - The Mexican / Dance Dance Dance 1978
WESI2113	Bettye Lavette - Doin' the Best That I Can 1978
WES22114	Karen Young - Bring on the Boys 1978
WES22114B	Karen Young - Baby You Ain't Nothin Without Me 1978
WES22115	The Bombers - (Everybody) Get Dancin' 1979
WES22116	Taana Gardner - Work That Body 1979
WES22117	Ednah Holt & Starluv - People Come Dance 1979
WES22118	Billy Nichols - Give Your Body Up to the Music 1979
WES22119	The Bombers - Let's Dance / Shake 1979
WES22120	Sugar & Spice - You're My Sugar, You're My Spice 1979
WES22121	Pico - Malaguena 1979
WES22122	Taana Gardner - When You Touch Me 1979
WES22123	Colleen Heather - On the Run 1979
WES22125	North End - Kind of Life (Kind of Love) 1979
WES22126	Billy Nichols - Diamond Ring 1980
WES22128	Loose Joints - Is It All Over My Face / Pop Your Funk 1980
WES22129	Loose Joints - Is It All Over My Face (Male / Female versions) 1980
WES22130	Bobby Youngblood - There's Never Been No One Like You 1980
WES22131	Master Boogies Song & Dance - When the Shit Hits the Fan 1980
WES22132	Taana Gardner - Heartbeat 1981
WES22133	People's Choice - Hey Everybody (Party Hearty) 1981
WES22134	Sweet G - A Heartbeat Rap 1981
WES22135	Sparque - Let's Go Dancin' 1981
WES22136	Inez Brooks - Chillin' Out 1981
WES22137	Taana Gardner - No Frills 1981
WES22138	Ednah Holt - Serious, Sirius Space Party 1981

WES22139	Stone - Time 1981
WES22140	Peech Boys - Don't Make Me Wait 1982
WES22141	Sparque - Music Turns Me On 1982
WES22142	Al McCall - Hard Times 1982
WES22143	Forrrce - Keep On Dancin' 1982
WES22144	George and Glen Miller - Touch Your Life 1982
WES22145	Glass - Let Me Feel Your Heartbeat 1982
WES22146	Debbie Trusty - Searchin' For Some Lovin' 1982
WES22147	Stone - Girl I Like the Way that You Move 1982
WES22148	Raw Silk - Do it to the Music 1982
WES22149	B.T. (Brenda Taylor) - You Can't Have Your Cake and Eat It Too 1982
WES22150	Mahogany - Ride on the Rhythm 1982
WES22151	Johnson & Youngblood - The Funk is in the Music 1983
WES22152	India - Stay With Me 1983
WES22153	Julius Brown - Party 1983
WES22154	Sean Taylor - I Can't Live Without You/Come Back to Me 1983
WES22155	Shirley Lites - Heat You Up (Melt You Down) 1983
WES22156	Sweet Life - I Get Lifted 1983
WES22157	Julius Brown - Diana 1983
WES22158	Love Club - Hot Summer Nights 1983
WES22159	Raw Silk - Just In Time 1983
WES22160	Sybil Thomas - Rescue Me 1983
WES22161	L.J. Waiters - Make it Feel Like [Never released] 1983
WES22162	DJ Divine - Get Into the Mix1983
WES22163	B+ - B-Beat Classic 1983
WES22164	Barbara Mason - Another Man 1983
WES22165	Angie - Let's Get on With It 1983
WES22166	Janet Daily and Senses - If You Can Count 1983
WES22167	Spyder C - Unity/Hollis Rock 1983
WES22168	Julius Brown - Never Too Late 1983
WES22169	Steve Pickett and the Post Nuclear Orchestra - Hello it's 1984 (1983)
WES22170	AOK - Style 1984
WES22171	D'Bora - No Sense 1984
WES22172	Sparque - Take Some Time 1984
WES22173	Diamond D - Fresh Avenue 1984
WES22174	Barbara Mason - Don't I Ever Cross Your Mind Sometime 1984
WES22175	Fantasy Machine - Fantasy Machine 1984

| WES22176 | Mona Ray - I Been Watchin' You 1984 |
| WES22177 | Karen Young - Come-A-Running 1985 |

West End Records catalog (currently available)

WES1001	Taana Gardner - I'm Comin' 1998
WES1001RE	Taana Gardner - I'm Comin' [Nicky Siano Remix] 1998
WES1002	Taana Gardner - Work That Body [Angel Moraes Remix] 2000
WES2001	Larry Levan/Various Artists - Larry Levan's Classic West End Remixes [CD/3XLP] 1999
WES2002	Taana Gardner - Anthology of a Diva: The Classics & More [CD] 2000
WES5001	Taana Gardner - Heartbeat [Remastered] 1999
WES5002	Loose Joints - Is It All Over My Face (Male/Female versions Remastered) 1999
WES5003	Ednah Holt - Serious, Sirius Space Party (Remastered) 1999
WES7001	Classic '77 West End T-shirt w/catalog titles spiral on back. Brown on gray. M,L,XL
GAR1001	Larry Levan/Various Artists - Larry Levan Live at the Paradise Garage [DBL CD] 2000
GAR7001	Paradise Garage T-shirt white glo-in-dark on black. M,L,XL. Front: logo Back: "Paradise Garage" Sleeve: "Guaranteed Genuine Garage Gear" logo (All profits go to charity)

music to read by

Larry Levan Live at the Paradise Garage
Double CD & Limited Edition Triple Vinyl Set

CD-1

Bourgie Bourgie - Ashford & Simpson
It's Music - Diamond Harris
At Midnight - T Connection
Put Your Body In It - Stephanie Mills
Dreaming A Dream - Crown Heights Affair
By The Way You Dance - Bunny Sigler
Right In The Socket - Shalamar
Take Me Home - Cher
Pick Me Up I'll Dance - Melba Moore

CD-2

Funk Train - Munich Machine
Here I Go Again - People's Choice
Bad Mountain - Motown Sounds
Let Yourself Go - Supremes
Angel In My Pocket - Change
Smack Dab In The Middle - Janice McCain
Sun, Sun - Jakki
Trinidad - John Gibbs & U.S. Steel Band
My First Mistake - Chilites
Erucu - Jermaine Jackson

Larry Levan's Classic West End Records Remixes
(Made Famous at the Legendary Paradise Garage)
CD & Limited Edition Triple Vinyl Set

Heartbeat - Taana Gardner
Serious, Sirius, Space Party - Ednah Holt
No Frills - Taana Gardner
Don't Make Me Wait - New York Citi Peech Boys
Let's Go Dancin' - Sparque
Is It All Over My Face - Loose Joints
Work That Body - Taana Gardner
Give Your Body Up To The Music - Billy Nichols
When You Touch Me - Taana Gardner

Information on how to purchase the items listed above plus the most current catalog,
release dates, news and much more, can be found at http://www.westendrecords.com.